NOTTING HILL GATE

Textbook 8
Allgemeine Ausgabe

Erarbeitet von:
Nathan Giles (Thedinghausen), Penelope Pedder (Köln),
Maike Pegler (Sarstedt/Gödringen), Susanne Quandt (Bremen),
Dr. Stefanie Quinlan (Frankfurt am Main)

sowie Denise Arrandale (Neumünster), Michael Biermann (Hamburg),
Hannelore Debus (Mörfelden-Walldorf), Phil Mothershaw-Rogalla
(Volkmarsen-Külte), Dr. Ivo Steininger (Wetzlar)

Fachliche Beratung:
Angela Berkenkamp (Wetzlar), Imke del Federico (Kerpen),
Dr. Matthias Munsch (Frankfurt am Main), Anke Riemer (Hamburg),
Kathleen Unterspann (Halstenbek)

Notting Hill Gate 8
Allgemeine Ausgabe
Textbook

Zusatzmaterialien zu Notting Hill Gate 8

Für Lehrkräfte:

- Textbook für Lehrkräfte 8 (ISBN 978-3-14-128287-0)
- Materialien für Lehrkräfte 8 (ISBN 978-3-14-128297-9)
- Lernerfolgskontrollen 8 (ISBN 978-3-14-128323-5)
- CD für Lehrkräfte 8 (ISBN 978-3-14-128307-5)
- DVD für Lehrkräfte 8 (ISBN 978-3-14-128317-4)
- Online-Diagnose zu Notting Hill Gate 8
  www.onlinediagnose.de

Für Schülerinnen und Schüler:

- Workbook 8 (inkl. Audios) (ISBN 978-3-14-128213-9)
- Workbook 8 mit interaktiven Übungen (inkl. Audios) (ISBN 978-3-14-145261-7)
- Interaktive Übungen 8 (WEB-14-128223)
- Arbeitsbuch Inklusion 8 (inkl. Audios) (ISBN 978-3-14-128233-7)
- Klassenarbeitstrainer 8 (ISBN 978-3-14-128249-8)
- Grammatiktrainer 8 (ISBN 978-3-14-128389-1)
- Wortschatztrainer 8 (ISBN 978-3-14-128243-6)

Das digitale Schulbuch und digitale Unterrichtsmaterialien für Schülerinnen und Schüler und für Lehrkräfte finden Sie in der BiBox – dem digitalen Unterrichtssystem passend zum Lehrwerk. Mehr Informationen über aktuelle Lizenzen finden Sie auf www.bibox.schule.

www.westermann.de/nhg

Alle digitalen Ergänzungen zum Buch erkennen Sie an dem Symbol **DIGITAL+**.
Dazu zählen Audiotracks, Videoclips, Arbeitsblätter zur Medienbildung, zusätzliche Übungen zu den Practise-Seiten und Zusatzmaterialien zum Buch. Gehen Sie auf www.westermann.de/webcode und geben Sie den Webcode **WES-128203-001** ein. Sie können auch den QR-Code scannen.

© 2025 Westermann Bildungsmedien Verlag GmbH, Georg-Westermann-Allee 66, 38104 Braunschweig
www.westermann.de

Das Werk und seine Teile sind urheberrechtlich geschützt. Jede Nutzung in anderen als den gesetzlich zugelassenen bzw. vertraglich zugestandenen Fällen bedarf der vorherigen schriftlichen Einwilligung des Verlages. Wir behalten uns die Nutzung unserer Inhalte für Text und Data Mining im Sinne des UrhG ausdrücklich vor. Nähere Informationen zur vertraglich gestatteten Anzahl von Kopien finden Sie auf www.schulbuchkopie.de.
Für Verweise (Links) auf Internet-Adressen gilt folgender Haftungshinweis: Trotz sorgfältiger inhaltlicher Kontrolle wird die Haftung für die Inhalte der externen Seiten ausgeschlossen. Für den Inhalt dieser externen Seiten sind ausschließlich deren Betreiber verantwortlich. Sollten Sie daher auf kostenpflichtige, illegale oder anstößige Inhalte treffen, so bedauern wir dies ausdrücklich und bitten Sie, uns umgehend per E-Mail davon in Kenntnis zu setzen, damit beim Nachdruck der Verweis gelöscht wird.

Druck A[1] / Jahr 2025
Alle Drucke der Serie A sind im Unterricht parallel verwendbar.

Redaktion: Lisa Fast und Dr. Katja Nandorf sowie Doris Bos
Vokabelanhang: Doris Bos
Illustrationen: Mario Ellert, Bremen
Umschlaggestaltung: LIO Design GmbH, Braunschweig
Layout: LIO Design GmbH, Braunschweig
Druck und Bindung: Westermann Druck GmbH, Georg-Westermann-Allee 66, 38104 Braunschweig

ISBN 978-3-14-**128203**-0

Erklärungen

So arbeitest du mit dem Buch

Im Buch findest du folgende Verweise:

1 audio — Hier gibt es einen Audiotrack, den du auch online abrufen kannst.

2 video — Hier gibt es einen Videoclip, den du auch online abrufen kannst.

3 workbook — Hier siehst du, auf welcher Seite im Workbook es weitere Übungen gibt.

4 wordbank — In den Wordbanks findest du Wörter nach Wortfeldern geordnet.

5 skill — Auf den Skills-Seiten findest du Tipps und Strategien fürs Lernen.

6 grammar — Zu dieser Aufgabe gibt es Erklärungen und Beispiele im Grammatik-Teil.

7 media worksheet — Dieser Hinweis kennzeichnet Aufgaben, in denen du Medienkompetenz aufbaust und trainierst. Zu diesen Aufgaben gibt es Arbeitsblätter, die du über den Webcode oder den QR-Code auf Seite 2 abrufen kannst.

DIGITAL+ practise more — Dieser Hinweis zeigt, dass es zusätzliches Material auf der Webseite gibt.

In den Units gibt es verschiedene Arten von Aufgaben:

8 CHOOSE YOUR LEVEL — Bei diesen Aufgaben gibt es drei unterschiedliche Schwierigkeitsgrade:

I leicht   II mittel   III schwierig

9 GET TOGETHER — Hier arbeitest du mit einem Partner oder einer Partnerin zusammen. Entscheidet, wer Partner A und wer Partner B ist und wählt jeweils einen Schwierigkeitsgrad. Geht dann zur entsprechenden Seite und bearbeitet die Aufgabe.

Partner A
I Go to page 130.
II Go to page 133.
III Go to page 136.

Partner B
I Go to page 139.
II Go to page 142.
III Go to page 145.

10 CHOOSE YOUR TASK — Hier gibt es drei Aufgaben, von denen du dir eine aussuchen kannst. Du kannst auch mit einem Partner oder einer Partnerin oder in einer Gruppe arbeiten.

TARGET TASK — In der Target Task (Zielaufgabe) wendest du an, was du gelernt hast. Du erarbeitest ein kleines Produkt, das du in der Klasse vorstellen und in deinem Portfolio aufbewahren kannst.

> **!** In Notting Hill Gate 8 wird der Unterschied zwischen britischem und US-amerikanischem Englisch thematisiert. Die US-amerikanische Schreibweise findet sich dort, wo die Texte aus einem US-amerikanischen Kontext stammen, ansonsten folgt das Buch der britischen Rechtschreibung.

Quiz	**6**
Quiz 1: What do you know about the USA?	6
Quiz 2: Landscapes and cities in the USA	8
Unit 1 – Welcome to the USA	**9**
Part A: Impressions of the USA	10
Part B: New York City	20
Challenge: What is the real story of Thanksgiving?	30
Challenge: Fighting against racism	31
Challenge: The father of hip-hop – DJ Kool Herc	32
Unit 2 – High school	**33**
Part A: Welcome to high school!	34
Part B: After-school activities	44
Challenge: You should see me in a crown	54
Challenge: Prom dress	56
Unit 3 – My world today	**57**
Part A: Relationships	58
Part B: Digital communication	68
Challenge: Every Day	78
Challenge: Cyberbullying – FAQs	80
Unit 4 – Our world tomorrow	**81**
Part A: The power of hope	82
Part B: The world of work	92
Challenge: Interview "Hope is a discipline"	102
Challenge: Unusual jobs	104
Unit 5 – New horizons	**105**
Part A: Immigration	106
Part B: The Republic of Ireland	116
Challenge: Enrique's journey	126
Challenge: Annie Moore	128
Challenge: Isle of Hope, Isle of Tears	129
Get together	**130**
Projects	**148**
Project 1: Hollywood	148
Project 2: Green cities	150
Skills	**152**
1. Wortschatzarbeit	152
2. Hören	153
3. Mit anderen sprechen	154
4. Schreiben	155
5. Lesen	156
6. Sprachmittlung	157
7. Videoclips verstehen	158
8. Im Internet recherchieren	159
9. Präsentationen halten	160
10. Eine Szene vorspielen	161

Kurzes Inhaltsverzeichnis für den schnellen Überblick

Wordbanks — 162

- Around the world — 162
- Travelling — 163
- Descriptions — 163
- School life — 164
- American and British English — 165
- Feelings — 166
- Seeking and giving advice — 166
- (Digital) communication — 167
- Expressing opinions — 168
- Presenting something — 168
- Hopes and dreams — 169
- The world of work — 170
- Numbers — 171

Classroom phrases — 172

Grammar — 174

1. Die einfache Vergangenheit: Aussagen *(revision)* — 174
2. Die einfache Vergangenheit: Fragen *(revision)* — 175
3. Das Perfekt: Aussagen *(revision)* — 176
4. Das Perfekt: Fragen *(revision)* — 177
5. Das Passiv *(revision)* — 178
6. Die Vorvergangenheit — 179
7. Bedingungssätze Typ 1 *(revision)* — 180
8. Reflexivpronomen — 181
9. Indirekte Rede 2 — 182
10. Adverbien der Art und Weise *(revision)* — 183
11. Die Steigerung von Adverbien — 184
12. Bedingungssätze Typ 2 — 185
13. Modalverben *(revision)* — 186
14. Bedingungssätze Typ 3 *(optional)* — 187
15. Indirekte Befehlssätze — 188
16. Die Verlaufsform der Vergangenheit *(revision)* — 189
17. Die Verlaufsform des Perfekts: Aussagen — 190
18. Die Verlaufsform des Perfekts: Fragen — 191

Words — 192

- Einleitung — 192
- Wortlisten nach Units — 195
- *Dictionary* — 231
- *Names* — 271
- *Numbers* — 274
- *Irregular verbs* — 275

Ausführliches Inhaltsverzeichnis — 278

Bild- und Textquellen — 284

Ein ausführliches Inhaltsverzeichnis befindet sich auf den Seiten 278 bis 283.

Quiz 1

What do you know about the USA?

In this book you will learn a lot about the USA. What do you already know about the country? Try to answer the questions. The correct letters make a sentence.

1 In the USA there are …
- **B** 5 states.
- **A** 25 states.
- **W** 50 states.

2 The capital of the USA is …
- **E** Washington, D.C.
- **A** New York City.
- **P** Chicago.

3 The first president of the USA was …
- **L** Arnold Schwarzenegger.
- **A** George Washington.
- **N** John F. Kennedy.

4 The USA has a population of …
- **E** about 33 million people.
- **R** about 330 million people.
- **H** about 3.3 billion people.

5 The most important American film awards are called …
- **J** the Adams.
- **T** the Leonardos.
- **E** the Oscars.

6 An important American holiday in November is …
- **G** Thanksgiving.
- **B** Independence Day.
- **M** Pancake Day.

7 The Statue of Liberty is in …
- **O** New York City.
- **U** Los Angeles.
- **E** San Diego.

8 The very first people who came to America were probably from …
- **S** Antarctica.
- **I** Asia.
- **C** Australia.

9 Martin Luther King Jr. …
- **W** was a US president.
- **N** fought for equal rights for African Americans.
- **R** was the first US-American to win an Olympic gold medal.

10 In New York City there are …
- F about 2.5 million people.
- I about 5.5 million people.
- G about 8.5 million people.

11 What is the official language of the USA?
- I English.
- Q Spanish.
- T There is no official language.

12 In the 1850s the first jeans in America were made by …
- A Billy Jean.
- D Johnny Blue.
- O Levi Strauss.

13 'Moccasins', 'anorak' and 'kayak' are words from …
- T indigenous languages.
- L Asian languages.
- R European languages.

14 The letter 'B' in 'NBA' stands for …
- P bowling.
- O baseball.
- H basketball.

15 Cheerleaders …
- E shout, dance and do stunts at games.
- O play American football at school.
- N run around the stadium.

16 The first hamburger in America was sold in …
- V 1495.
- J 1605.
- U 1885.

17 Hip-hop originated in …
- D Hawaii.
- S New York City.
- Z Hollywood.

18 The Super Bowl can be won in …
- A American football.
- G mini golf.
- K cooking.

Your sentence:

seven 7

Quiz 2

Landscapes and cities in the USA

Match the photos to the places on the map. The correct letters make a word. You can find help on the map in the front of your book.

L — Golden Gate Bridge in San Francisco
C — Desert in Arizona
M — Statue of Liberty and skyline in New York City
E — Alligator in Florida
W — Surfing in Hawaii
E — Dog sled ride in Alaska
O — Farmland in Kansas

Your word:
① ② ③ ④ ⑤ ⑥ ⑦ !

8　eight

1

1. Describe the pictures. What are the people doing?
2. Where do you think the people are?
3. If you could be in one of the places, which one would you choose? Why?

Welcome to the USA

Part A Impressions of the USA

- You will learn about some aspects of US-American history and culture.
- You will listen to a podcast about national holidays that are celebrated in the USA.
- You will create a fact file about a US state.

Part B New York City

- You will find out about sights in New York.
- You will read about what people living in New York say about their neighbourhood.
- You will create a digital travel guide of New York.

1   Part A   Part B   Challenge

Welcome to the USA

1a   skill: talking with people p. 154
How much USA is there in your life?
Talk to a partner and make notes.

1b   workbook p. 4/1
Share your ideas in class and make a word web.

Spotlight on ...

2a
Look at the pictures and talk about them in class.

2b
Read the info texts. What do you find most interesting?

... geography

The United States of America is located in North America and covers an area of 3.8 million square miles (9.83 million square kilometres) which is about 27.5 times bigger than Germany. The USA has six time zones from east to west, so when it is noon in Boston, a city in the eastern state Massachusetts, it is only six o'clock in the morning in Honolulu, Hawaii, in the west. There is a wide variety of climate zones and landscapes: deserts, beaches, mountains, forests and tropical islands, to name just a few. There are big cities like New York and Philadelphia in the east and San Francisco and Los Angeles in the west, and long stretches of farmland in the states of Kansas and Oklahoma. In California there are sunny beaches, and in Alaska you can see mountain peaks covered with snow all year round.

... technology

US-American innovations have had a huge impact on the world. In 1913, for example, Henry Ford installed the very first assembly line in his car factory in Highland Park, Michigan. His innovation changed the whole industry because it significantly reduced the time it took to build a car and thus made cars a lot more affordable. In the 1960s, American innovation even extended into outer space, and in 1969, Neil Armstrong became the first man to set foot on the moon. American companies have also contributed to groundbreaking innovations in the field of information technology (IT). Companies located in Silicon Valley, south of San Francisco, California, have played an important role not only in developing Internet technology but also in the field of artificial intelligence.

Impressions of the USA 1

... national parks

In 1872, Ulysses S. Grant, the 18th president of the USA, signed a bill that established the world's first national park in the state of Wyoming: Yellowstone. Politicians wanted to preserve and protect natural beauty, geological wonders and diverse ecosystems and provide public areas for people to have fun and relax. Today, there are 63 national parks and hundreds of state parks all over the USA, for example Grand Canyon National Park in Arizona or the Everglades in Florida, famous for its tropical wetlands and alligators.

... food

There is a lot more to US-American food than just hamburgers and hot dogs. You can find a wide variety of regional specialities like huckleberry pie from the state of Montana or Philly cheesesteak sandwich from Philadelphia, Pennsylvania. Immigrants from all over the world also influenced eating habits in the USA with the recipes they brought with them. In recent years, organic food that puts more emphasis on healthy eating and the use of fresh ingredients, less meat and lots of vegetables has become more and more popular. Portland, Oregon, for example, is well known for its vegetarian and vegan food scene.

... pop culture

American pop culture has influenced and inspired people all over the world. Many different music styles originated in the US, especially in the last century. Country music, for example, evolved in the 1920s, and Nashville, Tennessee, became one of its hotspots. Another genre that has its roots in the USA is hip-hop, which started in New York City in the 1970s. American films, TV series and TV shows have also had a huge influence on youth culture with Hollywood being the birthplace of the American film industry. Famous film directors from the US whose films became popular all over the world include Steven Spielberg and George Lucas.

2c CHOOSE YOUR LEVEL skill: reading p. 156, workbook p. 4/2

I Take notes on three of the states mentioned in the texts. Then find the states on a map.
II Take notes on four of the cities mentioned in the texts. Then find the cities on a map.
III Take notes on four places mentioned in the texts and find them on a map. Then take notes on what is written about one of the people in the texts.

ACTIVATE PRACTISE DEVELOP PRACTISE APPLY

1   Part A   Part B   Challenge

> **GRAMMAR HELP**   the simple past (R) p. 174–175
>
> Das *simple past* kennst du bereits. Erinnerst du dich noch, wie es gebildet und verwendet wird? Sieh dir die Beispielsätze an. Woran erkennst du, dass hier das *simple past* benötigt wird?
>
> In 1969, Neil Armstrong became the first man to set foot on the moon.
> Many different music styles originated in the US, especially in the last century.
> Hip-hop started in New York City in the 1970s.
>
> Auf den Seiten 174–175 findest du weitere Erklärungen und Beispiele zum *simple past*, und auf den Seiten 275–277 gibt es eine Liste mit unregelmäßigen Verben.

A trip to Yellowstone National Park

3   grammar: simple past (R) p. 174, workbook p. 5/3, 4

Copy the text and fill in the gaps with the correct verb form.

Hi everyone, greetings from Yellowstone! We ??? (arrive) here three days ago. On our first day, we ??? (drive) around a lot and ??? (see) some of the highlights of the park. The views ??? (be) really amazing. We ??? (have) a fantastic day yesterday, too. We ??? (walk) so much that our feet ??? (hurt) in the evening. We all ??? (sleep) really well last night because we ??? (be) so tired. And there is so much more to see – I ??? (not expect) the park to be so big! And I ??? (not know) that Yellowstone ??? (be) actually the first national park in the US. It's definitely an amazing place!

Innovations

4   grammar: simple past (R) p. 175, workbook p. 6/5

Unscramble the questions and write them in your exercise book. Then answer them.

1. groundbreaking – was – What – innovation – Ford's – ?
2. the very first assembly line – Where – Ford – install – did – ?
3. the car industry – Why – the assembly line – change – invention of – did – the – ?
4. the – first – moon – on – Who – man – the – was – ?
5. country music – evolve – When – did – ?
6. the 1970s – What – in – started – New York City – in – ?

How to pronounce the letters *-ed*

5   audio 1/1

Listen to the words and repeat them. Then sort them into three lists according to the sound at the end of the words.

installed · changed · reduced · influenced · evolved ·
extended · played · inspired · established · originated

/-t/	/-d/	/-ɪd/
...	installed	...
...	...	...

DIGITAL+ practise more 1–2

12   twelve   ACTIVATE   **PRACTISE**   DEVELOP   PRACTISE   APPLY

Impressions of the USA 1

Sightseeing in the USA

6a
Look at the three travel ads. Which destination do you find the most interesting? Why?

Welcome to Arizona, the land of natural wonders!
With breathtaking landscapes and endless adventures, Arizona is a must-see destination for nature lovers. Start your trip at the Grand Canyon, one of the most magnificent natural wonders in the world. For the ultimate thrill, step out onto the Skywalk, a glass bridge that takes you out 70 feet over the canyon's edge.
→ Find out more in the video clip

Experience the ultimate adventure in Alaska!
Enjoy outdoor activities and stunning natural beauty in the northernmost state of the USA. Visit the charming town of Skagway and step back in time to the gold rush era. If you're feeling more adventurous, why not take a dog sled ride?
→ Find out more in the video clip

Discover the magic of Pennsylvania!
Pennsylvania is perfect if you are looking for a state rich in history and charming small towns. Visit the historic town of Gettysburg where the famous Civil War battle took place, and enjoy the delicious local food in Lancaster. If you prefer bigger cities, you can learn about American history at Independence Hall in Philadelphia.
→ Find out more in the video clip

6b CHOOSE YOUR LEVEL video 1, 2, 3, skill: watching a video clip p. 158, media worksheet 8

I Watch the video clips. Take notes on the sights that you can visit in the three states.

II Watch the video clips and take notes on what you can see and do in the three states.

III Watch the video clips and take notes on the history, geography and tourist attractions of the three states.

6c
Collect the information from the video clips on the board.

6d workbook p.6/6, 7
Which state would you like to go to? What would you like to see and do there?

Some glimpses of US-American history

7a

Look at the pictures. What aspects of US-American history do you expect to learn about in the texts? Then read the texts.

1 Archaeological findings suggest that the first people appeared on the American continent about 20,000 years ago.

2 Around 1,000 AD, people from Scandinavia reached the part of North America that is known as Canada today. There they lived in small settlements for about 100 years.

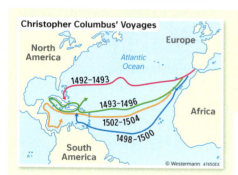

3 In 1492, Christopher Columbus landed in the Caribbean. Although there were already people living there, he claimed the land for Spain. His "discovery" marks the beginning of the European colonization of the American continent.

4 In the 17th century, people from Britain and other European countries began to settle on the east coast of what is the USA today. Many of them came to America for political or economic reasons and some wanted to escape religious suppression. One of the most well-known of these groups were the British Pilgrim Fathers, who reached America in November 1620 on the ship *Mayflower*.

5 When the settlers from Europe arrived, there were hundreds of different Native American nations in North America who spoke different languages and had different ways of living. The European settlers not only took their land from them, often using violence, but they also brought diseases with them that the Native Americans were not familiar with. In the following centuries, millions of Native Americans died from diseases and violence.

6 By 1733, there were 13 British colonies on the east coast of North America. These colonies were governed by Great Britain and had to pay taxes to the British government. In 1775, the colonies began a war for their independence from Great Britain. On 4 July, 1776, the Founding Fathers of the United States declared the United States of America an independent nation. The American War of Independence lasted until 1783.

Impressions of the USA 1

7 Until 1865, slavery was a legal institution in the USA. Slaves from Africa were forced to work under inhumane conditions in almost every field of work. This practice ended after the Civil War. It was fought from 1861 to 1865 between the more industrialized northern states that wanted freedom for the slaves and the agricultural southern states that were in favour of slavery.

8 In the first half of the 20th century, the USA was involved in World War I (1914-1918) and World War II (1939-1945). In 1941, Germany declared war on the USA, and the USA entered the Second World War. In 1945, after years of fighting in Europe, Africa and the Pacific, the USA and its allies won the war. Since then, there has always been a US-American military presence in Europe.

9 The end of slavery in the 19th century did not lead to complete equal rights for black and white people, especially in the south of the USA. Until the mid-1960s, there was racial segregation in public places and institutions. In the 1950s and 1960s, the civil rights movement gained momentum, with Martin Luther King Jr. being one of its leaders.

10 On 11 September 2001, terrorists hijacked four planes and flew two of them into the twin towers of the World Trade Center in New York. Around 3,000 people died in the attack, and the World Trade Center was completely destroyed. In 2006, rebuilding began, and the One World Trade Center is now the main building of the rebuilt complex.

11 In 2009, Barack Obama, born in Honolulu, Hawaii, in 1961, became the first African American president of the United States. He served as the 44th president until 2017.

7b CHOOSE YOUR LEVEL skill: reading p. 156

I Write down these events in the correct chronological order.

- The end of slavery
- The first people on the American continent
- The Pilgrim Fathers reach America aboard the "Mayflower"
- The colonies become independent
- Columbus arrives in the Caribbean

II Write headings for six or more of the texts.
III Make a timeline of the events mentioned in the texts.

7c workbook p. 7/8

Have you heard of any other historical events in US-American history that you think are important? Talk about them in class in German.

1 Part A   Part B   Challenge

PEOPLE & PLACES 1 video 4, 5, workbook p. 8/9

The Trail of Tears

The arrival of the settlers from Europe completely changed the lives of the estimated seven million indigenous people in what is known as the USA and Canada today. Not only did the settlers bring diseases that killed many Native Americans, but they also stole their land by driving them away with violence or even murdering them. Native Americans resisted, but by 1900 the number of Native Americans had been reduced to about 300,000. In the 19th century, the US government established the reservation system and forced Native Americans to live in certain areas, on land that was often of poor quality and sometimes far away from where they used to live.

Trail of Tears / Jerome Tiger 1961

One of the most terrible examples of what this meant for the Native Americans took place between 1830 and 1850. White settlers wanted to grow cotton in the southeast of the USA, and the US government forced about 60,000 Native Americans to leave their land there and walk across the Mississippi River, over 1,000 miles to the west. Thousands of them died on the way and the long and hard route was named the "Trail of Tears".

Talk to a partner. What was new to you?

National holidays

8a audio 1/5, skill: listening p. 153

Listen to the podcast about four American holidays. Write down the names of the holidays in the order they are presented in the podcast.

| Independence Day | | Thanksgiving | | Martin Luther King Jr. Day | | Juneteenth |

8b skill: mediation p. 157, workbook p. 8/10

Listen again and take notes. What does each of the four holidays commemorate? Tell someone in German what you have learnt about the holidays.

American history and culture

9 CHOOSE YOUR TASK B: wordbank: descriptions p. 163, B+C: skill: searching the internet p. 159, presentations p. 160, B+C media worksheet 6

A Make a collage about one event or person from American history and label it.
B Prepare a one-minute talk on an American sportsperson, actor or actress, musician, …
C Find out about the American flag and tell your class about it.

Impressions of the USA

The American Dream

10a

Read the quote. What is the "American Dream" according to James T. Adams?

> *"The American Dream, that dream of a land in which life should be better and richer and fuller for every man, with opportunity for each."*
>
> James T. Adams

James T. Adams (1878 – 1949) was an American historian and author.

10b CHOOSE YOUR LEVEL

I What do you think: what do you need to lead a "better and richer and fuller life"? Choose three of the topics from the box and rank them.

II What do you think: what do you need to lead a "better and richer and fuller life"? Choose three of the topics from the box. Give reasons for your choice.

money · health · education · personal freedom · security · peace · tolerance · …

III What do you think: What topics from the box would a teenager decide to be the most important for a "better and richer and fuller life"? Which ones would a 40- and a 70-year-old person choose? Make three lists and give reasons for your choices.

10c

Read this passage from a dictionary entry about the American Dream.
According to the dictionary entry, what do you have to do to achieve the American Dream?

> The American Dream is a set of ideals such as democracy, rights, freedom and equality. Freedom in this case means that everyone – regardless of his or her social class or origin – can become rich and successful if he or she just works hard enough.

10d wordbank: expressing opinions p. 168, workbook p. 8/11, 12

Read what some people have said about the American Dream.
Who do you agree or disagree with most? Say why.

"Only in America can someone start with nothing and achieve the American Dream. That's the greatness of this country."

Rafael Cruz, born 1939

"The American Dream of rags to riches is a dream for a reason – it is hard to achieve; were everyone to do it, it wouldn't be a dream but would rather be reality."

Robert Fulton 1765 – 1815

"No person can maximize the American Dream on the minimum wage."

Benjamin Todd Jealous, born 1973

ACTIVATE   PRACTISE   **DEVELOP**   PRACTISE   APPLY

seventeen 17

1 Part A · Part B · Challenge

Mixed numbers

11 wordbank: numbers p. 171, workbook p. 9/13

Copy the sentences and fill in the correct words and numbers from the box.

1776 · 44th · 13 · 2009 · first ·
20,000 · 27.5 · 18th · 4th · 9.83 million

1. The USA is about ??? times bigger than Germany.
2. It is about ??? square kilometres big.
3. The ??? people appeared on the American continent about ??? years ago.
4. Ulysses S. Grant was the ??? president of the USA.
5. Barack Obama became the ??? US president in ???.
6. In the year ???, the ??? British colonies declared themselves independent.
7. Independence Day is celebrated on ??? July.

Discover more

12 CHOOSE YOUR LEVEL workbook p. 9/14

I Write about Florida. Fill in the gaps with words from the box.

1. The first people ??? Florida more than 12,000 years ago.
2. Today, about 20 million people ??? in Florida.
3. Florida ??? one of the most popular tourist destinations in the USA.
4. Millions of people ??? Disneyworld in Orlando each year.
5. Another name for Florida ??? "sunshine state".

is ·
visit ·
reached ·
live ·
is

II Write about Nevada. Fill in the gaps with words from the box. There is one more word than you need.

1. The first people ??? to settle in Nevada at least 14,800 years ago.
2. Nevada ??? a US state in 1864.
3. Las Vegas ??? the most famous and the biggest city in Nevada.
4. Nevada ??? the driest state in the US and ??? large desert areas.
5. Nevada ??? also called the "Silver State".

is ·
brought ·
is ·
is ·
started ·
became ·
has

III Write about Massachusetts. Fill in the gaps with the words from the brackets. Use the simple present or the simple past.

1. The first people ??? (come) to what today is called Massachusetts about 12,000 years ago.
2. In 1620, settlers called the Pilgrim Fathers ??? (arrive) on the ship Mayflower.
3. Boston, one of oldest cities in today's USA, ??? (be established) in 1630.
4. Massachusetts ??? (become) a US state in 1788.
5. Today, Boston ??? (be) the biggest city and the capital of Massachusetts.
6. Boston ??? (be situated) on the east coast of the USA.
7. Massachusetts ??? (be known) for its many different landscapes.
8. It ??? (be sometimes called) the "Baked Bean State".

Impressions of the USA 1

Presenting a state TARGET TASK

13 workbook p. 10/15, wordbank: around the world p. 162, numbers p. 171

Your task is to present one of the fifty states of the USA. Create a fact file.
Before you start, look at these steps:

STEP 1
Which states would you like to learn more about? Make a list in class.

STEP 2
Work in groups or with a partner. In class, decide which team is going to work on which state.

STEP 3
Do your research. You could focus on some of these categories:
- geography (area, population, capital, big cities/rivers/mountains, climate)
- history (important events)
- economy (which industries, where most people work)
- tourist attractions (sights, events)
- famous people (actors or actresses, musicians, sportspersons, writers, politicians)
- …

STEP 4
Decide which information you want to include in your fact file.

STEP 5
Make a first draft. Decide on a suitable layout and add pictures.

STEP 6
Get peer feedback and edit your fact file if necessary.

STEP 7
Display your fact files in class.

Fact file – Iowa

Capital: Des Moines
Area: 145.743 km²
Longest river:
Missouri River
Highest mountain:
Hawkeye Point
Population: about
3,000,000 people

ACTIVATE PRACTISE DEVELOP PRACTISE **APPLY** nineteen 19

First impressions

1a video 6, media worksheet 8

Watch the video clip. What is your first impression of New York City?

1b wordbank: around the world p. 162

Which words would you use to describe New York?

busy · sleepy · noisy · fascinating · quiet · boring · multicultural · lively · fabulous · …

1c workbook p. 11/1

Can you imagine living in a big city like New York? Why? Why not?

Messages from New York

2a audio 1/6, skill: reading p. 156

Listen to the tourists and read along. Who is where? Take notes, then find the places on the map of New York at the back of your book.

Ben: The show was awesome! I haven't seen anything like it before. The costumes, the music – fabulous! And all of the actors were so good. Now I know why Broadway is so famous for its theater productions. I'm definitely going to see another show while I'm here. It's been the best part of my trip to New York so far.

Suri: Hi everyone! Can you see me? I'm up here – yes, that's right, I'm INSIDE Lady Liberty's crown. I've wanted to do this since I was a kid and I can't believe that I'm really here on Liberty Island now. I've had to climb 162 steps to get up here, but it's definitely worth it! The trip on the ferry was great as well – the view over the harbor and the skyline of New York was amazing, but I can see even better from up here inside the Statue of Liberty. Next stop is Ellis Island, the place where so many immigrants entered the United States in the late 19th and early 20th century.

Kim: This is so cool. I'm riding a bike across Brooklyn Bridge right over the East River. I always thought New York would be too dangerous for cycling, but apparently that has changed. There are now so many good bike lanes that I've decided to tour the city on a bike. This bike lane across the bridge is a great way to get from Manhattan to Brooklyn.

New York City

Andrea: It's lovely here in Central Park. It's so green and calm. I think it was a brilliant idea to build such a big park right in the middle of the busiest part of New York. There are even lakes, a zoo and museums inside the park. We've been on our feet all day long to see as much of New York as possible, but I'm really happy that we've rented this boat and can relax a little. I don't think my feet have ever hurt as much as today.

Fabio: I'm at the 9/11 Memorial, at the site where the Twin Towers were hit by a terrorist attack in 2001. It's amazing what has been rebuilt here since then. I'm standing at the North Pool that was built in the footprint of the former North Tower, and there are new skyscrapers all around me. There's also a South Pool where the South Tower used to stand and inside the pools are the largest man-made waterfalls in North America. They're really impressive, and the atmosphere here is quite moving.

2b
Talk about the places in class. What do the tourists like about them?

2c CHOOSE YOUR LEVEL

I Read Ben and Suri's statements again and answer the questions.

1 What is Broadway famous for?
2 How many steps do you have to climb to get to the top of the Statue of Liberty?
3 How did Suri get to Liberty Island?
4 Where does Suri want to go next?

II Read the first four statements again and answer the questions.

1 What has been the best part of Ben's trip to New York so far?
2 Since when has Suri wanted to visit the Statue of Liberty?
3 How does Kim tour New York?
4 What can you rent in Central Park?

III Read the statements again and answer the questions.

1 What does Ben say about the show that he has just seen on Broadway?
2 What do you learn about Ellis Island?
3 Which boroughs of New York does Brooklyn Bridge connect?
4 What does Andrea say about Central Park?
5 What can you see at the 9/11 Memorial?

2d workbook p. 11/2
Which of the places would you like to visit? Say why.

ACTIVATE   PRACTISE   DEVELOP   PRACTISE   APPLY

1   Part A   **Part B**   Challenge

> **GRAMMAR HELP**   the present perfect (R) p. 176-177
>
> Das *present perfect* kennst du bereits. Erinnerst du dich noch, wie es gebildet wird und wann man es benutzt? Sieh dir die Beispielsätze an. Woran erkennst du, dass hier das *present perfect* benötigt wird?
>
> I **haven't seen** anything like it before.
> It's **been** the best part of my trip to New York so far.
> I've **wanted** to do this since I was a kid.
>
> Auf den Seiten 176-177 findest du weitere Erklärungen und Beispiele zum *present perfect*.

Visiting New York

3a   grammar: present perfect (R) p. 176

Copy the sentences and fill in the gaps. Use the present perfect.

1. Ben ??? (not see) such a fantastic show before.
2. Many people ??? (visit) Broadway since the first show in 1866.
3. Suri ??? (climb) 162 steps, and now she has an amazing view over the harbour.
4. Riding a bike in New York ??? (become) much safer in the last years.
5. Andrea's feet ??? (never hurt) like that before.

3b   grammar: present perfect (R) p. 176, workbook p. 11/3

Complete the sentences. Use the present perfect or the simple past.

I ??? (already see) many cities in the US, but I ??? (not be) to New York yet. My friend ??? (go) there last month, and she ??? (enjoy) it a lot.
She ??? (show) me some amazing pictures yesterday. She also ??? (recommend) a hotel and I ??? (just check) it out on the Internet.
I ??? (always want) to go to New York, so I think I'll book a room right now!

Have you ever …?

4a   grammar: present perfect (R) p. 177

Write down five or more questions for a partner.

Have you ever	travelled seen been visited …	by ferry? a musical? …

4b   grammar: present perfect (R) p. 177, workbook p. 12/4

Work with a partner and ask and answer questions. React to your partner's answers by asking follow-up questions.

You can answer:
Yes, I have.
No, I haven't.

You can ask follow-up questions:
What was it like? What did you do there?
Would you like to … one day? Why?/Why not?

Brandon's vlog about New York

5a video 7, skill: watching a video clip p. 158, media worksheet 8

Watch the video clip.
What is Brandon's favourite time of the year?
Why?

5b CHOOSE YOUR LEVEL video 7, skill: watching a video clip p. 158

I Read the statements. Then watch the video clip again and choose the right information.

1 This building is 1,776 feet high and has 102 floors.
    A One World Trade Center   B Empire State Building

2 An old railroad has been turned into this park.
    A Central Park   B The High Line

3 In winter, they put up a huge Christmas tree here.
    A Chinatown   B Rockefeller Center

II Read the statements. Then watch the video clip again and match them to the sights.

1 From up there, you have a great view of the whole city.
2 It is often called the "Freedom Tower".
3 You've probably seen it in films or on TV.
4 It is also a great example of New York City's multicultural history.
5 In winter, a huge Christmas tree is put up in front of it.

| Central Park | Chinatown | Empire State Building | Rockefeller Center | One World Trade Center |

III What do you learn about the High Line, Chinatown and the Staten Island Ferry?
Watch the video clip again and take notes.

5c skill: searching the internet p. 159, media worksheet 6

Choose one of the sights from the video clip and find out more about it.
Work with a partner and tell each other what you found most interesting.

5d wordbank: (digital) communication p. 167, workbook p. 12/5, 6

Imagine you are a tourist in New York.
Write a text message to a friend and recommend one or more of the sights to them.

You can write:
Hi ..., I'm here at the ... It's ...
Did you know that it was built ...?
You should come and see it yourself.

Boroughs and people

6a audio 1/7

Listen and read along. Which teenager lives in which borough: the Bronx, Manhattan, Brooklyn, Queens and Staten Island? Find the boroughs on the map at the back of your book.

My family is originally from Lebanon, but we've lived in Manhattan for eight years now. There are a lot of different neighborhoods in Manhattan. Our apartment is in the north, in the part called Harlem. You can see many of the typical New York brownstone houses here. Harlem is not a bad place to live. It's still not as expensive as many other parts of the city. My dad has an old food truck, and we sell hot dogs at different places in Harlem. It's hard work and we don't make a lot of money. *(Bilal Hinawy, 16)*

Brooklyn is the best. I grew up around here. I go to high school in downtown Manhattan, but I'm glad to get back here in the evenings. It's not as loud as Manhattan, the sidewalks are clean and there are lots of parks and beaches. Brooklyn also has cool little stores with clothes and shoes. To me, Brooklyn's special – there's no other neighborhood like it. I wouldn't want to live anywhere else. *(Marian Jones, 14)*

I think there is no better place than Staten Island. I don't know of anybody who grew up here who doesn't like it. It's not as loud and busy as Manhattan or Brooklyn, and there are lots of lakes and parks. Some people think that living on Staten Island must be boring because it's so quiet. But it's near downtown Manhattan with all its great entertainment. There's a ferry so you can get there fast. And you don't have to pay for the ferry! *(Tami Webb, 18)*

I moved to Queens from the Caribbean. I've lived here for ten years, and I'm really proud of my borough. People from all over the world live here, so you can hear a lot of different languages and eat all kinds of food. People learn to get along with each other or just leave each other in peace. *(Paul Beliard, 17)*

I'm from the Bronx. It's a busy and culturally diverse place with lots of street art. Many people here are Hispanics. My family is from Puerto Rico, and at home we speak Spanish. Lots of people who work in Manhattan live in my borough. Many years ago, the Bronx had a bad reputation because of its high crime rate, but now it's a good place to be. Hip-hop started around here, and that's my favorite kind of music. We also have the best baseball team in the world – the Yankees. Whenever I have enough money, I go and watch a game.
(Joshua Rodriguez, 16)

New York City 1

6b skill: reading p. 156

Do you think the teenagers are happy where they live? Find statements in the texts that show how they feel about their boroughs. Copy the statements into your exercise book.

6c workbook p. 14/7, 8

Which borough would you like to live in? Give some reasons for your answer.

An open letter to NYC

7a wordbank: around the world p. 162

Read this extract from the song "An open letter to NYC" by the Beastie Boys. Describe the picture of New York that comes to mind while reading it.

(…)
Brooklyn, Bronx, Queens and Staten
From the Battery to the top of Manhattan
Asian, Middle-Eastern and Latin
Black, White, New York you make it happen

Brownstones, water towers, trees, skyscrapers
Writers, prizefighters and Wall Street traders
We come together on the subway cars
Diversity unified, whoever you are, uh

(…)
Dear New York, I hope you're doin' well
I know a lot's happened, and you've been through hell
So, we give thanks for providin' a home
Through your gates at Ellis Island, we passed in droves

(…)
Dear New York, this is a love letter
To you and how you brought us together
We can't say enough about all you do
'Cause in the city we're ourselves and electric, too

(…)
I see you're still strong after all that's gone on
Lifelong we dedicate this song
Just a little somethin' to show some respect
To the city that blends and mends and tests, uh

Since 9/11, we're still livin'
And lovin', life we've been given
Ain't nothin' gonna take that away from us
We lookin' pretty and gritty 'cause in the city we trust

Dear New York, I know a lot has changed
Two towers down, but you're still in the game
Home to the many, rejectin' no one
Acceptin' peoples of all places, wherever they're from

(…)

7b CHOOSE YOUR LEVEL skill: reading p. 156

I Find words and phrases in the lyrics that show how the speaker feels about New York.
II In the song, the speaker addresses New York like a person. Find words and phrases in the lyrics that describe the city's character and copy them into your exercise book.
III What places, landmarks and people are mentioned in the lyrics? What do you think: why were they included in the song?

7c skill: writing p. 155, workbook p. 15/9, 10, media worksheet 11

Write a (love) letter to the place where you live or would like to live.

ACTIVATE PRACTISE **DEVELOP** PRACTISE APPLY

Part B

PEOPLE & PLACES 2 video 8

Culture for everyone

New York has a lively cultural scene. There are thousands of theatres, art galleries and museums, and you can enjoy musicals, concerts and lots of other cultural events. Everyone has heard of Broadway, home to many musical theatres.
The Metropolitan Opera, known as the Met, has world-famous performances. If you want to see world-class modern art, visit the MoMA, the Museum of Modern Art in Manhattan. It was opened in 1929 and is one of the world's leading art museums.

Hip-hop originated in the Bronx. In 1973, DJ Kool Herc played soul and funk music in a new and special way at a party, which is today seen as the birth of hip-hop.
You can visit the Universal Hip-Hop Museum, where you'll find records, musical equipment, clothing and hip-hop magazines on display.

Find out what's on at Broadway at the moment. Which show would you like to see?

New York tips

8 skill: mediation p. 157, workbook p. 15/11

Help someone who does not speak English understand this flyer. Tell them in German about the opening times, fees and activities you can do at the three places.

TIPS FOR THE CITY THAT NEVER SLEEPS

YANKEE STADIUM ○ BRONX   *Tour times vary – please book in advance on our website*

Take a tour of the Yankee Stadium and visit the exhibition to experience the rich history of New York's baseball champions. Each tour is led by one of our passionate tour guides.
- Standard Adult Tour Admission: $35
- Seniors aged 65 & above: $24
- Kids aged 14 & under: $24

The B, D and 4 trains stop at 161st Street / Yankee Stadium. Follow the signs within the station to Yankee Stadium.

MUSEUM OF MODERN ART ○ MANHATTAN   *Sat 10:30am–7:00pm, Sun–Fri 10:30am–5:30pm*

Enjoy one of the largest collections of modern art in the world, including works of architecture and design, drawings, paintings, sculptures, photographs, prints, illustrated and artists' books, films, and electronic media.
- Adults: $30
- Students: $17 (full-time with ID, including international students)

Please note: Due to renovations, the cafeteria on the 2nd floor will be closed from March.

CENTRAL PARK ○ MANHATTAN   *open 6am to 1am daily*

Enjoy a walk in one of the most famous parks of the world or book an official Central Park tour like *the Statues and Monuments Tour, the Bike Tour* or *the Playground Adventure*.
- Prices starting at $25.

Check our website for special offers.

At Grand Central Station

9 GET TOGETHER

Get together with a partner. Buy and sell train tickets at Grand Central Station.

Partner A
- I Go to page 130.
- II Go to page 133.
- III Go to page 136.

Partner B
- I Go to page 139.
- II Go to page 142.
- III Go to page 145.

Immigrant Heritage Week

10a

Look at the poster. What is celebrated during Immigrant Heritage Week?

10b audio 1/10, skill: listening p. 153

Listen to the podcast episode. Which of these events are mentioned by the hosts?

1. Coney Island walking tour
2. Mexican art exhibition
3. Stories from Home
4. Parade of Flags
5. Home-made

IMMIGRANT NEW YORK

Join us for a week of events to honor New York's legacy as a **city of immigrants** and celebrate New York's cultural diversity!

Discover how essential immigrants have always been and still are to the city's life.

IMMIGRANT HERITAGE WEEK

10c workbook p. 16/12

Listen again and write down the statements with the correct information.

1. Coney Island is famous for its forests / amusement parks / art galleries.
2. At the "Stories from Home" event, memories / drinks / hot dogs were shared.
3. At the "Parade of Flags", each flag represented a different community / language / nationality that can be found in Brooklyn.
4. At the "Home-made" event in Harlem, you could see flags / fireworks / live performances.

New York, New York

11 CHOOSE YOUR TASK   C: skill: searching the internet p. 159

A Write an acrostic about New York.
B Write multiple-choice quiz questions about New York for your classmates.
C Find out about the many nicknames New York has been given in its history. Tell your class about them.

A **D**IFFERENT **N**EIGHBOURHOODS
IN THE CITY THAT **NE**VER SLEEPS,
AWESOME AND
YOUNG,
OPEN AND
F**R**IENDLY.
MY **K**IND OF PLACE!

1   Part A   **Part B**   Challenge

New York facts

12 grammar: passive (R) p. 178

Copy the statements and choose the correct passive forms from the brackets.
1. Many languages ??? (are spoken / have been spoken) in New York.
2. Many brownstone houses ??? (have been seen / can be seen) in Harlem.
3. The Empire State Building ??? (was built / is built) from 1930 till 1931.
4. A new exhibition at the museum ??? (will be opened / has been opened) in June next year.
5. The Immigrant Heritage Week ??? (has been celebrated / was celebrated) every year since 2004.
6. The High Line is an old railroad which ??? (is turned / has been turned) into a park.

Curious tourist

13   **CHOOSE YOUR LEVEL** grammar: passive (R) p. 178, workbook p. 16/13

I   Unscramble the questions and write them down.
1. built – When – the – was – Statue of Liberty – ?
2. New York – How many – are – spoken – in – languages – ?
3. every year since 2004 – celebrated – has been – What – ?
4. will – Christmas tree – When – be put up – this year's – ?

II   Write questions in the passive.
1. How long ??? the café ????
2. Why ??? the Immigrant Heritage Week ??? each year?
3. When ??? the Empire State Building ????
4. When ??? we ??? again by the bus?
5. Where ??? many skyscrapers ??? since 2001?

will ... be picked up ·
have ... been built ·
will ... be closed ·
is ... celebrated ·
was ... completed

III   Write questions in the passive for these answers. There can be more than one solution.
1. The One World Trade Center was completed in 2014.
2. The café at the museum is closed due to renovations.
3. Lots of skyscrapers can be seen from the Statue of Liberty.
4. At the World Trade Center site many buildings have been rebuilt so far.
5. You will be taken back to the hotel by bus.
6. The tourists are going to be picked up at 12 o'clock.

Spelling

14a wordbank: American and British English p. 165

Sort the words into two lists: one for British spelling and one for American spelling.

     center · centre · favourite · favorite ·
     traveled · travelled · theatre · theater ·
     harbour · harbor

14b workbook p. 16/14

Are there similar words in German or another language that you speak? Tell the class.

A New York travel guide TARGET TASK

15 workbook p. 17/15, wordbank: around the world p. 162, skill: writing p. 155, media worksheet 1, 6, 13

Your task is to create a page for a (digital) travel guide of New York.
Before you start, look at these steps:

STEP 1
In class, collect ideas for your guide. Think about:
- places
- sights
- activities
- neighbourhoods to visit
- …

Get together with a partner or in a small group.
Decide who is going to work on which topic.

STEP 2
In your group, plan your page.
Make notes on what you already know and what you have to find out.

STEP 3
Do your research. You can also look for pictures.

STEP 4
Make a first draft. Then check and edit your texts.

STEP 7
Present your pages in class. Give each other feedback.

STEP 8
You can put all your pages together to create a (digital) travel guide.

You can use phrases like:

Make sure you visit …

… is a must-see because …

… is the biggest / best / most exciting / …

… is a perfect place to relax / enjoy / see / experience / …

… is the ideal place to watch …

Check out

1. Kannst du kurze Infotexte über die USA verstehen? Workbook, p. 18
2. Kannst du einen Podcast über amerikanische Feiertage verstehen? Workbook, p. 18
3. Kannst du die Aussagen von Zitaten verstehen? Workbook, p. 19
4. Kannst du Informationen über Sehenswürdigkeiten in New York verstehen? Workbook, p. 20
5. Kannst du jemandem sprachlich aushelfen, der touristische Informationen nicht versteht? Workbook, p. 20
6. Kannst du mit passenden Redewendungen über Sehenswürdigkeiten schreiben? Workbook, p. 21

What is the real story of Thanksgiving?

For a long time, history books told a story of "The First Thanksgiving" as shown in this picture painted by US-American painter Jean Ferris in 1915. The story goes like this:
In 1620, the Pilgrim Fathers arrived in what is now the state of Massachusetts.
That winter was very cold and the Pilgrims did not know how to find food in their new country. Many died from hunger, the cold and disease. The same area was home to Native Americans – the Wampanoag. In March 1621, two Wampanoag men called Samoset and Squanto decided to help the new settlers. They showed the Pilgrims how to hunt, catch fish, grow food and build houses. Squanto stayed with them and assisted the settlers. Thanks to Squanto, the Pilgrims learnt how to grow food such as pumpkins and corn. In November 1621, the Pilgrims invited the Wampanoag to celebrate their first harvest with them. Many Wampanoag chiefs came with their families and brought food with them. They all ate, sang and celebrated together for three days – and that was the first Thanksgiving.

Jean Ferris: The First Thanksgiving, 1621. The scene is not historically accurate.

But did it really happen like that? And what does the story leave out? Today, it is told differently. Although there is evidence that Chief Massasoit of the Wampanoag had a peaceful relationship with the Pilgrims when they arrived, and it seems that many Wampanoag did teach the Pilgrims how to grow food and survive in the harsh New England climate, there is no evidence of a harvest celebration during the second Pilgrim winter in America.
Also, the relationship between the settlers and the Native American population in that area did not stay peaceful for long. In 1657, a chain of events led to a massive conflict and about 5 per cent of the White population and 40 per cent of the Native American population in the region were killed.
It is difficult to find out what happened exactly, and there is not one single story of the first Thanksgiving dinner – as is often the case with historical events. But it is quite obvious that the first Thanksgiving did not take place as many people believed it did. Thanksgiving was not even an American holiday until the Civil War era, and it did not become a formal federal holiday until 1941.

Look at the picture and describe it. What do you think: what is not accurate?
Collect ideas and talk about them with a partner.

> **NOTE:** In contrast to Canada, where it was officially decided to use the term "First Nation" only, there is an ongoing discussion in the USA about the best words to use when talking or writing about Native Americans. In his book "Everything you wanted to know about Indians but were afraid to ask", Anton Treuer, a member of the Ojibwe First Nation, explains that "there is no way to solve the terminology debates to everyone's satisfaction right now, and it is even more important to make safe spaces for everyone to start asking questions." Besides Indigenous and Native American, he himself uses the terms Native American and Indian, but it is highly controversial to use these terms as an outsider.

accurate = *genau, richtig*; to hunt = *jagen*; to assist = *unterstützen*; corn (AE) = *Mais*; harvest = *Ernte*; chief = *Herrscher/in (Fremdbezeichnung)*; evidence = *Beweis*; relationship = *Beziehung*; to survive = *überleben*; harsh = *streng*; massive = *enorm, riesig*; per cent = *Prozent*; obvious = *offensichtlich*; formal = *offiziell*; federal holiday = *Bundesfeiertag*; in contrast to = *im Unterschied zu*; ongoing = *laufend*; Indian = *Indianer/in (generalisierende Fremdbezeichnung)*; satisfaction = *Zufriedenheit*; highly controversial = *stark umstritten*; outsider = *Außenseiter/in*

Fighting against racism

After the end of enslavement in 1865, Black people in the USA still suffered from racist discrimination by Whites. Many Black Americans lived in poverty, and laws limited their freedom while White people were privileged.

There was segregation – the practice of keeping Black and White people apart from each other and treating them differently – in many places. Cinemas, hotels, restaurants, buses and other places had separate entrances and seating areas for African Americans and Whites. Public schools for Black students only were created to keep them separate from White students.

"Colored" referred to Black people during segregation. It is considered offensive today.

In 1909, a group of Black and White people in New York City founded the National Association for the Advancement of Colored People (NAACP). They wanted to fight against racism. Black leaders began to initiate marches, demonstrations and court cases to stop racist laws.

One very famous case that was brought to court with the support of the NAACP in 1951 was that of seven-year-old Linda Brown from Topeka, Kansas. She was not allowed to go to a school which was just a few blocks away from her home because she was Black. Linda's father went to the Supreme Court, and in the end it was ruled that segregation in public schools was illegal.

Another important battle that the NAACP fought took place in Montgomery, Alabama in 1955. Rosa Parks, a Black woman, was told to give up her bus seat to a White man. She refused and was arrested. In response to this, the NAACP started the Montgomery bus boycott. For 381 days, Black people did not use the buses in Montgomery and the bus companies lost a lot of money. Finally, in another case, the Supreme Court decided that Montgomery could no longer have a segregated public transportation system.

On August 28, 1963, about 250,000 people, Black and White, led by Martin Luther King Jr., marched to the Lincoln Memorial in Washington to protest peacefully against racism and segregation – a milestone for the civil rights movement.

Two years later, President Lyndon B. Johnson signed a law which promised equal rights for Black Americans in jobs, voting and the use of public facilities.

But although open segregation is a thing of the past, there is still no complete equality. Racism continues to exist, and statistically, Black Americans are poorer, less well educated and more often victims of crime than White Americans.

Find out more about Linda Brown, Rosa Parks or Martin Luther King Jr. and the times they were living in. Share your findings in class.

racism = *Rassismus*; enslavement = *Versklavung*; to suffer from = *erleiden*; racist = *rassistisch*; discrimination = *Diskriminierung*; poverty = *Armut*; law = *Gesetz*; to limit = *einschränken*; to keep apart = *getrennt halten*; seating area = *Sitzbereich*; public school *(AE)* = *staatliche Schule*; to found = *gründen*; to initiate = *gründen*; march = *Marsch*; court case = *Gerichtsverfahren*; support = *Unterstützung*; Supreme Court = *Oberstes Bundesgericht*; to refuse = *sich weigern*; to arrest = *verhaften*; segregated = *getrennt*; voting = *Wählen*; facility *(AE)* = *Einrichtung*

Part A   Part B   Challenge

The father of hip-hop – DJ Kool Herc

It is not often that you can say when and where exactly a certain style was invented. But in the case of hip-hop (although it was not called hip-hop yet) that is actually possible.

On the evening of 11 August 1973, 15-year old Cindy Campbell organized a "back to school" party in the community room of her apartment house at 1520 Sedgwick Avenue in New York. She sold tickets for her party and persuaded her brother Clive, known as DJ Kool Herc, to provide the music. Because there were few other options for teenagers to party in safe surroundings in New York City at that

DJ Kool Herc

time, her party was a huge success. Over 300 people showed up, and DJ Kool Herc became a local celebrity overnight.

His special innovation was what he called the Merry-Go-Round. He had noticed that people waited for the moments in a song when you can only hear the beat – the drum breaks – to hit the dance floor. In order to enable them to move longer to the beat, DJ Kool Herc used two turntables and two identical records. This allowed him to make the drum breaks last longer by switching between the records – playing one, while rewinding the other.

Breakdancers on a street in New York in 1984

Party-goers developed a special dance style to these longer drum breaks. They became known as b-boys and b-girls, and the thing they were doing became b-boying and b-girling, or breaking, or breakdancing. Some say that the breaking we know today started as a way for rival street gangs to fight without having to use violence. Dancers from each gang would show off their moves, and the one with the most innovative and complex moves would win. By the summer of 1973, DJ Kool Herc had been using and refining his break-beat style for about a year, but his sister's party put him before his biggest audience yet. It was the success of that party that would begin a musical revolution, a full six years before the term "hip-hop" entered popular vocabulary.

Since then, hip-hop has been going strong. DJ Kool Herc is still performing and producing music today. He is just as much of a crowd pleaser as he was before.

Explain in a few sentences what role DJ Kool Herc played in the history of hip-hop.

option = *Möglichkeit*; to party = *feiern*; surroundings (pl) = *Umgebung*; to show up = *erscheinen*; celebrity = *Berühmtheit*; beat = *Takt*; to hit the dance floor = *auf die Tanzfläche gehen*; to enable = *ermöglichen*; turntable = *Plattenspieler*; to switch = *wechseln*; to rewind = *hier: erneut spielen*; rival = *rivalisierend*; to show off = *zeigen*; innovative = *originell, neu*; to refine = *verbessern*; audience = *Publikum*; to enter = *Eingang finden in*; popular = *allgemein*; to go strong (informal) = *erfolgreich sein*; crowd pleaser = *Publikumsliebling*

2

1. What do you think: who are the people and where are they?
2. What are the people doing?
3. What looks familiar to you? What looks different?

High school

Part A Welcome to high school!

- You will read entries from an American high school yearbook.
- You will find out about school life in the USA.
- You will create a yearbook entry.

Part B After-school activities

- You will find out about after-school activities at an American high school.
- You will read about an afternoon at an American football match.
- You will do a role play about an interview.

2 | Part A | Part B | Challenge

School life in the USA

1

What comes to mind when you think of school life in the USA?
Think about what you know from films, songs, books etc. Share your ideas in class.

A high school yearbook

2a
Look at these yearbook photos from a high school in Philadelphia and talk about them.

2b skill: reading p. 156
Now read the yearbook entries.
What do you find interesting or surprising?

Last year's highlights!

Student exchange program
"There are no strangers here; only friends you haven't met yet." This quote is the motto of the school exchange program. Last year, we welcomed five new exchange students who had traveled all the way to Philadelphia from different parts of the world. They all had a great time with their host families.

1 — Welcoming new friends

2 — Good summer reads

Summer reading challenge
In June, the library club published a list of great summer reads and organized a competition for the keenest readers. There were prizes for readers who had finished at least five books over the summer vacation. Eric Johnson from the 9th grade had read the most books – twelve in total! Congratulations!

Marching band
For decades, our marching band has been a great support for our football team, and it has taken part in parades and competitions. One highlight was the Pennsylvania state championship last fall where our marching band came second. Thanks for some awesome moments in the past year!

3 — The new homecoming queen Linda Chang and homecoming king Bradey Parekh

4 — Our marching band in full swing!

Homecoming
In October, we celebrated homecoming week. Lots of students who had graduated from high school in June came back to visit us. This included the previous homecoming king and queen who won the last homecoming election. They crowned the new king and queen, and once the cheerleaders had finished their dance, there was a fantastic football game. What an awesome week!

Welcome to high school! 2

Cheerleading classes
Before cheerleading trials began, the cheer team had held beginners' classes for the freshmen, who then presented their new skills in a short demonstration at the school basketball tournament in November after they had practiced cheer basics and a dance in the weeks before.

Swimming club
In January, the swimming team won the state championship. Our top athlete Katie Miller broke her personal record after she had trained hard. She won gold in the singles in a thrilling final with her strongest competitor Dana Simmons and later won bronze in the team event. Congratulations to all!

5 Cheer for our team!

6 Swimming to the top

8 A spectacular night celebrating the end of high school for our senior students!

7 Great success for our fundraisers!

Fundraising
The Fundraiser Club has always been very creative and full of energy when it comes to finding ways to raise money. Last year's motto was "Enjoy a great meal for a great cause." Once a week the members of the club provided a healthy lunch for all students. They raised $9,200 to help graduates from our school with their college fees – what a success!

Prom night
What a glamorous night! A big thank you to the prom committee for organizing a fantastic prom night to celebrate our senior students' graduation. Everyone looked fabulous in their best suits and dresses! After the formal dinner had ended, the party continued with the traditional dance and the crowning of the prom king and queen.

2c CHOOSE YOUR LEVEL skill: mediation p. 157

A friend has questions about the yearbook. Answer them in German.

I Choose three or more questions.
II Choose five or more questions.
III Choose seven or more questions.

1 Was hat das Zitat mit dem Austauschprogramm zu tun?
2 Was musste man machen, um einen Preis fürs Lesen zu bekommen?
3 Was ist denn Homecoming und was haben die da gemacht?
4 Was macht denn die Band auf Bild 4?
5 Das sieht ja interessant aus, wofür trainieren die denn da auf Bild 5?
6 Wie erfolgreich war der Schwimmclub?
7 Was steht da mit 9200 Dollar?
8 Noch eine Frau mit Krönchen auf dem Kopf? Was war denn da der Anlass?

2d workbook p. 22 / 1, 2

What is similar and what is different to your school? Talk about it with a partner and take notes. Then share your ideas in class.

ACTIVATE PRACTISE DEVELOP PRACTISE APPLY

| **2** | Part A | Part B | Challenge |

GRAMMAR HELP — the past perfect p. 179

In den Beispielsätzen wird über Ereignisse berichtet, die in der Vergangenheit geschehen sind. Wie würdest du die Sätze auf Deutsch formulieren? Welches der beiden Ereignisse in einem Satz fand jeweils zuerst statt? Was fällt dir an den farbig markierten Formen auf?

<u>Before</u> cheerleading trials began, the cheer team had held beginners' classes.

Katie Miller broke her personal record <u>after</u> she had trained hard.

<u>After</u> the formal dinner had ended, the party continued with the traditional dance.

Die Zeitform, die verwendet wird, um anzuzeigen, dass ein Ereignis in der Vergangenheit vor einem anderen Ereignis stattgefunden hat, heißt *past perfect*. Auf Seite 179 findest du weitere Erklärungen und Beispiele.

High school life last year

3 grammar: past perfect p. 179, workbook p. 22/3–5

Match the sentence parts and write down the sentences.
Underline the part of each sentence that tells you what happened first.

1. Before the exchange students arrived in the USA,
2. Eric Johnson won the reading competition
3. After the cheerleaders had shown their best dance moves,
4. The marching band was very successful
5. After they had trained hard for many weeks,

A. the swimming team won the state championship.
B. the homecoming football game started.
C. because they had spent a lot of time practising.
D. because he had read twelve books over the summer holidays.
E. they had only talked to their host families online.

Chain game: Suzie's dream

4 grammar: past perfect p. 179, workbook p. 24/6

Look at what Suzie did and write about a chain of events.

1. come home
2. talk to mum
3. do homework
4. lie down
5. fall asleep
6. dream of winning prize with cheerleading team

You can write:
After Suzie had come home, she talked to her mum.
After she had talked to her mum, she …

DIGITAL+ practise more 7

ACTIVATE **PRACTISE** DEVELOP PRACTISE APPLY

Welcome to high school! 2

PEOPLE & PLACES 3 video 9

High schools in the USA

The way high schools are organized can vary across the USA. In general, students have to collect a number of credits during the last four years of high school in order to graduate. Some subjects are obligatory, like maths and English, but there are also optional subjects (electives) that students get credits for, such as a foreign language, art or home economics. During the graduation ceremony – when students get their high school diploma – they normally wear special clothes: "caps and gowns". Graduation is celebrated with a huge formal dance called prom, which is usually held at the end of the high school year. Students wear traditional evening dress, and at many schools a prom king and queen are elected.

Watch the video clip. What is different to the school systems that you know?

Amy in Philadelphia

5a audio 1/14-16, workbook p. 24/7a

Amy, 16, from Bath in England is going to spend one year in the USA.
Listen to the three scenes and find out: who are the people? Where are they in each scene?

5b CHOOSE YOUR LEVEL skill: listening p. 153

I Listen again and choose the correct word.

1 The Bakers have brought **flowers** / **a welcome sign** with them for Amy.
2 Amy likes the **pumpkin pie** / **burger**.
3 Amy is a bit nervous about her first day **at school** / **at her host family's house**.
4 Jenna's school has no **dress code** / **café**.

II Listen again and complete the sentences.

1 Amy is a bit ??? about her first school day.
2 Jenna thinks Amy's accent sounds ???.
3 You do not have to wear a ??? at the school.
4 "French fries" is what Americans call ???.
5 Jenna's room is ??? ??? Amy's room.

III Listen again and answer the questions.

1 How do the Bakers welcome Amy?
2 What do they have for dinner?
3 What do they talk about during dinner?
4 What is Amy nervous about?
5 Where is Amy's room?
6 What is Amy looking forward to?

5c wordbank: American and British English p. 165

Listen again.
What differences between American and British English do you notice?

5d workbook p. 24/7b, 8

Imagine you are Amy. At the end of your first day in the USA, write a text message home and tell your family or friends about your first day.

ACTIVATE   PRACTISE   **DEVELOP**   PRACTISE   APPLY

2 Part A Part B Challenge

Amy's first day at school

6a skill: reading p. 156

**Amy has promised her friends and family to blog about her experiences.
Read about her first day at school. Who does she meet?**

Philadelphia, 2 September
Hi everyone,

Today was my first day at school. It did NOT begin with putting on my school uniform.
It took me some time to decide on an outfit, but I really liked wearing my own clothes to school. After breakfast (there are soooo many different kinds of cereal here, I hope I can try them all before the year is over), we went to the school bus stop.

We were picked up by a yellow school bus that looked exactly like the ones you see in American films. These yellow buses are for schoolchildren only. Almost everyone goes to school by bus, or they drive their own car if they are over 16.
I was a bit nervous, but luckily my host sister, Jenna, was with me. She thinks that it is really cool that I can cycle to school at home. Hardly anyone cycles to school over  here – either the journey is too long or their parents think it's too dangerous. The trip to school was fun. Jenna introduced me to some of her friends and they were all really friendly.

At school, I had to go to the school registrar's office first. The registrar gave me my ID card that I have to have with me all the time, my timetable (which is called a 'schedule' over here), all the books I need for my courses and the combination number for my locker.
Then I had to put all my books in my locker and go to homeroom. That's where they check attendance and give out important information first thing in the morning. It's a bit like registration at home. My trip to the office made me late. And the school building is huge! There are over 1,000 students here. My new class was right in the middle of the Pledge of Allegiance when I opened the door.

 American students begin their day by saying: "I pledge allegiance to the flag of the United States of America, and to the republic for which it stands, one nation under God, indivisible, with liberty and justice for all." I guess I'll have to learn that by heart although, strictly speaking, it's not my flag. But I guess it would be rude not to join in. Maybe I'll ask my host family what's best.

Well, anyway, when I walked into the classroom late, everyone stared at me and I felt a bit uncomfortable. But my homeroom teacher Mr de Sousa was very nice. He introduced me to the students in my homeroom and asked a girl to help me find my classrooms.

Welcome to high school! 2

My first lesson was maths (or math as it is called here …). It's good that I like maths because unlike at home, school days here are more or less the same every day. So I have maths in first period every single day! Apart from maths, I have science, gym (we would say PE) – that's only on Tuesdays and Thursdays – history, English and my elective, robotics. The electives are only on the schedule twice a week, too.

Schedule Student ID 130970 Name: Amy Milligan Grade: 11				
	Mon–Fri	Subject	Room	Teacher
1	7:25 – 8:15	Homeroom, math	W276	de Sousa, Enrico
2	8:20 – 9:10	Science	W161	Birk, Wendy
3	9:15 – 10:05	Geography	W223	Mulvern, Jack
4	10:10 – 11:00	History	W262	Pearce, Sandra
5	11:05 – 11:55	English	W140	Alvarez, Ramos
6	11:55 – 12:45	Lunch; Study period	Cafeteria; Study hall	
7	12:50 – 1:40	Gym (Tue and Thur)	W220	Kracinski, Lea
8	1:45 – 2:35	Elective: robotics (Mon and Fri)	W105 (lab)	Monterres, Patsy

After every lesson I have to go to my locker in the hallway outside my homeroom and get the books for my next lesson. We're not allowed to carry big bags around in the school building. For lunch, Jenna met me at my locker. She took me to the school cafeteria, which was very busy. There is an early lunch for freshmen and sophomores (students in grade 9 and 10) and a late lunch for juniors and seniors (students in grade 11 and 12).

Jenna and her friends invited me to sit outside with them. The school has an outside lunch area where you can eat when the weather is good. There's a wide variety of food on the menu to choose from. It tastes really good, much better than the food at my school in Bath. Jenna told me that the school's fundraiser club had organized something they called "great meal, great cause" last year. They served healthy meals to raise money, and they were so successful that the school now takes part in a "farm to table" programme which means that they serve organic food that is produced locally.

6b wordbank: American and British English p. 165

Look at Amy's blog post again and find words that are different in British and American English. Write them in a list. Do you know any more words in British and American English? Add them.

6c CHOOSE YOUR LEVEL skill: reading p. 156, writing p. 155, media worksheet 16

I Read Amy's blog post again and write one or two sentences for each picture.
II What did Amy do on her first school day? Read her blog post again and take notes.
III Write a short summary of Amy's day.

6d wordbank: school life p. 164, workbook p. 25/9-11

What did you learn about school life in the USA? Write it down.

ACTIVATE   PRACTISE   DEVELOP   PRACTISE   APPLY   thirty-nine 39

2 Part A Part B Challenge

A video chat

7a audio 1/18

Listen and read along. What is the difference between clubs and electives?

Amy is videochatting with her best friend Emma in Bath.

Emma: Hi Amy, great to see you. How are you? Are you homesick? How was your first week at school?
Amy: I'm fine. I'm not homesick at all. I'm doing OK at school although I'm a bit behind in geography and American history. But I really like my elective.
Emma: What's an elective?
Amy: Electives are subjects that you can choose. They're not optional like clubs. You need electives like all your other subjects to collect credits. For your elective you can choose something you really like.
Emma: Ah, OK. So what's your elective?
Amy: Robotics. It's so good. They have a robot in the lab here that's like one of those used in car factories. Our teacher has already shown us how to program it to pick up a pen and draw a line on a piece of paper. That was so amazing. But we also get to build robots ourselves. In January, there's going to be a science fair at the school. There will be a display of different science projects and we'll try to program a short cheerleading routine for our robot. It will involve waving a flag – I'll send you a video of it!

Emma: Wow, that sounds so cool! Yes, please do send me a video. So, what other electives do they offer?
Amy: There are so many! There are different languages, business law, IT stuff like computer repairing and web programming, but also vocational training like auto body repair.
Emma: Business law? That sounds like university.
Amy: Jenna, my host sister, is doing business law for her elective because she's thinking about doing law or business at university.
Emma: Can you do more than one elective? Or a different one next term?
Amy: I'm not sure. I'll have to talk to my school guidance counsellor about it. There are no terms over here. We have two semesters per school year. If possible, I'd really like to try plumbing, women's studies and Chinese next semester. Or video game development, fashion design and world literature? Tough choice …
Emma: You're so lucky! The only choice I had this year was between French and Spanish.

7b CHOOSE YOUR LEVEL skill: reading p. 156, workbook p. 26/12, 13

I Read the dialogue again. Make a list of all the electives that Amy mentions.

II Read the dialogue again. What do you learn about Amy's elective? Take notes.

III Read the dialogue again and answer the questions.
1 What does Amy tell Emma about her elective?
2 What was Jenna's motivation for choosing her elective?
3 Why does Amy want to talk to her guidance counsellor?
4 Why does Amy think that electives are good?

Welcome to high school! 2

High school electives

8a
Read the descriptions of different high school electives.
Which one would you choose? Why?

Electives
all electives two semesters, 2 credits, open to grades 10 to 12

PERSONAL FINANCE
Students will learn useful tools for managing their own finances.

MARKETING
This course covers an introduction to marketing and marketing ethics. Students will learn about marketing plans and strategies that businesses use to market their products.

MOVIE PRODUCTION
Students will learn to write scripts and get to know the techniques needed to produce a movie.

MAINTENANCE
Students will learn basic maintenance and repair skills and how to use different tools on household machines.

CULINARY ART
This course will give students hands-on experience in the field of food preparation.

BASIC WOODWORKING
This course will provide students with the skills needed for wood processing while also introducing them to the design process and safety precautions.

8b
Which of these electives do you think is most useful? Which is least useful? Why?

8c workbook p. 27/14
What electives are there at your school? What other electives would you like to have? Say why.

Different schools

9 skill: talking with people, p. 154
Mill around and talk about what you know about schools in the UK and the USA. What is the same at your school? What is different? What would you like to have at your school, too?

School life

10 CHOOSE YOUR TASK wordbank: school life p. 164

A Design a poster for prom night.

B Write a radio commercial advertising a student exchange programme to the USA. Record it.

C 🔍 Choose one aspect of American school life that you would like to know more about, for example the Pledge of Allegiance, homecoming or prom night. Do some research and give a short presentation of your findings.

COME TO **PROM** *Night*
WHEN: 30 July
WHERE: in the auditorium
HOW MUCH: $50.00 – $80.00 per ticket
DRESS CODE: evening dress

2 | Part A | Part B | Challenge

British or American?

11 audio 1/20, wordbank: American and British English p. 165

Listen to the five mini dialogues. For each dialogue, say whether the first or the second speaker is American. Compare your results in class.

A German elective

12 skill: mediation p. 157

Read the description of an elective from a German school. Explain in English what it is about.

Technik im Haushalt

In diesem **Wahlpflichtkurs** untersuchen wir elektrische Haushaltsgegenstände. Wir schauen uns zum Beispiel Mixer, Taschenlampen, elektrische Zahnbürsten und Toaster genauer an.
Ihr könnt kaputte Gegenstände mitbringen, die wir dann zerlegen, um ihre Funktionsweise zu verstehen und sie vielleicht sogar zu reparieren. Außerdem finden wir heraus, wie die Geräte möglichst lange halten und nachhaltig eingesetzt werden. Dazu beschäftigen wir uns mit verschiedenen Möglichkeiten des Energiesparens im Haushalt, bestimmen den Energieverbrauch der Geräte und überlegen, wie möglichst wenig Strom verbraucht wird.

The yearbook club

13a audio 1/22

Listen to the meeting of the yearbook club. What do the students and the teacher talk about?

13b CHOOSE YOUR LEVEL skill: listening p. 153, workbook p. 27/15

Read the questions. Then listen again and take notes. Answer the questions.

I
1. What team is Catherine writing about?
2. What club is Carlos writing about?
3. What is Li writing about?
4. What does the teacher ask the club members to do?

II
1. What teams and clubs are Catherine, Carlos and Li writing about?
2. What does the teacher ask the club members to do?
3. How long should the texts be?
4. What problem does Michael mention?

III
1. How does the teacher organize the writing?
2. What does she say about pictures?
3. What is the problem with the first deadline the teacher gives?
4. Apart from sports teams and clubs, what else does the teacher want the students to cover?
5. What does the teacher suggest for the page about the registrar's office?

DIGITAL+ practise more 7

Welcome to high school! 2

A yearbook entry TARGET TASK

14 workbook p. 28/16, wordbank: school life p. 164, wordbank: American and British English p. 165, media worksheet 1, 6

Your task is to create one page for an American high school yearbook.
Before you start, look at these steps:

STEP 1
Work with a partner or in a small group.

STEP 2
Imagine you are American high school students. Choose a topic for your page.
You can think of:
- a typical American sport like baseball, football, lacrosse, …
- an elective like welding, business law, light and sound technology, …
- an event like prom night, homecoming, …
- …

STEP 3
Research your topic and take notes.
Make sure to write down the sources of your information.

STEP 4
Write a first draft. Add matching pictures. Think of a good headline.

STEP 5
Ask classmates for feedback.
Edit your page.
Then create the final version of your page.

STEP 6
Present your page in a gallery walk.
You can put all your pages together
and make a (digital) yearbook.

The **Fundraiser Club** came up with a lot of fun ideas to raise money. Everyone's favourite was **PAJAMA DAY** in June.

ACTIVATE   PRACTISE   DEVELOP   PRACTISE   **APPLY**   forty-three 43

Your school clubs

1 skill: talking with people p.154, workbook p.29/1

Are you a member of a club at your school? Work in small groups and tell each other which clubs you go to, what you do there and what you like about the clubs.

High school clubs

2a workbook p.29/2, 3

Read about some of the clubs that students at Amy and Jenna's school in Philadelphia can join. Which of them do you find interesting? Say why.

Clubs and activities

Mathletics club
Come and stretch your brain muscles! We compete in mathematics competitions for all levels. Classroom 4b, Wednesdays at 4pm.

Baseball club
Are you our next best pitcher or catcher? Join the best baseball team in the state of Pennsylvania! Sports hall, Thursdays, 3-5pm.

Glee club
We love singing! If you love spreading joy through music, too, you should join us in the music room on Tuesday afternoons from 4pm.

Model congress
A role-playing simulation of the United States congress is not only fun but also a place to debate the latest topics.
We meet Mondays, 3-5pm in room 201.

Theater group
Do you love acting, performing and improvising? Then come and join our theater group. Meet us in the auditorium on Tuesdays, 4-5:30pm.

Debating society
Bring your best arguments and help us succeed in the state-wide Pennsylvania debate tournament.
We meet Thursdays from 4pm in room 201.

Future Business Leaders of America
FBLA High School is a program that helps high school students prepare for careers in business through academic competitions, leadership development and educational programs.
Fridays, 3-5pm in room 405.

After-school activities 2

2b 🔊 audio 1/24

Listen to Amy and Jenna and read along. What school clubs are they talking about?

Jenna: Hi Amy, what are you up to?
Amy: Hey Jenna, I'm just looking at the after-school clubs. Do you think I should join one while I'm here?
Jenna: Yes, definitely. You'll have a lot of fun if you join a club. Don't you have clubs at your school in the UK?
Amy: Not exactly. We have a few clubs, but most of them are only lunchtime clubs. We can't choose from so many cool things like you can here. We also start later in the mornings and don't finish lessons until 3pm, so there's less time for after-school clubs. And we definitely have fewer sports clubs.
Jenna: What about younger kids with working parents? Are there any school clubs at elementary school?
Amy: When I was in primary school, I went to an after-school club. It was *at* my school, but it wasn't run *by* my school. My parents had to pay for it, and we did lots of different activities there, not just one.
Jenna: I don't think there are clubs you have to pay for around here. Anyway, let's find a good one for you at our school. Is there anything you're especially interested in?
Amy: Not really. It all sounds good. What do you think of the mathletics club? I like maths, but I've never tried competing in it.
Jenna: I did that in my first year at high school, my freshman year. It was fun, but I'm just not good enough at math so I dropped out. But if you're really good at math, I think you'll enjoy it.
Amy: I don't think I'm THAT good at maths. Which other clubs have you tried?
Jenna: A lot. Cheerleading, history club, chemistry club, drama, glee club and Future Business Leaders of America.
Amy: Wow! That *is* a lot. What exactly is a "glee club"?
Jenna: It's a singing group! You get together once a week to sing all kinds of songs. The club usually organizes a concert in the fall. If you're interested, you could try it out – or we can go to the concert together.
Amy: That sounds good. I'm not great at singing, but I'd love to see the club perform.

2c

Look at the dialogue again. What does Amy say about her experience with school clubs in the UK?

2d CHOOSE YOUR LEVEL 🔊 audio 1/25, skill: listening p. 153

I Listen to the rest of the dialogue. Which club is Jenna going to this year?
II Listen to the rest of the dialogue. Which clubs does Amy choose in the end?
III Listen to the rest of the dialogue. Which clubs do the girls choose? Why?

2e workbook p. 30/4

Talk about the clubs at Amy's, Jenna's and your school. What is the same? What is different? Are there any clubs you would like to have at your school?

You can say:
At Jenna's school there is / are …
We also have … / We don't have …
I would love to have … at our school.

ACTIVATE PRACTISE DEVELOP PRACTISE APPLY

2 Part A | Part B | Challenge

GRAMMAR HELP — conditional clauses type 1 (R) p. 180

Bedingungssätze kennst du bereits. Sie drücken aus, was unter einer bestimmten Bedingung geschehen wird oder geschehen kann. Sieh dir die Beispielsätze an: In welchem Teil wird die Bedingung genannt? In welchem Teil wird ausgedrückt, was passiert, wenn die Bedingung erfüllt ist? Was kannst du über die Verbformen sagen?

If you're really good at maths, you'**ll enjoy** the mathletics club.
You **will have** a lot of fun **if** you **join** a club.
If you **love** spreading joy through music, too, you **should join** us in the music room.

Auf Seite 180 kannst du nachlesen, was bei dieser Art von Bedingungssätzen zu beachten ist.

Choosing a club

3 grammar: conditional 1 (R) p. 180, workbook p. 31/5

Match the sentence parts and write down the sentences.

1. If you love singing,
2. If you're interested in how a government works,
3. You'll enjoy the debating society
4. If you see yourself as a future leader,

A if you like competing in debate tournaments.
B the FBLA could be a good club for you.
C you should join the glee club.
D you can join the model congress.

What if …?

4 grammar: conditional 1 (R) p. 180, workbook p. 31/6

David from London is thinking about spending a year in another country as an exchange student. Copy the sentences and fill in the gaps to make conditional sentences (type 1).

1. If I ??? (go) to Germany as an exchange student, I ??? (be able to) improve my German.
2. If I ??? (spend) a year in Australia, I ??? (not be able to) fly home for Christmas.
3. I ??? (not be) here for my best friend's birthday if I ??? (go) abroad.
4. If my friend ??? (have) a party for his birthday, I ??? (miss) it.
5. If I ??? (stay) at home, I ??? (not know) what it is like to go to school in another country.
6. If I ??? (go) to another country, my friends and family ??? (miss) me and I ??? (miss) them.
7. But I ??? (make) lots of new friends if I ??? (decide) to go.
8. And if my host family ??? (be) nice, I ??? (have) a great time.

Different languages?

5a workbook p. 31/7

Unscramble these American English words and write them down.

prgraom · lfal · viemo · mhat · csheudle

5b wordbank: American and British English p. 165

Find the British English words for the American words and write them down.

After-school activities 2

Plans for next Friday

6a

Amy and her host family are talking about their plans for next Friday.
Look at the pictures. What do you think are they going to do?

6b audio 1/27

Listen to Amy and her host family. What is a "tailgate party"?

6c CHOOSE YOUR LEVEL skill: listening p. 153, workbook p. 32/8

I Listen again and take notes. Then complete the sentences with the words from the box.

1. The family is having ??? for dinner.
2. Ben is going to ??? with the marching band at the football game next Friday.
3. Before the football game, there will be a ??? in the parking lot.
4. Jenna's dad is going to make ??? for the tailgate party.

perform
tailgate party
chilli
salad and baked potatoes

II Listen again and take notes.
Then write about what each family member is going to do on Friday.

III Listen again and take notes. Then write a text message from Amy to her parents telling them about each family member's plans for Friday.

ACTIVATE   PRACTISE   **DEVELOP**   PRACTISE   APPLY

forty-seven 47

A high school football game

7a skill: writing p. 155, media worksheet 7, 10

Read what Amy wrote about the football game in her blog. Write down at least three words from the blog entry that you would hashtag.

Wow, I have so much to tell you about the football game last Friday. It was brilliant – not only the game but the whole afternoon and evening.

Before the game, I experienced my very first tailgate party and I LOVED it! A tailgate party is like an opening act for the game and starts earlier. It's called a tailgate party because it all happens in the school's parking lot (that's a car park) around the cars. "Tailgate" is the American English word for car boot. They also call it "trunk". Sometimes these different words are a bit confusing …

My host family and I and a lot of other families drove up to the school and took out camping tables and chairs from our car boots. Everyone unpacked lots of tasty food and drinks to share, like popcorn and chips (I mean crisps), and some people even barbecued hotdogs and burgers. It smelt delicious. We brought a large pot of "the best chilli in the world", which I had helped my host dad prepare. The chilli was REALLY good. Lots of people came back for second helpings.

Getting to know people and chatting to them in such a relaxed and chilled atmosphere was really nice. Everyone was so friendly, they all made sure to introduce themselves to me. I also met some more of Jenna and Ben's friends and ate way too many hot dogs …

Then we went to our seats in the stadium, which looks like a stadium for professional football, not like a school playing field at all. Jenna had explained the rules to me, but I'm still not sure if I understand everything correctly. But watching the players, the cheerleaders and the brilliant marching band was amazing anyway. The atmosphere in the stadium was great, too. It was really exciting. Everyone seemed to be enjoying themselves so much. There is an incredible team spirit at the high school – most of the students and many of their families come out to watch, cheer for the team and have a good time. My host brother, Ben, is a member of the

marching band, who performed before the match and at half-time. They played their instruments while walking in patterns on the field – it all looked quite complicated.

Ben had been a bit nervous beforehand, but everything went well, and he was really happy with himself afterwards.

The cheerleading was also really cool. I hadn't expected it to be so athletic. I have never seen such high jumps and impressive flips before. There are both boys and girls in the team, and they did a really good job in cheering the players on to do their best. They created a very special atmosphere.

After-school activities 2

There was so much going on – it was almost like a carnival! I also liked the cheerleaders' chant. Everyone in the stadium knew it and shouted it really loudly. It goes like this:

Hey, hey

Hey, hey are you ready? *(double clap)*

Are you ready? *(double clap)*

To play *(clap)*

Say go team *(clap)*

Go team *(clap)*

Panthers all the way!

"The Panthers" is the name of the school team. They won the match, and the stadium went crazy! I'm really looking forward to the next football game, and I'll make sure I know the rules by then!

7b CHOOSE YOUR LEVEL skill: reading p.156

I Read the blog entry again and answer the questions.
1 Where does a tailgate party take place?
2 What two other words for the word "tailgate" are mentioned?
3 What did Amy and her host family take to the tailgate party?
4 What does the high school stadium look like?
5 Who comes to the stadium to watch the game?

II Read the blog entry again and answer the questions.
1 What do people take to a tailgate party?
2 What do people do at a tailgate party?
3 What does Amy say about the stadium?
4 What did the marching band do?
5 What did the cheerleaders do?
6 How did the game end?

III Read the blog entry again and answer the questions.
1 What do you need for a tailgate party?
2 What happens at a tailgate party?
3 What did Amy like about the tailgate party?
4 What did the marching band and the cheerleaders do?
5 What did Amy find impressive about the marching band and the cheerleading?
6 What was the atmosphere like during the game? What did it make Amy think of?
7 What is Amy going to do before the next game?

7c

Find words and phrases in Amy's blog post that can be used to describe an atmosphere.

7d wordbank: descriptions p. 163, media worksheet 13, workbook p. 32/9, 10

What other words or phrases to describe an atmosphere can you think of?
Add them to your list. Use your list to write a short text about a school event at your school.

ACTIVATE PRACTISE **DEVELOP** PRACTISE APPLY

2 | Part A | **Part B** | Challenge

PEOPLE & PLACES 4 video 10

Sports in the USA

Sport plays an important role in the USA, especially at school. For many American students it is as important to be good at sports as it is to be good at maths, science or English.
Some holidays are also sports highlights. On New Year's Day and Thanksgiving, the American football games of the colleges take place. Each team has their own cheerleaders, chants and dance performances to animate the spectators to cheer them on.

Some sports events are even national events that are shown on TV and watched by millions of people, for example the Super Bowl (American football) or Opening Day (baseball).

**Watch the video clip.
What do you find out about baseball?
Talk about the game in class.**

American football

8a video 11, skill: watching a video clip p. 158, media worksheet 8

Watch the video clip. What is the main aim in American football?

8b workbook p. 33/11

Watch the video clip again and answer the questions.

1 When was the first football match?
2 How many players are on the field?
3 Why can a 60-minute game actually take up to 3 hours?
4 What is a full-contact sport?
5 What equipment do you need for a full-contact sport?
6 What does NFL stand for?

Sports

9 CHOOSE YOUR TASK   C: media worksheet 6

A **Create a poster for a sports event.**
B **Write your own cheerleading chant. You can perform it if you like.**
C **Choose one sport that is popular in the USA. Do some research, make a fact file and tell your class about the sport.**

B
Go Panthers!
S is for Super
U is for Unique
P is for Perfect,
'cause you know we are sweet.
E is for Enthusiasm
R is for Rap
So come on all you Panther fans
Let's hear you clap!

After-school activities 2

Exchange challenges

10 GET TOGETHER

Get together with a partner.
Do a role play about an exchange student's problems.

Partner A	Partner B
I Go to page 131.	I Go to page 140.
II Go to page 134.	II Go to page 143.
III Go to page 137.	III Go to page 146.

A video call

11a skill: mediation p. 157

Your school has invited some exchange students from the USA. Before they travel, you and your mother have a video call with your exchange partner, Aaron. Your mother cannot speak English very well. Help her and Aaron to understand each other.

Aaron: How will I get to your house? Is there a bus from the airport?
(1) You: *Er fragt, wie …*

Your mother: Sag ihm, dass er sich keine Sorgen machen muss – wir holen ihn natürlich mit dem Auto vom Flughafen ab.
(2) You: *Don't worry. We'll …*

Aaron: That's very kind of you. I'm already looking forward to my trip.
(3) You: *Er sagt, dass …*

Your mother: Frag doch mal, was er gerne isst oder gar nicht mag. Und ob wir irgendwelche Allergien berücksichtigen müssen.
(4) You: …

Aaron: I'm not allergic to anything. But I am a vegan so I don't eat any animal products. I like to eat toast and jam in the morning so I don't need any special milk. The only thing I really don't like, aside from animal products, is carrots.
(5) You: …

Your mother: Sag ihm, dass das gar kein Problem ist. Er kann auch gern mit zum Einkaufen kommen und sich ein paar Sachen aussuchen.
(6) You: …

Aaron: Oh great. Thank you very much.
(7) You: …

11b workbook p. 34/12

What could you do to make your exchange student feel welcome?
Collect ideas and write a dos and don'ts list.

2 Part B

Enjoy yourself!

12 grammar: reflexive pronouns p. 181, workbook p. 34/13

Choose the correct reflexive pronouns from the box and complete the sentences.
There are more pronouns than you need.

1 After their performance, the cheerleaders were happy with ???.
2 I cut ??? when I was making the chilli.
3 Before the game, the coach told his team: "Enjoy ???!"
4 Ben was proud of ??? after his performance.
5 We really enjoyed ??? at the game.

> myself
> yourself
> himself, herself, itself
> ourselves
> yourselves
> themselves

Doing an interview

13a skill: talking with people p. 154, media worksheet 17

Look at the tips on how to do an interview. Find a good order and write the tips down.

A Thank your interview partner politely.
B Give your partner enough time to answer your questions.
C Say goodbye.
D Explain to your interview partner why you want to do the interview.
E Ask him or her to repeat their answer if you don't understand it.
F Prepare interview questions.
G Ask your questions.
H Introduce yourself politely.
I Think about an interview topic.

13b

Compare your results with a partner. Edit them if necessary.

Preparing for an interview

14 CHOOSE YOUR LEVEL

I Match the sentence parts and write down the questions.

1 Did you
2 What did you enjoy most
3 Was there
4 What was
5 What could have been

A about your exchange experience?
B like your exchange experience?
C surprising about your exchange experience?
D better?
E anything you didn't like?

II Complete the questions with question words and write them down.

1 ??? did you contact when you started planning your exchange?
2 ??? did you start planning your exchange?
3 ??? did you like your exchange experience?
4 ??? exactly did you like or not like?
5 ??? could have been better?
6 ??? do you think of life in the United States?

III Write eight questions for someone who did a student exchange. Use the words in the box.

> favourite subject · special events · problems · host family · food · friends · be homesick · new hobbies

After-school activities 2

Interviewing an exchange student TARGET TASK

15 workbook p. 35/14, skill: performing a scene p. 161, media worksheet 2, 5, 17

Your task is to carry out a role play of an interview with an exchange student. Before you start, look at these steps:

STEP 1
Work with a partner. Imagine you get the chance to interview Amy or another exchange student about their experiences.

STEP 2
Collect questions and answers.
Think about:
- the host family
- new friends
- lessons at the new school
- electives and school clubs
- sports and activities
- …

> **TIP**
> - Choose questions that make your interview partner talk, like questions with questions words such as "What do you think …?", "How was …?" or "When did you …?"
> - Avoid questions that he or she can answer with a simple "Yes." or "No."

STEP 3
Plan your role play.
- Decide who is playing which role.
- Decide on the questions you are going to ask and in which order to ask them.
- Write cue cards if you need help.

STEP 4
Practise your role play.

STEP 5
Present your role play as an audio recording or a video clip or act it out in class.

Check out

1. Kannst du kurze Texte aus einem Jahrbuch verstehen?	Workbook, p. 36
2. Kannst du darüber sprechen, was du über den Schulalltag in den USA weißt?	Workbook, p. 37
3. Kannst du den Inhalt einer deutschen Kursbeschreibung auf Englisch wiedergeben?	Workbook, p. 38
4. Kannst du einem Gespräch über Schul-AGs wichtige Informationen entnehmen?	Workbook, p. 38
5. Kannst du einen kurzen Text über eine Schulveranstaltung schreiben?	Workbook, p. 39
6. Kennst du Unterschiede zwischen dem britischen und dem amerikanischen Englisch?	Workbook, p. 39

ACTIVATE   PRACTISE   DEVELOP   PRACTISE   **APPLY**

You should see me in a crown

Liz Lighty, the main character in Leah Johnson's novel You should see me in a crown, *had it all planned out. She's going to win a scholarship to Pennington, the college she's always wanted to go to, and leave her old life behind as quickly as possible. When she gets the letter telling her that she didn't get that scholarship, all her plans blow up. But there might still be a chance for her to get another scholarship – the one her school gives out every year to prom king and queen.*

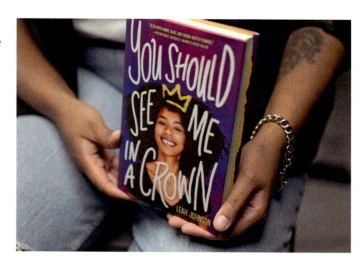

"I'm not running for prom queen." I fold the paper and shove it back into his hand. Now I am laughing. I seriously can't help it. "Are you kidding me?"

"I'm serious (…), big sis. (…) You need the money, and they're giving money away. It seems like the perfect solution to me." Other schools have huge endowments for athletics or the arts, but Campbell County High School has one for prom. It's such a big deal, our rich alums give back faithfully to ensure that we have the biggest, most elaborate spectacle of a prom season in Indiana every year. And part of that spectacle happens to be the massive scholarships they give to the prom king and queen, for what they like to call the "outstanding service and community engagement" the winners must display.

But mostly, the alums are just writing checks to one anothers' stuck-up kids – checks in the neighbourhood of ten grand. Robbie is right: It's almost exactly what I need to make Pennington work.

"Look, this money could be enough to at least get you to Pennington, you know? You win, and Granny and Grandad keep the house."

My stomach churns at the thought of one of my classmates getting that scholarship. All that money just for playing dress-up and picking up trash on the playground. All that money going to another Campbell County rich kid with too much time on their hands and no fear of the spotlight. It isn't fair. None of it is fair.

I think about the speeches and the public events and how visible the prom court candidates are every year. (…) There's no way to hide when you run for prom queen; there's no way to fly under the radar when you want that title. And I've never been one to break from the ensemble to go solo. Everything about the idea is ridiculous, but I

---

novel = *Roman*; scholarship = *Stipendium*; to blow up *(informal)* = *sich zerschlagen*; to run = *kandidieren*; prom queen *(AE)* = *Ballkönigin*; I can't help it. = *Ich kann nicht anders.*; Are you kidding me? *(informal)* = *Ist das dein Ernst?*; to be serious = *es ernst meinen*; sis *(informal)* = *Schwester*; endowments *(pl)* = *Stiftungsgelder*; big deal *(informal)* = *große Sache*; alum *(informal)* = *Absolvent/in*; faithfully = *zuverlässig*; to ensure = *garantieren*; elaborate = *raffiniert*; to happen to be = *zufällig sein*; outstanding = *außergewöhnlich*; check = *Scheck*; stuck-up = *eingebildet*; grand *(informal)* = *tausend Dollar*; to churn = *sich heftig drehen*; trash *(AE)* = *Müll*; fear = *Angst*; none = *nichts*; visible = *sichtbar*

can't stop thinking about it. (…)
"Ro, be realistic." I shake my head and slip down to the floor. "I'm nobody's prom queen."
"Pennington is important to you, right?" He sits down next to me and bumps my shoulder with his.
I nod, even though he already knows the answer to that. Pennington has always been my North Star, the place where all my missing pieces would suddenly fit. (…)
"You got three days to get thirty signatures and declare yourself a candidate. You've got my vote, big sis. Don't count yourself out."

The next day, when they meet at the store where Liz works in the afternoons, Liz tells her friends that she hasn't gotten the scholarship to Pennington.

Their reactions are immediate.
Britt cracks her knuckles. "That's such garbage! Nobody deserves that scholarship more –"
Gabi shakes her head. "I'm going to take care of this, I'll have my parents' lawyer call –"
Stone grabs the crystal pendant hanging from her necklace. "I have palo santo in my purse. We can cleanse your clarinet and –"
I wave my hands in front of me with a quiet laugh. These weirdos are the best sometimes. "Guys, it's cool. It's fine. Well, not fine. It's pretty awful actually. But it'll be okay. I have a plan."
Like a lightbulb, Gabi's face instantly shifts from rage to recognition.
"We're going to make you prom queen," she says simply, reading my mind.
"We're gonna what?" Britt narrows her eyes.
"My sentiment exactly," I mumble. I add so that Gabi can hear me, "Robbie said the same thing, and I'm starting to believe that I'm in some alternate universe in which I am a viable option for prom court."
In a concert band, you're arranged into sections so that the instruments and sounds in your ear are the most similar to your own – so that what surrounds you is you, to a degree. It's easier to know your clarinet part when you're not fighting against a cello on one side and a tuba on the other.
High school friend groups are something like an ensemble in that way. My friends are certified oddballs, the inkblots on an otherwise pure white page, and it's why we work together so well. Because as long as they're my people, as long as they're the ones on my left and my right, sometimes I can forget that I don't fit in anywhere else in this town. (…)
"Lizzie; I was born to be a fairy godmother; it's my destiny." Gabi plops her highlighter yellow (…) bag next to the register and pulls her phone out of it. Her fingers fly across the screen so quickly, I almost don't notice she's speaking. "A couple slight changes, and you'll be as good as new. Certifiably prom queen ready." (…)
And just like that, I'm Campbell County High School's newest prom queen contender.

What is Liz's first reaction to her brother's suggestion?
What do you think: how will the novel end? Why?

---

solo = *allein*; ridiculous = *albern*; North Star = *Polarstern*; signature = *Unterschrift*; vote = *Stimme*; gotten *(AE)* = *Partizip von get*; to crack = *knacken*; knuckle = *Knöchel*; garbage *(AE)* = *Müll*; to deserve = *verdienen*; lawyer = *Rechtsanwalt/Rechtsanwältin*; purse *(AE)* = *Handtasche*; to cleanse = *reinigen*; clarinet = *Klarinette*; weirdo = *seltsame Person*; rage = *Wut*; recognition = *Anerkennung*; to read one's mind = *Gedanken lesen*; sentiment = *Meinung*; to mumble = *murmeln*; viable = *realisierbar*; to surround = *umgeben*; oddball = *Verrückte/r*; inkblot = *Tintenklecks*; fairy godmother = *Märchenfee*; destiny = *Schicksal*; register *(AE)* = *Kasse*; slight = *gering*; certifiably = *nachweisbar*; contender = *Bewerber/in*

prom dress

I'm nearing the end of my fourth year
I feel like I've been lacking crying too many tears
Everyone seemed to say it was so great,
but did I miss out
Was it a huge mistake?

I can't help the fact I like to be alone
It might sound kinda sad, but that's just what I seem to know
I tend to handle things usually by myself
And I can't ever seem to try and ask for help

I'm sitting here, crying in my prom dress
I'd be the prom queen, if crying was a contest
Make-up is running down, feelings are all around
How did I get here? I need to know

I guess I maybe had a couple expectations
I thought I'd get to them, but no, I didn't
I guess I thought that prom was gonna be fun
But now I'm sitting on the floor and
all I wanna do is run

I keep collections of masks upon my wall
To try and stop myself from revealing it all
Affecting others is the last thing I would do
I keep to myself, though I want to break through

I hold so many small regrets
And what-ifs down inside my head
Some confidence it couldn't hurt me
My demeanor is often misread

I'm sitting here, crying in my prom dress
I'd be the prom queen, if crying was a contest
Make-up is running down, feelings are all around
How did I get here? I need to know

I guess I maybe had a couple expectations
I thought I'd get to them, but no, I didn't
I guess I thought that prom was gonna be fun
But now I'm sitting on the floor and
all I wanna do is run

All I wanna do is run
All I wanna do is run
All I wanna do is run

I'm sitting here, crying in my prom dress
I'd be the prom queen, if crying was a contest
Make-up is running down, feelings are all around
How did I get here? I need to know

I guess I maybe had a couple expectations
I thought I'd get to them, but no, I didn't
I guess I thought that prom was gonna be fun
But now I'm sitting on the floor and all I wanna do is run

All I wanna do is run

Listen to the song by mxmtoon.
How does it make you feel?

---

to near = *sich nähern*; to lack = *nicht haben*; to miss out = *verpassen*; to tend to = *neigen zu*; to handle = *bewältigen*; by oneself = *allein*; crying = *Weinen*; contest = *Wettbewerb*; expectation = *Erwartung*; to get to = *hier: erfüllen*; mask = *Maske*; upon = *an*; to reveal = *enthüllen*; to affect = *Einfluss haben auf, schaden*; to keep to oneself = *ein/e Einzelgänger/in sein*; to break through = *durchbrechen*; regret = *Bedauern*; confidence = *Vertrauen, Zuversicht*; to hurt = *schaden*; demeanor (AE) = *Benehmen, Auftreten*; to misread = *falsch verstehen*

3

1. Describe the pictures. What situation do you think the people are in?
2. What do the pictures have in common?
3. Think of a caption for each picture.

My world today

Part A Relationships

- You will talk about friendship and what makes a good friend.
- You will listen to a podcast episode on friendship.
- You will create a text for a friendship tree.

Part B Digital communication

- You will talk about digital communication.
- You will listen to a podcast episode on cyberbullying.
- You will collect tips for online communication.

3 Part A · Part B · Challenge

Friends and friendship

1 workbook p. 40/1

What comes to mind when you think about the terms "friends" and "friendship"?
Collect ideas in class and talk about them.

What is going on?

2a wordbank: feelings p. 166

Look at the pictures and describe what you see. How do you think the teenagers are feeling?

depressed · lonely · happy · helpless · excited · angry · glad · upset · worried · unhappy · …

2b

What do you think happened before each picture was taken?
What is going to happen next?

Friends

3a skill: reading p. 156

Read what these teenagers say. Who says that their brothers are their best friends?
Who says that their best friend has just moved to another city?

Janet: I don't have one best friend. I have a group of friends and some other kids I talk to sometimes, but there is no one I would call my BFF. I always have someone I can talk to or do things with. I actually like it that way.

Linh: I have a good friend called Ruby, but I also have another good friend called Anne. They are both great! The problem is: Ruby and Anne can't stand each other. That can be quite difficult for me because we can never do things as a group. It's always either the one or the other. I really wish they'd get along with each other.

58 fifty-eight   ACTIVATE PRACTISE DEVELOP PRACTISE APPLY

Relationships 3

Arda: My friends are the guys I play games with online. A while ago, my mom said I should try and make some friends in real life. I've really tried, but there's just no one who's interested in the same things. My online friends are all into the same stuff as I am. They just don't live near me. So I explained to my mom why I was sticking with my online friends for the time being, and she said she understood that it's not that easy to make friends. I told her that I would keep on trying to make some "offline friends", though.

Reese: Some people think it's strange, but my brothers are my best friends. We are pretty close in age: Matt is in 7th grade, and Andy is one year older than me. We spend almost all our free time together. Who needs other friends when you have the best brothers in the world?

Luis: Jake and Mason were my friends in 7th grade, but this year they only want to hang out with their other friends from the basketball team. I'm not good at basketball, and I don't really like those other guys. I've been on my own a lot lately. I told Jake and Mason that I was unhappy with the situation, but nothing has changed so far.

Lucia: I've been a little sad lately because my best friend Tom moved to another city two weeks ago. We used to do everything together, and now I'm mostly by myself. I mean, I know other classmates at school, and there are a few kids I hang out with, but it's just not the same without Tom. I didn't think it would be so hard! I talked to him yesterday, and he told me that most of his classmates seemed OK but that he hadn't made any new friends yet. He said that the first week had been really boring and that he missed me a lot. I wonder if I'll ever be able to make a new best friend …

3b CHOOSE YOUR LEVEL

I Read the statements again. Who is unhappy with their situation? Why?

II Read the statements again. Choose one of the unhappy teenagers and give them some advice.

III Read the statements again. Choose one of the people the teenagers talk about and write a statement about the situation from their point of view.

3c skill: writing p. 155, workbook p. 40/2

Choose one of the teenagers. Imagine their situation four weeks later and write another statement from their point of view.

ACTIVATE PRACTISE DEVELOP PRACTISE APPLY fifty-nine 59

3 Part A   Part B   Challenge

> **GRAMMAR HELP** reported speech 2 p. 182
>
> Indirekte Rede *(reported speech)* verwendest du, wenn du wiedergeben möchtest, was jemand sagt bzw. gesagt hat. Du hast bereits den Fall kennengelernt, dass das Verb im einleitenden Satz in der Gegenwart steht. Bei den folgenden Beispielen steht dieses in der Vergangenheit. Was fällt dir auf? Was verändert sich?
>
> | Direkte Rede: | Indirekte Rede: |
> |---|---|
> | Arda: "I am sticking with my online friends." | Arda said that he was sticking with his online friends. |
> | Arda: "I will keep on trying to make some offline friends." | Arda said that he would keep on trying to make some offline friends. |
> | Tom: "Most of my classmates seem OK." | Tom told me that most of his classmates seemed OK. |
> | Tom: "I haven't made any new friends yet." | Tom told me that he hadn't made any new friends yet. |
> | Tom: "The first week was really boring." | He said that the first week had been really boring. |
>
> Auf Seite 182 findest du weitere Beispiele und Erklärungen zur indirekten Rede.

What Tom said

4 grammar: reported speech 2 p. 182

Imagine you met Tom at a party and talked to him. The next day, you report to another friend what Tom told you.

1. Tom: "I moved here two weeks ago."
2. Tom: "I have lots of hobbies."
3. Tom: "I like music and basketball."
4. Tom: "I haven't played basketball for two weeks."
5. Tom: "I'm also thinking of joining a band."
6. Tom: "My best friend Lucia and I were in a band together."
7. Tom: "I will hopefully see Lucia in August."

You can write:
Tom told me that he had …
He also said …
…

Reporting statements

5 grammar: reported speech 2 p. 182, workbook p. 41/3, 4

Write down what the people said. Underline the words that you had to change in reported speech.

1. Janet: "I don't have one best friend."
2. Linh: "Ruby and Anne have had lots of arguments."
3. Linh: "They aren't talking to each other at the moment."
4. Arda: "My online friends are my best friends."
5. Reese: "My brothers are very important to me."
6. Luis: "I spoke to Jake and Mason yesterday."
7. Jake and Mason: "We will spend more time with you in the future."
8. Luis: "They want to meet me next weekend for a game of basketball."

You can write:
Janet said that she …
Linh said that …
She also mentioned …
…

 DIGITAL+ practise more 10-11

ACTIVATE **PRACTISE** DEVELOP PRACTISE APPLY

Relationships 3

Penny's podcast

6a
How would you finish this sentence: "Friends are people who …"?
Share your ideas in class.

6b audio 2/1
Listen to the podcast episode about friendship.
Which of your ideas from 6a are mentioned
in the podcast?

6c CHOOSE YOUR LEVEL   skill: listening p. 153, workbook p. 42/5, 6

I Listen again and complete the sentences with the words from the box.

1 Friends are people who are ??? in you.
2 Friends are people you feel ??? around.
3 Friends are people who are ??? with you.
4 Friends are people who accept that you aren't ???.
5 Friends could be people who you don't ???.

honest · perfect ·
expect · good ·
interested

II Listen again and complete the sentences with the words from the box.

1 Friends ask lots of ??? and are interested in your ???.
2 Friends always make you feel ??? to talk about ??? stuff, too.
3 Friends don't talk about you behind your ???.
4 Friends understand that you have ??? and ???.
5 Any new ??? you ??? might ??? a friend.

strengths · back ·
weaknesses · become ·
meet · difficult ·
safe · person ·
questions · answers

III Listen again and take notes on the five aspects of friendship that Penny talks about.

Your opinion

7a   wordbank: expressing opinions p. 168
What are your thoughts on what makes a
good friend? Why do you think so?
Make notes.

You can write:
· honest — because you don't want to be
  friends with someone who lies to you
· loyal — because you want to be able to rely
  on them in difficult situations
· …

7b   media worksheet 15
Using your notes from 7a, write a short
comment. Make sure to include an
introduction, a main part and a conclusion.

*There are many opinions on what makes a
  really good friend. Some people say that …,
  others think that …
In my opinion, …
To sum it all up, …*

ACTIVATE   PRACTISE   **DEVELOP**   PRACTISE   APPLY

An interview

8a skill: reading p. 156

Scan the interview with Professor Miller about friendship. How many readers have sent in questions? What do they ask?

1 *Professor Rosanne Miller is a child psychologist and friendship expert based in Wisconsin. Jo, a reporter for a teen magazine, asked her to answer some readers' questions.*

5 **Jo:** First, we have an email from a girl named Ashley from Buffalo, New York. Her question is: "Why do some people have best friends, and others have just friends?"

Professor Miller: That's a very good question.
10 It's important to know that not everybody has a best friend. Many of us wish to have one, but it's just not the case for everybody. If you look at the research on the topic, only one out of four kids say that they have a best friend.
15 So, although it's fantastic to have a best friend, it's actually quite rare. It's completely fine not to have a best friend.

Jo: Could you give us an example of what you mean by that exactly?

20 **Professor Miller:** Sure. Even if you don't have that one person in your life, remember that you may have all kinds of other friends. You may have a neighborhood friend, or a friend you see every week at swim practice. You may
25 have several school friends with whom you get along well. And all of those friendships are important. Focus on what you have, not on what you think you're missing.

Jo: Great, thanks. So, next up, we have a
30 question from a reader in Denver, Colorado. Christopher writes: "I had a friend for a long time, but then he started acting strangely. He wasn't a good friend anymore, and he said some mean stuff or ignored me. I finally told
35 him I didn't want to be friends anymore. Was that the right thing to do?"

Professor Miller: Now, that's a difficult situation Christopher has found himself

in. Maybe other readers have had similar
40 experiences. If you feel very hurt, or you feel like your friend is not listening to you at all, then it might be the right choice to end the friendship. It is essential, however, to stay fair.
45 Remember that this situation might be difficult for your former friend, too. Do not say bad things about them to other people. Try to keep it between yourself and the other person.

50 **Jo:** You said that other kids might have experienced the situation Christopher describes. Do you think it is common for teenagers to end friendships?

Professor Miller: Absolutely. If we look at
55 the research again, we see that in 8th grade, for example, one out of four friendships does not last until the end of the year.
It can be difficult to get along with others, for anyone at any age. And sometimes, if things
60 do not seem to work out at all over a longer period of time, and you are unhappy all the time, you may have to do what Christopher did and end a friendship.

Jo: That's quite sad, but it makes sense. Our
65 next question picks up on what you have just

said. Sarah from Davis, California, asks: "What if a friend is being mean to you, but you still want them to be your friend?"

Professor Miller: This is important for all young people to know. In any friendship, you're definitely going to experience difficult situations. But let me remind you that no person on earth is perfect. And we have to forgive our friends – and ourselves! – for not being perfect. If you do not seem to be getting along with a friend, it is important that you talk about your situation. If you, or your friend, are sorry about what happened, you have to tell each other. Sometimes it helps to spend a few days apart, and if you feel like you have had enough time to think about what happened, it might be a good moment to talk. Talking, being honest, acting responsibly and being fair are important behaviors in staying friends.

8b CHOOSE YOUR LEVEL

I Read the interview and answer the questions.

1 What is Rosanne Miller's job?
2 How did Christopher's friend hurt him?
3 How should you behave when you end a friendship?
4 How many friendships do not last during 8th grade?

II Read the interview and answer the questions.

1 Why did Jo talk to Professor Miller?
2 If you look at the research on the topic, how many teenagers have a best friend?
3 How did Christopher's friend's behaviour change?
4 When should you think about ending a friendship?
5 According to studies, how many friendships end during the 8th grade?

III Read the interview and answer the questions.

1 In what way is Professor Miller qualified to be interviewed about the topic of friendship?
2 According to studies, how many teenagers have a best friend?
3 What should you focus on if you do not have a best friend but would like to have one?
4 What should you do if you are unhappy with a friend all the time?
5 What is an important thing to remember in a friendship?
6 What should you do when there is a difficult situation in your friendship?

8c

Look at the readers' questions again. Write down the one or two statements from Professor Miller's answers that you think sum up each answer best.

8d wordbank: expressing opinions p. 168, workbook p. 43/7-9

Professor Miller says that sometimes it is better to end a friendship. Do you agree with her? Write a text in which you say why or why not.

| Part A | Part B | Challenge |

Six-word stories

9a

You can tell a very long, very interesting story in only six words.
Read the stories and collect ideas in class what they could be about.
Who could be talking? What could have happened?

1. Strangers, friends, best friends, lovers, strangers
2. Love her? Hate her? Said nothing …
3. Painfully he changed "is" to "was".
4. You. Me. Her? I don't know.
5. Found true love. Married someone else.

9b

Choose the six-word story you like best.
What longer story might be hidden within it? Write down your ideas.

9c skill: writing p. 155, workbook p. 44/10

Write your own six-word story.
You can present your stories in class if you like.

A video about friendship

10 video 12, skill: watching a video clip p. 158, mediation p. 157, workbook p. 44/11

Watch the video clip and take notes on the most important information. Tell someone who does not understand English the most important information in German.

What makes a good friendship?

Friendship

11 CHOOSE YOUR TASK A+B: wordbank: feelings p. 166, B: media worksheet 11

A Create a picture or collage about what "friendship" means to you and label it.
   You can also include sayings and quotes.
B Write a letter or a text message to a friend and tell them why they are such a good friend.
C Present a song or song lyrics about friendship to your class. Tell the class about the message of the song and what you like or dislike about it.

Relationships 3

A poem

12a

Read the poem. What is your first reaction? What do you think about it?

On the Discomfort of Being in the Same Room as the Boy You Like

1 Everyone is looking at you looking at him.
Everyone can tell. He can tell. So you
spend most of your time not looking at him.
The wallpaper, the floor, there are cracks
5 in the ceiling. Someone has left a can of
iced tea in the corner, it is half empty,
I mean half full. There are four light bulbs
in the standing lamp, there is a fan. You
are counting things to keep from looking
10 at him. Five chairs, two laptops, someone's
umbrella, a hat. People are talking so you
look at their faces. This is a good trick. They
will think you are listening to them and not
thinking about him. Now he is talking. So
15 you look away. The cracks in the ceiling are
in the shape of a whale or maybe an elephant
with a fat trunk. If he ever falls in love with
you, you will lie on your backs in a field
somewhere and look up at the sky and he will
20 say, *Baby, look at that silly cloud, it is a whale!*
and you will say, *Baby, that is an elephant
with a fat trunk,* and you will argue for a bit,
but he will love you anyway.
He is asking a question now and no one has
25 answered it yet. So you lower your eyes from
the plaster and say, *the twenty first, I think,*
and he smiles and says, *oh, cool,* and you
smile back, and you cannot stop your smiling,
oh you cannot stop your smile.

Sarah Kay

12b CHOOSE YOUR LEVEL skill: reading p. 156, wordbank: feelings p. 166

I Read the poem again and answer the questions.
1 What is the person in the poem trying *not* to do?
2 What do you think: how is the person feeling at the end of the poem?
3 How would you describe the person in the poem? Write down adjectives to describe him or her.

II Read the poem again and answer the questions.
1 What is the person in the poem doing to avoid looking at the boy?
2 What is the "trick" the person in the poem is talking about?
3 Why do you think the person cannot stop smiling at the end of the poem?
4 What is the person in the poem like? Describe him or her.

III Read the poem again and answer the questions.
1 How is the discomfort mentioned in the title expressed in the poem?
2 What is the connection between the cracks in the ceiling and the clouds the person imagines?
3 What is the person in the poem daydreaming about?
4 What do you think: how is the person feeling in the beginning? How is he or she feeling in the end? Why do you think that?

12c workbook p. 45/12

**Imagine that the person in the poem and the boy talk to each other after school.
Write their dialogue.**

ACTIVATE   PRACTISE   **DEVELOP**   PRACTISE   APPLY

He said, she said

13 CHOOSE YOUR LEVEL grammar: reported speech 2 p. 182

I Write down what the people said and fill in the verb in the correct tense.

1. Camila: "I like Taylor." – Camila said that she ??? Taylor.
2. Taylor: "I saw Camila yesterday." – Taylor said that he ??? ??? Camila the day before.
3. Taylor: "I will ask Camila on a date." – Taylor said that he ??? ask Camila on a date.
4. Camila: "I have always liked Taylor." – Camila said that she ??? always ??? Taylor.
5. Camila: "I am thinking about Taylor a lot." – Camila said that she ??? ??? about Taylor a lot.

II Write down what the people said. Use the verb in the correct tense.

1. Lauren: "I can't sleep because I am so excited."
2. Gabriel: "I am going to the cinema with Lauren next weekend."
3. Lauren: "I have already bought the tickets."
4. Gabriel: "Maybe we will share some popcorn."
5. Lauren: "I spent all my pocket money on the tickets."
6. Gabriel: "I don't really like romantic comedies."

You can write:
Lauren said that she …
Gabriel …
…

III Steve is telling his cousin about his best friend Taylor.
Write down the underlined sentences in direct speech.

Taylor has been my best friend for the last three years. Last week he told me that <u>he was going out with this girl from our school</u>. He said that he <u>had been in love with her since 6th grade</u> and that <u>he wanted to spend more time with her</u>. He said that <u>I would always be his best friend</u> but that <u>he needed more time for his relationship now</u> and <u>that he hoped I would understand</u>.

You can write:
Taylor: "I am …"
…

Quotes on friendship

14a audio 2/4

Listen to the quotes and pay particular attention to the way the underlined parts are connected when you speak. What do you notice? Talk about it in German.

1. True <u>friends are</u> <u>never apart</u>, maybe in distance but <u>never in</u> heart. *(Unknown)*
2. Good <u>friends are</u> like stars. You <u>don't always</u> see them, but you know <u>they are always</u> there. *(Unknown)*
3. <u>There are</u> friends, <u>there is</u> family, and then <u>there are</u> friends that become family. *(Unknown)*
4. <u>Friends are</u> those rare people who ask how we <u>are and</u> then wait to hear <u>the answer</u>. *(Ed Cunningham)*

14b
Listen again and repeat the quotes.

14c workbook p. 45/13
Learn the quote you like best by heart.

A friendship tree TARGET TASK

15 workbook p. 46/14, wordbank: feelings p. 166, skill: writing p. 155, media worksheet 1, 9–16

Your task is to write one or more texts for a friendship tree.
Before you start, look at these steps:

STEP 1
Plan your tree. Decide in class:

- how to make the tree
- what materials to use
- how big it will be
- where to put it
- …

STEP 2
Decide what kind of text or texts you would like to write. For example:

- collages with pictures and texts
- slogans or quotes
- song lyrics
- poems
- six-word stories
- stories
- texts about your own experiences
- …

STEP 3
Write your text or texts.

STEP 4
Hang your texts on the friendship tree and talk about them. You can also read out some of the texts in class.

"Many people will walk in and out of your life, but only true friends will leave footprints on your heart."
Eleanor Roosevelt

"Only a true friend would be that truly honest."
Donkey, Shrek

"It's not enough to be friendly. You have to be a friend."
R.J. Palacio

"You can count on me like one, two, three I'll be there."
Bruno Mars

Forever
help each otheR
lIsten to music together
watch moviEs
haNg out
play viDeo games

friend friend friend
football friend
friend LIAN friend
friend video games
friend biking friend

ACTIVATE   PRACTISE   DEVELOP   PRACTISE   **APPLY**

3 Part A | Part B | Challenge

Digital communication

1 workbook p. 47/1

What kinds of digital communication channels do you use and what for? How much do you rely on digital communication in your everyday life?

You can say:
I like to share …
I prefer voice messages to text messages because …
I check our class group chat for …
…

Virtual connections

2a skill: reading p. 156

Skim the texts. What are they about? Take notes.

Teens on their smartphone habits

I'm **Jayden** and I live in Chicago. I usually spend around three hours a day using my phone, mostly messaging friends, playing games and listening to podcasts. I'm really glad I live in an era with so much technology because it means I can keep in touch more easily with my friends that live further away. I also often watch videos mindlessly – without really paying attention – because it helps me relax.

I'm **Olivia** from Tulsa, Oklahoma. I spend very little time on my phone compared to most people I know. I find staring at a little screen all day just so boring – I live my life more happily in the real world, not online! I still have a phone for contacting people though, and I like the fact that it's fast since they usually reply right away.

I'm **Liam** from Pittsburgh, Pennsylvania, and I'm a self-confessed phone addict. It never leaves my side; I even sleep with it under my pillow! I probably send more than 200 messages a day, and I can text faster than anyone I know. I also look up everything on the Internet – I love the fact that today we can access information more easily and more quickly than ever before.

GLUED TO OUR SCREENS

According to a recent study, the majority of US-Americans spend at least **five hours on their smartphone each day.** That's almost as much time as they spend at school or work! Our cell phones are never far from reach, with the **average person sending 13 text messages per day.** In fact, 95% of text messages are read and responded to within three minutes of being received.

ACTIVATE   PRACTISE   DEVELOP   PRACTISE   APPLY

Digital communication 3

299 Comments

 Pete, 43 from Michigan
I am a parent to two teenagers, and I was shocked to learn this week that 59% of US teens have been bullied or harassed online. They are humiliated, or they receive nasty messages and even physical threats, or false rumors are spread about them. Apparently, most of this cyberbullying happens over social media. It has become a major problem. Why can't social media companies react more quickly once you show them proof, and ban bullies from their platforms or block their social media accounts? Why can't schools be stricter and expel students who bully others?

Communication in a digital age

In today's digital age, our communication habits are constantly evolving. It seems that what was once unacceptable can become normal very quickly. A new survey has shown that many young adults are now choosing to end relationships via text or social media – in fact, up to 30% of teenagers admit to breaking up with their partner via text. The reason? Many say that it's less awkward than having a face-to-face conversation and it allows them to choose their words more carefully.

2b CHOOSE YOUR LEVEL

I Read the texts and answer the questions.

1 What does Jayden often do to relax?
2 What does Olivia like about her phone?
3 How many messages does Liam usually send per day?
4 How many messages does the average person send every day?
5 How many US teens have been bullied or harassed online?

II Read the texts and answer the questions.

1 What does Jayden mostly do with his phone?
2 What does Olivia use her phone for?
3 What does Liam love about the Internet?
4 How much time do the majority of US-Americans spend on their phone every day?
5 What was Pete shocked about?
6 How many teenagers admit to breaking up with someone via text?

III Read the texts and answer the questions.

1 What does Jayden say is good about technology?
2 What does Olivia say about her life in the real world?
3 What does Liam say about his smartphone habits?
4 How many messages are read within three minutes of being received?
5 What are the most common forms of harassment online?
6 What does Pete want social media companies to do?
7 Why do teenagers break up with their partner via text?

2c workbook p. 47/2, 3

**When do you prefer face-to-face communication, when digital?
Give reasons for your answer.**

ACTIVATE   PRACTISE   DEVELOP   PRACTISE   APPLY

3   Part A   **Part B**   Challenge

GRAMMAR HELP   adverbs of manner (R) p. 183, comparison of adverbs p. 184

Mit Adverbien der Art und Weise *(adverbs of manner)* kannst du Tätigkeiten näher beschreiben. Adverbien werden in der Regel aus Adjektiven gebildet, indem man *-ly* hinzufügt (z. B. *quickly, easily*), allerdings gibt es auch unregelmäßige Formen (z. B. *fast*).

We can access information *easily* and *quickly*.
I can text *fast*.

Adverbien der Art und Weise können auch gesteigert werden. Was fällt dir bei den folgenden Beispielen auf?

We can access information today *more easily* and *more quickly* than ever before.
I can text *faster* than anyone I know.

Auf den Seiten 183-184 findest du weitere Erklärungen und Beispiele zu den Adverbien der Art und Weise, auch dazu, wie man den Superlativ bildet.

Modern communication

3a   grammar: adverbs of manner (R) p. 183

Copy the sentences and fill in the gaps with adverbs of manner.

1. I can text very ???. (fast)
2. I can keep in touch with my family ??? via video calls. (easy)
3. I reply to text messages very ???. (quick)
4. You should think ??? about what you post online. (careful)

3b   grammar: comparison of adverbs p. 184, workbook p. 48/4

Copy the sentences and fill in the gaps with the comparative forms of the adverbs of manner.

1. I can contact my family ??? over the phone than by writing letters. (easy)
2. I live my life ??? in the real world than online. (happy)
3. Texting allows me to choose my words ???. (careful)
4. I can concentrate ??? when I switch my smartphone off. (good)
5. Students who spend a lot of time online often do ??? in school than students who do not. (bad)

Who?

4a   grammar: comparison of adverbs p. 184

Copy the questions and fill in the gaps with the superlative forms of the adverbs of manner.

1. Who can run ??? in your family? (fast)
2. Who can sing ??? of all your friends? (beautiful)
3. Who can draw ??? in your class? (good)
4. Who cooks ??? in your family? (bad)

4b   workbook p. 48/5

Choose two or more of the questions from 4a and answer them.

Digital communication 3

Emoji misunderstandings

5a skill: talking with people p. 154

What is your favourite emoji and what do you use it for? Talk about it with a partner.

5b

Read the article. What is new to you? Talk about it in class.

Emojis – a universal language?

Why are they called emojis?
Nowadays, we are very familiar with the little yellow hands and faces we frequently see in our digital communication – emojis. But do you know where the word "emoji" comes from? Did you know it was connected to the word "emotion"? While it's true that we often use emojis to help express our emotions, the word "emoji" is actually a combination of two Japanese words: picture (絵 pronounced "eh") and character (文字 pronounced "moji").

History of the emoji
In 1999, the first set of Japanese emojis had just 176 icons. Today, there are over 3,000 emojis. They are used so often that the "face with tears of joy" emoji 😂 was named the Oxford Dictionary's "word of the year" in 2015!

Different interpretations
Many people think that emojis are like a universal language, but your culture can influence your understanding and use of emojis. Take the angel emoji, 😇 for example – in the west, many people understand this to portray innocence or doing a good deed, whereas in China it can be a signal for death and may feel threatening! The hand sign 👌 which is used to mean "OK" in many European countries is an insult in Brazil!

A less harmful example of different emoji interpretations is the folded hands 🙏. In Japanese culture this represents gratitude and may refer to prayer before a meal, but many Internet users have been using it to represent a high five! What do you think it means?

There are so many subtle cultural differences in emoji use, that in 2017 a translation agency hired the world's first emoji translator!

What are their limits?
So, while emojis can add emotion and help replace the facial expressions and tone of voice that are lacking in digital communication, you should be aware that there is no guarantee they will be understood the way you intended! 😉

5c CHOOSE YOUR LEVEL skill: reading p. 156

I What do you learn about the folded hands emoji from the article? Take notes.

II What emojis are mentioned in the article? What do you learn about them? Take notes.

III What do you learn about the history and the use of emojis in the article? Take notes.

5d workbook p. 49/6, 7

Do you think it is helpful to use emojis? Give reasons for your answer.

Communicating online

6a
Look at the pictures and the headline of the article. What do you expect it to be about?

6b
Read the article. Were you right in 6a?

Getting connected

In a world where many of us are beginning to feel more comfortable communicating online than offline, how is this impacting our relationships?

The advantages of digital communication

"There are definitely some positives," says sociologist Savannah Redford. "Many of us are more connected than ever before since we can easily reach our loved ones via a text or a phone call. Also, we can share more of our lives with more people – such as posting holiday photos for the whole family to see, instead of sending a postcard to your closest relatives."

Digital communication is also a cheap and time-saving way to keep in touch with friends and family when there is physical distance, which can often mean older relatives are much less isolated. For young people too, online environments can represent new opportunities to make new friends or find people who share the same hobbies or interests. Marcus, a 15-year-old from Texas, agrees: "I am quite shy at school which means I haven't made many friends there, but when I come home, I have plenty of friends to talk to online. We have met a few times in person, but I actually prefer talking to them from the comfort of my bedroom."

The disadvantages of digital communication

While the digital age of communication clearly has some benefits, it is important to think about how else it is affecting us. "First of all, we now have different expectations of how connected we should be," says Savannah. "We used to have clear boundaries between school or work, home life and friendships, since they were physically separate environments. Now the boundaries are blurred, and people expect that they can contact us at all times and that we respond immediately. I don't think this is always a good thing."

Digital communication 3

Digital media also seems to be affecting our social skills. Without face-to-face interaction, misunderstandings are more likely to happen, and people are more likely to feel protected from the consequences of acting carelessly. Laura, a 14-year-old from Philadelphia, has learned that the hard way. "I once lost a best friend because of something I said to her online. In real life, I would not have said it, but without having the person right there in front of you, it can be easier to say something offensive."

How to maintain good relationships online

It is important to remember that the digital world is still a part of our offline lives, and we should act responsibly in both environments. "My top tips for maintaining good relationships, online and offline, are all about respect," says Savannah. "Think carefully about not just what you are saying, but how you are saying it. Just as you wouldn't shout all the time in a real conversation, you shouldn't write in an aggressive way, using all capital letters or too many exclamation points or question marks.

Always be polite, even if it means taking another few seconds to check your messages before you click send. And most of all – be authentic. Digital communication should enhance our life, not harm it."

6c CHOOSE YOUR LEVEL skill: reading p. 156

I Read the article again. Take notes on the advantages of digital communication.

II Read the article again. What are the advantages and disadvantages of digital communication? Take notes.

III Read the article again. Take notes on what it says about:
- the advantages of digital communication.
- the disadvantages of digital communication.
- how to maintain good relationships online.

6d wordbank: (digital) communication p. 167, expressing opinions p. 168, workbook p. 50/8

In class, collect advantages and disadvantages of digital communication. Discuss: what are the biggest advantages and disadvantages of digital communication in your opinion?

6e skill: writing p. 155, media worksheet 15

What do you think: do the advantages of digital communication outweigh the disadvantages? Write a comment.

You can write:
Some people say ..., but I think ...
I'm not so sure that ...
On the one hand ..., but on the other hand ...
Although I can understand ..., I think ...
...

ACTIVATE PRACTISE **DEVELOP** PRACTISE APPLY

seventy-three 73

School rules

7a skill: mediation p. 157

An exchange student from the US is at your school. You are showing her how to use your school's online communication platform. Explain to her the following rules in English.

- Achte auf die Lesbarkeit deiner Nachrichten. Benutze nicht zu viele Emojis oder Abkürzungen.
- Vermeide Missverständnisse, indem du klar und eindeutig kommunizierst.
- „Schreie" andere nicht an, indem du nur Großbuchstaben verwendest.
- Schreibe keine albernen oder überflüssigen Nachrichten in Gruppenchats.
- Teile und poste Fotos von anderen nur mit deren Erlaubnis.
- Denke immer daran, dass du für gepostete Inhalte verantwortlich bist. Verbreite Texte oder Fotos nicht gedankenlos.

7b

Which rule(s) do you find most important? Why?

7c workbook p. 50/9, 10

Which of the rules are often broken at your school? How do you feel about it?

An interview about cyberbullying

8a audio 2/8

Listen to the interview.
Why is cyberbullying a topic that is close to Asher's heart?

8b skill: listening p. 153

Listen again. What ways does Asher mention to protect yourself and others against cyberbullying? Take notes.

8c workbook p. 51/11, 12

Which piece of advice from Asher is the most important in your opinion? Talk about it in class.

Texting

9 GET TOGETHER

Work with a partner. Text each other to make plans for the afternoon.

Partner A	Partner B
I Go to page 131.	I Go to page 140.
II Go to page 134.	II Go to page 143.
III Go to page 137.	III Go to page 146.

Digital communication 3

Writing an email

10a video 13, skill: watching a video clip p. 158

Watch the video clip. What is important when you write a formal email?

10b skill: writing p. 155, media worksheet 14

Work with a partner. Choose one or more of these situations and write emails.

1. You are going on a trip to London with your family and would like to stay at a youth hostel. You need a family room for four people from 4 July to 8 July, your little sister needs a crib and your father is a vegan.
2. You are taking part in an exchange programme and would like to ask your host family if they will pick you up from the airport, if they have a bike you could use while staying with them and if you should bring anything such as a sleeping bag.
3. You would like to take part in a dance workshop with a famous American choreographer. You started dancing five years ago, and you are not sure if you are good enough. You would also like to know how much it costs.

10c

Swap your emails and give each other feedback. You can find a feedback sheet at www.westermann.de/webcode if you enter the webcode WES-128203-001.

Communication

11 CHOOSE YOUR TASK

A Work with a partner. Send your partner a text message. In it, describe your day using only emojis. Then "translate" the emoji message into an English text about each other's day and read out your texts to each other.

B Write a polite text message or email to tell your teacher that you cannot come to the class party. Think of a very good or funny reason.

C What do you find annoying about other people's communication behaviour? Why? Write a short text about it.

ACTIVATE   PRACTISE   **DEVELOP**   PRACTISE   APPLY

| Part A | Part B | Challenge |

Non-stop communication

12a audio 2/10, skill: listening p. 153

Listen to Sofia talking about her friend Liam. What does she find annoying about his behaviour?

12b CHOOSE YOUR LEVEL wordbank: seeking and giving advice p. 166, workbook p. 52/13

I Listen again. What do you think Sofia should do?
Send her a text message with one piece of advice.

You can write:
Hi Sofia, I think you should …

II Listen again. What do you think Sofia should do?
Write a text message to Sofia with advice on what she could do and say.

III Listen again. What do you think Sofia should say to Liam?
Write a text message from Sofia to Liam.

What's the opposite?

13a skill: working with words p. 152

Copy the words in the box into your exercise book and write down their opposites by adding a prefix. You can use a dictionary for help.

You can write:
friendly – **un**friendly
…

friendly · polite · healthy · possible · important · advantage · agree · understand · acceptable

13b workbook p. 52/14

Underline the prefixes. What are the different prefixes that can change the meaning of a word to the opposite?

How to pronounce *ea*

14a audio 2/12

Listen to the words and repeat them.

easily · healthy · break up · spread · reason · reach · threat · great · clean · instead of · dream · heavy

14b

Make lists in your exercise book and listen again. Write the words in your lists.

/e/	/iː/	/eɪ/
healthy	easily	break up
…	…	…

14c audio 2/13, workbook p. 52/15

Listen and check your lists.

DIGITAL+ practise more 12–14

76 seventy-six   ACTIVATE   PRACTISE   DEVELOP   **PRACTISE**   APPLY

Tips for online communication TARGET TASK

15 workbook p. 53/16, wordbank: seeking and giving advice p. 166, skill: presentations p. 160, media worksheet 4

Your task is to collect tips for online communication and present them.
Before you start, look at these steps:

STEP 1
What is important in order to communicate respectfully and politely online?
Get together with a partner or in a small group. Collect your ideas and make notes together.

STEP 2
Use your notes to write down a list of tips.

> **Tips for online communication**
> It's important to think first before sending …
> You should …
> Take care to …
> Be careful not to …
> You shouldn't …
> Never …
> …

STEP 3
Decide how to present your tips. It could be:

- a poster
- a digital presentation
- a short video
- …

STEP 3
Work on your product. Edit it if necessary.

STEP 4
Present your work.

STEP 5
As a class, compare the different tips from the groups. Together, decide on the five most important tips. If you like, you can create a poster and put it up in your classroom.

Check out

1. Kannst du persönliche Aussagen zum Thema Freundschaft verstehen?	Workbook, p. 54
2. Kannst du wiedergeben, was jemand gesagt hat?	Workbook, p. 55
3. Kannst du deine Meinung in einer kurzen Aussage ausdrücken?	Workbook, p. 55
4. Kannst du kurze Zeitungsartikel zum Thema digitale Kommunikation verstehen?	Workbook, p. 56
5. Kannst du ein Interview zum Thema Mobbing im Internet verstehen?	Workbook, p. 56
6. Kannst du eine förmliche E-Mail schreiben?	Workbook, p. 57

ACTIVATE   PRACTISE   DEVELOP   PRACTISE   **APPLY**

Every Day

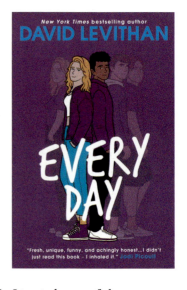

Each morning, A wakes up in a different body. There's never any warning about who it will be, but A is used to that. Never get too attached. Avoid being noticed. Do not interfere.

And that's fine – until A wakes up in the body of Justin and meets Justin's girlfriend, Rhiannon. From that moment, the rules by which A has been living no longer apply. Because, finally, A has found someone he wants to be with – every day …

Day 5994

I wake up.
Immediately I have to figure out who I am. It's not just the body – opening my eyes and discovering whether the skin on my arm is light or dark, whether my hair is long or short, whether I'm fat or thin, boy or girl, scarred or smooth. (…)
Every day I am someone else. I am myself – I know I am myself – but I am also someone else.
It has always been like this.
The information is there. I wake up, open my eyes, understand that it is a new morning, a new place. (…)
Today I am Justin. (…)
I'm never the same person twice, but I've certainly been this type before. Clothes everywhere. Far more video games than books. Sleeps in his boxers. (…)
"Good morning, Justin," I say. Checking out his voice. Low. The voice in my head is always different.
Justin doesn't take care of himself. His scalp itches. His eyes don't want to open. He hasn't gotten much sleep.
Already I know I'm not going to like today. It's hard being in the body of someone you don't like, because you still have to respect it. I've harmed people's lives in the past, and I've found that every time I slip up, it haunts me. So I try to be careful.
From what I can tell, every person I inhabit is the same age as me. I don't hop from being sixteen to being sixty. Right now, it's only sixteen. I don't know how this works. Or why. I stopped trying to figure it out a long time ago. (…)
The alarm goes off. I reach for a shirt and some jeans, but something lets me see that it's the same shirt he wore yesterday. I pick a different shirt. I take the clothes with me to the bathroom, dress after showering. His parents are in the kitchen now. They have no idea that anything is different.
Sixteen years is a lot of time to practice. I don't usually make mistakes. Not anymore.
I read his parents easily: Justin doesn't talk to them much in the morning, so I don't have to talk to them. (…) I shovel down some cereal, leave the bowl in the sink without washing it, grab Justin's keys and go.
Yesterday I was a girl in a town I'd guess to

---

warning = *Warnung*; to get attached = *sich binden*; to interfere = *stören*; to apply = *gelten*; to figure out = *verstehen, begreifen*; skin = *Haut*; light = *hell*; scarred = *vernarbt*; smooth = *glatt*; low = *tief*; scalp = *Kopfhaut*; to itch = *jucken*; to slip up = *einen Fehler machen*; to haunt = *verfolgen*; to inhabit = *bewohnen*; alarm = *Wecker*; to reach for = *greifen nach*; to pick = *aussuchen*; to shovel = *schaufeln*; sink = *Spülbecken*

be two hours away. The day before, I was a boy in a town three hours farther than that. I am already forgetting their details. (…)

I access [Justin's] memory to show me the way to school. (…) As I take Justin's books out of his locker, I can feel someone hovering on the periphery. I turn, and the girl standing there is transparent in her emotions – tentative and expectant, nervous and adoring. I don't even have to access Justin to know that this is his girlfriend. (…) Her name is Rhiannon. And for a moment – just the slightest beat – I think that, yes, this is the right name for her. I don't know why. I don't know her. But it feels right.

This is not Justin's thought. It's mine. I try to ignore it. I'm not the person she wants to talk to. (…)

A and Rhiannon spend the day together and both feel that there is something special going on between them. In the evening, A realizes that their life has changed.

This is hard for me.
I have gotten so used to what I am, and how my life works.
I never want to stay. I'm always ready to leave.
But not tonight.
Tonight I'm haunted by the fact that tomorrow he'll be here and I won't be.
I want to stay.

A breaks their own rules and tells Rhiannon that they wake up in a different body every day. After not believing it at first, Rhiannon finally accepts what A's life is like, and the two try to see each other as often as possible. A very much wants to be in a real relationship with Rhiannon and sometimes it seems to be working. But there are other days when it is difficult.

Day 6005
(…) "You never get involved in the people's lives? The ones you're inhabiting."
I shake my head.
"You try to leave the lives the way you found them."
"Yeah."
"But what about Justin? What made that so different?"
"You," I say.

Day 6016
"(…) Are you really not a boy or a girl?" (…)
It's interesting to me that this is the thing she's hung up on.
"I'm just me," I tell her. "I always feel at home and I never feel at home. That's just the way it is."

Day 6026
"(…) I mean, you're a different person every day. And I just can't love every single person you are equally. I know it's you (…). I know it's just the package. But I can't, A. (…) I want you to know, if you were a guy I met – if you were the same guy every day, if the inside was the outside – there's a good chance I could love you forever. This isn't about the heart of you – I hope you know that. But the rest is too difficult. (…) I just can't do it."

What do you think: can a relationship like this work? Why? Why not?

Cyberbullying – FAQs

How do you tell the difference between a joke and bullying?
If you feel hurt or think others are laughing at you instead of with you, then the joke has gone too far. If it continues even after you've asked them to stop, then this could be bullying. Whether it is happening online or offline, if you are not happy about it, you should not have to put up with it.

Who should I talk to if someone is bullying me online? Why is reporting important?
If you think you're being bullied, the first step is to seek help from someone you trust. If you are not comfortable talking to someone you know, search for a helpline to talk to a professional counsellor. If the bullying is happening on a social platform, consider blocking the bully and formally reporting their behaviour on the platform itself. Social media companies are obligated to keep their users safe.

How do we stop cyberbullying without giving up access to the Internet?
If you experience cyberbullying, you may want to delete certain apps or stay offline for a while. But getting off the Internet is not a long-term solution. You did nothing wrong, so why should you be disadvantaged? It may even send the bullies the wrong signal – encouraging their unacceptable behaviour. We all want cyberbullying to stop, which is one of the reasons reporting cyberbullying is so important. But creating the Internet we want is more than calling out bullying. We need to be kind to one another online and in real life. It's up to all of us!

Is there a punishment for cyberbullying?
Schools take bullying seriously and will take action against it. If you are being cyberbullied by other students, report it to your school. Laws against bullying, particularly on cyberbullying, are relatively new and still do not exist everywhere. In countries that have specific laws on cyberbullying, it is seen as criminal activity. However, it is important to remember that punishment is not always the most effective way to change the behaviour of bullies. Sometimes, focusing on repairing the harm and mending the relationship can be better.

Are there any online anti-bullying tools for children or young people?
Each social platform offers different tools that allow you to restrict who can comment on or view your posts and to report cases of bullying. Also, the first line of defence against cyberbullying could be you. Think about where cyberbullying happens in your community and ways you can help – by raising your voice, calling out bullies, reaching out to trusted adults or by raising awareness of the issue.

If you are worried about your safety or something that has happened to you online, urgently speak to an adult you trust.

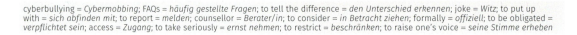

cyberbullying = *Cybermobbing*; FAQs = *häufig gestellte Fragen*; to tell the difference = *den Unterschied erkennen*; joke = *Witz*; to put up with = *sich abfinden mit*; to report = *melden*; counsellor = *Berater/in*; to consider = *in Betracht ziehen*; formally = *offiziell*; to be obligated = *verpflichtet sein*; access = *Zugang*; to take seriously = *ernst nehmen*; to restrict = *beschränken*; to raise one's voice = *seine Stimme erheben*

4

1. What can you see in the pictures? Talk about them in class.
2. How do the pictures relate to the topic of this unit: "Our world tomorrow"?
3. In what way do the pictures relate to your hopes and dreams for the future?

Our world tomorrow

Part A The power of hope

- You will talk about hopes and dreams.
- You will read about people who are taking action for a better future.
- You will present your ideas about an ideal world in the future.

Part B The world of work

- You will talk about different jobs.
- You will find out about hard and soft skills.
- You will create a page for a booklet about jobs.

4   Part A   Part B   Challenge

Talking about the future

1   wordbank: hopes and dreams p. 169, skill: talking with people p. 154, workbook p. 58/1

What are your hopes and dreams for your personal future? What are your hopes and dreams for the future of the world? Talk to a partner.

Hopes and dreams

2a   skill: reading p. 156

Read what these teenagers say about their hopes and dreams for the future.
Write down two or three keywords for each person.

2b

Read out your keywords for one person to a partner. How many keywords do you have to read out before your partner can guess the person? Take turns.

I'm Chenoa. That's "white dove" in Navajo. I'm 15 and I live in Los Angeles with my parents. My dream for the future is to become a famous director and create movies that make people dream or help them escape reality for a while but also inspire and motivate them. I've chosen "camerawork" as one of my electives at school, and I've become even more interested in the technical side of movie making, especially in animation.
If I had the choice, I would go to the California Institute of the Arts and learn from the best. I would have to win a scholarship, though. The fees are so high that my family could never afford them – even if I had a job.

My name is José. I'm 13 years old and I hope to be able to become a teacher. My parents are from Honduras originally. They came to the USA before I was born because they could get jobs here. Both of my parents never went to college. They work a lot, but they don't earn very much money because they don't have any good qualifications. But I'm really glad they emigrated to the USA anyway. If we were still living in Honduras, things would be more difficult and I wouldn't have the opportunities I have here. It would be great if I won a scholarship for a really good college. I'm trying to keep my marks up, but it's really difficult and my parents can't help me. They just don't have the time and the knowledge. But even if that doesn't work, I could still go to community college. Sometimes I dream about what I would do if I was rich. If I had a billion dollars, I would try to help students all over the world to get a good education. I think that would solve a lot of problems.

ACTIVATE   PRACTISE   DEVELOP   PRACTISE   APPLY

The power of hope 4

My name is Robert. I'm 17 and I would love to become a professional paraclimber. I had to overcome some difficulties when I started climbing because I was born with a disability and use a wheelchair, so I had to find a gym with special equipment, for example. But I made it! I've been climbing for three years now, and I love it. Luckily, there is a large paraclimbing community in the USA, so I can take part in competitions and share my experiences with other people who have similar difficulties. I'm also really grateful to my family. They always support me. My dad drives me to all my competitions and my mom and my brothers watch me as often as they can and cheer for me. My dream is to compete in the Paraclimbing National Championships – I train five times a week to reach that goal. It would be so cool if paraclimbing became a Paralympic sport. Not just because it's my sport but also to raise awareness for the fact that a disability does not necessarily mean that you cannot do what you want to do!

I'm Miriam and I'm 15 years old. My dream is to make the world a better place, especially by fighting against climate change. When I've finished school, I want to train as a sustainability manager because I might be able to really change something then.
For the time being, I became a member of the student council at my school last year, and I really like to see our ideas and actions having at least a small impact. At the moment, we're campaigning for our school to become a "Green School". I know that one school going green won't stop climate change, but at least we're doing something. I just wish that things would change faster sometimes. If it wasn't so difficult and didn't take so much time to make politicians, or basically most grown-ups, listen to young people's ideas and concerns about the future, a lot of things would improve. If I was the president of the United States, I would definitely make better climate laws.

2c CHOOSE YOUR LEVEL

I Read the statements again. What are the teenagers' hopes and dreams?

II Read the statements again. What are the teenagers' hopes and dreams? What are they doing or planning to do to reach their goals?

III Read the statements again. What are the teenagers' hopes and dreams? What are they doing or planning to do to achieve their goals? What problems do they talk about?

2d workbook p. 58/2

If you had a lot of money, which one of the teenagers would you like to help?
Why? How?

You can say:
If I had a lot of money, I would like to help …
  because …
I would support …

4 | Part A | Part B | Challenge

GRAMMAR HELP — conditional clauses type 2 p. 185

Conditional clauses type 1 kennst du schon. Du benutzt sie, um auszudrücken, was unter bestimmten Bedingungen höchstwahrscheinlich geschehen wird, z. B.: *If you miss the bus, you will be late.*

Conditional clauses type 2 verwendest du, um zu sagen, was unter einer nur gedachten Bedingung passieren würde. Dies ist nicht so wahrscheinlich wie bei den *conditional clauses type 1*. Was fällt dir bei den Sätzen auf?

If I had the choice, I would go to the California Institute of the Arts.
If I had a billion dollars, I would try to help students all over the world.
If it did not take so much time, things would improve faster.

Auf Seite 185 findest du weitere Beispiele und Erklärungen zu den *conditional clauses type 2*.

If …

3a grammar: conditional 2 p. 185

Match the sentence parts and write down the sentences.

1 If Chenoa was a famous director,
2 If paraclimbing became a Paralympic sport,
3 If José and his parents still lived in Honduras,
4 If it did not take so much time to make politicians listen,
5 It would be great

A he would not be able to go to college.
B if there were better climate laws.
C things would be better.
D it would show that people with a disability can do amazing things.
E she would create films that make people dream.

3b grammar: conditional 2 p. 185, workbook p. 59/3

Complete these conditional sentences (type 2) with the correct forms of the verbs.

1 If Chenoa ??? (be) a student at the California Institute of the Arts, she ??? (learn) how to direct films.
2 If there ??? (not be) a paraclimbing community in the USA, Robert ??? (not be able to) take part in competitions.
3 If there ??? (not be) any gyms with special equipment, Robert ??? (not be able to) do his dream sport.
4 If José's parents ??? (have) more qualifications, they ??? (get) better jobs.
5 If Miriam ??? (can) change the world, she ??? (make) better climate laws.

If I had the chance …

4 grammar: conditional 2 p. 185, workbook p. 59/4

What would you do if you had the chance?
Make notes, then talk to a partner.

You can say:
If I had the chance, I would …
… ride my bike around the world.
… become an engineer.
…

 DIGITAL+ practise more 15

ACTIVATE **PRACTISE** DEVELOP PRACTISE APPLY

The power of hope 4

Working towards change

5a skill: reading p. 156
Read this article from an American magazine. What does it say about imagination? Do you agree?

5b
In class, collect ideas for actions that you can take on each of the four levels of climate action.

Working towards change – the four levels of climate action

Thinking about the future and challenges like climate change can make us feel helpless. Sometimes combating climate change just seems too big a task.

If you feel like this too, it can help to know that you are not alone. Many of us feel that way about the climate crisis. There is even a name for it: climate anxiety. The best way to do something about it? Climate action!

But what can we actually do to make a difference? It is important to know that even small things can help. First, we need to imagine a better future in order to be able to work towards it. Our imagination is a powerful tool. So, try and imagine in detail what a green and livable future would look like to you. Also find out about what experts say on the topic and about what we can do about climate change.

Then, before you get going, it is helpful to know the four levels of climate action and decide on which level you can get involved.

LEVEL 1 is about individual action, for example when you decide for yourself to eat less meat or buy fewer new clothes in order to reduce the CO_2 output that you are responsible for. Every action for reducing our ecological footprint counts.

LEVEL 2 is action in your direct circle, for example when your family decides to use public transport as often as possible.

On **LEVEL 3**, you take actions to your community. One example for this is establishing a recycling system at your school. Other institutions can then copy or adapt the system. Thus, your actions can influence many people in a positive way.

LEVEL 4 is the systemic level. It is about trying to change the system as a whole. You could sign petitions or join an existing movement. Actions on this level usually have the biggest impact because they take place on a larger scale, for example when a whole country decides to ban short-distance flights. Actions on this level are often the ones that you need the most stamina and patience for.

LEVELS OF CLIMATE ACTION
LEVEL 1: Individual action
LEVEL 2: Our direct circle
LEVEL 3: Community action
LEVEL 4: Systemic action

Although action is needed to save our planet, fighting climate change can be exhausting, so remember to take breaks. Burned-out people cannot really help in saving a burned-out planet.

5c CHOOSE YOUR LEVEL   skill: writing p. 155, wordbank: seeking and giving advice p. 166, workbook p. 60/5-7
What could you tell someone who feels helpless about climate change?
Read the article again to get ideas.

- **I** Write a message of about 60 words and tell them what actions they could take.
- **II** Write a message of about 80 words and tell them what actions they could take.
- **III** Write a message of about 100 words and tell them what actions they could take.

4 Part A

Turning a vision into reality

6a
Look at the pictures and the headline. What do you expect to read about in the article?

6b
Read the article. What was the "spark" that is mentioned in the headline?

The spark that led to a global movement

1 Americans purchase nearly 3 billion batteries every year to power radios, toys, cell phones, watches and laptops. But what happens with these batteries when they are empty? After learning of the potential dangers of batteries that are not properly disposed of, a young boy from New Jersey decided to take action.

How did it all begin?

5 Back in 2019, right around his 10th birthday, Sri Nihal Tammana was watching the news about a huge fire in a Californian waste disposal plant, causing not only millions of dollars worth of damage but also massive harm to the environment, and it was all started by a battery. He asked his dad how we could prevent this from happening again, and he was told that that
10 was possible if all people recycled their batteries instead of just throwing them away in their household garbage. In the following weeks, Sri Nihal saw more stories about batteries causing fires around the world, and he found out how
15 the chemicals in different kinds of batteries cause terrible pollution when they end up in landfills instead of being collected and taken to recycling plants. He also learned that as many as 15 billion batteries are thrown in the trash each
20 year globally although they contain valuable chemicals and rare metals that can be used again.

First steps

Sri Nihal decided he had to try and do something to help. He began by collecting batteries in his
25 school and community and taking them to free recycling points. Eventually, he collected so many that he was told he couldn't use the bins anymore. So, in June 2019, he started his own non-profit organization "Recycle My Battery." He began by
30 installing free-to-use battery bins in his school in Edison, New Jersey, which were successful right away.

The power of hope 4

Thinking further

Sri Nihal realized that collecting the batteries was a good starting point but that real change was only going to happen if as many people as possible knew about the dangers of batteries and saw how important it is to recycle them. Because of that, he also started running awareness campaigns to educate both adults and young people about the importance of battery recycling. He also spread the word in his inner circle, among friends and family and encouraged them to join him for his campaign.

Where they are today

By today, he and his friends have collected and recycled more than 300,000 used batteries, keeping them out of landfills. They have also reached an estimated 15 million people via their campaigns and recruited over 500 volunteer kids from schools globally. Back in 2019, he never believed his little idea about recycling batteries would grow the way it has, just because he wanted to make a difference and started to do something about it. It turns out that this commitment was infectious. People just began listening and joining in. This shows that everyone can be a changemaker – even young people. So if you care about something, first believe that you can change things, and second, take the first step to make that change happen. You'll be amazed by where those two small steps could lead.

6c CHOOSE YOUR LEVEL skill: reading p. 156

I Read the article again. What are the problems with batteries? Take notes from the text.

II Read the article again. What are the problems with batteries? How can they be solved? Take notes from the text.

III Read the article again. What are the problems with batteries? What did Sri Nihal and his friends do to help solve these problems? What have they achieved so far? Take notes from the text.

6d
What did you find out about Sri Nihal and his project from the article? Talk about it in class.

6e
Sri Nihal had a vision. Look at the four levels of action on page 85 again. Which level has Sri Nihal reached with his organization?

6f workbook p. 61/8, 9
How would you define a "changemaker" (line 54)? What kind of attitude do changemakers need?

4 Part A

Changing the world

7 CHOOSE YOUR TASK B+C: skill: searching the internet p. 159, media worksheet 6, wordbank: presenting something p. 168

A What could be done in your neighbourhood to make your area more environmentally friendly? Collect ideas and present them in class.
B There are many songs about how to change the world. Find and present one or more to your class.
C All over the world, you can find people who are changing things for the better. Do some research. Find out where and how things actually got better and tell your class about it.

PEOPLE & PLACES 5

Student councils in the USA

Most elementary and secondary schools in the USA have student councils that enable students to become involved in the affairs of the school.

Student councils help share students' ideas, interests and concerns with teachers and school principals. They often also help raise funds for school activities, including social events, community projects, helping people in need and school reform. For example, many schools organize food drives, fundraisers such as charity runs and parties.

A very important aspect of the work of student councils is that they not only help with improving school life for everyone but that students also learn about democracy and about taking on responsibility.

Is there a similar organization at your school? What does it do? Do you think it is a good idea to have a student council?

A charity run

8 skill: mediation p. 157, workbook p. 62/10, 11

Your little brother's school is organizing a charity run. Your American aunt, Mia, who is staying with your family, does not understand what your brother, Eric, is asking for. Help them.

Eric: Kannst du Tante Mia fragen, ob sie mich sponsert?
(1) You: *Mia, would you sponsor …?*
Mia: Oh, I'd love to, but what for exactly?
(2) You: *Sie …*
Eric: Für unseren Wohltätigkeitslauf! Mama macht schon mit, und Oma rufe ich gleich an.
(3) You: …
Mia: A charity run, that sounds cool. I think it's great that he's taking part. So, what would I have to do?

(4) You: …
Eric: Sie muss sich überlegen, wie viel sie für jede Runde, die ich laufe, spenden würde, und das dann hier auf diesem Formular eintragen und unterschreiben.
(5) You: …
Mia: OK. What about €1.50?
(6) You: …
Eric: Das wäre toll. Vielen Dank, Mia. Jetzt habe ich schon zwei Sponsoren!
(7) You: …
Mia: You're welcome.

4 The power of hope

The power of hope

9a

What do you know about Michelle Obama? What was her job from 2009 to 2017? Talk about her in class.

9b

Read this excerpt from a speech by Michelle Obama. What are the topics she addresses?

1   (…) So for all the young people in this room (…) know that this country belongs to you — to all of you, from every background and walk of life. If you or your parents are immigrants, know that you are part of a proud American tradition — the infusion of new cultures, talents and ideas, generation after generation (…). If your family doesn't have much money, I want you to remember
5   that in this country, plenty of folks, including me and my husband — we started out with very little. But with a lot of hard work and a good education, anything is possible — even becoming President. That's what the American Dream is all about. (…)

Right now, you need to be preparing yourself (…). You need to prepare yourself to be informed and engaged as a citizen, to serve and to lead, to stand up for our proud American values and
10 to honor them in your daily lives. And that means getting the best education possible so you can think critically, so you can express yourself clearly, so you can get a good job and support yourself and your family, so you can be a positive force in your communities.

And when you encounter obstacles, (…) when you are struggling and you start thinking about giving up, I want you to remember something (…) and that is the power of hope — the belief that
15 something better is always possible if you're willing to work for it and fight for it.

It is our fundamental belief in the power of hope that has allowed us to rise above the voices of doubt and division, of anger and fear that we have faced (…). Our hope that if we work hard enough and believe in ourselves, then we can be whatever we dream (…). So that's my final message to young people (…). Don't be afraid. Be focused. Be determined. Be hopeful.
20 Be empowered. Empower yourselves with a good education, then get out there and use that education to build a country worthy of your boundless promise. Lead by example with hope, never fear. (…)

9c CHOOSE YOUR LEVEL skill: reading p. 156

I Read the first two paragraphs again and copy the words that express the main idea of each paragraph best. In which lines did you find them?
II Read the first three paragraphs again and copy the words that express the main idea of each paragraph best. In which lines did you find them?
III Read the excerpt again and copy the words that express the main idea of each paragraph best. In which lines did you find them?

9d media worksheet 18, workbook p. 62/12

Find a video clip of the speech on the Internet and watch it. Do you think it is a good speech? Do you agree with Michelle Obama that hope can help you reach your goals? Why or why not?

ACTIVATE   PRACTISE   **DEVELOP**   PRACTISE   APPLY

4 Part A — Part B — Challenge

Word pairs

10a
Combine words from box A and box B to make expressions from this unit. Write them down.

A climate · student · ecological · battery · public · non-profit · awareness · charity

B council · transport · change · campaign · organization · footprint · run · recycling

10b
Think of three or more two-word expressions like that and write them down.

10c
Choose three or more of your expressions from 10a or 10b. Write down one sentence for each expression to show what it means.

What would happen if …?

11 CHOOSE YOUR LEVEL grammar: conditional 2 p. 185

I Complete the conditional sentences (type 2) with the correct forms of the verbs.
1. If people ??? (grow) more trees, our cities ??? (become) greener.
2. If politicians ??? (make) better climate laws, things ??? (change) faster.
3. If people ??? (recycle) more, fewer products ??? (have to be) produced.
4. If people ??? (use) public transport more often, there ??? (be) fewer cars on the streets.

II Write about what you would do if …
1. you could wish for three things.
2. a thousand people were willing to help you make the world a better place.
3. you were the president of the United States.
4. you had a billion euros.

III If you could change five things in the world, what would you do and why? Write about it.

The world in 50 years

12a audio 2/18
Listen to the people talking about the future. Which of these topics do they talk about?

schools · houses · travelling · food · animals · work

12b skill: listening p. 153, workbook p. 63/13, 14
Listen again and take notes. Then write down what the people say about the topics.

You can write:
John says that in 50 years there might be …
Sarah thinks there could also be …
Bill says that maybe no more … will be used in 50 years.
…

DIGITAL+ practise more 15

90 ninety   ACTIVATE PRACTISE DEVELOP **PRACTISE** APPLY

4 The power of hope

My ideal future world TARGET TASK

13 workbook p. 64/15, wordbank: hopes and dreams p. 169

Your task is to present to your class what your ideal world in the future would look like.
Before you start, look at these steps:

STEP 1
Imagine your ideal world. What does it look like? You could:
- make notes
- sketch it
- create a digital word web
- find pictures and make a digital mood board
- …

STEP 2
Prepare a presentation of your ideas.
Make notes on what you would like to say about your ideal world.

STEP 3
Use your notes to present your work to your classmates.

You can say:
In my ideal future world, there would be no more …
…

ACTIVATE   PRACTISE   DEVELOP   PRACTISE   **APPLY**

4 Part A | Part B | Challenge

Jobs

1a
Work with one or two partners. Write down all the jobs you know in English. You have three minutes.

1b
How many jobs have you collected? Compare your lists in class.

1c audio 2/20, skill: listening p. 153
Listen to the job descriptions and match them to the pictures.

A animal keeper

B physiotherapist

C electrician

D gardener

E nursery teacher

F construction worker

G accountant

H lawyer

1d workbook p. 65/1, 2
What do you think are the advantages and disadvantages of each of these jobs? Discuss in class.

What do they do for a living?

2a
Read the statements. Which job do you find the most interesting? Give reasons.

Damian

1 Registered nurse: I work in a hospital in a small town in Ohio on the children's ward as a registered nurse. We look after children aged two to twelve with all sorts of problems here. I take blood samples, change wound dressings, take temperatures and try to make our patients feel as comfortable as possible.
I'm also allowed to carry out and interpret diagnostic tests. I can't prescribe any medication though, only qualified doctors are allowed to do that. I like working here. It's always great when a kid can leave the hospital because we've helped them get better. The only thing that's sometimes a bit difficult for me is that I have to work shifts.

92 ninety-two   ACTIVATE PRACTISE DEVELOP PRACTISE APPLY

The world of work 4

Cody

2 Fashion designer: I really like fashion – that's why I became a fashion designer. My job is very creative, and I design clothing and accessories. I create original new designs or adapt fashion trends. I have to be able to work with different materials. For example, I have recently started working with recycled and sustainable materials. Big cities like New York are famous for their fashion designers – only the best are allowed to host their own fashion shows. That's also my big dream: I hope I will be able to present my own designs in a big fashion show one day – but I know that I will have to work hard to achieve that goal.

John

3 Forest worker: I am a forest worker in Oregon. There are many forests here, and I do lots of different things. For example, I cut down trees, load them onto big tractors and drag them out of the forest. That's why I must be able to drive big trucks and tractors. I can also operate machinery that drags logs. We also create firebreaks – areas without trees where forest fires can be stopped. We remove sick trees from the forest as well so that the forest as a whole stays healthy. I like my job because it is outdoors and it is very physical. I also like the fact that I'm able to do something useful for the ecological system here. Oregon has so many beautiful forests and we need to look after them.

Tamara

4 Surf instructor: Surf instructors teach people of all ages the proper techniques for surfing. You need to be a very good swimmer to do this job, and you also have to know a lot about safety and have life-saving skills because you have to make sure everyone is safe at all times. I had to get a number of safety certifications before I was allowed to become a surf instructor. Two years ago, I was able to start my own surf school in Santa Cruz, California, so I'm my own boss now which I really like. But that also means that I have to do a lot of office work as well like planning, advertising and managing surfing courses. I love my job because I can do what I am passionate about for a living, and I meet new people all the time which is very inspiring.

2b CHOOSE YOUR LEVEL skill: reading p. 156, workbook p. 65/3-5

I What do the people do in their jobs? Take notes.
II What do the people do in their jobs? Why do they like their jobs? Take notes.
III Choose three or more of the people and write about them and their jobs.
Where do the people work? What do they do? What skills do they need for their job? What are their duties? Why do they like their jobs?

My future job

3a   wordbank: the world of work p. 170

Talk to a partner about what is important to you in a job. Think about:
- money and working hours
- working indoors or outdoors
- working in a team or on your own
- …

3b   skill: working with words p. 152

Together with your partner, collect jobs that each of you could do that fit your ideas from 3a.
Look up the names of the jobs in a dictionary if necessary.

ACTIVATE   PRACTISE   DEVELOP   PRACTISE   APPLY

4 Part A | **Part B** | Challenge

> **GRAMMAR HELP** modal verbs (R) p. 186
>
> Du hast bereits verschiedene Modalverben kennengelernt. Für die Modalverben *must* und *can* gibt es Ersatzformen. Erinnerst du dich daran, wie die Ersatzformen für *must* und *can* lauten und wie sie verwendet werden? Schau dir dazu die folgenden Beispielsätze an.
>
> I *will have to* work hard to achieve that goal.
> I *had to* get a number of safety certifications.
> I hope I *will be able to* present my own designs in a big fashion show one day.
> Two years ago, I *was able to* start my own surf school.
> Only doctors *are allowed to* prescribe medication.
> I had to get a number of safety certifications before I *was allowed to* become a surf instructor.
>
> Auf Seite 186 findest du weitere Erklärungen und Beispiele zu den Modalverben und ihren Ersatzformen.

Talking about jobs

4 grammar: modal verbs (R) p. 186

Copy the sentences and fill the gap with modal verbs from the box.

1 In order to become a vet, you ??? study at university.
2 I study medicine so I hope I ??? work as a doctor some day.
3 I had saved some money so I ??? start my own business three months ago.
4 I can speak French so I hope I ??? find a job in France in the future.
5 I ??? do lots of different courses before I ??? become a nurse last year.
6 I quickly found a new job. I ??? wait long.
7 In my old job, I had to go to the office every day. I ??? work from home.
8 As a registered nurse, you ??? prescribe medication, only doctors can do that.

> will be able to (2x) ·
> was able to (2x) ·
> aren't allowed to ·
> wasn't allowed to ·
> have to ·
> had to ·
> didn't have to

Asking questions

5 grammar: modal verbs (R) p. 186, workbook p. 67/6

Unscramble the questions. Then look at the texts on page 92 and 93 again and answer them.

1 are you allowed to – what – Damian, – at work? – carry out
2 your goal? – will you have to – do – Cody, – to achieve – what
3 what kind – John, – operate? – are you able to – of machinery
4 your own surf school? – when – were you able to – start – Tamara,

What's the job?

6a audio 2/22

Listen to the job words and repeat them. Where is the stress? Make three lists.

first syllable	second syllable	third syllable
g<u>a</u>rdener	phot<u>o</u>grapher	elec<u>tri</u>cian
…	…	…

6b workbook p. 67/7

Choose four or more of the job words from 6a and write one sentence each explaining what people in the jobs do.

The world of work 4

Everybody has skills

7a skill: reading p. 156

Read this article from an American magazine and take notes. Work with a partner and summarize the main points in German.

Everybody has skills

Ever thought about what it takes to apply for a job? Employers usually look for two kinds of skills: soft skills and hard skills. Everybody has soft and hard skills – but what exactly are they?

Hard skills (also called *job skills*) are skills that help you do particular jobs. Examples are: computer software knowledge, being able to repair cars or bicycles, foreign languages, or computer programming.

People learn hard skills at school, on the job or from life experience. You can even try and teach yourself skills like using a particular computer program.

Soft skills (also called *people skills* or *personal skills*) have to do with your personality, attitude and manners. Examples are: politeness, good communication, reliability, and the ability to work in a team.

hard skills

soft skills

Recognizing your hard and soft skills

As a high school student you may have learned skills through school, volunteering, or sport. If you play a sport, you probably have good teamwork skills. Good at presentations? Your communication skills are likely to be great! Do you babysit for neighbors? For that you have to be reliable and responsible.

Improving your skills

You can always improve your hard and soft skills! To practice soft skills, talk to friends and family and ask them for feedback. To practice or learn hard skills, take a course, buy a book or watch tutorials. And when it comes to applying for a job, don't just list these skills in your application – make sure you show how you have used them and give examples to show what you can do. Good luck!

7b CHOOSE YOUR LEVEL workbook p. 67/8-10

I Make one list with examples of hard skills and one list with examples of soft skills.
II Collect the examples of hard and soft skills mentioned in the article. Try to add your own examples. Explain the difference between the two types of skills.
III Collect examples of hard and soft skills. Explain the difference between the two types of skills. Then choose a job and write about the hard and soft skills you need for this job.

4 Part B — A soft skill check

8a

Find out if you have good soft skills! What would you do in each situation? Write down the letters. Then check your result on page 230.

1. You're late for school.
   a) You enter the classroom without saying anything and sit down.
   b) You enter the classroom and say good morning to everyone.
   c) You apologize to the teacher and promise it won't happen again.

2. You start group work in class.
   a) You choose a group with good classmates so that you don't have to work so hard.
   b) You choose classmates that you know you can work well with.
   c) You are not happy about the situation and ask your teacher for an individual task.

3. Your class has to tidy the school grounds every day for a week.
   a) You wait and hope that others will volunteer.
   b) You immediately say that you will do it.
   c) You say you definitely won't do it.

4. Your teacher wants to explain something to the whole class.
   a) You listen carefully and ask specific questions.
   b) You quietly talk to your neighbour and don't listen at all.
   c) You don't pay much attention and look out of the window.

5. Some of your classmates are arguing on the school bus.
   a) You don't do anything but you later complain to your close friends at school.
   b) You try to end the argument peacefully.
   c) You shout at your classmates and tell them to stop fighting.

6. Your group work is due tomorrow. Some of you haven't done the assignments.
   a) You help the others in order to get a good individual and group result.
   b) You work all night long on your own and your partners' assignments.
   c) You shout at your partners and do your own part of the presentation.

8b

Look at the soft skill check again. What soft skills do you need in each situation? Discuss.

organisational skills · taking initiative · ability to work in a team · politeness · being on time · listening skills · …

8c skill: talking with people p. 154

Which skills do you need to work on? How could you improve them? Talk to a partner.

You can say:
I need to work on being on time. I could …
What about you?

4 The world of work

What to do?

9a audio 2/24

Nick, a 17-year-old high school student, is talking to his aunt Leah. Listen and read along. What are they talking about?

Leah: Hi Nick, how are you doing? What are you up to?
Nick: Hi Auntie Leah. I want to go to that really cool music festival in summer, but the tickets are so expensive. I really need to find a job as soon as possible to add to my pocket money.
Leah: OK – what kind of job are you looking for?
Nick: Well, it needs to be something I can do after school or on the weekends. I was thinking about filling shelves at a supermarket or helping people pack their bags at the cash register. Do you have any other ideas?
Leah: Yes, I do actually. You could mow people's lawns or you could get a job as a paper boy – those jobs are before or right after school. I heard that supermarket jobs are often in the evenings, and working late might tire you out too much. I know that you have trouble getting up in the mornings anyway!
Nick: I hate to say that you are right – I really don't like getting up early. So I don't think working as a paper boy is for me.

Leah: Don't worry, you'll find a job that is for you. Hmm, let me think: have you considered being a busboy at a restaurant? Your dad did that when he was a teenager.
Nick: I know – and he hated it! So much hard work, and the pay was really bad – and I don't think that has changed much. I'd much rather work outside and keep fit at the same time to be honest. Dog walking for example! I love dogs, and I am quite good with them.
Leah: Yes, that's a good idea! You're also fun around younger kids. Babysitting could be for you. Or how about tuition? You are good at math and French – and you are patient. Why not help students who are struggling at school?
Nick: That is an awesome idea! Why have I never considered that until now? I used to help my neighbor with his homework, and I liked it. Well, you have given me some really good ideas – I'll see if there are any job openings nearby. Thanks, Auntie Leah!
Leah: I'm always happy to help! Now good luck, and don't forget to update me on the progress of your job hunt!

9b CHOOSE YOUR LEVEL skill: reading p. 156

I Look at the dialogue again. List the jobs that Nick and Leah mention.
II Look at the dialogue again. Which jobs does Nick like? What does he like about them? Which jobs does he not like?
III Look at the dialogue again. What are the advantages and disadvantages of the jobs that Nick and Leah mention?

9c workbook p. 68/11

What soft skills does Nick need for the jobs? Which skill that Leah mentions is a hard skill?

ACTIVATE   PRACTISE   **DEVELOP**   PRACTISE   APPLY

ninety-seven

| Part A | **Part B** | Challenge |

A job application form

10a

Read Nick's application form. What kind of job is he applying for?

APPLICATION FORM

Name: *Nick Adams*
Address: *12 Washington Rd, Philadelphia, PA 19147*
Phone: ~~512-28763238~~
Email: *N.Adams@xyyy.com*
Age: *17*
Current grade at high school: *12th grade*
Subjects you feel comfortable tutoring / last grade achieved in report: *French (A), math (A)*
Grades you feel comfortable tutoring: *up to 11th grade*
Experience in tutoring: *helping my neighbor with his homework*
Other relevant experience: *boy scout camp counselor at the age of 17 (boy scout since the age of 7), spent 2 months in French-speaking Canada last summer, member of the Mathletics club at high school*
Why do you want to work with us? *I like helping others and can work well with younger students. I enjoyed helping my younger neighbor do his homework and prepare for tests. That is why I would enjoy working as a tutor for Top Tutoring.*
References: *Mr. Curtis from Boys Scouts of America and Mrs. Newman, my neighbor*

TOP TUTORING
Working towards better grades

10b workbook p. 69/12

Do you think that Nick is the right person for the job? Why or why not?

A job interview

11a wordbank: seeking and giving advice p. 166

Nick is invited to a job interview at Top Tutoring. What tips can you give Nick for his interview? What should he do or say, and what should he definitely not do or say during the interview?

You can say:
During the job interview, Nick should …
He shouldn't …
He must …
But he certainly must not …

11b audio 2/25, workbook p. 69/13

Listen to Nick's interview. Did he follow the tips?
Would you give him the job?

ACTIVATE PRACTISE **DEVELOP** PRACTISE APPLY

The world of work 4

PEOPLE & PLACES 6 video 14

Vocational training in the USA

In many American high schools, students can take part in organized educational programmes to prepare them for their professional lives. Vocational training typically starts in career and technical education (CTE) programmes. These programmes provide students with specific skills and practical experience that prepare them for employment or further education after high school. The places students work at can include auto shops, farms, offices and hospitals. In these environments students get an idea of what it is like working in that specific field. While Germany has a very good dual vocational training system with fixed standards for apprenticeships, in the USA there is no single set of apprenticeship standards that all programmes offering on-the-job training have to follow. In general, fewer high school graduates start an apprenticeship after high school than go to college or university.

What practical training would you like to get at school?

Help wanted

12 skill: mediation p. 157

An American exchange student sees this ad and asks you what it is about. Tell them the most important information in English.

> **Helfende Hand gesucht!**
>
> Du bist Schülerin oder Schüler und möchtest dein Taschengeld aufbessern? Du bist 14 Jahre oder älter und kannst gut mit Menschen umgehen? Dann melde dich bei uns. Wir suchen für meine Mutter (76 Jahre) jemanden, der für ein paar Stunden in der Woche kleinere Tätigkeiten für sie übernimmt, wie z. B. einkaufen gehen oder den Hund ausführen. Wir bezahlen einen guten Stundenlohn. Näheres erfährst du in einem persönlichen Gespräch (Tel.: ▓▓▓▓▓▓▓▓). Wir freuen uns auf deinen Anruf!

The world of work

13 CHOOSE YOUR TASK A+C: skill: searching the internet p. 159, B: wordbank: expressing opinions p. 168

A Do some research on unusual jobs and present your top three in class.
B Do you think it is a good idea to turn your hobby into a profession? Write a short text about the pros and cons.
C Do some research on the future of the world of work. What jobs will probably become more important? What jobs might disappear? Give a one-minute talk about your findings.

A role play

14 GET TOGETHER

Get together with a partner.
Do a role play of a job interview.

Partner A	Partner B
I Go to page 132.	I Go to page 141.
II Go to page 135.	II Go to page 144.
III Go to page 138.	III Go to page 147.

ACTIVATE   PRACTISE   **DEVELOP**   PRACTISE   APPLY

4   Part A   **Part B**   Challenge

A very bad job interview

15   grammar: conditional 3 (optional) p. 187, workbook p. 70/14, 15

Read about Ella's job interview. Write down some tips for Ella to use in the future.

1. Ella was late for the interview. If she hadn't missed the bus, she would have been on time.
2. Ella's clothes were not appropriate. If her trousers hadn't been full of holes, she would have made a better impression.
3. Ella didn't ask any questions. If she had asked some questions, it would have been better.
4. Ella didn't know much about the company. If she had done some research, she would have known more about the company.
5. Ella didn't get the job. If she had prepared well for the job interview, maybe she would have got the job.

You can write:
Be on time.
Wear …
…

Skills and jobs

16   **CHOOSE YOUR LEVEL**   wordbank: the world of work p. 170, workbook p. 70/16

I   Read what the people say about themselves. What could be a good job for each person? Why?

II   Read what the people say about themselves. Take notes on what they like or dislike and what they are good at. What could be a good job for each person?

III   Read what the people say about themselves. Describe their personalities and skills. What job or jobs would suit each person?

Rebecca: My favourite subject at school is art, and I've never been really good at sports. I love using my imagination to create and invent new things. I enjoy making things with my own hands. I wouldn't like working outdoors a lot though.

Aaron: It's very important to me that I can help other people. My friends say that I'm a friendly and patient person, and I love being around people. I also see myself as a team player. I wouldn't like doing a job where I have to sit alone at a desk in an office the whole day.

Reza: I like solving problems, and I'm really good with computers. For example, I like writing computer programs, and if something isn't working, I won't stop looking for a solution until I've found and solved the problem. At school, I'm in the maths club. I have never really liked history, and I'm not very good at art or music.

Jasmine: I just love sports. I go running almost every day, and I'm also really good at sports at school. My favourite team sport is basketball, and I've started training young children at our local sports club. I really like helping other people improve their skills. It's important to me to be active, and I don't like sitting still very much.

DIGITAL+ practise more 18

ACTIVATE   PRACTISE   DEVELOP   **PRACTISE**   APPLY

The world of work 4

Our job booklet TARGET TASK

17 workbook p. 71/17, wordbank: the world of work p. 170

Your task is to create one page for a (digital) booklet about jobs for people with different personalities and skills. Before you start, look at these steps:

STEP 1
In class, make a list of jobs you would like to include in your booklet.

STEP 2
Get together in small groups. Choose the job you would like to write about.
Make sure that each job is only presented once in the booklet.

STEP 3
Collect information about the job.
Think about:
- what you do in the job
- where you work
- what hard and soft skills you need
- …

STEP 4
Create your page. Add pictures and / or photos.

STEP 5
Put all your pages together in a (digital) booklet.

> **Tip**
>
> Your page will be good if you …
> - keep information short and precise.
> - present information clearly.
> - use headings.
> - use different colours.
> - use pictures and / or photos.
> - do not overload it with too much information.

Physiotherapist

A physiotherapist
- helps people after an injury or operation
- helps people to improve movement
- gives massages

Hard skills needed:
- medical knowledge

Soft skills needed:
- listening skills and good communication
- ability to understand patients' feelings

Check out

1. Kannst du einem Zeitschriftenartikel wichtige Informationen entnehmen?	Workbook, p. 72
2. Kannst du ausdrücken, was unter bestimmten Bedingungen passieren würde?	Workbook, p. 73
3. Kannst du in einem Gespräch zwischen zwei Personen sprachlich aushelfen?	Workbook, p. 73
4. Kannst du darüber sprechen, was dir bei einem Job wichtig ist?	Workbook, p. 74
5. Kannst du beschreiben, welche Fähigkeiten und Kenntnisse man für einen Job braucht?	Workbook, p. 74
6. Kannst du ein Bewerbungsgespräch verstehen?	Workbook, p. 75

ACTIVATE   PRACTISE   DEVELOP   PRACTISE   **APPLY**

Interview

"Hope is a discipline": youth climate case plaintiff on why he's suing the US government
Dharna Noor

Nathan Baring of Alaska is part of a group of young activists suing the US, which they say "willfully ignored" dangers of fossil fuels

Nathan Baring is [an] Alaskan climate activist. He is also a plaintiff in Juliana v United States, *a lawsuit (…) brought by 21 young Americans. [Lawsuits in the USA are named after at least one of the plaintiffs, in this case Kelsey Juliana, and the defendant.]*

How did you become aware of the climate crisis?
(…) It's incredible the changes that have happened within my lifetime. When I was growing up, it used to be very normal to have two-week periods of 40-below temperatures during the winter. Now it seems like it's rare that we get those temperatures at all. As a Nordic skier and as someone who grew up in Fairbanks, I see it's become so much milder and wetter. (…)

How did you get involved in climate organizing? Tell me a little bit about your political journey.
(…) When I was 12 or 13, I attended some climate-science discussions at the University of Alaska, Fairbanks. It freaked me out. At that point, I got involved in an organization called *Alaska Youth for Environmental Action* (…). Julia Olson, the head lawyer for the Juliana case, reached out to my organization. (…) It's been quite a journey since then!

Students Nathan Baring and Avery McRae participate in a Senate Climate Change Task Force.

You're the only Juliana plaintiff from Alaska. Could you tell me a little bit about what that's like?
The organizations I was part of growing up were almost exclusively led by Indigenous organizers who always centered (…) climate justice. I realized that was kind of unique when I (…) got into the broader climate movement. But in Juliana, there are a number of plaintiffs who are Indigenous and grew up with much more of that cultural background than I did as a white person. I also (…) focus on labor justice because

---

youth = *Jugendliche/r*; plaintiff = *Kläger/in*; to sue = *verklagen*; willfully *(AE)* = *absichtlich, mutwillig*; fossil fuel = *fossiler Brennstoff*; v (= versus) = *gegen*; to bring a lawsuit = *Anklage erheben*; to become aware of = *sich einer Sache bewusst werden*; period = *Zeitraum*; temperature = *Temperatur*; Nordic skier = *Skiläufer/in*; to freak out *(informal)* = *jemanden ausflippen lassen*; environmental = *Umwelt-*; head lawyer = *leitende/r Anwalt/Anwältin*; to reach out = *Kontakt aufnehmen*; to lead = *leiten*; to center = *die Aufmerksamkeit richten auf*; broad = *vielseitig*; to focus on = *sich konzentrieren auf*; labor *(AE)* = *Arbeit*; to participate in = *teilnehmen an*; senate = *Senat*; task force = *Arbeitsgruppe*

Alaska is probably the most oil-dependent state in the nation. The state is largely paid for by taxes on the oil industry. (…) I have friends that don't believe in climate change. I have friends who work in the oil industry (…) or have family members who do. But the issue is really not that people don't believe in climate change. It's that they've been given no vision for a future without oil. (…) Alaska, West Virginia, Louisiana, Texas, these states have been (…) the resource bucket for the rest of the nation. If we're going to (…) move beyond that, we have to be there for the states that have not seen, in decades, any economic diversion away from fossil fuels.

Kelsey Juliana, a lead plaintiff in Juliana v United States, speaks during a news conference outside the Supreme Court in Washington, D.C.

We recently saw a landmark victory for youth climate suits out of Montana, which like Alaska is a fossil fuel-rich red state. What did you make of the Montana victory?

I have the privilege of knowing the plaintiffs in that case. I was absolutely thrilled for them. They really got to make history. This win in a state like Montana, which is, in a lot of ways, economically similar to Alaska, it's especially exciting. (…) It came from a state with a really rich coal industry. (…) The Montana case really emphasized the (…) importance of a trial. (…) We need that kind of sunlight. (…)

Juliana could go to trial sometime soon. How are you feeling about that prospect?

(…) It's been eight years of pushing for a trial. I sunk to quite a low in February 2020, (…). And then boom, March 2020, was the beginning of Covid. I had to de-center a lot of my own grief and big feelings about climate change. It's like that famous quote: "Hope is a discipline." I really took that to heart.

Still, it would be nice to finally have a trial! In a funny way, the longer we've waited, the stronger we've become. The evidence of climate change is so clear now. (…)

Protesters attend a rally outside the Supreme Court in support of the Juliana v United States lawsuit.

What levels of activism does Nathan talk about? How is he trying to change the world?

dependent = *abhängig*; largely = *größtenteils*; resource = *Ressource*; beyond = *jenseits*; diversion = *hier: Richtungswechsel*; landmark = *Meilenstein*; suit = *Zivilprozess*; red state = *Bundesstaat, in der die Mehrheit der Menschen die Republikanische Partei unterstützt*; to be thrilled = *sich wahnsinnig freuen*; to make history = *Geschichte schreiben*; win = *Sieg*; economically = *wirtschaftlich*; coal = *Kohle*; to emphasize = *hervorheben*; trial = *Prozess, Gerichtsverhandlung*; to go to trial = *vor Gericht gehen*; prospect = *Aussicht*; to sink = *sinken*; low = *Tiefpunkt*; grief = *Kummer*; to take to heart = *sich zu Herzen nehmen*; lead = *führend*; conference = *Konferenz*; Supreme Court = *Oberstes Bundesgericht*; rally = *Versammlung*; lawsuit = *Gerichtsverfahren*

Unusual jobs

Snake milker
Around the world, an estimated 4.5 million people are bitten by snakes every year, and about 120,000 of them die. That makes the jobs of snake milkers very important. They "milk" snakes, not for real milk but for their venom, which can then be used to produce an antidote.

Train pusher
The first train pushers worked in New York City. They made sure that people did not get caught in the doors when the train departed. Automatic door technology replaced them about 100 years ago. Today, you can still meet professional train pushers in Tokyo. Their job is to get as many people as possible into every subway train during rush hour.

Ethical hacker
When you think of hackers, you probably think of cybercrime. But there are also "good hackers" who hack into computer programs to find security gaps. They also test software for big companies to make it as safe as possible.

Water slide tester
When a hotel or water park first installs a new slide, someone has to make sure that it's safe to use, so you need a water slide tester. You just have to be at least 18 years old, love a good adrenaline rush, and have great attention to detail so you can notice and report potential dangers.

What do you think: which of these jobs is the most important? Why?
Which one would you like or not like to do? Why?

---

snake milker = *Schlangenmelker/in*; around the world = *weltweit*; to bite = *beißen*; snake = *Schlange*; to milk = *melken*; venom = *Gift*; antidote = *Gegenmittel*; train pusher = *jemand, der Menschen in U-Bahnen und Züge schiebt*; to get caught = *eingeklemmt werden*; to depart = *abfahren*; automatic = *automatisch*; rush hour = *Stoßzeit*; ethical = *ethisch*; cybercrime = *Internetkriminalität*; to hack = *hacken*; water slide = *Wasserrutsche*; adrenaline rush = *Adrenalinstoß*; to have great attention to detail = *große Aufmerksamkeit fürs Detail haben*

5

1. Look at the pictures. What can you see?
2. Where do you think the people are?
3. Choose one of the people in the pictures and write a speech bubble for them.

New horizons

Part A Immigration

- You will read different immigration stories.
- You will watch a presentation about statistics on immigration in the USA.
- You will write a text from an immigrant's point of view.

Part B The Republic of Ireland

- You will listen to people talking about life in Ireland.
- You will find out about sights in Ireland.
- You will give a five-minute talk about one interesting aspect of Ireland.

5 Part A

Leaving home

1a

What do you think: why do people leave their home and begin a new life in a different country? Work in small groups and write down possible reasons.

flee from war ·
go and live with a partner ·
go to university · …

1b workbook p. 76/1

Share your ideas in class and talk about them.

A new beginning

2a skill: reading p. 156

Scan the stories of three immigrants to the USA. What countries did they come from?

1   My name is Mary O'Donnell and I'm from Kilkenny in Ireland. There, I lived on a small farm with my parents and two brothers. In 1846, we lost our complete harvest due to potato blight (a disease that causes potatoes to rot). The same happened in the next couple of years – not
5   only to us but to farmers all over Ireland. By 1851, we were desperate. Because of the size of the farm and the quality of the soil we could not grow anything else. Without potatoes, our staple food, we were literally starving. We also couldn't pay the rent for the farm, and our landlord threatened to throw us out. But we were luckier than most. My dad's brother, Uncle Joe, had
10 emigrated to America in 1839, and in 1852 he managed to buy prepaid tickets to New York for all of us and told us to come to the USA as quickly as possible. The journey from Cork to New York on a sailing ship in cold and stormy weather took one month. The boat was overcrowded, many were seasick, there was little fresh air, our cabin was tiny and the food was horrible. We were so happy when we arrived in New York and saw Uncle Joe standing at the harbour!

Mary in New York in 1858

15 My name is Simon Goldschmidt, and I was born in Germany in 1925. When I was eight years old, the Nazis came to power and my whole life changed. Because we are Jewish, my father was not allowed to practice as a doctor anymore, and I was forced to leave school. In the beginning, my mother told us not to worry and that it would all be over soon. But
20 it only got worse, and it didn't take us that long to realize that staying in Germany would be dangerous for us. After the November Pogrom of 1938, it was clear that we had to leave our home to save our lives. My parents applied for visas to the USA, but it took until 1940 to finally get them. On May 11th 1940, we boarded a ship in Hamburg together with many other emigrants, and I can still
25 remember standing on the deck, being happy to escape, although it was terrible for me that I had to leave all my friends, and I was really worried for my grandparents in Berlin.

Simon in the USA in 1943

My name is Ji-Hoon Choi. I was born in South Korea in 1951 and lived there until I was 23. Korea was a very poor country at that time. The unemployment rate was very high, and my father advised me to try to
30 find work in the USA. Thanks to my parents' financial support, I was able to leave Korea and move to Los Angeles in 1974. I did not speak much English then, so I was glad that I found a job in a small shop that belonged to a Korean family. I worked in their shop for five years and saved as much money as I could. Although I sent some money
35 to my family in Korea, by 1979 I had saved so much that I was able to open my own shop. By then I had married. My wife is Korean, too. She came here in 1977, and our son was born in 1981. We kept working in the shop together until our two children had finished university. They both got very good jobs. My son is a lawyer and my daughter is a consultant. My wife and I sold our shop in 2016 and retired. Although we thought about going back to Korea, we decided to stay here with our
40 children and grandchildren. My grandson has just started college, and my granddaughter is going to finish high school in two years. Leaving home and starting out on my own was very hard for me in the beginning, but when I look at my children and grandchildren today, I'm glad that my parents told me to come here and that I was able to provide my children with a good education.

Ji-Hoon and his wife in 1978

2b CHOOSE YOUR LEVEL

I Read the stories and finish the sentences. In which line did you find the information?

1 Mary's family lost their harvests due to …
2 By 1851, they were literally …
3 Simon Goldschmidt's life changed when …
4 His family left Germany because …
5 Ji-Hoon went to the USA to …
6 Today, he is glad …

II Read the stories and finish the sentences. In which line did you find the information?

1 When Mary O'Donnell's family lost their harvests, they …
2 In 1852, Mary's uncle Joe …
3 The boat to New York was …
4 Simon Goldschmidt's life changed in 1933 because they …
5 Simon and his parents realized that …
6 When he left Germany, Simon was …
7 In the 1970s, Korea was …
8 Ji-Hoon first worked …
9 After they retired, Ji-Hoon and his wife decided …

III Read the stories and take notes on the following questions. In which line did you find the information you needed? Then use your notes to write a short text about the people.

– Why did the people leave their home countries?
– How did they feel at what point?

2c workbook p. 76/2

What do you think: how did Mary and Simon's lives go on? Collect ideas in class.

GRAMMAR HELP

reported commands p. 188

Wenn du einen Befehl, eine Bitte, eine Aufforderung oder eine Warnung wiedergeben möchtest, bildest du einen indirekten Befehlssatz. Schau dir die Beispiele an. Was fällt dir auf?

Uncle Joe: "**Come** to the USA."
Simon's mother: "**Don't worry**."
Ji-Hoon's father: "**Try** to find work in the USA."

Uncle Joe told us **to come** to the USA.
My mother told us **not to worry**.
My father advised me **to try** to find work in the USA.

Weitere Erklärungen zu indirekten Befehlssätzen findest du auf Seite 188.

Boarding the ship

3a grammar: reported commands p. 188

It is very noisy at the harbour. Mary's mother asks Mary to repeat what they are told to do when they board the ship.

1. Please board the ship.
2. Bring your suitcase with you.
3. Go to the first cabin on the left.
4. Stay below deck during storms.
5. Use the third-class toilets only.

You can write:
1. They told us to board the ship.
2. …

3b grammar: reported commands p. 188, workbook p. 77/3, 4

Report what the passengers are told not to do.

1. Do not fall overboard.
2. Please do not use too much fresh water.
3. Do not start a fire.
4. Do not walk around on deck.
5. Do not climb the ship's mast.

You can write:
1. They warned us not to fall overboard.
2. They asked us …
3. …

Verbs and nouns

4a skill: working with words p. 152

Look at the verbs in the box. Find nouns from the same word family and write down the verbs and nouns. There can be more than one solution. Use a dictionary for help.

emigrate · begin · live · arrive ·
advise · rent · marry · change ·
escape · use · work

You can write:
emigrate – emigration
begin – …
…

4b

Choose five or more of the words and write statements using them. You can look at the texts on page 106 and 107 for help.

Immigration 5

The USA, an immigration country

5a wordbank: numbers p. 171

Look at this graph from a presentation about immigration to the USA. Has there been an increase or decrease in the number of immigrants over the years? What could be the reasons for this?

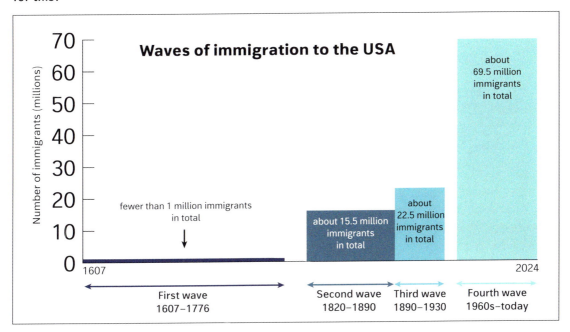

5b CHOOSE YOUR LEVEL video 15, skill: watching a video clip p. 158, workbook p. 77/5

I   Watch the presentation and take notes. Then complete the sentences.

1 There have been four ??? of immigration to the USA.
2 From 1820 to 1890, most immigrants came from ???, ??? and Scandinavia.
3 During the third immigration wave, the number of people who immigrated to the USA from Eastern and Southern ??? increased.
4 In ???, a quota system was introduced.
5 In 2022, most immigrants came from ???.

II   Watch the presentation and take notes. Then answer the questions.

1 How many waves of immigration to the USA have there been?
2 Why did many people emigrate from Ireland to the USA in the 1840s and 1850s?
3 When did the second immigration wave peak?
4 What per cent of immigrants came from Italy during the third wave?
5 Why did immigration decrease after 1924?
6 Where did most immigrants come from in 2022?

III   Watch the presentation and take notes on the four immigration waves to the USA. Where did the immigrants come from? Why did they leave their home countries?

ACTIVATE   PRACTISE   **DEVELOP**   PRACTISE   APPLY

5 — Part A | Part B | Challenge

Elizabeth Flynn – diary of an immigrant

6a
Look at the pictures.
What do you expect to read about?

6b
Read the diary entries.
Were you right in 6a?

New Orleans, Louisiana, May 1st, 1889
Our ship from Dublin arrived in New Orleans after five horrible weeks of travel. **I'm so glad to be back on land!**

New Orleans, May 2nd, 1889
Today, we were questioned by immigration officials and had a medical inspection. One Russian family has to return home because they all have tuberculosis.
Thank God we are all healthy and fit!

New Orleans, July 4th, 1889
The Americans celebrated Independence Day today. There were fireworks, a parade and a band.
I have never seen anything so wonderful!

St. Louis, July 10th, 1889
We took a steamboat up the Mississippi river to St. Louis. Father couldn't find work in New Orleans, and the city was full, noisy and very busy. The south is very hot and humid. There are alligators and poisonous snakes there. It is strange and exciting and not like Ireland at all.

St. Louis, July 17th, 1889
We are going southwest to Oklahoma Territory in a wagon train tomorrow. Father saw an advertisement promising free farmland in Oklahoma. He said that we will have fresh air, a farm and no one to tell us what to do. My parents bought a wagon, oxen to pull it, a milk cow, a horse and some chickens. Everything we own is in the wagon: food, clothes, tools, guns and a few books. We will sleep under the stars and cook over a fire. I'm so excited!

6c   skill: reading p. 156
Read the diary entries again. What people, places and events does Elizabeth mention? What are her family's plans for the future? Take notes.

6d   workbook p. 78/6, 7
Why do you think people write diaries? Do you keep a record of your life?
If you do, in what form? Talk about it in class.

A letter home

7a skill: reading p. 156
Scan Elizabeth's letter home to Ireland and find the elements that show you that this is a letter.

7b
Read Elizabeth's letter. Where is she now? What topics does she write about?

West of Oklahoma City, March 3rd, 1890

Dear family,

I hope you're all well. It took us most of August and September to reach Oklahoma Territory. The Great Plains are beautiful. There is green grass everywhere, but almost no trees. We saw lots of bison, deer and rabbits. The weather was extremely hot and dry, but we had some rain and even a thunderstorm once. The thunder and lightning were very scary. Luckily we had no tornadoes because there is nowhere to hide on the open plains! At night the wolves and coyotes were howling. Everyone was nervous.

Life in a wagon train was hard. Emily and I walked to Oklahoma. I am glad that our shoes were new because we walked over 500 miles to reach our new home. Mama and baby James rode in the wagon, and Father rode the horse. We had been warned not to take unnecessary things with us, and after the first week on the trail I understood. Every day, we saw things that people had left behind. We walked by chairs, tables and even a piano in the grass next to the trail. Some people gave up and went back east.

We had a daily routine to keep us busy. Every day, we woke up before the sun. Emily and I collected buffalo chips for our fire. Father milked the cow while mother was cooking breakfast. Then we rode 10 or 15 miles and made camp again. Once, we had to fix a wagon wheel that had broken. We finally made it to Oklahoma City in September, and we've also managed to survive the winter. Now it is spring. Yesterday, Father got a good piece of farmland in a land race. It was exciting. He rode his horse as fast as he could. Then he put a wooden stake in the ground on our new land. The rest of us were following him slowly in our wagon. Now we will build a house and barn, plant a vegetable garden and start farming.

Hope to hear from you soon. Give all our love to family and friends. I will send you some drawings of our new home as soon as I have time.

Love,
Elizabeth

7c CHOOSE YOUR LEVEL

I Read the letter again. What does Elizabeth tell her family about nature? Take notes.

II Read the letter again. What does Elizabeth tell her family about nature and life on the trail? Take notes.

III Read the letter again. What does Elizabeth tell her family about nature, life on the trail and the family's plans for the future? Take notes.

7d workbook p. 79/8-10

If you had to leave your home country to start a new life somewhere else and could only pack one bag, what would you take with you? Write a list and talk about it with a partner.

PEOPLE & PLACES 7 video 16, workbook p. 80/11

Ellis Island

For millions of immigrants the first sights of the USA were the Statue of Liberty and Ellis Island in the harbour of New York. The Statue of Liberty faces southeast, making it a perfect symbol for the welcoming of immigrants who come to the USA hoping to find a better life. While everyone who had travelled in first and second class was taken directly to the piers in New York harbour by smaller boats, every immigrant who arrived as a third class passenger had to pass through the immigration station on

Ellis Island

Ellis Island from 1892 onwards. It is estimated that more than 12 million immigrants passed through its gates up until 1954 when the station was closed. Immigration officers wrote down information on name, age, country of origin etc., and everyone had to have a medical examination. If you failed at either point, you were sent back. That is why Ellis Island became known as the 'Island of Tears'. Today, Ellis Island is a museum, the "Ellis Island Immigration Museum".

Medical examination at Ellis Island

What do you think: how did people feel before their journey, on the boat and after they had passed the examination on Ellis Island?

A meme

8a

Look at the meme. Who could the man be? Who do you think he is addressing? What is the message of the meme?

8b

What do you think about the message of the meme?
Talk about it in German.

On the move

9 **CHOOSE YOUR TASK** B: skill: searching the internet p. 159, medoa worksheet 6, wordbank: presenting something p. 168

A If you could choose any country in the world to emigrate to, where would you go? Why? Write a short text about your reasons.

B Choose one of the people on pages 106 to 107. Find out more about the situation in their home country around the time they emigrated and present your findings.

C Make your own family tree. Ask your parents and grandparents about your family and where everyone came from. What did you find out that you did not know before? You can add interesting facts about your family's past and history if you like.

Life in the USA

10a audio 3/2

Listen to Roberto's story. Where does he live?
Where does his family live?
Why did he move to the USA?

10b **CHOOSE YOUR LEVEL** skill: listening p. 153

I Listen again and complete the sentences.
1 Roberto's father ??? (keeps animals / works in a factory).
2 Roberto's mother is a ??? (teacher / secretary).
3 Life in Paraguay is ??? (easy / difficult).
4 Roberto ??? (can / cannot) see his family very often.
5 Roberto tutors students in ??? (French / Spanish) to earn some extra money.

II Listen again and complete the sentences.
1 Roberto is in the USA in order to ???.
2 He managed to get a scholarship from a ???.
3 Roberto likes to ??? with his friends.
4 Roberto likes to listen to ???.
5 Roberto will be away from home for ??? years.
6 After his studies, Roberto plans to ???.

III Listen again and take notes. Write down two or more facts about:
1 Roberto's family
2 Why Roberto goes to university in the USA
3 What Roberto likes about the USA
4 Roberto's future plans

10c skill: talking with people p. 154, workbook p. 81/12

What do you miss when you are away from home? Do you get homesick?
Talk about it with a partner.

5 | Part A | Part B | Challenge

What was going on?

11 grammar: past progressive (R) p. 189, workbook p. 81/13

Copy the sentences and fill in the correct verb forms. Decide whether to use the simple past or the past progressive.

1 While he ??? (live) in Paraguay, Roberto ??? (go) to a small school in his village.
2 While the passengers ??? (board) the ship, a suitcase suddenly ??? (fall) into the water.
3 Elizabeth's parents ??? (work) on the field when it ??? (start) to rain.
4 Mary's uncle ??? (wait) at the harbour when the ship ??? (arrive) at Ellis Island.
5 A little child ??? (begin) to cry while the passengers ??? (wait).
6 It ??? (rain) when Ji-Hoon ??? (leave) the airport.

You can write:
1. *While he was living in Paraguay, Roberto went to …*

Adjectives and more

12 **CHOOSE YOUR LEVEL** workbook p. 81/14

I Copy the sentences and add adjectives to make the sentences more interesting. You can use words from the box or think of your own.

1 Carlos took a/an ??? plane to the USA.
2 The ??? journey to the airport had taken six hours.
3 He was thinking about the ??? town that he had left to start a/an ??? life in the USA.
4 He felt ??? when the plane landed in Los Angeles.
5 He sent a/an ??? message to his parents as soon as he arrived.

happy · big · small · long · new · old · difficult · exhausting · dangerous · excited

II Copy the adjectives and add opposites. Then combine five of the adjectives with nouns and write down expressions that could be used in a story about immigration.

sad · poor · expensive · new · slow · friendly · cold · difficult · tiny

III Copy the adjectives and add opposites. Then choose five of the adjectives and write sentences that could be used in a story about immigration.

sad · legal · poor · expensive · new · slow · healthy · friendly · unnecessary · cold · difficult · tiny

Countries

13 skill: working with words p. 152, wordbank: around the world p. 162

Write down eight or more names of countries and add the matching adjectives. Compare your list with a partner.

You can write:
Ireland – Irish
China – …

DIGITAL+ practise more 20-21

Immigration 5

An immigration story TARGET TASK

14 workbook p. 82/15, skill: writing p. 155, wordbank: around the world p. 162, media worksheet 1, 9–16

Your task is to write from the point of view of someone who moved to another country. Before you start, look at these steps:

STEP 1
Collect ideas for your text, for example in a list, a word web, a table, a (digital) mood board, …
Keep the following questions in mind:
- Who moved?
- When did they move?
- Where did they move to?
- Why did they move?
- What …?
- How …?
- What happened then?

STEP 2
Decide what kind of text you would like to write:
diary entries, a letter, an email, a blog post, …?
You can go to www.westermann.de/webcode and enter the webcode WES-128203-001 to find worksheets if you need help.

STEP 3
Make a draft of your text.
Ask a classmate for feedback and edit it if necessary.

STEP 4
Write your text. Check it for mistakes.
You can add pictures or photos if you like.

STEP 5
Present your text to the class.

> *My immigration story*
>
> *Three years ago, I moved from England to Japan. Why Japan? Well, I got a job offer from a company in Tokyo. I've always been interested in Japanese culture and the job offer was good, so I moved to Tokyo.*
> *In my free time I'm taking part in language classes. I do lots of sightseeing and enjoy experiencing the cultural differences. Japan is an amazing country and I love living here! Tokyo now feels like a second home to me, but of course I sometimes miss England.*
> *Find more details on my website: #emma_o_intokyo*

ACTIVATE   PRACTISE   DEVELOP   PRACTISE   **APPLY**

5 | Part A | **Part B** | Challenge

A map of Ireland

1 workbook p. 83/1

What do you know about Ireland? What can you find out by looking at this map? Talk about it in class.

Ireland

2a audio 3/4

Listen to the people and read along. Where do they live?

1 Hello, I'm Finn and I'm from Galway. I'm a Gaelic football player. My team is the St John's Juniors, and I'm the goalkeeper. You haven't heard of Gaelic football? There are 15 players on each team, and the players can throw, kick and carry the ball. It's the best game in the world! I'm still in school, and my mum says I haven't been studying enough since I started playing football: I spend all of my time on the football field. My dream is to play in the All-Ireland Senior Championship one day.

2 My name's Patrick O'Toole. I'm from the USA, and I'm visiting Ireland for the first time in my life. Tonight, I'm in Limerick, but I will be travelling all over the island during the next few weeks. I want to find out all about my family history. My great-great-grandparents emigrated from Wexford to the USA over a hundred years ago. I have been trying to find out more about them for years, and now I'm finally here. It's very exciting to find out where they came from and to discover this beautiful country for myself.

3 Hi, I'm Declan. I have a band together with my friends Noah and Lucy – the Shamrocks! We like all kinds of music, but we mostly play Irish folk. I've been playing the fiddle since I was a child. We make our money playing in pubs all over Cork, our home town. I enjoy every show, but my favourite concerts are the ones we play for our family and friends. It's a wonderful feeling to play the songs we have known all our lives and to hear our loved ones sing along. That, to me, is Ireland. That, to me, is home.

4 I'm Anna. I'm 34 years old and I live in Sligo. I was born in Poland but moved to Dublin with my parents when I was a little child. Did you know that Polish is the largest non-Irish nationality in Ireland? I speak English and Polish with my family and love to visit Poland on my holidays. I think you could say that I feel Polish and Irish at the same time. For a few months, my partner has been talking about moving to another country, but I know that I want to stay right where I am. Ireland will always be my home.

2b CHOOSE YOUR LEVEL skill: reading p. 156

I Choose two or more of the texts and read them again. What do you learn about the people? Take notes.

II Choose three or four of the texts and read them again. What do you learn about the people? Take notes.

III Read the texts again. What do you learn about the people? Take notes.

2c workbook p. 83/2

Use your notes to talk about the people in class.

5 Part B

GRAMMAR HELP — the present perfect progressive p. 190-191

Das *present perfect progressive* verwendest du, wenn du über etwas sprechen möchtest, das in der Vergangenheit begonnen hat und immer noch andauert bzw. immer noch zutrifft. Schau dir die Beispiele an und beschreibe, wie die Formen gebildet werden.

I've been playing the fiddle since I was a child.
I have been trying to find out more about my great-great-grandparents for years.
For a few months, my partner has been talking about moving to another country.
My mum says I haven't been studying enough since I started playing football.

Auf den Seiten 190 und 191 findest du weitere Erklärungen und Beispiele zum *present perfect progressive*.

What have they been doing?

3 grammar: present perfect progressive p. 190, workbook p. 84/3

Copy the sentences and complete them with the verbs in the present perfect progressive.

1 Finn ??? (do) his homework since he came back from football training this afternoon.
2 Finn and his best friend ??? (play) football in the same team for five years.
3 Patrick O'Toole ??? (wonder) about his family history for a long time.
4 Patrick ??? (walk) around Limerick for two hours.
5 Declan ??? (play) the fiddle for many years.
6 Anna ??? (live) in Ireland since she was a little child.

Since or for?

4a grammar: present perfect progressive p. 190

Look at the pictures. Write down what the people have been doing or have not been doing.

Patrick – travel – for 7 hours

Anna – not watch TV – for 2 hours

Finn – not play Gaelic football – since 5 o'clock

Declan – give a concert – since 8 o'clock

4b grammar: present perfect progressive p. 190

Complete the sentences by using a verb from the box and decide if you have to use "since" or "for".

talk · dream · play · live

1 The Shamrocks ??? in pubs (since / for) six years.
2 Finn ??? about playing in the All Ireland Senior Championship (since / for) he was ten.
3 Anna ??? in Sligo (since / for) three years.
4 Anna's partner ??? about moving to another country (since / for) a while.

5 The Republic of Ireland

Sightseeing in Ireland

5a audio 3/5

Listen to the descriptions and match the names of Irish sights to the pictures.

A Powerscourt Estate C Lemon Rock E Dingle Peninsula G Sea Adventure
B Hook Lighthouse D Blarney Castle F Connemara National Park Waterpark

1

2

3
7

4

5

6

5b CHOOSE YOUR LEVEL skill: listening p. 153

I Listen again and complete the sentences with the correct information.

1 Powerscourt Estate is ??? minutes away from Dublin.	A 13	B 30
2 At Blarney Castle, you can listen to the mystical story about the Blarney ???.	A stone	B horse
3 Dingle is the perfect place for ??? lovers.	A car	B animal
4 Connemara National Park is on the ??? coast.	A Atlantic	B Pacific

II Listen again and take notes. Then match the information with the sights.

1 Here you can see magnificent gardens.
2 At this sight, you should kiss a stone.
3 Some people say that ghosts live here.
4 Some scenes in a famous film were filmed here.
5 Here you can choose one of many hiking trails.
6 If you want to watch dolphins or seals, you should come here.

**III Listen again and take notes. What do you learn about the sights?
Write down two or more facts for at least five of the sights.**

5c workbook p. 84/4

Which of the sights would you like to visit? Tell a partner and say why.

ACTIVATE PRACTISE **DEVELOP** PRACTISE APPLY

5   Part A   **Part B**   Challenge

What to do in Dublin

6a   wordbank: descriptions p. 163
Look at these photos from a travel guide. Talk about what you see.

6b
Read the texts. Which sights do you find interesting? Where would you like to go?

Right at the heart of Dublin, you will find the beautiful campus of **Trinity College**. Roughly 20,000 students – young people from Ireland and all around the world – study here. Trinity College is not only Ireland's oldest and most famous university, it is also the home of the Book of Kells, a beautifully illustrated manuscript of the bible which dates back to around the year 800. Over a million tourists come to see it every year.

Go shopping in **Grafton Street**. Spend your money on the latest fashion or buy some traditional Irish sweaters. Listen to the many street musicians playing music up and down this beautiful shopping area.
Have some cake at Bewley's, Dublin's most famous café, or relax at St Stephen's Green, a big public park next to Grafton Street.

If you like cool arts and music, visit **Temple Bar**. This area in the centre of Dublin has arts centres and theatres, a fashion and design market, hip second-hand shops and countless pubs and bars. While Temple Bar is a lively centre of activity for young people and tourists, it is also a famous nightlife spot.

The Republic of Ireland 5

Visit **EPIC, the Irish Emigration Museum,** and find out about the many Irish people – some unknown, some famous – who left the island and made their mark in the USA and all over the world.
Explore what "being Irish" means from the outside and the inside, in Ireland and all around the world.

Do you like swords, shields and historic battles? Check out **Dublinia Viking Museum** and experience all aspects of Viking life. Try Viking clothes, find out about life on a Viking ship and learn to fight like a Viking warrior. Learn about Dublin's medieval past by getting to know the city as it was 700 years ago. Play medieval games, find out about medieval food and walk along a medieval Dublin street.

Follow in the footsteps of those who fled the potato famine. 2,500 of them sailed across the Atlantic on the **Jeanie Johnston** – a nightmare of a voyage. Take a journey back in time, find out about the horrible living conditions on board a famine ship and hear the stories of the people who had to leave their home country in order to escape starvation.

6c CHOOSE YOUR LEVEL skill: reading p. 156

I Choose at least three of the attractions. Write down no more than three keywords for each.
II Choose at least four of the attractions. Write down no more than three keywords for each.
III Choose at least five of the attractions. Write down no more than three keywords for each.

6d workbook p. 85 / 5, 6

Work with a partner. Can they guess which attractions your keywords describe? Take turns.

PEOPLE & PLACES 8 video 17, workbook p. 86/7

Ireland

Ireland is divided between Northern Ireland, which belongs to the United Kingdom, and the Republic of Ireland with its capital Dublin.

For about 750 years, Ireland was under British rule. Many Irish people wanted Ireland to become an independent country, but there was also a strong minority who wanted to remain part of the United Kingdom. These were mainly Protestants in the northern part of Ireland.

In 1922, after the *Irish War of Independence*, the 26 counties in the southern part of Ireland became independent from the UK as the *Irish Free State*, while the six counties in the north of Ireland stayed part of the UK. For a long time, this led to unrest and

violence, especially in Northern Ireland between the late 1960s and 1998 – a time known as *The Troubles*.

In 1948, the official name *Republic of Ireland* was established, and in 1973 the Republic of Ireland joined the European Union at the same time as the UK and Denmark.

After the Brexit in 2020, Ireland is besides Malta the only country with English as an official language in the EU.

Watch the video clip. What aspect of Irish history would you like to learn more about?

A song for Ireland

7a

Listen to the "Song for Ireland" by Phil and June Colclough and read the first few lines of the lyrics. What do you imagine the person speaking to be like? What situation are they in?

Walking all the day
Near tall towers where falcons build their nests
Silver-winged they fly
They know the call of freedom in their breasts
Soar Black Head against the sky
Where twisted rocks run down to the sea
Living on your western shore
Saw summer sunsets asked for more
I stood by your Atlantic sea
And sang a song for Ireland

Talking all the day
With true friends, who try to make you stay
Telling jokes and news
Singing songs to pass the night away
Watched the Galway salmon run
Like silver dancing darting in the sun
Living on your western shore
Saw summer sunsets asked for more
I stood by your Atlantic sea
And sang a song for Ireland (...)

7b wordbank: feelings p. 166

How does the song make you feel? Make a list of five words that describe the feelings that the song evokes in you.

7c workbook p. 86/8, 9

Share your list with a partner. Explain to each other why you chose these words.

5 The Republic of Ireland

Gaelic football

8 skill: mediation p. 157, workbook p. 87/10

Imagine you and your friend are talking to Finn, the Gaelic football player. Your friend is very interested in Gaelic football, but his English is not as good as yours. Help him and Finn understand each other.

Your friend: Ich wüsste schon gerne, ob Gaelic Football das Gleiche wie Fußball ist.
(1) You: Finn, is Gaelic football the same as …?

Finn: It's a bit like football, but it is also like rugby and basketball. It's a bit complicated to explain!
(2) You: Es ist ein bisschen …

Your friend: Spielen da denn 11 Spieler mit?
(3) You: …

Finn: No, there are 15 players on the field.
(4) You: …

Your friend: Und wenn das ein bisschen wie Basketball ist, gibt es dann auch Körbe?
(5) You: …

Finn: No, there are no baskets. The players kick or punch the ball into or above a goal.
(6) You: …

Your friend: Und wie lange dauert so ein Spiel?
(7) You: …

Finn: A game has two halves of 30 minutes and a short half-time break.
(8) You: …

Your friend: Ich kann mir das alles immer noch nicht vorstellen. Frag ihn bitte, ob wir mal zu einem Spiel kommen können.
(9) You: …

Finn: That's an epic idea! Why don't you come to our game on Friday?
(10) You: …

Planning a trip

9 GET TOGETHER

Get together with a partner.
Read the travel information about Ireland and make a travel itinerary.

	Partner A	Partner B
I	Go to page 132.	Go to page 141.
II	Go to page 135.	Go to page 144.
III	Go to page 138.	Go to page 147.

More about Ireland

10 CHOOSE YOUR TASK A: wordbank: travelling p. 163, B+C: skill: searching the internet p. 159, C: wordbank: descriptions p. 163

A Design a poster advertising Ireland as a holiday destination.
B   Do some research on the languages spoken in Ireland and present your findings in class.
C   Find information about a famous Irish person (actor, musician, writer, …) and tell your class about them.

ACTIVATE   PRACTISE   **DEVELOP**   PRACTISE   APPLY

5 Part B

Facts about Ireland

11 CHOOSE YOUR LEVEL workbook p. 87/11, 12

I **Match the sentence parts and write down the sentences.**

1 Dublin is
2 The river in Dublin
3 The Republic of Ireland
4 Ireland is
5 Northern Ireland

A an island.
B belongs to the UK.
C is called the river Liffey.
D is a member of the European Union.
E the capital of the Republic of Ireland.

II **Unscramble the sentences and write them down.**

1 part of – Northern Ireland – the UK. – is
2 Cork – Ireland. – in the south of – is a city
3 Ireland – and hills. – its green fields – is known for
4 is – an important part of – Music – Irish culture.
5 is – Gaelic football – one of the most popular – in Ireland. – sports
6 the official – of the Republic of Ireland. – English and Irish – languages – are

III **Finish the sentences with information from this unit.**

1 The Book of Kells is a book which …
2 If you want to go shopping in Dublin, you can …
3 There is a Viking Museum in Dublin where …
4 In the 19th century, many Irish people left Ireland because …
5 The Republic of Ireland joined the European Union in …
6 The UK left the European Union in 2020, whereas the Republic of Ireland …
7 Gaelic football …

Preparing a talk

12 workbook p. 88/13, 14

Read the phrases. Then copy them into your exercise book in the order in which you would hear them in a talk.

A Thank you very much for listening.
B Hello everyone.
C Finally, I would like to talk about …
D Have you got any questions?
E My next point is …
F To sum everything up, …
G First, let me show you …
H Today, I would like to talk about …

DIGITAL+ practise more 22–23

The Republic of Ireland 5

A five-minute talk TARGET TASK

13 workbook p. 89/15, skill: presentations p. 160, wordbank: presenting something p. 168, media worksheet 4

Your task is to give a five-minute talk about one interesting aspect of Ireland.
Before you start, look at these steps:

STEP 1

Decide what you would like to talk about. Think about:
- music
- people
- food
- sights
- history
- …

STEP 2

Do your research.
- Do some research on your topic using books or the Internet.
- Do not forget to list your sources.
- Choose texts in English which are easy to understand.
- Take notes on the most important facts.

STEP 3

Prepare your presentation.
- Read through your findings and organize the information. What is important? What is not?
- How and in which order do you want to present the facts? Decide on a structure for your talk.
- Find some good pictures.
- You can make a (digital) presentation or a poster and show pictures or videos during your talk.
- Make notes on cue cards.

STEP 4

Practise your talk with a partner.
- Use your notes.
- Give each other feedback.

STEP 5

Give your talk.

Check out

1. Kannst du Schaubildern wichtige Informationen entnehmen?	Workbook, p. 90
2. Kannst du verstehen, was Immigrantinnen und Immigranten über ihr Leben erzählen?	Workbook, p. 91
3. Kannst du einen Text mit Adjektiven interessanter machen?	Workbook, p. 91
4. Kannst du Texte aus einem Reiseführer verstehen?	Workbook, p. 92
5. Kannst du über Sehenswürdigkeiten in Irland sprechen?	Workbook, p. 92
6. Kennst du nützliche Redewendungen für eine Präsentation?	Workbook, p. 93

ACTIVATE PRACTISE DEVELOP PRACTISE **APPLY**

Enrique's journey

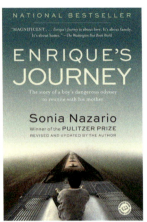

Every year, more than one million immigrants come to the USA. An estimated 500,000 of them enter the USA illegally, and about 120,000 of these are "unaccompanied minors" – children who travel without an adult. Most of them come across the southern border from Mexico after a long journey in constant fear of being caught and deported back home. One of these minors was Enrique, who left Honduras in the year 2000 in search of his mother. In 2002, his story, reported and written by Sonia Nazario, was published as a six-part series in the Los Angeles Times and later made into a book.

In Honduras

The boy does not understand.
His mother is not talking to him. She will not even look at him. Enrique has no hint of what she is going to do.
Lourdes [his mother] knows. She understands, as only a mother can, the terror she is about to inflict, the ache Enrique will feel and finally the emptiness.
What will become of him? (…)
They live on the outskirts of Tegucigalpa, in Honduras. She can barely afford food for him and his sister, Belky, who is 7. Lourdes, 24, scrubs other people's laundry in a muddy river. She fills a wooden box with gum and crackers and cigarettes, and she finds a spot where she can squat on a dusty sidewalk next to the downtown Pizza Hut and sell the items to passersby. (…)
They have a bleak future. He and Belky are not likely to finish (…) school. Lourdes cannot afford uniforms or pencils. Her husband is gone. A good job is out of the question. So she has decided: She will leave. She will go to the United States and make money and send it home. She will be gone for one year, less with luck, or she will bring her children to be with her. It is for them she is leaving, she tells herself, but still, she feels guilty.
She kneels and kisses Belky and hugs her tightly. (…)
But Lourdes cannot face Enrique. He will remember only one thing that she says to him: "Don't forget to go to church this afternoon."
It is Jan. 29, 1989. His mother (…) walks away.
"Donde esta mi mami?" Enrique cries, over and over. "Where is my mom?"
His mother never returns.

In the following years, Enrique lives first with his father, then with his grandmother. He talks to his mother on the phone from time to time. She is able to send money but never comes back and Enrique misses her. Eleven years after his mother left Honduras, when he is 16 years old, Enrique decides to leave home and try to get to the USA on his own. Because they have to cover long distances and have little to no money, many people trying to get to the USA from Central America ride on freight trains – a dangerous thing to do.

---

illegally = *ungesetzlich, illegal*; unaccompanied = *unbegleitet*; minor = *Minderjährige/r*; border = *Grenze*; to deport = *ausweisen*; hint = *Hinweis*; terror = *Schrecken*; to be about to do something = *im Begriff sein, etwas zu tun*; to inflict = *zufügen*; ache = *Schmerz*; emptiness = *Leere*; outskirts (pl) = *Randbezirke*; barely = *kaum*; to scrub = *schrubben*; laundry = *Wäsche*; muddy = *matschig*; wooden box = *Holzkiste*; gum = *Kaugummi*; to squat = *hocken*; dusty = *staubig*; passersby = *Vorübergehende*; bleak = *trostlos*; to be out of the question = *nicht in Frage kommen*; guilty = *schuldig*; to kneel = *knien*; to hug = *umarmen*; tightly = *fest*; to cover = *zurücklegen*; Central America = *Mittelamerika*; freight train = *Güterzug*

Facing the beast

Enrique looks ahead on the train. Men and boys are hanging on to the sides of tank cars, trying to find a spot to sit or stand. Some of the youngsters could not land their feet on the ladders and have pulled themselves up rung by rung on their knees, which are bruised and bloodied.

Suddenly, Enrique hears screams.

Three cars away, a boy, 12 or 13 years old, has managed to grab the bottom rung of a ladder on a fuel tanker, but he cannot haul himself up. Air rushing beneath the train is sucking his legs under the car. It is tugging at him harder, drawing his feet toward the wheels.

"Don't let go!" a man shouts. He and others crawl along the top of the train to a nearby car. They shout again.

The boy dangles from the ladder. He struggles to keep his grip.

Carefully, the men crawl down and reach for him. Slowly, they lift him up.

The rungs batter his legs, but he is alive. He still has his feet.

Enrique tries several times to get to Mexico. On his journey, he is robbed, beaten, caught by the immigration police and deported, but he never gives up. On his eighth try he finally makes it as far as the banks of the Rio Grande, the river that forms part of the border between Mexico and the USA. There he stays in a camp with other people who wait for a chance to cross the river into US territory. Enrique manages to call his mother, who is living in North Carolina by now, and she sends him money so he can pay smugglers to take him to Texas.

Across the border

Lourdes has not slept. (…)

Now a female smuggler is on the phone. The woman says: "We have your son in Texas, but $1,200 is not enough. $1,700." Lourdes grows suspicious. Maybe Enrique is dead, and the smugglers are trying to cash in. "Put him on the line." she demands.

"He is out shopping for food," the smuggler says.

Lourdes will not be put off. "He is asleep," the smuggler says.

"How can he be both?" Lourdes demands to talk to him.

Finally, the smuggler gives the phone to Enrique.

"Sos tu?" his mother asks anxiously. "Is it you?"

"Si, Mami, it's me."

What do you think: how does the story go on?

_{beast = *Bestie*; ahead = *voraus*; to hang on = *sich festhalten an*; ladder = *Leiter*; rung = *Sprosse*; bruised = *geprellt*; bloodied = *blutverschmiert*; scream = *Schrei*; bottom = *untere(r, s)*; fuel = *Benzin*; tanker = *Tankwagen*; to haul = *ziehen*; beneath = *unter*; to suck = *saugen*; to tug at = *zerren an*; to draw = *ziehen*; toward = *in Richtung*; to let go = *loslassen*; to crawl = *kriechen*; to dangle = *herabhängen*; grip = *Griff*; to batter = *böse zurichten*; to rob = *berauben*; to beat = *schlagen*; police = *Polizei*; bank = *Ufer*; smuggler = *Schmuggler/in*; suspicious = *misstrauisch*; dead = *tot*; to cash in = *Kapital schlagen aus*; to demand = *verlangen*; to be put off = *sich vertrösten lassen*; anxiously = *besorgt*}

Annie Moore

After the opening of the new immigration building on Ellis Island on 1 January 1892, the New York Times reported that the "first immigrant to register was fifteen-year-old Annie Moore, from Cork, Ireland." Annie had arrived on the steamboat *Nevada* with her two younger brothers, Anthony and Philip. They were going to join their parents and two older siblings, who had arrived in New York two years earlier.

Ellis Island was decorated in red, white and blue that day to celebrate its opening. Whistles and foghorns were blowing, and it must have been overwhelming to a young girl coming from Ireland. Little did she know that she was the first of twelve million people who would enter the United States through Ellis Island in search of a better life and that she would become an iconic symbol of Irish immigration to the USA in the years to come.

The article that appeared in the New York Times on January 2, 1892

Today, you can see statues of Annie Moore in New York, inside the Ellis Island National Museum of Immigration and in Cobh, a small town just outside Cork in Ireland, the place where Annie and her brothers set off on their journey to the USA.

The sculpture at Cobh is of Annie and her two brothers, the one in New York shows Annie holding a small suitcase in one hand and looking expectantly at the scene before her.
Both statues were created by the famous Irish sculptor Jeanne Rynhart.

In 1993, Irish sculptor Jeanne Rynhart created two statues of Annie Moore. One stands at the Cobh Heritage Centre in Cork ...

... the other in Ellis Island, New York

opening = *Eröffnung*; the New York Times = *Name einer Tageszeitung*; to register = *anmelden*; sibling = *Geschwister*; whistle = *Pfeife*; foghorn = *Nebelhorn*; to blow = *ertönen*; overwhelming = *überwältigend*; did = *hier als Verstärkung benutzt*; in search of = *auf der Suche nach*; iconic symbol = *hier: Inbegriff*; to set off = *sich auf den Weg machen*; sculpture = *Skulptur*; expectantly = *erwartungsvoll*; sculptor = *Bildhauer/in*

Isle of Hope, Isle of Tears

Annie's story inspired writers and musicians. One of the most famous songs about her is "Isle of Hope, Isle of Tears" by Brendan Graham.

On the first day of January
Eighteen ninety-two
They opened Ellis Island
And they let the people through
And the first to cross the threshold
Of that Isle of hope and tears
Was Annie Moore from Ireland
Who was only fifteen years

Isle of Hope, Isle of Tears
Isle of Freedom, Isle of Fears
But it's not the Isle you left behind
That Isle of Hunger, Isle of Pain
Isle you'll never see again
But the Isle of home is always on your mind

In a little bag she carried
All her past and history
And her dreams for the future
In the Land of Liberty
And courage is the passport
When your old world disappears
But there's no future in the past
When you're fifteen years

Isle of Hope, Isle of Tears
Isle of Freedom, Isle of Fears
But it's not the Isle you left behind
That Isle of Hunger, Isle of Pain
Isle you'll never see again
But the Isle of home is always on your mind

When they closed down Ellis Island
In Nineteen Fourty-Three
Seventeen million people
Had come there for Sanctuary
And in springtime when I came here
And I stepped onto its piers
I thought of how it must have been
When you're fifteen years

Isle of Hope, Isle of Tears
Isle of Freedom, Isle of Fears
But it's not the Isle you left behind
That Isle of Hunger, Isle of Pain
Isle you'll never see again
But the Isle of home is always on your mind

Isle of Hope, Isle of Tears
Isle of Freedom, Isle of Fears
But it's not the Isle you left behind
That Isle of Hunger, Isle of Pain
Isle you'll never see again
But the Isle of home is always on your mind

What do you think: how did Annie feel when she arrived in the USA? Write her diary entry.

isle = *kleine Insel*; threshold = *(Tür)schwelle*; to leave behind = *zurücklassen*; pain = *Schmerz*; to be on one's mind = *an etwas denken*; courage = *Mut*; passport = *(Reise)pass*; to close down = *schließen*; sanctuary = *Zufluchtsort*; springtime = *Frühling*

At Grand Central Station

9 UNIT 1, p. 27 PARTNER A, wordbank: travelling p. 163, skill: performing a scene p. 161

You work at the ticket office at Grand Central Station in New York.
Your partner would like to go to New Haven.
Look at the boxes and do a role play. You are the first to start.

1. Begrüße deinen Kunden / deine Kundin und frage, wie du helfen kannst.
   You can say:
   Hello. How can I …?

2. Partner B möchte Fahrkarten kaufen.

3. Sage, dass das kein Problem ist und frage, wie viele Personen fahren möchten.
   You can say:
   … How many …?

4. Partner B antwortet.

5. Sage, dass es ein Sonderangebot für Familien gibt und frage, wie alt die Kinder sind.
   You can say:
   There's a special offer for …
   How old …?

6. Partner B antwortet.

7. Sage, dass die Fahrkarten für Kinder zwischen 5 und 11 nur $1 kosten, wenn sie mit einem Erwachsenen zusammen fahren.
   You can say:
   Tickets for children between … are only
   … if they are travelling with an adult.

8. Partner B hat eine weitere Frage.

9. Sage, dass Hin- und Rückfahrkarten für alle $75 kosten.
   You can say:
   Return tickets are …

10. Partner B reagiert.

11. Überreiche die Fahrkarten und frage, ob Partner B mit Karte oder Bargeld zahlen möchte.
    You can say: :
    Would you like to pay with card or cash?

12. Partner B hat noch eine Frage.

13. Sage, dass der nächste Zug um 11:45 auf Gleis 17 fährt.
    You can say:
    … leaves at … from platform …

14. Partner B reagiert.

15. Verabschiede dich.

Partner A

Exchange challenges

10 UNIT 2, p. 51 PARTNER A, wordbank: seeking and giving advice p. 166, skill: performing a scene p. 161

Imagine you are an exchange student at an American high school and you are unhappy. You have made an appointment with the school counsellor. Choose one problem or more from the list below or make up your own. Talk to your partner about your situation.

Problems
→ I haven't made any friends at my new school yet.
→ My host parents are always at work and I'm alone all the time.
→ I don't like the food my host parents cook.
→ I'm homesick.
→ …

You can say:
I'm very unhappy because …
I have a problem. I …
I don't know how to tell them that …
…

Texting

9 UNIT 3, p. 74 PARTNER A

You and your partner are texting each other to make plans for the afternoon. Look at the ideas below and write two or more messages to your partner. You are the first to start.

Cinema
watch film and go for pizza afterwards

Swimming
spend the afternoon at the pool

Gaming
play video games

???

You can write:
What about …?
Let's …
Why don't we …?
Do you have another idea?
…

Arguments for
→ It's fun.
→ It's not too expensive.
→ We've never tried it before.
→ You can meet friends there.
→ It's so nice outside.
→ …

Arguments against
→ It's boring.
→ I didn't like it last time.
→ It's too expensive.
→ My parents will never say yes.
→ The weather is not good enough.
→ …

Get together | Project 1 | Project 2

A role play

14 UNIT 4, p. 99   PARTNER A, wordbank: the world of work p. 170, skill: performing a scene p. 161

You are applying for a job as a dogsitter. Your partner is looking for a dogsitter. Use your role card and do a role play. Your partner is the first to start.

Role card partner A

- You have some experience because your grandmother has always had dogs.
- You are free on Tuesdays and Thursdays.
- You can also sometimes work at the weekend.
- …

You can say:
I love dogs.
I have some experience with dogs.
I used to look after …
…

Planning a trip

9 UNIT 5, p. 123   PARTNER A, skill: talking with people p. 154

Read the flyers and tell your partner about the sights. Then listen to what partner B tells you about *Dolphin Discovery Boat Trips* and *Marble Arch Caves* – two tourist attractions in Ireland. Decide on two sights you would both like to visit.

The Ring of Kerry

This route in County Kerry takes you to some of the most beautiful places in Ireland. Here are some:
- Derrynane Beach, one of the world's cleanest beaches
- Cahergal, a stone ringfort from the Iron Age
- 110-metre long Torc Waterfall

You can do the tour by car or bus, but there are walking paths, too.

You can say:
At … there is …
You can see …
I would like to go to … because …
I don't like … that much. I'd rather go to …
…

The Zoological Museum Dublin

- An interactive exhibition of animals from Ireland and abroad.
- Learn how scientists in Australia are trying to use DNA to recreate the Tasmanian Wolf.
- Have your photograph taken through the jaws of a Great White Shark.

Partner A

At Grand Central Station

9a UNIT 1, p. 27 PARTNER A, wordbank: travelling p. 163, skill: performing a scene p. 161

You work at the ticket office at Grand Central Station in New York.
Your partner would like to go to New Haven.
Look at the boxes and do a role play. You are the first to start.

1 Begrüße deinen Kunden / deine Kundin und frage, wie du helfen kannst. **You can say:** *Hello. How …?*	9 Sage, dass Hin- und Rückfahrkarten für alle $75 kosten. **You can say:** *Return tickets are …*
2 Partner B möchte Fahrkarten kaufen.	10 Partner B reagiert.
3 Sage, dass das kein Problem ist und frage, wie viele Personen fahren möchten. **You can say:** *… How …?*	11 Überreiche die Fahrkarten und frage, ob Partner B mit Karte oder Bargeld zahlen möchte. **You can say:** *… with card or cash?*
4 Partner B antwortet.	12 Partner B hat noch eine Frage.
5 Sage, dass es ein Sonderangebot für Familien gibt und frage, wie alt die Kinder sind. **You can say:** *There's a special offer …* *How …?*	13 Sage, dass der nächste Zug um 11:45 auf Gleis 17 fährt. **You can say:** *… from platform …*
6 Partner B antwortet.	14 Partner B reagiert.
7 Sage, dass die Fahrkarten für Kinder zwischen 5 und 11 nur $1 kosten, wenn sie mit einem Erwachsenen zusammen fahren. **You can say:** *Tickets … between … are only …* *if they … with an adult.*	15 Verabschiede dich.
8 Partner B hat eine weitere Frage.	

one hundred and thirty-three 133

Get together | Project 1 | Project 2

Exchange challenges

10 UNIT 2, p. 51 PARTNER A, wordbank: seeking and giving advice p. 166, skill: performing a scene p. 161

Imagine you are an exchange student at an American high school and you are unhappy. You have made an appointment with the school counsellor. Choose one problem or more from the list below or make up your own. Talk to your partner about your situation.

Problems
→ *I haven't made any friends at my new school yet.*
→ *My host parents are always at work and I'm alone all the time.*
→ *I don't like the food my host parents cook.*
→ *I'm homesick.*
→ *My host brother is not very nice.*
→ *…*

Texting

10a UNIT 3, p. 74 PARTNER A

You and your partner are texting each other to make plans for the afternoon. Look at the ideas below and write two or more messages to your partner. You are the first to start.

Cinema
watch film and go for pizza afterwards

Swimming
spend the afternoon at the pool

Gaming
play video games

???

You can write:
What about …?
Let's …
Why don't we …?
…

Arguments for
→ *fun*
→ *not too expensive*
→ *never tried it before*
→ *can meet friends there*
→ *good for your health*
→ *weather so good*
→ *…*

Arguments against
→ *boring*
→ *too expensive*
→ *didn't like it last time*
→ *what we always do*
→ *people there I don't want to meet*
→ *parents will never say yes*
→ *…*

Partner A

A role play

14 UNIT 4, p. 99   PARTNER A, wordbank: the world of work p. 170, skill: performing a scene p. 161

II You are applying for a job as a dogsitter. Your partner is looking for a dogsitter. Use your role card and do a role play. Your partner is the first to start.

Role card partner A

- You have some experience because your grandmother has always had dogs.
- You are free on Tuesdays and Thursdays.
- You can also sometimes work at the weekend.
- …

Planning a trip

9 UNIT 5, p. 123   PARTNER A, skill: talking with people p. 154

II Read the flyers and tell your partner about the sights. Then listen to what partner B tells you about *Dolphin Discovery Boat Trips* and *Marble Arch Caves* – two tourist attractions in Ireland. Decide on two sights you would both like to visit.

The Ring of Kerry

This 179-kilometre-long route takes you to some of the most beautiful places in County Kerry, Ireland. Here are just a few:
- Derrynane Beach, near the village of Caherdaniel, is one of the world's cleanest beaches.
- Make sure to go to Cahergal, a stone ringfort from the Iron Age.
- Torc Waterfall is a 110-metre long waterfall surrounded by fantastic woodland.

You can do the tour by car or bus, but there are walking paths, too.

The Zoological Museum Dublin

- A collection of animals from Ireland and abroad in an interactive exhibition.
- Learn how scientists in Australia are trying to use DNA to recreate the Tasmanian Wolf.
- Hold one of the world's strangest teeth.
- Have your photograph taken through the jaws of a Great White Shark.

| Get together | Project 1 | Project 2 |

At Grand Central Station

9 UNIT 1, p. 27 PARTNER A, wordbank: travelling p. 163, skill: performing a scene p. 161

III You work at the ticket office at Grand Central Station in New York.
Your partner would like to go to New Haven.
Look at the boxes and do a role play. You are the first to start.

1. Begrüße deinen Kunden / deine Kundin und frage, wie du helfen kannst.

2. Partner B möchte Fahrkarten kaufen.

3. Sage, dass das kein Problem ist und frage, wie viele Personen fahren möchten.

4. Partner B antwortet.

5. Sage, dass es ein Sonderangebot für Familien gibt und frage, wie alt die Kinder sind.

6. Partner B antwortet.

7. Sage, dass die Fahrkarten für Kinder zwischen 5 und 11 nur $1 kosten, wenn sie mit einem Erwachsenen zusammen fahren.

8. Partner B hat eine weitere Frage.

9. Sage, dass Hin- und Rückfahrkarten für alle $75 kosten.
   You can say:
   Return tickets are …

10. Partner B reagiert.

11. Überreiche die Fahrkarten, frage, ob Partner B mit Karte oder Bargeld zahlen möchte.

12. Partner B hat noch eine Frage.

13. Sage, dass der nächste Zug um 11:45 auf Gleis 17 fährt.

14. Partner B reagiert.

15. Verabschiede dich.

Partner A

Exchange challenges

10 UNIT 2, p. 51   PARTNER A, wordbank: seeking and giving advice p. 166, skill: performing a scene p. 161

III Imagine you are an exchange student at an American high school and you are unhappy. You have made an appointment with the school counsellor. Choose one problem or more from the list below or make up your own. Talk to your partner about your situation.

Problems
→ *no friends at new school*
→ *host parents always at work*
→ *don't like the food*
→ *homesick*
→ *host brother not very nice*
→ *very strict host parents*
→ *…*

Texting

9 UNIT 3, p. 74   PARTNER A

III You and your partner are texting each other to make plans for the afternoon. Look at the ideas below and write two or more messages to your partner. You are the first to start.

Cinema
watch film and go for pizza afterwards

Swimming
spend the afternoon at the pool

Gaming
play video games

???

Arguments for
→ *fun*
→ *not too expensive*
→ *never tried before*
→ *nearby*
→ *can meet friends there*
→ *good for your health*
→ *…*

Arguments against
→ *boring*
→ *too expensive*
→ *didn't like it last time*
→ *what we always do*
→ *people there I don't want to meet*
→ *parents will never say yes*
→ *…*

| Get together | Project 1 | Project 2 |

A role play

14 UNIT 4, p. 99   PARTNER A, wordbank: the world of work p. 170, skill: performing a scene p. 161

III You are applying for a job as a dogsitter. Your partner is looking for a dogsitter. Use your role card and do a role play. Your partner is the first to start.

Role card partner A

- You have some experience because your grandmother has always had dogs.
- You are free on Tuesdays and Thursdays.
- You can also sometimes work at the weekend.
- You would like to earn at least £5.00 per hour.
- …

Planning a trip

9 UNIT 5, p. 123   PARTNER A, skill: talking with people p. 154

III Read the flyers and tell your partner about the sights. Then listen to what partner B tells you about *Dolphin Discovery Boat Trips* and *Marble Arch Caves* – two tourist attractions in Ireland. Decide on two sights you would both like to visit.

The Ring of Kerry

This 179-kilometre-long route in County Kerry takes you to some of the most beautiful spots in Ireland. You can do the round trip by car, bus or bike, but there are walking paths, too.
Here are just a few of its attractions: Derrynane Beach, near the village of Caherdaniel, is one of the world's cleanest beaches. If you are interested in history, make sure to go to Cahergal, which is a stone ringfort dating back to the Iron Age. Another must-see sight is Torc Waterfall. The 110-metre long waterfall is just a five-minute walk off the N71 Killarney Kenmare road and is surrounded by stunning woodland scenery.

The Zoological Museum Dublin

- A collection of animal displays from Ireland and abroad in a highly interactive exhibition – lots of exhibits can be picked up and handled.
- Learn how scientists in Australia are attempting to use DNA to recreate the Tasmanian Wolf.
- Hold one of the world's strangest teeth.
- Have your photograph taken through the jaws of a Great White Shark.
- Don't miss the tragic tale of Ireland's Last Great Auk. Extinct since 1844, only a handful of these beautiful birds can be found in museums today.

Partner B

At Grand Central Station

9 UNIT 1, p. 27 PARTNER B, wordbank: travelling p. 163, skill: performing a scene p. 161

You are at the ticket office at Grand Central Station in New York and would like to go to New Haven. Look at the boxes and do a role play. Your partner is the first to start.

1 Partner A begrüßt dich.	10 Sage, dass du die Fahrkarten kaufen möchtest. **You can say:** *OK. Then I'd like to …*
2 Begrüße den Ticketverkäufer / die Ticketverkäuferin und sage, dass du gern Fahrkarten nach New Haven kaufen möchtest. **You can say:** *Hello. I would like to …, please.*	11 Partner A reagiert.
	12 Sage, dass du mit Karte zahlen möchtest und frage, wann und wo der nächste Zug nach New Haven fährt. **You can say:** *With card, please. Here …* *When … leave? From which …?*
3 Partner A benötigt weitere Informationen.	
4 Sage, dass vier Personen fahren möchten, zwei Erwachsene und zwei Kinder. **You can say:** *… adults and …*	13 Partner A reagiert.
	14 Bedanke und verabschiede dich.
5 Partner A hat noch eine Frage.	15 Partner A reagiert.
6 Sage, dass die Kinder 7 und 9 Jahre alt sind. **You can say:** *They are …*	
7 Partner A reagiert.	
8 Sage, dass das großartig ist und frage, wie teuer Fahrkarten für Hin- und Rückfahrt für die ganze Familie sind. **You can say:** *Great.* *So how much are return tickets for …?*	
9 Partner A beantwortet deine Frage.	

| Get together | Project 1 | Project 2 |

Exchange challenges

10 UNIT 2, p. 51 PARTNER B, wordbank: seeking and giving advice p. 166, skill: performing a scene p. 161

Imagine you are a school counsellor at an American high school. An exchange student from Germany is unhappy and has come to talk to you. Give them some advice.

Advice
→ join school club or sports team
→ talk to host family, stay polite and friendly
→ cook your favourite food for host family, go shopping for food with them
→ …

You can say:
Why don't you …?
You could …
It can be helpful if you …
…

Texting

9 UNIT 3, p. 74 PARTNER B

You and your partner are texting each other to make plans for the afternoon.
Look at the ideas below and write two or more messages to your partner.
Your partner is the first to start.

Studying
prepare for maths test

Hanging out
meet friends and just chill

Biking
go on a bike tour and enjoy nature

???

You can write:
What about …?
Let's …
Why don't we …?
Do you have another idea?
…

Arguments for
→ I really need a good mark in maths.
→ It's fun.
→ It's not too expensive.
→ We've never tried it before.
→ It's so nice outside.
→ …

Arguments against
→ It's boring.
→ I didn't like it last time.
→ It's too expensive.
→ My parents will never say yes.
→ The weather is not good enough.
→ …

Partner B

A role play

14 UNIT 4, p. 99 PARTNER B, wordbank: the world of work p. 170, skill: performing a scene p. 161

You are looking for a dogsitter. Your partner has applied for the job and has come to your place for a job interview. Use your role card and do a role play. You are the first to start.

Role card partner B

- You have a new job and now you don't have enough time for your dog anymore.
- You are looking for a dogsitter with some experience.
- You need someone who takes your dog for walks on at least two afternoons a week and sometimes at the weekend.
- …

You can say:
What's your experience with dogs or other pets?
When can you …?
Could you …?
…

Planning a trip

9 UNIT 5, p. 123 PARTNER B, skill: talking with people p. 154

Read the flyers. Then listen to what your partner tells you about the *Ring of Kerry* and the *Zoological Museum* in Dublin – two tourist attractions in Ireland. Tell your partner about the *Marble Arch Caves* and the *Dolphin Discovery Boat Trip*. Together, decide on two sights you both would like to visit.

Marble Arch Caves

- Explore a natural underworld of rivers, waterfalls and passages.
- Our guides take you on exciting tours through the caves.
- Take a ride on one of our electric boats along a river through the caves.

You can say:
At … there is …
You can see …
I would like to go to … because …
I don't like … that much. I'd rather go to …
…

Dolphin Discovery Boat Trip

- Where the river Shannon flows into the Atlantic Ocean lives a group of bottlenose dolphins.
- We take you on a tour to watch them and their calves.

| Get together | Project 1 | Project 2 |

At Grand Central Station

9 UNIT 1, p. 27 PARTNER B, wordbank: travelling p. 163, skill: performing a scene p. 161

II You are at the ticket office at Grand Central Station in New York and would like to go to New Haven. Look at the boxes and do a role play. Your partner is the first to start.

| 1 | Partner A begrüßt dich. |

| 2 | Begrüße den Ticketverkäufer / die Ticketverkäuferin und sage, dass du gern Fahrkarten nach New Haven kaufen möchtest.
You can say:
…, please. |

| 3 | Partner A benötigt weitere Informationen. |

| 4 | Sage, dass vier Personen fahren möchten, zwei Erwachsene und zwei Kinder.
You can say:
… adults and … |

| 5 | Partner A hat noch eine Frage. |

| 6 | Sage, dass die Kinder 7 und 9 Jahre alt sind.
You can say:
They … |

| 7 | Partner A reagiert. |

| 8 | Sage, dass das großartig ist und frage, wie teuer Fahrkarten für Hin- und Rückfahrt für die ganze Familie sind.
You can say:
… are return tickets for …? |

| 9 | Partner A beantwortet deine Frage. |

| 10 | Sage, dass du die Fahrkarten kaufen möchtest.
You can say:
OK. Then I'd … |

| 11 | Partner A reagiert. |

| 12 | Sage, dass du mit Karte zahlen möchtest und frage, wann und wo der nächste Zug nach New Haven fährt.
You can say:
With card, please.
When …? From which …? |

| 13 | Partner A reagiert. |

| 14 | Bedanke und verabschiede dich. |

| 15 | Partner A reagiert. |

Partner B

Exchange challenges

10 UNIT 2, p. 51 PARTNER B, wordbank: seeking and giving advice p. 166, skill: performing a scene p. 161

ll Imagine you are a school counsellor at an American high school. An exchange student from Germany is unhappy and has come to talk to you. Give them some advice.

Advice
→ join school club or sports team, try to be more open
→ talk to host family, stay polite and friendly
→ cook your favourite food for host family, go shopping for food with them
→ …

You can say:
Why don't you …?
It can be helpful if you …
…

Texting

9 UNIT 3, p. 74 PARTNER B

ll You and your partner are texting each other to make plans for the afternoon. Look at the ideas below and write two or more messages to your partner. Your partner is the first to start.

Studying
prepare for maths test

Hanging out
meet friends and just chill

Biking
go on a bike tour and enjoy nature

???

You can write:
What about…?
Let's …
Why don't we …?
…

Arguments for
→ need a good mark in maths
→ fun
→ not too expensive
→ never tried it before
→ so nice outside
→ …

Arguments against
→ boring
→ didn't like it last time
→ too expensive
→ parents will never say yes
→ weather is not good enough
→ …

| Get together | Project 1 | Project 2 |

A role play

14 UNIT 4, p. 99 PARTNER B, wordbank: the world of work p. 170, skill: performing a scene p. 161

You are looking for a dogsitter. Your partner has applied for the job and has come to your place for a job interview. Use your role card and do a role play. You are the first to start.

Role card partner B

- You have a new job and now you don't have enough time for your dog anymore.
- You are looking for a dogsitter with some experience.
- You need someone who takes your dog for walks on at least two afternoons a week and sometimes at the weekend.
- …

Planning a trip

9 UNIT 5, p. 123 PARTNER B, skill: talking with people p. 154

Read the flyers. Then listen to what your partner tells you about the *Ring of Kerry* and the *Zoological Museum* in Dublin – two tourist attractions in Ireland. Tell your partner about the *Marble Arch Caves* and the *Dolphin Discovery Boat Trip*. Together, decide on two sights you both would like to visit.

Marble Arch Caves

- Explore a natural underworld of rivers, waterfalls and winding passages.
- Our guides take you on exciting tours through the caves.
- Take a ride on one of our electrically powered boats along a river that flows through the caves.

Dolphin Discovery Boat Trip

- Where the river Shannon flows into the Atlantic Ocean lives Ireland's only resident group of bottlenose dolphins.
- Book a tour on one of our five boats and enjoy an afternoon of watching them and their calves.

At Grand Central Station

9 UNIT 1, p. 27   PARTNER B, wordbank: travelling p. 163, skill: performing a scene p. 161

III You are at the ticket office at Grand Central Station in New York and would like to go to New Haven. Look at the boxes and do a role play. Your partner is the first to start.

1 Partner A begrüßt dich.	8 Sage, dass das großartig ist und frage, wie teuer Fahrkarten für Hin- und Rückfahrt für die ganze Familie sind. **You can say:** *… are return tickets for …?*
2 Begrüße den Ticketverkäufer / die Ticketverkäuferin und sage, dass du gern Fahrkarten nach New Haven kaufen möchtest.	
	9 Partner A beantwortet deine Frage.
3 Partner A benötigt weitere Informationen.	10 Sage, dass du die Fahrkarten kaufen möchtest.
4 Sage, dass vier Personen fahren möchten, zwei Erwachsene und zwei Kinder.	11 Partner A reagiert.
	12 Sage, dass du mit Karte zahlen möchtest und frage, wann und wo der nächste Zug nach New Haven fährt.
5 Partner A hat noch eine Frage.	
6 Sage, dass die Kinder 7 und 9 Jahre alt sind.	13 Partner A reagiert.
	14 Bedanke und verabschiede dich.
7 Partner A reagiert.	15 Partner A reagiert.

| Get together | Project 1 | Project 2 |

Exchange challenges

10 UNIT 2, p. 51 PARTNER B, wordbank: seeking and giving advice p. 166, skill: performing a scene p. 161

Imagine you are a school counsellor at an American high school. An exchange student from Germany is unhappy and has come to talk to you. Give them some advice.

Advice
→ join school club or sports team, try to be more open
→ talk to host family, stay polite and friendly
→ cook your favourite food for host family, go shopping for food with them
→ …

Texting

9 UNIT 3, p. 74 PARTNER B

You and your partner are texting each other to make plans for the afternoon.
Look at the ideas below and write two or more messages to your partner.
Your partner is the first to start.

Studying
prepare for maths test

Hanging out
meet friends and just chill

Biking
go on a bike tour and enjoy nature

???

Arguments for
→ good mark
→ fun
→ not too expensive
→ never tried it before
→ so nice outside
→ …

Arguments against
→ boring
→ didn't like it last time
→ too expensive
→ parents will never say yes
→ weather not good enough
→ …

Partner B

A role play

14 UNIT 4, p. 99 PARTNER B, wordbank: the world of work p. 170, skill: performing a scene p. 161

III You are looking for a dogsitter. Your partner has applied for the job and has come to your place for a job interview. Use your role card and do a role play. You are the first to start.

Role card partner B

- You have a new job and now you don't have enough time for your dog anymore.
- You need someone with experience who takes your dog for walks on at least two afternoons a week and sometimes at the weekend.
- Sometimes you have to go on business trips overnight. Your dogsitter should be able to take care of your dog then.
- You would pay £4.50 per hour.
- …

Planning a trip

9 UNIT 5, p. 123 PARTNER B, skill: talking with people p. 154

III Read the flyers. Then listen to what your partner tells you about the *Ring of Kerry* and the *Zoological Museum* in Dublin – two tourist attractions in Ireland. Tell your partner about the Marble *Arch Caves* and the *Dolphin Discovery Boat Trip*. Together, decide on two sights you both would like to visit.

Marble Arch Caves

- Explore a a fascinating natural underworld of rivers, waterfalls and winding passages.
- Our guides take you on exciting tours through the caves.
- Take a ride on one of our electrically powered boats along a river that flows through the caves under the ground.

Dolphin Discovery Boat Trip

- Where the river Shannon flows into the Atlantic Ocean lives Ireland's only resident group of more than 100 bottlenose dolphins.
- Book a tour on one of our five boats and enjoy an exciting afternoon of watching them and their calves.

Get together | **Project 1** | Project 2

Hollywood DIGITAL+

Introduction

Hollywood is a neighbourhood in Los Angeles and the heart of the world-famous American film industry. It is home to many influential film companies and continues to attract creative minds who want to try their luck in the entertainment industry.
So why not take a closer look at what lies behind the glitz and glamour of the red carpet and find out more about Hollywood and the American film industry?

Plan it

1 In class, think about what you would like to do in your project. You can collect ideas in a list, for example:

- Prepare a presentation or a podcast about the history of the film industry in Hollywood.
- Present a famous Hollywood film director, producer, film music composer, actor or actress.
- Write about jobs in the film industry.
- Prepare a presentation or a podcast about important film awards.
- Present facts about a famous Hollywood film in a fact file.
- Write a film review about a Hollywood production.
- …

> **Tip**
>
> You can make a class product, for example a film magazine: every group creates one page, and then you can put everything together at the end.

Hollywood

2 Now get together in small groups and make a detailed plan. Write down:

- what information you need
- how you can find information
- how you want to present your work
- what material you need for your project work (for example: computer, paper, glue, ...)
- who does what and when

Tip

When you as a group have a plan about what to do and how to present your work, you can ask your classmates from other groups for feedback on your plan.

Do it
skill: searching the Internet p. 159, media worksheet 6

And ... action! Do research, collect pictures, write texts, ... and create an interesting film review, fact file, poster, computer presentation, ... Here is an example of a film review:

Film review: La La Land

United States, 2016
Running time: 128 minutes
Cast: Ryan Gosling, Emma Stone, John Legend, Rosemarie DeWitt
Director: Damien Chazelle
Genres: romance, comedy, drama, musical

The film follows a hopeful actress (Mia, played by Emma Stone) and a jazz musician (Sebastian, played by Ryan Gosling). The pair meet accidentally in Los Angeles several times. They are both trying to make their dreams come true – Mia wants to star in big films and Sebastian wants to play music at his own concerts. While they are trying to make these things happen, they fall in love. There are problems for the couple, though. Trying to make their dreams come true takes a lot of energy, and they find that they don't have any energy left for their relationship.

"La La Land" is a lovely film with lots of singing and dancing. I enjoyed it because it shows the world of Hollywood in a realistic and exciting way. Some people don't like the film because of how some of the acting is done, but I think you should watch it and form your own opinion about it!

★★★☆☆

Check it

Check everything. Are there any spelling or grammar mistakes? Are the pictures big enough?
Is everything easy to understand? If you want to give a presentation, practise it before you give it.

Present it
skill: presentations p. 160

Present your work. You can ask your classmates for feedback after the presentation.

| Get together | Project 1 | **Project 2** |

Green cities DIGITAL+

Introduction

Cities not only in the US, but all around the globe are trying to become "greener" in order to improve their citizens' quality of life, become more sustainable and combat climate change. So how can cities become "greener", and what are good examples of measures cities can take? Why not do some research and find out more?

Plan it

1 In class, collect ideas for topics you could work on. You can make notes in a word web. Here is an example:

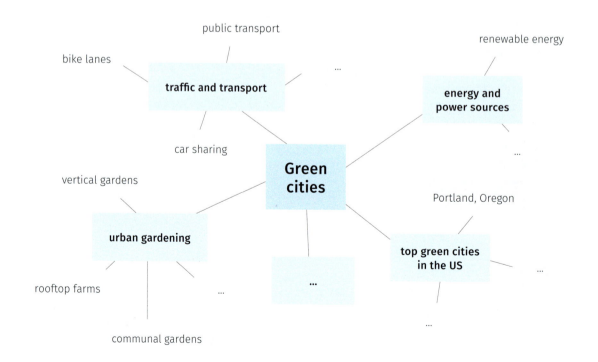

Green cities

2 Now collect ideas about what you could create. For example:

- fact files
- articles
- podcasts
- posters
- …

Tip

You can make a class product, for example a wall newspaper with lots of different articles, pictures and fact files.

Urban gardening in NYC – The 'edible' city

There are more than 700 urban farms and gardens in New York City – and they're not only on the ground. Many are high above the streets on rooftops! These urban farms are growing fresh, local produce right in the city. They're good for the environment and they look nice. But there's more to urban gardening than fresh vegetables, fruit, beautiful flowers and bees. Gardens like these help people to live a better life because it's also about creating a community, about caring and sharing.

3 Now get together in small groups and make a detailed plan. Write down:

- what information you need
- how you can get the information
- how you want to present your work
- what material you need for your project work (for example: computer, paper, glue, …)
- who does what and when

Tip

When you as a group have a plan about what to do and how to present your work, you can ask your classmates from other groups for feedback on your plan.

Do it   skill: searching the Internet p. 159, media worksheet 6

Do research, collect pictures, write texts, … and create an interesting fact file, article, …

Check it

Check everything. Are there any spelling or grammar mistakes? Are the pictures big enough? Is everything easy to understand? If you want to give a presentation, practise it before you give it.

Present it   skill: presentations p. 160

Present your work. You can ask your classmates for feedback after the presentation.

| Skills | Wordbanks | Grammar | Words |

1 WORKING WITH WORDS
Wortschatzarbeit

Im *Dictionary* ab Seite 231 kannst du die Wörter aus diesem Buch und die Lernwörter aus den vorigen Bänden nachschlagen. Wenn du ein Wort suchst, das dort nicht steht, kannst du ein Wörterbuch benutzen. Oft kannst du dir aber auch ein Wort erschließen, weil du schon ein ähnliches Wort kennst.

Wörterbücher

▸ Die Wörter sind alphabetisch geordnet. Du darfst nicht nur auf den ersten Buchstaben achten, sondern musst auch die folgenden Buchstaben angucken: *face* steht beispielsweise vor *false*.

▸ Hinter den Einträgen stehen Lautschrift und Wortart. Dann folgen in einsprachigen Wörterbüchern eine Definition oder Erklärung des Wortes, in zweisprachigen Wörterbüchern die Übersetzung und Beispiele zur Verwendung des Wortes.

▸ Du musst immer alle Einträge durchlesen. Dann entscheidest du, welche Übersetzung am besten passt. Wenn du zum Beispiel ein Rezept liest und dort das Wort *season* findest, schlag im Wörterbuch unter „s", dann „se" / „sea" usw. nach, bis du das Wort findest.

> *Method:*
> *1. Cut the chicken into slices. Then season the chicken with salt, pepper and curry powder.*

▸ *season* als Nomen mit der Bedeutung „Jahreszeit" oder „Saison" ergibt hier keinen Sinn. Weiter unten findest du das Verb *season*. Dort steht unter anderem der Eintrag „würzen" – das passt hier gut als Übersetzung.

Erschließungsmethoden

▸ Manche Wörter musst du gar nicht nachschlagen, denn du kannst sie dir herleiten. Du kennst beispielsweise „*friendly*" – „*unfriendly*" ist das Gegenteil. Oder du kennst „*organization*" – „*organize*" ist das zugehörige Verb.

Tipp: Nutze elektronische Hilfsmittel! (media worksheet 3)

• Im Internet gibt es viele Seiten, auf denen du Wörter nachschlagen und dir die richtige Aussprache anhören kannst. Oft gibt es ausführliche Erklärungen zu den unterschiedlichen Bedeutungen in verschiedenen Zusammenhängen.

2 LISTENING
Hören

In Klasse 5 bis 7 hast du schon einige Strategien für
Hörübungen kennengelernt.
Hier ist eine Zusammenfassung der wichtigsten Punkte:

1. Vor dem Hören
▸ Gibt es eine Höraufgabe im Buch? Dann lies sie dir genau durch. Was sollst du herausfinden?
▸ Wie lautet die Überschrift des Hörtextes? Welche Hinweise gibt sie dir?
▸ Gibt es Bilder? Was ist darauf zu sehen? Vielleicht kannst du vor dem Hören schon etwas über die Situation herausfinden.
▸ Überlege: Worum könnte es gehen? Was weißt du schon über das Thema?

2. Während des Hörens
▸ Höre dir den Hörtext einmal ganz an und verschaffe dir einen Überblick.
Wer ist beteiligt? Was ist passiert? Vielleicht kannst du auch schon etwas heraushören, das du für die Bearbeitung der Aufgabe brauchst.
▸ Dabei musst du nicht jedes einzelne Wort verstehen. Versuche erst einmal herauszufinden, worum es ganz allgemein geht *(listening for gist)*.
▸ Achte auch auf die Stimmen der Sprechenden. Selbst Hintergrundgeräusche können dir helfen zu verstehen, worum es geht.
▸ Sieh dir noch einmal an, was du herausfinden sollst. Dann höre wieder zu. Achte diesmal auch auf Details *(listening for detail)* und mache dir Notizen. Notiere nur Stichwörter, keine ganzen Sätze.

Who?	Where?	When?	What?
Wer spricht? Um wen geht es?	Wo findet das Gespräch / die Geschichte statt?	Wann findet das Gespräch / die Geschichte statt?	Was wird besprochen? Was passiert?

3. Nach dem Hören
▸ Vergleicht eure Ergebnisse. Was habt ihr herausgefunden?

Tipp: Nutze jede Gelegenheit, um Englisch zu hören!

· Alle Hörtexte zum Buch findest du, wenn du auf www.westermann.de/webcode den Webcode WES-128203-001 eingibst oder den QR-Code scannst, den du auf Seite 2 findest.
· Versuch doch mal, dein Lieblingsbuch als Hörbuch auf Englisch anzuhören.
· Es gibt verschiedene Möglichkeiten, sich Texte in verschiedenen Geschwindigkeiten vorlesen zu lassen. Du kannst probieren, das Tempo nach und nach zu erhöhen.

| Skills | Wordbanks | Grammar | Words |

3 TALKING WITH PEOPLE
Mit anderen sprechen

Um dein Englisch zu trainieren, solltest du jede Gelegenheit nutzen, Englisch zu sprechen. Auch wenn es dir vielleicht komisch vorkommt – sprich so viel Englisch wie möglich mit deinen Mitschülerinnen und Mitschülern.

1. Versuche, so viel wie möglich auf Englisch auszudrücken
▶ Wenn du über ein bestimmtes Thema sprechen willst, überlege dir vorher einige Ausdrücke, die du im Gespräch verwenden kannst. Die *wordbanks* ab Seite 162 können dir dabei helfen.
▶ Wenn du etwas nicht verstanden hast, bitte darum, dass es wiederholt wird:
"Can you say that again, please?" oder: *"Can you repeat that, please?"*
▶ Wenn dir ein Wort nicht einfällt, kannst du es umschreiben:
"Excuse me, could you pass me the … erm … it's not a fork or a knife. You can eat soup with it."

2. Präge dir Redewendungen und Sätze ein
▶ Es gibt eine Reihe von Redewendungen und Sätzen, die du im Englischunterricht häufig verwenden kannst.
▶ Viele davon findest du bei den *classroom phrases* auf den Seiten 172-173.

3. Wenn du Interviews durchführst
▶ Schreibe deine Fragen auf und überlege, was mögliche Antworten sein könnten.
▶ Stelle offene Fragen, die mehr als ein Wort als Antwort erfordern.
Verwende Fragewörter wie *what, when, where, who, how* oder *why*.
▶ Wenn etwas unklar ist oder du es nicht richtig verstanden hast, stelle weitere Fragen oder bitte um Wiederholung.

4. Sprich so oft Englisch, wie du kannst
▶ Höre dir die Hörtexte aus deinem Englischbuch an und lies die Texte laut mit. Versuche, die Aussprache der Sprecherinnen und Sprecher nachzuahmen.
▶ Singe englischsprachige Lieder mit.
▶ Unterhalte dich auf Englisch mit jemandem, der ebenfalls Englisch sprechen kann.

Tipp: Nimm dich auf! (media worksheet 2, 5, 17)
- Lies einen Text aus dem Buch laut vor oder sprich Englisch und nimm dich auf. Dann kannst du dich selbst anhören und überprüfen, wie dein Englisch klingt.
- Wenn ihr zu zweit zusammenarbeitet, könnt ihr Dialoge und Interviews aufnehmen und gemeinsam prüfen, ob es noch etwas zu verbessern gibt.

4 WRITING
Schreiben

Auch zum Erstellen unterschiedlicher Texte hast du schon einige Methoden kennengelernt. Wichtig ist, dass du deinen Text planst und nicht einfach losschreibst. Hier sind die wichtigsten Schritte:

1. Planen
▷ Überlege: Was für einen Text willst du schreiben – eine E-Mail, eine Textnachricht, eine Geschichte, einen Brief? Auf www.westermann.de/webcode kannst du den Webcode WES-128203-001 eingeben und dort Anleitungen zu verschiedenen Textsorten finden.
▷ Wenn du eine Geschichte schreiben willst, kannst du mithilfe von *who, what, where, when* und *why* Ideen sammeln und die Geschichte planen.
▷ Außerdem kann es helfen, in einem *word web* oder einer Liste passende Wörter zu sammeln. Du kannst auch in den *wordbank*s im Buch oder in einem Wörterbuch nachschauen.
▷ Überlege: Was sollte am Anfang stehen, wie weckst du Interesse? Was folgt darauf? Wie könnte das Ende der Geschichte sein?
▷ Auch wenn du einen Artikel oder Bericht schreibst, solltest du dir vorher überlegen, wie du ihn gliedern möchtest und wichtige Wörter sammeln.

2. Schreiben und überarbeiten
▷ Bei jeder Art von Texten gilt, dass du zunächst einen Entwurf *(draft)* schreiben solltest – entweder handschriftlich oder am Computer.
▷ Überlege dir eine passende Überschrift. Möchtest du Bilder einfügen? Falls ja, suche passende und vergiss nicht, anzugeben, wo du sie gefunden hast.
▷ Überarbeite und verbessere *(edit)* dann deinen Text. Du kannst auch andere nach ihrer Meinung zu deinem Text und nach Verbesserungsvorschlägen fragen.
▷ Wenn dein Text fertig ist, schreibe ihn ins Reine. Das kannst du handschriftlich oder mithilfe eines Textverarbeitungsprogramms am Computer machen.

3. Veröffentlichen
▷ Dein fertiger Text sollte „veröffentlicht" werden *(publish)*. Zeige ihn deiner Lehrkraft, einem Mitschüler, einer Mitschülerin oder der Klasse.
▷ Du kannst deinen Text in deinem (digitalen) Portfolio aufbewahren.

> **Tipp: Texte digital erstellen und veröffentlichen** (media worksheet 1, 9-16)
>
> • Wenn du einen Text mithilfe eines Textverarbeitungsprogramms am Computer schreibst, kannst du zunächst Ideen und nützliche Wörter in einem Dokument sammeln und speichern. Du kannst deine Ideensammlung und deinen Text dann jederzeit bearbeiten, ändern und ergänzen.
> • Oft könnt ihr Texte, die in Einzel- oder Partnerarbeit entstanden sind, zu einem Klassenprodukt zusammenfügen. Vielleicht gibt es die Möglichkeit, dieses Produkt auf der Schul- oder Klassenwebseite zu veröffentlichen.

5 READING
Lesen

Es gibt viele Strategien, die dir helfen können, einen englischen Text zu verstehen. Sieh dir vor allem erst einmal die **Überschrift** und die **Bilder** an, die dir schon viel über den Inhalt verraten. Beim Text selbst kannst du zum Beispiel eine der folgenden Strategien anwenden:

1. Skimming
Beim *skimming* überfliegst du den Text erst einmal. Dafür brauchst du nicht jedes Wort zu verstehen. Du versuchst, dir schnell einen Überblick zu verschaffen: Worum geht es? Was passiert? Wer ist beteiligt?

2. Reading for detail
Du liest den Text gründlich, um möglichst viele Details herauszufinden. Mit den *wh*-Fragen kannst du die wichtigsten Informationen herausbekommen: Who? Where? When? What?

> **SWIMMING IS HIS LIFE**
>
> He's young, he's fast, he's great! This young man is going to make it to the top. Leroy Haffner will soon be one of Britain's best swimmers! Leroy was born in Bristol, UK. Swimming has always been his greatest love. He started swimming at the age of four. Three years later he had already won medals for his local club. The pool became the centre of his life and he took part in one national competition after another. Then last year, Leroy had an injury and couldn't swim for nearly two months. It was the worst time of his life. But Leroy is a fighter and he didn't give up. He started swimming again – and with great success.
> Next week, Leroy will participate in the National Championships. His coach, Ted Henley, knows that "Leroy will do really, really well".

Mache dir Notizen. Auf Kopien oder in deinen eigenen Büchern kannst du auch wichtige Textstellen markieren.

3. Scanning
Beim *scanning* suchst du einen Text gezielt nach ganz bestimmten Informationen ab, zum Beispiel nach speziellen Fakten.

> **Tipp:** Suche dir englische Texte zu Themen, die dich interessieren!
>
> - Du kannst im Internet und in Büchereien nach interessanten Texten auf Englisch suchen.
> - Lies so viel du kannst. Am Ende jeder Unit in diesem Buch findest du eine Kurzgeschichte und einen Sachtext oder ein Gedicht.

6 MEDIATION
Sprachmittlung

Manchmal gibt es Situationen, in denen du jemandem helfen musst, der deine Muttersprache oder eine Fremdsprache nicht so gut kann wie du. Hier erfährst du, wie das funktioniert:

1. Gib den Sinn wieder

Es kommt nicht darauf an, dass du alles Wort für Wort übersetzt. Wichtiger ist es, den Sinn wiederzugeben. Es muss klar werden, worum es geht.

Was gibt es heute Besonderes?

Our special recommendation today is fresh fish. Our chef was able to get some fresh trout that was caught this morning. We serve it with a lemon cream sauce, a side dish of rice and a light salad.

Es gibt frischen Fisch in Zitronensauce mit Reis und Salat.

2. Fasse dich kurz

Bilde einfache, kurze Sätze. Unwichtige Einzelheiten kannst du weglassen.

Was steht denn da?

**Science Museum –
New section open now**
Don't miss our brand new exhibition section on the history of the computer. From a model of Konrad Zuse's Z3, the first working computer in the world, to the latest tablets, there's a lot to see, learn and try out.

Sie haben eine neue Abteilung zur Geschichte des Computers eröffnet.

Tipp: Keine Angst vor Fehlern!

- Wenn dir ein wichtiges Wort nicht einfällt, kannst du es umschreiben.
- Versuche, dich an Redewendungen zu erinnern. Zum Beispiel kannst du mit *"What about ...?"* Vorschläge machen oder mit *"There is ... / There are ..."* etwas beschreiben.

| Skills | Wordbanks | Grammar | Words |

7 WATCHING A VIDEO CLIP
Videoclips verstehen

Englischsprachige Videoclips anzuschauen macht Spaß und ist eine tolle Möglichkeit, die Sprache noch besser zu lernen. Dabei solltest du einige Dinge beachten:

1. Bevor es losgeht
- Gibt es Bilder aus dem Videoclip in deinem Buch? Was ist zu sehen?
- Lies den Titel des Videoclips. Welche Hinweise gibt er auf den Inhalt?
- Worum könnte es gehen? Stelle Vermutungen an. Weißt du vielleicht schon etwas über das Thema?

2. Währenddessen
- Schaue dir den Videoclip in Ruhe an. Konzentriere dich dabei zunächst vor allem auf das, was du siehst.
  Who? Wer ist zu sehen? Um wen geht es?
  What? Worum geht es? Was passiert?
  Where? Wo findet es statt?
  When? Wann findet es statt?
- Was ist dein erster Eindruck? Mache dir Notizen. Es ist nicht schlimm, wenn du nicht alles verstehst. Achte auf die Stimmen, Körpersprache und Gesichtsausdrücke der Personen im Videoclip.
- Gibt es eine Aufgabe zu dem Videoclip in deinem Buch? Was sollst du herausfinden? Behalte die Fragen im Kopf, während du ein zweites Mal zuschaust. Konzentriere dich stärker auf das, was du hörst. Kannst du jetzt schon mehr verstehen? Gibt es Wörter, die immer wieder vorkommen? Notiere sie dir.
- Versuche, gleich danach die Fragen zu beantworten. Wenn nötig, schaue dir dann den Clip ein weiteres Mal an. Überprüfe dabei deine Antworten.

3. Hinterher
- Tausche dich mit deinen Mitschülerinnen und Mitschülern aus.
  Welche Eindrücke habt ihr bekommen? Was habt ihr herausgefunden?

Tipp: Schaue dir Videoclips und Filme auf Englisch an (media worksheet 8)

- Alle Videoclips zum Buch findest du, wenn du auf www.westermann.de/webcode den Webcode WES-128203-001 eingibst oder den QR-Code scannst, den du auf Seite 2 findest.
- Sieh dir Filme, Serien oder Berichte zu Themen, die dich interessieren, auf Englisch an.
- Auf DVDs oder bei Streaming-Diensten kannst du fast immer den englischen Ton und englische Untertitel einschalten. Nach und nach lernst du so besser zu verstehen, was gesagt wird.

8 SEARCHING THE INTERNET
Im Internet recherchieren

Hier erfährst du, wie du im Internet zu einem Thema recherchieren kannst.

---

1. Benutze eine Suchmaschine

▸ Gute Suchbegriffe erleichtern dir die Suche im Internet. Versuche, möglichst genau zu formulieren, wonach du suchst – und zwar auf Englisch.
▸ Gib die Suchbegriffe in eine Suchmaschine ein.
▸ Es kann sein, dass die Suchmaschine eine riesige Anzahl an Treffern anzeigt. Oft genügt es, sich die ersten 10 bis 20 Suchergebnisse anzuschauen.

2. Suche auf englischsprachigen Seiten

▸ Suche am besten direkt auf englischsprachigen Seiten – dann steht dir der nötige Wortschatz gleich zur Verfügung. Bei vielen Suchmaschinen kannst du Englisch als Sprache wählen.
▸ Es gibt Webseiten, auf denen du Informationen in einfacherem Englisch finden kannst. Deine Lehrkraft kann dir helfen, sie zu finden.

3. Halte nützliche Informationen fest

▸ Überfliege erst einmal die Seiten, die dir interessant erscheinen. Dafür brauchst du nicht jedes Wort zu verstehen.
▸ Wenn du interessante Webseiten gefunden hast, kannst du dir Notizen zu den Inhalten machen.
▸ Denke daran, dir auch das Datum deiner Recherche aufzuschreiben und die Quelle zu sichern. So weißt du später noch, wo du die Informationen gefunden hast.
▸ Wenn du Textausschnitte für deine eigenen Texte unverändert aus dem Internet übernimmst, musst du zeigen, dass es Zitate sind. Setze sie in Anführungszeichen und gib die Quelle an, sowie das Datum, an dem du sie gefunden hast.

4. Sei kritisch

▸ Informationen, die du im Internet findest, sind nicht immer richtig.
▸ Sei deshalb kritisch und überprüfe die Informationen noch einmal auf anderen Seiten oder in einem Lexikon.

Tipp: Nutze digitale Tools (media worksheet 6, 7)

- Es gibt viele sinnvolle Tools im Internet. Du kannst zum Beispiel Währungen und Maßeinheiten umrechnen oder dir Entfernungen anzeigen lassen.
- Viele englischsprachige Einrichtungen, vor allem Museen, bieten virtuelle Rundgänge an.
- Du kannst auch virtuell durch britische Städte spazieren.

| Skills | Wordbanks | Grammar | Words |

9 PRESENTATIONS
Präsentationen halten

Hier findest du einige Tipps und Tricks für gelungene Präsentationen.

1. Bevor du etwas präsentierst
- Überlege: Was möchtest du zu deinem Thema sagen? Wie viel Zeit hast du für deinen Vortrag?
- Bei einer sehr kurzen Präsentation, zum Beispiel einem *one-minute talk*, musst du dich auf das absolut Notwendige beschränken.
- Gliedere deinen Vortrag: Überlege, in welcher Reihenfolge du deine Ideen vorstellen und wie du anfangen möchtest.
- Fertige ein Poster oder eine Computerpräsentation an, um deinen Vortrag anschaulich zu machen. Wenn du Bilder oder Texte aus dem Internet oder aus einem Buch kopiert hast, dann vermerke immer, wo und wann du sie gefunden hast.
- Notiere Stichpunkte zu dem, was du sagen möchtest, auf Karteikarten.
- Übe deinen Vortrag vor dem Spiegel, vor Freunden oder vor deiner Familie.

2. Während du präsentierst
- Sprich langsam und deutlich.
- Sieh deine Zuhörerinnen und Zuhörer an, wenn du sprichst. Achte zum Beispiel bei einer Computerpräsentation darauf, nicht ständig auf den Bildschirm zu schauen.
- Versuche, frei zu sprechen. Du kannst die wichtigsten Punkte von deinen Notizen oder deinem Poster ablesen. Nützliche Redewendungen findest du in der *wordbank* auf Seite 168.

3. So wird dein Vortrag spannend und lebendig
- Musik, Videoclips, interessante Bilder oder Zitate machen deinen Vortrag abwechslungsreich.
- Achte auf eine lebendige Mimik, Gestik und Stimme.
- Zeige deinen Zuhörerinnen und Zuhörern auf deinem Poster oder auf den Seiten deiner Computerpräsentation, worüber du gerade sprichst. So wird dein Vortrag für die Klasse noch interessanter.

> *So sieht ein gelungenes Vortragsposter aus*
> - ansprechende Überschrift
> - relevante Informationen
> - verständliche Sätze, aber nicht zu viel Text
> - große Bilder und Schrift: Jeder im Raum muss sie sehen und lesen können.
> - saubere Schrift
> - Bilder mit Bildunterschriften

Tipp: Schau dir Tutorials an (media worksheet 4)

- Zum Präsentieren gibt es viele Tutorials im Internet. Schau dir einige an und überlege, was bei dir schon gut klappt und was du noch verbessern könntest.
- Zum Thema Computerpräsentationen kannst du dir ein passendes Arbeitsblatt herunterladen und dir Tutorials anschauen. Gehe dazu auf www.westermann.de/webcode und gib den Webcode WES-128203-001 ein.

10 PERFORMING A SCENE
Eine Szene vorspielen

Szenische Lesungen, Rollenspiele und Theaterstücke sind eine gute Methode, um dein Englisch zu trainieren. Hier findest du einige Tipps, damit du deine Rolle erfolgreich spielen kannst.

1. Szenische Lesung
- Für ein *dramatic reading* musst du deinen Text nicht auswendig lernen. Du solltest ihn aber so gut kennen, dass du auf Aussprache, Betonung und Mimik achten kannst, ohne den Faden zu verlieren.
- Achte darauf, dass Betonung, Lautstärke und Aussprache zu dem passen, was du liest. Überlege dir z. B., wie sich die Person fühlt und wie du beim Vorlesen Spannung erzeugen kannst.

2. Rollenspiele
- Mit der Methode *read – look up – speak* kannst du deine Rolle auswendig lernen: Du liest deinen Satz still, siehst dann auf und sprichst ihn.
- Halte beim Sprechen Augenkontakt zu deinem Gegenüber.
- Wechselt auch mal die Rollen und übt mit anderen Partnern. So lernt ihr, spontan zu reagieren.
- Wenn ihr *cue cards* verwendet, denkt daran, nur Stichworte zu notieren, keine ganzen Sätze!

3. Theaterstücke
- Bei Theaterstücken geht es noch mehr als bei Rollenspielen um das Schauspielern. Du solltest deinen Text gut auswendig lernen, damit du dich besser auf das Spielen konzentrieren kannst.
- Versetze dich in die Person hinein, die du darstellst. Überlege, in welcher Stimmung die Person ist. Denke beim Sprechen an die passende Mimik und Gestik.
- Mit Requisiten und Kostümen fällt es leichter, richtig in eine Rolle hineinzuschlüpfen.
- Denke immer daran, laut und deutlich und nicht zu schnell zu sprechen, damit das Publikum dich gut verstehen kann.

4. Präsentieren
- Rollenspiele, kleine Szenen, Sketche und Theaterstücke sind gute Mittel, um auch anderen zu zeigen, wie viel Englisch ihr schon könnt. Bei einem Schulfest oder an einem Tag der offenen Tür könnt ihr Eltern oder andere Klassen zu einer Vorführung einladen.

Tipp: Schaut euch selbst zu (media worksheet 2, 5)
- Rollenspiele könnt ihr aufnehmen und so gemeinsam überprüfen, ob es noch etwas zu verbessern gibt.

Around the world

Writing and talking about places

The capital of ... is ...

... is huge / small. It covers an area of ... km².

It has a population of ...

The longest river / highest mountain is ...

... is known as ... / famous for ... / also called ...

I would describe ... as a ... place.

When I think of ..., ... comes to mind.

In this area, you can see ...

... is a must-see / a perfect place to ... / an ideal ...

... is located / situated in ...

... is the biggest / best / least / one of the most ...

Countries and nationalities

Korea – Korean · Italy – Italian ·
Wales – Welsh · Scotland – Scottish ·
Poland – Polish · Paraguay – Paraguayan ·
Turkey / Türkiye – Turkish · France – French ·
England – English · Ireland – Irish ·
Germany – German · China – Chinese ·
the USA – US-American · Japan – Japanese · ...

There is / are ...

deserts · beaches · forests ·
cities · towns · villages ·
mountain peaks · tropical wetlands ·
long stretches of farmland · islands ·
a wide variety of climate zones ·
diverse ecosystems · natural beauty ·
different landscapes · national parks ·
a number of landmarks · geological wonders ·
interesting sights · cool events · ...

Places can be ...

awesome · sunny · covered with snow ·
huge · amazing · big · fantastic · small ·
noisy · breathtaking · stunning · charming ·
rich in history · well-known · cool · busy ·
far away · historic · sleepy · great · loud ·
fascinating · quiet · boring · lively · dirty ·
impressive · clean · famous · fabulous ·
pretty · multicultural · dangerous · lovely ·
a home · magnificent · large · a hotspot · ...

I left my home ...

... because I found a job in a different place.

... to find new opportunities.

... to start a new life.

... to get away from a difficult situation.

... because I wanted to be with my family.

... to search for a better life.

... to travel around the world.

... to flee from war.

Travelling

I would like to go to … / How do I get to …?

I would like to buy a ticket to …, please.

What's the quickest way to …?

How much is a single ticket / return ticket to …, please?

When does the next train / plane for … leave?

From which platform does the train to … leave?

There is a special offer for children between the ages of … and … travelling with an adult.

Come and visit the beautiful city of Galway!

- Discover **Galway's rich history**.
- Join a **food tour** and explore our restaurants, cafés, bistros and pubs.
- Visit the **beautiful beaches** in the Galway city area.
- Don't miss out on the **Galway festivals**.

Descriptions

Describing people

was born in … · got married in … ·
is famous because … · invented … ·
had … children · fought for … · worked … ·
went to school / university in … ·
encouraged other people to … · died in …

People can be …

adventurous · kind · happy · tall ·
angry · clever · smart · friendly · small ·
cool · funny · lazy · mean · active · …

Objects and things can be …

bright · colourful · big · small · cool
made of plastic / wood / paper / … · boring ·
expensive · cheap · interesting · …

A situation or atmosphere can be …

exciting · interesting · scary · inspiring ·
special · boring · happy · lively ·
relaxed · confusing · electric · …

Walt Disney

Walt Disney was an American film producer. He was born on December 5, 1901 in Chicago and is probably most famous for creating the cartoon character 'Mickey Mouse' in 1928.
Another famous cartoon character he invented is 'Dumbo', but he also produced films with real people such as the musical film 'Mary Poppins' in 1964.
Walt Disney died on December 15, 1966.

Talking about pictures

In the picture, there is / are … ·
The photo shows … · I can see … ·
In the photo, you can clearly see that … · …

School life

High school students in the USA ...

... often have a homecoming week at the beginning of the school year.

They crown a homecoming king and queen, and there are special events like a football game, a dance and performances by different clubs.

... usually go to school by bus or by car.

... do not have to wear uniform at school.

... have to carry their school ID card with them at all times.

... keep their bags and books in lockers.

... get their schedule / timetable at the registrar's office.

... go to homeroom for their first period. There their homeroom teacher checks attendance.

... begin their school day with the Pledge of Allegiance.

... can choose from a wide variety of electives such as art, foreign languages or video game development.

... can join a lot of different school clubs such as glee club, marching band or model congress.

... collect credits in order to graduate.

... wear caps and gowns during the graduation ceremony.

... celebrate graduation with a formal dance called prom.

Electives

home economics · robotics · business law · marketing · movie production · woodworking · maintenance · plumbing · culinary art · computer repairing · women's studies · light and sound technology · welding · IT · auto body repair · world literature · fashion design · personal finance · ...

School clubs

library club · fundraiser club · history club · mathletics club · drama / theater group · debating society · chemistry club · FBLA (future business leaders of America) · yearbook club · ...

American and British English

American English	British English
aside from	apart from
auditorium	assembly hall
on the weekend	at the weekend
fall	autumn
tailgate / trunk	car boot
parking lot	car park
French fries	chips
chips	crisps
movie	film
apartment	flat
soccer	football
principal	headteacher
vacation	holiday
period	lesson
grade	grade / mark
grade	year
cell (phone)	mobile (phone)
gym	PE
elementary school	primary school
trash / garbage	rubbish
store	shop
schedule	timetable
subway	underground

American English	British English
color / neighbor	colour / neighbour
favorite / to honor	favourite / to honour
to practice	to practise
center / theater	centre / theatre
percent	per cent
traveled / combating	travelled / combatting
math	maths
mom	mum
pajamas	pyjamas
program	programme
learned / dreamed	learnt / dreamt

Tipp

Es gibt ein paar Unterschiede zwischen dem Englisch, das in Großbritannien gesprochen wird *(BE)*, und dem Englisch, das in den USA gesprochen wird *(AE)*. Einige Wörter werden unterschiedlich buchstabiert, wobei es in manchen Fällen Regelmäßigkeiten gibt.
So werden Wörter aus dem Britischen Englisch wie *favourite* oder *harbour* im Amerikanischen Englisch nur mit *o* geschrieben: *favorite* oder *harbor*. Wörter mit der Endung *-re* (z. B. *centre* oder *theatre*) enden im Amerikanischen Englisch auf *-er (center, theater)*.
Bei anderen Wörtern muss man sich die Unterschiede einfach merken, wie zum Beispiel bei *per cent (BE) / percent (AE)*. Das gleiche gilt für einige Verben, deren Vergangenheitsformen im Amerikanischen Englisch regelmäßig sind *(learned, dreamed)*, im Britischen aber unregelmäßig *(learnt, dreamt)*.
Dann gibt es noch eine Gruppe von Wörtern, die komplett unterschiedlich sind, z. B. *fall (AE)* und *autumn (BE)*.
In einigen Fällen sind die Unterschiede nicht mehr so groß. Beeinflusst durch amerikanische Filme und Musik werden heutzutage auch im britischen Sprachraum Wörter wie *kid, movie* oder *post* verwendet. Auch Wörter, die im Britischen Englisch eigentlich mit *s* geschrieben werden (z. B. *organise, realise*), liest man mittlerweile häufig auch in Großbritannien in der amerikanischen Schreibweise mit *z*.

Du kannst dir die britische und amerikanische Aussprache der Wörter aus den Listen auf dieser Seite im Audiotrack anhören.

Feelings

People can be feeling ...

depressed · lonely · happy · helpless · excited · angry · glad · upset · worried · unhappy · sad · cheerful · ...

I am feeling sad because my best friend won't talk to me anymore.

They look like they are really angry. Maybe they are having an argument.

Friends are people you ...

... can trust.   ... like to spend time with.

... can rely on.   ... can talk to about anything.

When you love someone, ...

... you would do anything for them.

... you will listen to their problems.

... you will be there for them.

The girl in the yellow T-shirt seems to be very cheerful. I think she is happy to be with her friends.

Seeking and giving advice

I need your help with ...

I don't think you should worry about it too much because you'll find a solution.

If I were you, I would ...

Can you please give me some advice on ...?

You shouldn't / should ...

I'm having problems with ...

Why don't you ...?

What should I do when ...?

Have you tried talking to someone?

What's your advice on ...?

Make sure you don't make the same mistake twice.

What about finding new friends?

Don't ... / Never ...

I think it would be a good idea if you ...

It's important to ... / Be careful not to ...

(Digital) communication

Digital communication is a good thing …

- … because it is a cheap and time-saving way to keep in touch with friends and family – even if they are far away from you.
- … because it helps you to share pictures and memories easily.
- … because you can meet new people online, even if you are very shy offline.
- … because you can meet people who share your hobbies and interests.
- … because it can enhance your life.

Digital communication is a bad thing …

- … because people often spend too much time online.
- … because of cyberbullying.
- … because you can meet new people online who might be dangerous.
- … because the boundaries between school or work and home life are blurred and you are expected to be online at all times.
- … because misunderstandings are more likely to happen.

Digital communication can …   It makes people …   The best / worst thing about online communication is …

You can't … without using …   It causes …   … is a negative side of online communication because …

In my opinion, the advantages of digital communication (don't) outweigh the disadvantages.

Writing a letter

Dear …

How are you?
I am writing to you from …
I want to tell you all about …
Today we …

Lots of love, … / Love from …

Writing a text message

Hi Ben!
I'm at …
There are … It's …
You should …
See you soon! :)

Writing an email

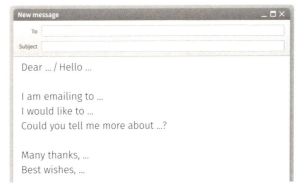

New message

To
Subject

Dear … / Hello …

I am emailing to …
I would like to …
Could you tell me more about …?

Many thanks, …
Best wishes, …

Expressing opinions

I think that ... because ...   In my opinion, it's a good / bad idea ... because ...   I believe that ... because ...

When you look at ... you can see that ...   One of the reasons for that is ...   If you ask me, ...

Another important point is that ...   The pros are ...

I think it's just as important to ... as to ...

I agree with that because ...   So I agree with ... the most.

On the one hand, you can say that ..., on the other hand, ...

However, you could say that ...   The cons are ...

I don't think you can ...   I think ... is more important than ...   I disagree with ...   I cannot agree with ...

I'd have to think some more about it.   I can't decide if I'm for or against it.

I'm not sure what I agree with.   To sum it all up, ...   Summarizing, I would say that ...

Presenting something

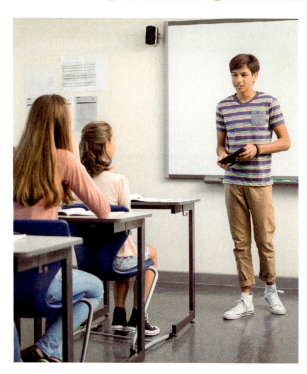

Hello and welcome to my presentation about ...
Today, I am going to be talking about ...
I would like to tell you about ...
First, I would like to introduce the topic of ...
In the second part of my presentation, I will ...
After that, I will talk about ...
Finally, I will look at ...
I will first give some information on ...
Here is an example of ...
On this slide, you can see ...
This is a photo of ...
This picture shows that ...
In this picture, you can clearly see ...
The most important point is ...
It is also important to mention that ...
You should know that ...
This shows how ...
The last aspect is ...
Thanks for listening. Are there any questions?

Hopes and dreams

I hope to …

have a good life · have a family ·
make the most out of life · travel the world ·
make a difference · help people ·
have some fun · be able to go abroad ·
change the world · improve things ·
make lots of money · become … · …

My hopes and dreams!

When I grow up, I'll …
When I have finished school, I …
My dream is to …
I want to …
I hope to …
I could …
If I …, I would …
It would be … if I had …

I am planning on doing … / going to …
I dream of being …

being successful in my job ·
doing something useful ·
becoming a vet / teacher / … ·
living in another country · …

starting my own business ·
getting rich ·
achieving my goals ·
having my own flat · …

Talking about the future

It would be great if there were …

In the future, I'll …

I think that more people will … in the future.

There will be more / less …

My ideal world in the future would look like this: …

I don't think there will be … anymore.

The world of work

Different jobs

doctor · teacher · lawyer · police officer · nursery teacher · photographer · electrician · gardener · waiter / waitress · engineer · (registered) nurse · bike mechanic · physiotherapist · coach · vet · dentist · fashion designer · forest worker · surf instructor · pilot · accountant · actor / actress · construction worker · …

You can work …

outdoors · indoors · in an office · on your own · in a team · with people · at a desk · from home · in a factory · in a hospital · at a school · with animals · …

A job should …

be fun · be interesting · pay well · have regular working hours · …

Soft skills

I can …
work under pressure · communicate · be a team leader · be a team member · …

I have …
lots of ideas · good manners · …

I am …
open to new ideas · creative · organized · good at … · good with people · polite · always on time · reliable · responsible · …

Hard skills

I can …
speak another language · repair cars · teach English · use technical language · drive a car · …

I have …
knowledge of IT programs · presentation skills · experience in / with … · …

A job interview

Thank you for inviting me.

Your application form looks very good.

I would like to get the job because …

Why don't you tell me a little about yourself?

I'm interested in / good at …

Why would you like to work for us?

I've worked for …

Do you prefer working indoors or outdoors?

What about working hours?

Have you got any more questions?

How much money will I earn?

Do you like working in a team or on your own?

How many days paid holiday do I get?

Numbers

Dates

by 1733 · until 1865 · in 1805 · after 1924 · between 1820 and 1890 · till 1783 · around 1,000 AD · about 20,000 years ago · in the 19th century · from 1820 to 1890 · during World War I · since the 1960s · …

Statistics

This graph clearly shows that … increased.
There is an increase in …

In this graph you can see that … decreased. The number of … became smaller. There is a decrease in …

This bar chart displays the number of people who … from … to …

This bar chart shows the development between … and …

This pie chart shows that 25 per cent of … are …
There are fewer … than …

Here you can see that there are more … than ….
The number of … is bigger.

There was a rise from … to …
The wave … then peaked in … and fell after …

The statistics prove/show that …

Tipp

you write	you say
1st March or 1 March	the first of March
2nd April or 2 April	the second of April
12th October	the twelfth of October

Tipp

Jahreszahlen sprichst du so aus:
1492   fourteen ninety-two
1939   nineteen thirty-nine
1951   nineteen fifty-one
2010   two thousand and ten

Tipp

Daten schreibst du im britischen Englisch so:
1 August, 2 January, 5 November
oder so:
1st / 1st August, 2nd / 2nd January, 5th / 5th November
Eine Jahreszahl schreibst du einfach dahinter:
1 August 2024 oder 01/08/24
Im amerikanischen Englisch ist es umgekehrt! Hier schreibt man den Monat VOR dem Tag:
August 1, August 1st oder 08/01/2024

Tipp

Du verwendest im Englischen Kommata, wenn du Ziffern gruppieren möchtest, keine Punkte!
The distance between New York and Los Angeles is 4,490 km.

Measurements

This box is 11cm wide, 6cm deep and 1cm tall.

| Skills | **Wordbanks** | Grammar | Words |

Classroom phrases

Which topic have you chosen?	Welches Thema hast du dir ausgesucht?
Which topic are you going to work on?	An welchem Thema hast du vor zu arbeiten?
Who is going to work on topic A / B / …?	Wer hat vor, an Thema A / B / … zu arbeiten?
I haven't decided yet.	Ich habe mich noch nicht entschieden.
I can't make up my mind.	Ich kann mich nicht entscheiden.
Do you want to work with me?	Willst du mit mir zusammenarbeiten?
You're good at … Why don't you …?	Du kannst gut … Warum machst du nicht …?

Sorry, I haven't got … with me.	Tut mir leid, ich habe … nicht dabei.
Sorry, I forgot to bring …	Tut mir leid, ich habe vergessen, … mitzubringen.

I've got a question.	Ich habe eine Frage.
Can you help me, please?	Können Sie / Kannst du mir bitte helfen?
I don't understand this.	Ich verstehe das hier nicht.
What's … in English / German?	Was heißt … auf Englisch / Deutsch?
What does … mean?	Was bedeutet …?
Can you spell that, please?	Kannst du das bitte buchstabieren?
Can you say that again, please?	Kannst du das bitte noch einmal sagen?
Sorry, I don't know.	Tut mir leid, das weiß ich nicht.
What page is it on?	Auf welcher Seite ist das?

Let's do the activities together.	Lass uns die Aktivitäten zusammen machen.
Let's compare …	Lass uns … vergleichen.
What do you think?	Was meinst du?
Whose turn is it?	Wer ist dran?

Are we allowed to use a dictionary?	Dürfen wir ein Wörterbuch benutzen?
Let's look it up in the dictionary.	Lass es uns im Wörterbuch nachschlagen.
What else do we need?	Was brauchen wir noch?

Classroom phrases

First we have to read up on … / investigate the idea about … / …	Als Erstes müssen wir uns über … informieren / die Idee über … untersuchen / …
I think we should first watch … / read … / explore … / …	Ich meine, wir sollten zuerst … anschauen / … lesen / … untersuchen / …
Do you know how to use the webcode?	Weißt du, wie man den Webcode benutzt?
Why don't we have a look at the website / on the Internet / … ?	Warum schauen wir nicht auf der Website / im Internet / … nach?

Who wants to keep the word list / take notes / prepare the fact file / … ?	Wer will die Wortliste führen / Notizen machen / den Steckbrief vorbereiten / … ?
Who is doing the presentation?	Wer übernimmt die Präsentation?
Who is writing down the results?	Wer notiert die Ergebnisse?
What do you think is the biggest problem / the most important fact / … ?	Was hältst du für das größte Problem / die wichtigste Tatsache / … ?
I think it would be a good idea to …	Ich finde, es wäre eine gute Idee, wenn wir …
Can I be the one to call / do the interview with / talk to / … ?	Kann ich … anrufen / das Interview mit … führen / mit … sprechen / … ?

Let me give you an example.	Lass mich dir ein Beispiel geben.
Well, it's a fact that …	Es ist nun mal eine Tatsache, dass …
I think that's a good point.	Ich denke, das ist ein guter Hinweis.
I wouldn't say so.	Das würde ich nicht sagen.
I see what you mean, but …	Ich verstehe, was du meinst, aber …
Sorry, I don't agree with you.	Tut mir leid, aber ich stimme dir nicht zu.
I'd rather focus on …	Ich würde mich lieber auf … konzentrieren.
We should do some more research on …	Wir sollten … besser untersuchen.
I'm sure there's more to it.	Ich glaube, da steckt mehr dahinter.
Only two of us seem to think that it's best to …	Nur zwei von uns scheinen der Ansicht zu sein, dass es am besten ist, wenn wir …
I agree with your idea / suggestion / …	Ich stimme deiner Idee / deinem Vorschlag / … zu.
You could make your text more interesting if you …	Du könntest deinen Text interessanter machen, wenn du …
I would use a different word here.	Ich würde hier ein anderes Wort verwenden.
We are running out of time.	Uns läuft die Zeit davon.
Well done!	Gut gemacht!

1 THE SIMPLE PAST: STATEMENTS (REVISION)
Die einfache Vergangenheit: Aussagen *(revision)*

Das *simple past* verwendet man, wenn man über etwas spricht, das in der Vergangenheit liegt und abgeschlossen ist.

a) Formen und bejahte Aussagesätze im *simple past*

Bei den regelmäßigen Verben hängst du -ed an die Grundform an:

DIGITAL+ video 18, 19

stay + **ed** → stay**ed** /steɪd/   look + **ed** → look**ed** /lʊkt/   visit + **ed** → visit**ed** /ˈvɪzɪtɪd/

Achte auf die Rechtschreibung: Endet die Grundform des Verbs auf -e, dann wird nur -d angehängt.
arriv**e** → arriv**ed** /əˈraɪvd/

Endet das Verb auf einen kurzen betonten **Vokal + Konsonant**, dann wird der Konsonant verdoppelt.
stop → sto**pped** /stɒpt/

Endet das Verb auf **Konsonant + y**, dann wird aus dem -y ein -i und die Endung lautet -ied.
tid**y** → tid**ied** /ˈtaɪdid/

Unregelmäßige Verben haben im *simple past* eine eigene Form (siehe Seite 275–277).

have → **had**   I **had** a great holiday.
go → **went**   We **went** to Yellowstone National Park.
do → **did**   We **did** lots of things.

Das Verb *be* hat zwei Formen im *simple past*: I / he / she / it **was** – you / we / they **were**
I **was** in New York last week, but my friends **were** in Boston.

b) Verneinte Aussagesätze im *simple past*

Sätze im *simple past* verneinst du im Allgemeinen mit *didn't (= did not)*.
Didn't ist bei allen Personen gleich. Danach kommt dann das Verb in der Grundform.
I **didn't go** to Boston last week.

Bei *was* und *were* hängst du nur *not* oder die Kurzform *n't* an.
I **wasn't** in Boston last week, and my friends **weren't** in New York.

2 THE SIMPLE PAST: QUESTIONS (REVISION)
Die einfache Vergangenheit: Fragen *(revision)*

Fragen im *simple past* bildest du in den meisten Fällen mit *did*. Eine Ausnahme sind Sätze mit *was* oder *were*.

a) Entscheidungsfragen und Kurzantworten im *simple past*

Bei Entscheidungsfragen im *simple past* stellst du *did* an den Satzanfang.
Did ist bei allen Personen gleich.
Achte auch hier darauf, das Verb danach in der Grundform zu verwenden.
In der Kurzantwort wird *did* wieder aufgegriffen.

DIGITAL+ video 18, 19

Entscheidungsfrage	Kurzantwort	Kurzantwort
Did you go to Yellowstone?	Yes, I did.	No, I didn't.
Did your friends come with you?	Yes, they did.	No, they didn't.

Bei Fragen mit *was* und *were* brauchst du kein *did*.
Hier steht *was* oder *were* am Satzanfang.
In der Kurzantwort wird *was* bzw. *were* wieder aufgegriffen.

Entscheidungsfrage	Kurzantwort	Kurzantwort
Were your parents in New York last year?	Yes, they were.	No, they weren't.
Was the weather good?	Yes, it was.	No, it wasn't.

b) Fragen mit Fragewort im *simple past*

Bei Sätzen mit Fragewort steht das Fragewort am Satzanfang. Es steht vor *did*.

What did you do in the holidays?
Where did you go?

Bei Fragen mit *who* braucht man jedoch kein zusätzliches *did*, wenn *who* nach dem Subjekt fragt.

Who went to the USA? – **My parents** went to the USA.

Bei Fragen mit *was* oder *were* brauchst du ebenfalls kein *did*.

How was your holiday?
What were your favourite places?

3 THE PRESENT PERFECT: STATEMENTS (REVISION)
Das Perfekt: Aussagen *(revision)*

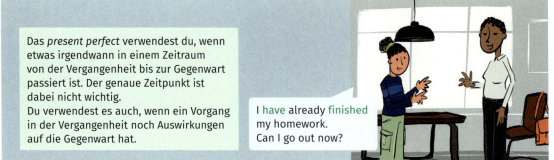

Das *present perfect* verwendest du, wenn etwas irgendwann in einem Zeitraum von der Vergangenheit bis zur Gegenwart passiert ist. Der genaue Zeitpunkt ist dabei nicht wichtig.
Du verwendest es auch, wenn ein Vorgang in der Vergangenheit noch Auswirkungen auf die Gegenwart hat.

I **have** already **finished** my homework.
Can I go out now?

a) Bejahte Aussagesätze im *present perfect*

Das *present perfect* bildest du mit *have / has* + Partizip Perfekt *(past participle)*.
Statt *have* bzw. *has* kannst du auch die entsprechende Kurzform benutzen.

I **have climbed** all the way up to the top of the Statue of Liberty.
I**'ve done** lots of sightseeing so far.
He **has finished** his dinner.
He**'s** just **seen** a fantastic Broadway show.

Bei regelmäßigen Verben bildest du das Partizip Perfekt, indem du an die Grundform des Verbs die Endung *-ed* anhängst. Beachte auch die Besonderheiten bei der Schreibung und Aussprache der *ed*-Endungen (s. auch Grammatik-Kapitel 1 auf Seite 174).

Grundform	simple past	past participle
climb	climbed	climbed
visit	visited	visited
stop	stopped	stopped
tidy	tidied	tidied
arrive	arrived	arrived

Die Formen der unregelmäßigen Verben musst du wie Vokabeln auswendig lernen.

Auf den Seiten 275-277 findest du hierzu eine Liste und auf Seite 277 einen Tipp, wie du die unregelmäßigen Formen gruppieren kannst, um sie dir leichter einzuprägen.

Grundform	simple past	past participle
be	was / were	been
do	did	done
have	had	had
buy	bought	bought

b) Verneinte Aussagesätze im *present perfect*

Die Verneinung bildest du mit *have not / has not* + Partizip Perfekt bzw. mit den Kurzformen *haven't / hasn't* + Partizip Perfekt.

I **have not been** to New York yet.
He **hasn't finished** his dinner yet.
We **haven't eaten** lunch yet.

4 THE PRESENT PERFECT: QUESTIONS (REVISION)
Das Perfekt: Fragen *(revision)*

Mit einer Entscheidungsfrage im *present perfect* kannst du z. B. fragen, ob jemand etwas irgendwann in der Vergangenheit schon einmal gemacht hat. Der genaue Zeitpunkt ist dabei nicht so wichtig.

a) Entscheidungsfragen und Kurzantworten im *present perfect*

Entscheidungsfragen im *present perfect* bildest du, indem du *have* bzw. *has* an den Satzanfang stellst.
In der Kurzantwort wird *have* bzw. *has* wieder aufgegriffen.

📱 **DIGITAL+** video 20

Entscheidungsfrage	Kurzantwort	Kurzantwort
Have you ever been to New York?	Yes, I have.	No, I haven't.
Has Ben ever seen a Broadway show?	Yes, he has.	No, he hasn't.
Have the children ever cycled across Brooklyn Bridge?	Yes, they have.	No, they haven't.

b) Fragen mit Fragewort im *present perfect*

Bei Fragen mit Fragewort steht das Fragewort am Satzanfang.

***What** have you done?*
***Where** have you been?*
***Why** hasn't she arrived yet?*

c) Adverbien der unbestimmten Zeit

Beim *present perfect* ist es nicht wichtig, wann genau in der Vergangenheit etwas passiert ist. Man betrachtet stattdessen den Zeitraum von der Vergangenheit bis zur Gegenwart. Daher werden bei Fragen und Aussagen im *present perfect* häufig Adverbien der unbestimmten Zeit verwendet, z. B. *ever* (= jemals), *never* (= nie), *already* (= schon), *just* (= gerade), *yet* (= schon) und *not yet* (= noch nicht).

Die meisten Adverbien stehen dann direkt vor dem Partizip Perfekt.

*Have you **ever** been to the USA? – No, I've **never** been there.*
*Has Suri **already** finished sightseeing? – Yes, she has **just** come back.*

Beachte die Ausnahme: *yet* steht am Satzende.

*Have you been to Central Park **yet**? – No, I have**n't** been there **yet**.*

5 THE PASSIVE (REVISION)
Das Passiv *(revision)*

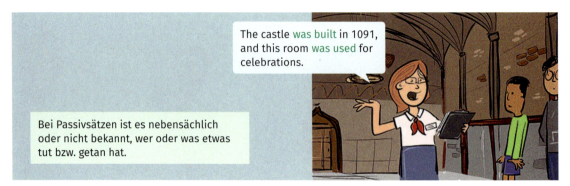

Bei Passivsätzen ist es nebensächlich oder nicht bekannt, wer oder was etwas tut bzw. getan hat.

Aktivsätze sagen uns, wer oder was handelt bzw. gehandelt hat.
In folgendem Beispiel sind das *thousands of workers*.

Thousands of workers **built** *the Empire State Building between 1930 and 1931.*

Wenn aber nicht betont werden soll oder wenn nicht bekannt ist, wer etwas tut oder getan hat, kannst du einen Passivsatz verwenden.

The Empire State Building **was built** *between 1930 and 1931.*

Das Objekt aus dem Aktivsatz, hier *the Empire State Building*, wird zum Subjekt des Passivsatzes.

	Subjekt	Verb	Objekt	
Aktivsatz:	Thousands of workers	built	the Empire State Building	between 1930 and 1931.
Passivsatz:	The Empire State Building	was built		between 1930 and 1931.

Das Passiv bildest du so: Form von **be** + **Partizip Perfekt** *(past participle)*

Englisch	Deutsch
English **is spoken** all over the world.	Englisch **wird** überall auf der Welt **gesprochen**.
My computer **was made** in China.	Mein Computer **wurde** in China **hergestellt**.
Since its opening, the museum **has been visited** by lots of tourists.	Seit seiner Eröffnung **ist** das Museum von vielen Touristen **besucht worden**.
The building **will be renovated** / **is going to be renovated** next year.	Das Gebäude **wird** nächstes Jahr **renoviert werden**.
The museum **is being renovated** at the moment.	Das Museum **wird** gerade **renoviert**.

In der Liste mit den unregelmäßigen Verben auf den Seiten 275-277 findest du das Partizip Perfekt *(past participle)* in der dritten Spalte.

Wenn du in einem Passivsatz doch einmal die handelnde Person oder die Ursache für etwas nennen willst, hängst du sie mit **by** („von", „durch") an den Satz an:

The Empire State Building was built **by** *thousands of workers.*   *The house was destroyed* **by** *a fire.*

6 THE PAST PERFECT
Die Vorvergangenheit

Du verwendest das *past perfect* z. B., wenn du über eine Handlung sprechen möchtest, die vor einer anderen Handlung in der Vergangenheit stattgefunden hat. Beide Handlungen sind dabei abgeschlossen.

Yesterday at 8am

After Noah **had taken** a shower, he **brushed** his teeth.

a) Aussagesätze im *past perfect*

Das *past perfect* bildest du mit *had* + Partizip Perfekt *(past participle)*.

Eric Johnson **had read** the most books.
Katie Miller **had trained** intensively.

DIGITAL+ video 22

Das Partizip Perfekt kennst du schon vom *present perfect* (s. Grammatik-Kapitel 3 auf Seite 176). Bei regelmäßigen Verben endet das Partizip Perfekt auf *-ed*. Bei unregelmäßigen Verben musst du die Formen auswendig lernen. Auf den Seiten 275-277 findest du eine Liste mit unregelmäßigen Verben.

Wenn du über zwei abgeschlossene Handlungen in der Vergangenheit sprechen möchtest, verwendest du für die weiter zurückliegende Handlung das *past perfect* und für die darauffolgende Handlung das *simple past*.

1. Handlung *(past perfect)*	2. Handlung *(simple past)*
After the formal dinner **had ended**,	the party **continued** with the traditional dance.
Once the cheerleaders **had finished** their dance,	there **was** a fantastic football game.

Die Verneinung bildest du mit *had not* + Partizip Perfekt *(past participle)* bzw. mit der Kurzform *hadn't* + Partizip Perfekt *(past participle)*.

Eric **hadn't expected** to win the prize.

b) Fragen im *past perfect*

Entscheidungsfragen im *past perfect* bildest du, indem du *had* an den Satzanfang stellst. In der Kurzantwort wird *had* wieder aufgegriffen.

Had Katie **trained** intensively? – Yes, she **had**. / No, she **hadn't**.

Bei Fragen mit Fragewort steht das Fragewort am Satzanfang.

How many books **had** Eric **read**?

7 CONDITIONAL CLAUSES TYPE 1 (REVISION)
Bedingungssätze Typ 1 *(revision)*

Mit Bedingungssätzen kannst du sagen, was unter bestimmten Bedingungen passieren wird bzw. passieren kann.

Ein Bedingungssatz besteht aus einem *if*-Satz und einem Hauptsatz. Der *if*-Satz nennt eine Bedingung. Der Hauptsatz drückt aus, was passiert, wenn die Bedingung erfüllt ist.
Im *if*-Satz vom Typ 1 steht das *simple present*, im Hauptsatz meist das *will-future*.

 DIGITAL+ video 23

if-Satz (Bedingung: Wenn …)	Hauptsatz (Folge: … dann …)
If you **miss** the bus,	you **will be** late.
If it **rains**,	the children **won't go** outside.

Bedingungssätze können entweder mit dem *if*-Satz oder mit dem Hauptsatz beginnen.
Wenn sie mit dem *if*-Satz beginnen, werden sie mit einem Komma getrennt.
Wenn sie mit dem Hauptsatz beginnen, verwendest du kein Komma.

If you go to the concert, I'll come with you.
I'll come with you if you go to the concert.

Im Hauptsatz kannst du auch Modalverben (z. B. *can, must, should, could*) oder den Imperativ verwenden.

*If you want, we **can go** to the concert together.*
*If you like acting, you **could join** the drama club.*
*If you have any questions, **ask** the teacher.*

8 REFLEXIVE PRONOUNS
Reflexivpronomen

Du verwendest Reflexivpronomen, wenn das Subjekt und das Objekt in einem Satz dieselbe Person bezeichnen.

Lucy was very proud of herself.

Reflexivpronomen beziehen sich auf das Subjekt in einem Satz.

*I enjoyed **myself** at the party.*

*My friends enjoyed **themselves**, too.*

*Ben was really proud of **himself**.*

Personalpronomen	Reflexivpronomen
I	myself
you	yourself
he	himself
she	herself
it	itself
we	ourselves
you	yourselves
they	themselves

Nicht immer sind Verben, die im Deutschen reflexiv sind, auch im Englischen reflexiv.

I can't concentrate. – Ich kann mich nicht konzentrieren. (*concentrate* = sich konzentrieren)
The friends met at school. – Die Freunde trafen sich in der Schule. (*meet* = sich treffen)

Im Englischen werden Reflexivpronomen auch benutzt, um ein Nomen oder Pronomen besonders zu betonen. Sie bedeuten dann im Deutschen „selbst" oder „selber".

*I can't repair this **myself**.* – Ich kann das nicht selber reparieren.
*You said that **yourself**.* – Du hast das selbst gesagt.

9 REPORTED SPEECH 2
Indirekte Rede 2

*... and then he told me that he **liked** me and that he **would call** me next weekend.*

Wenn du berichten willst, was jemand sagt oder gesagt hat, verwendest du indirekte Rede *(reported speech)*.

Indirekte Rede besteht aus einem Begleitsatz und der wiedergegebenen Aussage. Beide Satzteile können durch *that* verbunden werden.
Wenn im Begleitsatz das Verb in der Gegenwart steht, ändert sich die Zeitform in der wiedergegebenen Aussage nicht.

DIGITAL+ video 24

	Begleitsatz	wiedergegebene Aussage
Emily: "Chloe **is** angry with me."	Emily **says** (that)	Chloe **is** angry with her.

Oft steht jedoch das Verb im Begleitsatz in der Vergangenheit. Dann musst du die Zeitform in der wiedergegebenen Aussage anpassen. Sie rückt dann sozusagen eine Stufe weiter in die Vergangenheit (Zeitverschiebung = *backshift of tenses*).

	Begleitsatz	wiedergegebene Aussage
Tom: "Most of my classmates **seem** OK."	Tom **told** me (that)	most of his classmates **seemed** OK.
Tom: "The first week **was** really boring."	Tom **mentioned** (that)	the first week **had been** really boring.
Tom: "I **haven't made** any new friends yet."	Tom **told** me (that)	he **hadn't made** any new friends yet.
Linh: "Ruby and Anne **aren't talking** to each other."	Linh **said** (that)	Ruby and Anne **weren't talking** to each other.

Denke daran, Bezugswörter, die nur aus dem Zusammenhang richtig zu verstehen sind, wenn nötig in der wiedergegebenen Aussage anzupassen, wie z.B. Personalpronomen, Zeit- und Ortsangaben.

*Tom: "**I** will call **you** again **tomorrow**." → Tom told Lucia that **he** would call **her** again **the next day**.*

Aus diesen Tabellen kannst du ablesen, wie sich die Zeiten sowie Zeit- und Ortsangaben verändern.

Direkte Rede		Indirekte Rede
simple present	→	simple past
simple past	→	past perfect
present perfect	→	past perfect
present progressive	→	past progressive
will	→	would
can	→	could
should	→	should

Direkte Rede		Indirekte Rede
today	→	that day
this morning	→	that morning
yesterday	→	the day before
last week	→	the week before
tomorrow	→	the next day
next Friday	→	the following Friday
here	→	there

10 ADVERBS OF MANNER (REVISION)
Adverbien der Art und Weise *(revision)*

Lily is dancing **happily**.

Wenn du beschreiben möchtest, wie jemand etwas tut oder wie etwas geschieht, kannst du Adverbien der Art und Weise benutzen.

Adverbien der Art und Weise beziehen sich auf Verben und beschreiben, wie jemand etwas tut oder wie etwas geschieht. Diese Adverbien beschreiben also Tätigkeiten.

 DIGITAL+ video 25

Adjektiv: *Lily is **happy**.* **Adverb:** *Lily is dancing **happily**.*

Ein Adverb der Art und Weise bildest du, indem du an das Adjektiv die Endung *-ly* anhängst.

Adjektiv	Adverb
loud	loud**ly**
bad	bad**ly**
slow	slow**ly**

Manchmal ändert sich die Schreibweise, wenn *-ly* angehängt wird:
-y wird zu *-ily*
-le wird zu *-ly*
-l wird zu *-lly*.
-ic wird zu *-ically*

Adjektiv	Adverb
easy	eas**ily**
terrible	terrib**ly**
beautiful	beautifu**lly**
fantastic	fantast**ically**

Einige Adverbien haben Sonderformen, die du wie Vokabeln lernen musst. Manche Adjektive und Adverbien haben die gleiche Form (z. B. *fast* und *hard*)

Adjektiv	Adverb
good	**well**
fast	**fast**
hard	**hard**

Vorsicht: Nach einigen Verben der Sinneswahrnehmung (z. B. *look, taste, smell* und *feel*) verwendet man kein Adverb, sondern ein Adjektiv.

*This website **looks interesting**.*
*The cake **tastes delicious**.*
*The fish doesn't **smell good**.*
*I **feel great**.*

11 THE COMPARISON OF ADVERBS
Die Steigerung von Adverbien

The girl in the middle can run faster than the other girls.

Auch Adverbien, die beschreiben, wie jemand etwas tut, kann man steigern. Hier gelten die gleichen Regeln wie bei der Steigerung von Adjektiven.

a) Formen

Einsilbige Adverbien (z. B. *fast* und *hard*) werden durch das Anhängen von *-er* und *-est* gesteigert.

*Liam can text **faster** than anyone else.*
*He texts **the fastest**.*
*Olivia trains **harder** than her friends.*
*Olivia trains **the hardest**.*

	Komparativ	Superlativ
fast	fast**er**	(the) fast**est**
hard	hard**er**	(the) hard**est**

Es gibt auch unregelmäßige Steigerungsformen, die du wie Vokabeln lernen musst.

*Tony skates **better** than all the others.*
*He skates **the best**.*

	Komparativ	Superlativ
well	better	(the) best
badly	worse	(the) worst
much	more	(the) most

Zwei- und mehrsilbige Adverbien, die auf *-ly* enden, steigerst du mit *more* und *most*.

*Janet talks **more quickly** than Liz.*
*Emily talks **the most quickly**.*

	Komparativ	Superlativ
slowly	**more** slowly	(the) **most** slowly
quickly	**more** quickly	(the) **most** quickly
loudly	**more** loudly	(the) **most** loudly
happily	**more** happily	(the) **most** happily
beautifully	**more** beautifully	(the) **most** beautifully

b) Vergleichssätze

Vergleichssätze bildest du wie bei den Adjektiven mit *than* oder mit *as ... as*:

*Ann sings more beautifully **than** Janet.*
*Jason sings **as** beautifully **as** Ann.*

12 CONDITIONAL CLAUSES TYPE 2
Bedingungssätze Typ 2

Bedingungssätze können realistische oder unrealistische Bedingungen nennen. Ist eine Bedingung erfüllbar, verwendet man den Bedingungssatz Typ 1 (siehe auch Grammatik-Kapitel 7 auf Seite 180).

*If I **study** hard, maybe I **will win** a scholarship.*

Ist eine Bedingung jedoch unwahrscheinlich oder unmöglich, verwendet man den Bedingungssatz Typ 2.

*If I **had** a billion dollars, I **would support** students all over the world.*

Da die Person das Geld nicht hat, ist die Bedingung nicht erfüllbar.

Bei dieser zweiten Art von Bedingungssätzen steht der *if*-Satz im *simple past*. Im Hauptsatz steht *would* (oder *could*) mit einem Hauptverb im Infinitiv.

if-Satz *(simple past)* (Bedingung: Wenn …)	Hauptsatz *(would/could + infinitive)* (Folge: … dann …)
If Robert's family **wasn't** so supportive,	it **would be** more difficult for him.
If politicians **listened** more to young people,	maybe things **would change** more quickly.
If I **had** more time,	I **could train** even more.

Übrigens: Statt "*If I was …*" wird oft "*If I were …*" gebraucht. Beide Formen sind hier richtig.
*If I **were** still in Honduras, things would be more difficult.* Oder:
*If I **was** still in Honduras, things would be more difficult.*

Bedingungssätze können entweder mit dem *if*-Satz oder mit dem Hauptsatz beginnen. Wenn sie mit dem *if*-Satz beginnen, werden sie mit einem Komma getrennt. Wenn sie mit dem Hauptsatz beginnen, verwendest du kein Komma.

*Things would be more difficult **if I was** still in Honduras.*

13 MODAL VERBS (REVISION)
Modalverben *(revision)*

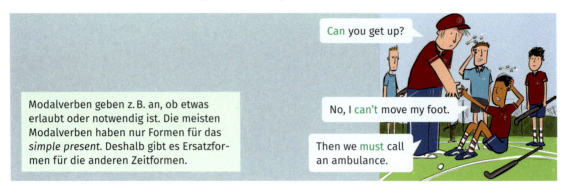

Modalverben geben z. B. an, ob etwas erlaubt oder notwendig ist. Die meisten Modalverben haben nur Formen für das *simple present*. Deshalb gibt es Ersatzformen für die anderen Zeitformen.

a) Fähigkeit: *can / be able to*

Wenn du sagen willst, dass jemand fähig ist, etwas zu tun, verwendest du *can* und die Ersatzform *be able to*. Im *simple past* kannst du auch *could* benutzen.

*John **can** cut down trees.* *John **could / was able to** stop a fire yesterday.*
*Tamara **will be able to** offer more surf courses in the future.*

DIGITAL+ video 27

b) Erlaubnis: *can, may / be allowed to*

Mit *can*, *may* und der Ersatzform *be allowed to* kannst du ausdrücken, dass etwas erlaubt ist.

***May** I open the window?* ***Can** I open the window?*
*Cody hopes that one day he **will be allowed to** present his designs in a fashion show.*

c) Verbot: *may not / can't / mustn't / not be allowed to*

Mit *may not*, *can't*, *mustn't* und der Ersatzform *not be allowed to* kannst du ein Verbot ausdrücken. Achtung! *mustn't* klingt wie im Deutschen „muss nicht", heißt aber „darf nicht"!

*Damian **can't** prescribe medication. = Damian **isn't allowed to** prescribe medication.*
*The patient **won't be allowed to** do sports for three weeks. The patient **may not** do sports.*

d) Notwendigkeit: *must / have to*

Mit *must* und der Ersatzform *have to* kannst du ausdrücken, dass etwas getan werden muss.

*A surf instructor **must** know a lot about safety. = A surf instructor **has to** know a lot about safety.*
*I **had to** get a number of safety certifications.* *I **will have to** work hard.*

Mit *needn't* und der Ersatzform *don't have to* kannst du sagen, dass etwas nicht notwendig ist.
*You **needn't** say that again. = You **don't have to** say that again.*

e) Empfehlung: *should / shouldn't*

Mit *should / shouldn't* drückst du aus, was deiner Meinung nach (nicht) passieren sollte.

*You **should** study for the test.* *You **shouldn't** talk behind your friend's back.*

f) Möglichkeit: *may / may not*

Mit *may / may not* drückst du aus, was vielleicht passiert.

*It **may** rain today.* *He is not feeling well. He **may not** come to school today.*

14 CONDITIONAL CLAUSES TYPE 3 (OPTIONAL)
Bedingungssätze Typ 3 *(optional)*

If she **had left** the house earlier, she **would have caught** the bus.

Wenn du beschreiben möchtest, was in der Vergangenheit unter einer bestimmten Bedingung hätte passieren können, aber nicht passiert ist, benutzt du einen Bedingungssatz Typ 3.

Bedingungssätze Typ 1 und 2 kennst du bereits (s. Grammatik-Kapitel 7 auf Seite 180 und Grammatik-Kapitel 12 auf Seite 185).

 DIGITAL+ video 28

Bei der dritten Art von Bedingungssätzen ist die Bedingung im *if*-Satz nicht mehr erfüllbar. Der *if*-Satz steht hier im *past perfect*.
Im Hauptsatz steht *would* (oder *could*) + *have* + Partizip Perfekt *(past participle)*.

if-Satz *(past perfect)* (Bedingung: Wenn …)	Hauptsatz *(would/could + have + past participle)* (Folge: … dann …)
If Ella **hadn't missed** the bus,	she **would have been** on time.
If Ella **had prepared** well for the interview,	maybe she **would have got** the job.

Bedingungssätze können entweder mit dem *if*-Satz oder mit dem Hauptsatz beginnen.
Wenn sie mit dem *if*-Satz beginnen, werden sie mit einem Komma getrennt.
Wenn sie mit dem Hauptsatz beginnen, verwendest du kein Komma.

*She **would have been** on time **if** she **hadn't missed** the bus.*

15 REPORTED COMMANDS
Indirekte Befehlssätze

Mit einem indirekten Befehlssatz kannst du zum Beispiel einen Befehl, eine Bitte, eine Aufforderung oder eine Warnung wiedergeben.

My mum is asking me **to get** some bread from the shop.

Wenn du einen Befehlssatz in der indirekten Rede wiedergeben willst, benutzt du den Infinitiv mit *to*.

Befehlssatz (direkte Rede)	Indirekter Befehlssatz
Uncle Joe: "**Come** to the USA."	Mary: "Uncle Joe told us **to come** to the USA."
Mary's mother: "**Pack** your bag."	Mary: "My mother told me **to pack** my bag."

Um einen Befehl oder eine Aufforderung wiederzugeben, kannst du im indirekten Befehlssatz das Verb *tell* verwenden. Bitten kannst du mit *ask*, Warnungen mit *warn* und Ratschläge mit *advise* wiedergeben.

Wenn der Originalsatz negativ ist, steht im indirekten Befehlssatz *not* vor dem Infinitiv mit *to*:

Befehlssatz (direkte Rede)	Indirekter Befehlssatz
Uncle Joe: "**Don't wait** too long."	Mary: "Uncle Joe warned us **not to wait** too long."
Mary's mother: "Please **don't put** too many things into your bag."	Mary: "My mother asked me **not to put** too many things into my bag."

Denke auch daran, gegebenenfalls Bezugswörter, wie zum Beispiel Pronomen, anzupassen.

Befehlssatz (direkte Rede)	Indirekter Befehlssatz
Mary's mother: "Please give **me your** bag."	Mary: "My mother told me to give **her my** bag."
Officer: "Give **me your** documents, please."	Mary: "The officer told us to give **him our** documents."

16 THE PAST PROGRESSIVE (REVISION)
Die Verlaufsform der Vergangenheit *(revision)*

Mit dem *past progressive* kannst du ausdrücken, was zu einem bestimmten Zeitpunkt in der Vergangenheit gerade passierte.

At 5pm, the girls were setting up their tent.

a) Bejahte Aussagesätze im *past progressive*

Das *past progressive* bildest du mit was / were + ing-Form.

 DIGITAL+ video 29

*The people **were boarding** the ship. A child **was crying**.*

So kannst du beschreiben, was gerade vor sich ging, als plötzlich etwas anderes geschah:

past progressive	simple past
While the people **were leaving** the ship, Elizabeth **was trying** to fall asleep	it **started** to rain. when she suddenly **heard** a noise.

was gerade passierte: neues Ereignis:
past progressive   simple past

b) Verneinte Aussagesätze im *past progressive*

Für die Verneinung fügst du **not** hinter die Form von be (**was** bzw. **were**) ein bzw. verwendest die entsprechenden Kurzformen.

*Elizabeth **wasn't** sleeping. Her parents **weren't** sleeping either.*

c) Entscheidungsfragen und Kurzantworten im *past progressive*

Entscheidungsfragen im *past progressive* bildest du, indem du was bzw. were an den Satzanfang stellst. In der Kurzantwort wird was bzw. were aufgegriffen.

***Was** Elizabeth **sleeping**?* — *Yes, she **was**. / No, she **wasn't**.*
***Were** her parents **cooking** breakfast?* — *Yes, they **were**. / No, they **weren't**.*

d) Fragen mit Fragewort im *past progressive*

Bei Fragen mit Fragewörtern stellst du das Fragewort an den Satzanfang.

***What was** Elizabeth **doing**?*
***Who was riding** the horse?*
***Where were** the people **going**?*

17 THE PRESENT PERFECT PROGRESSIVE: STATEMENTS
Die Verlaufsform des Perfekts: Aussagen

Das *present perfect progressive* verwendest du, wenn du über etwas sprechen möchtest, das in der Vergangenheit begonnen hat und immer noch andauert.

She **has been sleeping** for an hour.

a) Bejahte Aussagesätze im *present perfect progressive*

DIGITAL+ video 30

Das *present perfect progressive* bildest du mit *have / has + been + ing*-Form. Statt *have* bzw. *has* kannst du auch die entsprechende Kurzform benutzen.

I **have been doing** homework for hours.
We**'ve been listening** to the concert all evening.
Liam **has been playing** football all day.
Anna**'s been working** for the same company since she moved to Sligo.

b) Verneinte Aussagesätze im *present perfect progressive*

Bei Verneinungen fügst du *not* hinter *have* oder *has* ein bzw. verwendest die entsprechenden Kurzformen.

I **haven't been working** for long.
He **hasn't been practising** the guitar for a long time.

c) Die Zeitangaben *since* und *for*

Sätze im *present perfect progressive* enthalten oft eine Zeitangabe mit *since* oder *for*.

Since verwendest du, wenn es um einen genauen Zeitpunkt, an dem etwas begonnen hat, geht, wie z. B. *since 2021, since ten o'clock, since I was six years old*.
Dabei muss diese Tätigkeit nicht durchgängig stattgefunden haben.

*Declan has been playing the fiddle **since he was a child***.

Bei einem Zeitraum benutzt du *for*, z. B. *for six months, for ten years, for a long time*.

*Declan has been playing the fiddle **for many years***.

18 THE PRESENT PERFECT PROGRESSIVE: QUESTIONS
Die Verlaufsform des Perfekts: Fragen

a) Entscheidungsfragen im *present perfect progressive*

Entscheidungsfragen im *present perfect progressive* bildest du, indem du *have* bzw. *has* an den Satzanfang stellst.
Have bzw. *has* wird in den Kurzantworten aufgegriffen.

Entscheidungsfrage	Kurzantwort	Kurzantwort
Have you been waiting for a long time?	Yes, I have.	No, I haven't.
Has Patrick been travelling a lot during the last weeks?	Yes, he has.	No, he hasn't.
Have the children been playing all day?	Yes, they have.	No, they haven't.

b) Fragen mit Fragewort im *present perfect progressive*

Bei Fragen mit Fragewort steht das Fragewort am Satzanfang.

What have you been doing all day?
How long has Anna been living in Ireland?

| Skills | Wordbanks | Grammar | **Words** |

Nach Vokabeln suchen

Alphabetische Wortliste *(Dictionary)*: Du suchst nach der Bedeutung eines einzelnen englischen Wortes, das im Textbook vorgekommen ist? Dann nutze die alphabetische Wortliste ab Seite 231. Hier findest du auch die Wörter aus den Projekten, aus den *Wordbanks* und von den *Get together*-Seiten. Einige englische Wörter, die im Englischen und im Deutschen gleich sind, findest du auf Seite 194.

Wortlisten nach Kapiteln *(Vocabulary)*: Du möchtest die Vokabeln zu einem ganzen Abschnitt im Buch lernen? Dann nutze die chronologische Wortliste ab Seite 195. Nach Kapiteln und Seitenzahlen sortiert findest du hier alle Wörter, die neu im Buch vorkommen.

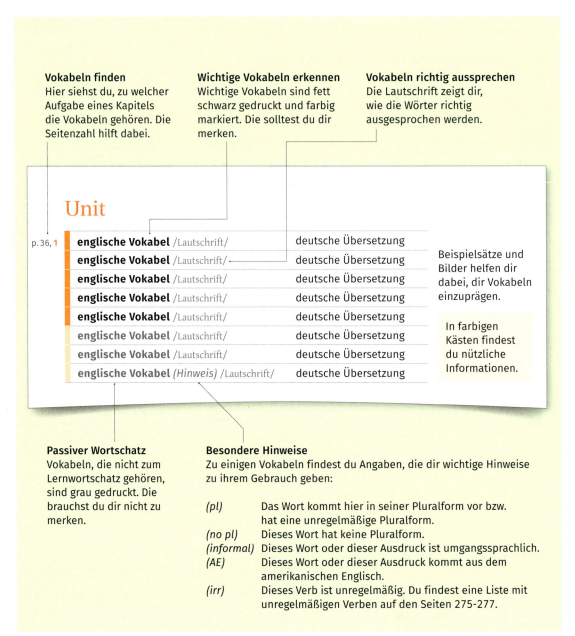

Vokabeln finden
Hier siehst du, zu welcher Aufgabe eines Kapitels die Vokabeln gehören. Die Seitenzahl hilft dabei.

Wichtige Vokabeln erkennen
Wichtige Vokabeln sind fett schwarz gedruckt und farbig markiert. Die solltest du dir merken.

Vokabeln richtig aussprechen
Die Lautschrift zeigt dir, wie die Wörter richtig ausgesprochen werden.

Beispielsätze und Bilder helfen dir dabei, dir Vokabeln einzuprägen.

In farbigen Kästen findest du nützliche Informationen.

Passiver Wortschatz
Vokabeln, die nicht zum Lernwortschatz gehören, sind grau gedruckt. Die brauchst du dir nicht zu merken.

Besondere Hinweise
Zu einigen Vokabeln findest du Angaben, die dir wichtige Hinweise zu ihrem Gebrauch geben:

(pl)	Das Wort kommt hier in seiner Pluralform vor bzw. hat eine unregelmäßige Pluralform.
(no pl)	Dieses Wort hat keine Pluralform.
(informal)	Dieses Wort oder dieser Ausdruck ist umgangssprachlich.
(AE)	Dieses Wort oder dieser Ausdruck kommt aus dem amerikanischen Englisch.
(irr)	Dieses Verb ist unregelmäßig. Du findest eine Liste mit unregelmäßigen Verben auf den Seiten 275-277.

Introduction

Die richtige Aussprache

Im Englischen spricht man Wörter oft anders aus als man sie schreibt.
Die Aussprache der Wörter wird mithilfe der Lautschrift in jedem Wörterbuch angegeben.
Man kann so auch neue Wörter richtig aussprechen, ohne sie vorher gehört zu haben.
Die Lautschrift ist eine Schrift, deren Symbole jeden Laut genau bezeichnen.
Hier ist eine Liste mit den Symbolen dieser Lautschrift zusammen mit Beispielwörtern.

The English alphabet

a	/eɪ/
b	/biː/
c	/siː/
d	/diː/
e	/iː/
f	/ef/
g	/dʒiː/
h	/eɪtʃ/
i	/aɪ/
j	/dʒeɪ/
k	/keɪ/
l	/el/
m	/em/
n	/en/
o	/əʊ/
p	/piː/
q	/kjuː/
r	/ɑː/
s	/es/
t	/tiː/
u	/juː/
v	/viː/
w	/ˈdʌbljuː/
x	/eks/
y	/waɪ/
z	/zed/

English sounds

Vokale

/ɑː/	**arm**
/ʌ/	b**u**t
/e/	d**e**sk
/ə/	**a, an**
/ɜː/	g**ir**l, b**ir**d
/æ/	**a**pple
/ɪ/	**i**n, **i**t
/i/	happ**y**
/iː/	**ea**sy, **ea**t
/ɒ/	**o**range, s**o**rry
/ɔː/	**all**, c**all**
/ʊ/	l**oo**k
/u/	Jan**u**ary
/uː/	b**oo**t

Doppellaute

/aɪ/	**eye**, b**y**, b**uy**
/aʊ/	**our**
/eə/	**air**, th**ere**
/eɪ/	t**a**ke, th**ey**
/ɪə/	h**ere**
/ɔɪ/	b**oy**
/əʊ/	g**o**, **o**ld
/ʊə/	t**our**

Konsonanten

/b/	**b**ag, clu**b**
/d/	**d**uck, car**d**
/f/	**f**ish, laug**h**
/g/	**g**et, do**g**
/h/	**h**ot
/j/	**y**ou
/k/	**c**an, du**ck**
/l/	**l**ot, smal**l**
/m/	**m**ore, **m**u**m**
/n/	**n**ow, su**n**
/ŋ/	so**ng**, lo**ng**
/p/	**p**resent, to**p**
/r/	**r**ed, a**r**ound
/s/	**s**ister, cla**ss** (stimmlos)
/z/	no**s**e, dog**s** (stimmhaft)
/t/	**t**ime, ca**t**
/ʒ/	televi**s**ion
/dʒ/	**s**au**s**age
/ʃ/	fre**sh**
/tʃ/	**ch**ild, **ch**eese
/ð/	**th**ese, mo**th**er (stimmhaft)
/θ/	ba**th**room, **th**ink (stimmlos)
/v/	**v**ery, ha**v**e
/w/	**w**hat, **w**ord

Betonungszeichen für die folgende Silbe

/ˈ/	**Hauptbetonung**
/ˌ/	**Nebenbetonung**

| Skills | Wordbanks | Grammar | **Words** |

Bekannte Wörter

Viele Wörter sind im Englischen und im Deutschen so gut wie gleich. Manche unterscheiden sich nur durch die Groß- bzw. Kleinschreibung – im Englischen werden die meisten Nomen kleingeschrieben. Viele dieser Wörter, die in deinem Buch vorkommen, findest du hier. Bei denen, die anders ausgesprochen werden als im Deutschen, ist die Lautschrift farbig hervorgehoben.

action /'ækʃn/
adverb /'ædvɜːb/
alligator /'ælɪˌgeɪtə/
animation /ˌænɪ'meɪʃn/
anorak /'ænəræk/
anti- /'ænti/
app /æp/
arm /ɑːm/
audio /'ɔːdiəʊ/
baby /'beɪbi/
babysitting /'beɪbiˌsɪtɪŋ/
ball /bɔːl/
band /bænd/
bar /bɑː/
baseball /'beɪsˌbɔːl/
basketball /'bɑːskɪtˌbɔːl/
bistro /'biːstrəʊ/
block /blɒk/
blog /blɒg/
boom /buːm/
boss /bɒs/
bowling /'bəʊlɪŋ/
bronze /brɒnz/
burger /'bɜːgə/
bus /bʌs/
café /'kæfeɪ/
cafeteria /ˌkæfə'tɪəriə/
camping /'kæmpɪŋ/
car sharing /'kɑː ˌʃeərɪŋ/
cartoon /kɑː'tuːn/
cello /'tʃeləʊ/
champion /'tʃæmpjən/
chance /tʃɑːns/
chat /tʃæt/
cheerleader /'tʃɪəˌliːdə/
cheerleading /'tʃɪəˌliːdɪŋ/
clever /'klevə/
clip /klɪp/
coach /kəʊtʃ/
collage /'kɒlɑːʒ/
computer /kəm'pjuːtə/
cool /kuːl/
deadline /'dedˌlaɪn/
deck /dek/
demonstration /ˌdemən'streɪʃn/
designer /dɪ'zaɪnə/
digital /'dɪdʒɪtl/
DJ /'diːˌdʒeɪ/
DNA /ˌdiːˌen'eɪ/
dollar /'dɒlə/

drama /'drɑːmə/
element /'elɪmənt/
email /'iːmeɪl/
emoji /ɪ'məʊdʒi/
engagement /ɪn'geɪdʒmənt/
ensemble /ɒn'sɒmbl/
episode /'epɪsəʊd/
etc. (= et cetera) /et 'setrə/
euro /'jʊərəʊ/
fair /feə/
fan /fæn/
film /fɪlm/
finger /'fɪŋgə/
fit /fɪt/
flyer /'flaɪə/
food truck /'fuːd ˌtrʌk/
form /fɔːm/
gaming /'geɪmɪŋ/
gang /gæŋ/
generation /ˌdʒenə'reɪʃn/
glamour /'glæmə/
global /'gləʊbl/
gold /gəʊld/
hacker /'hækə/
hamburger /'hæmˌbɜːgə/
hand /hænd/
high five /ˌhaɪ 'faɪv/
hip-hop /'hɪp hɒp/
hobby /'hɒbi/
hot dog /ˌhɒt 'dɒg/
hotel /həʊ'tel/
hunger /'hʌŋgə/
icon /'aɪkɒn/
ideal /aɪ'dɪəl/
illegal, legal /ɪ'liːgl, 'liːgl/
info /'ɪnfəʊ/
instrument /'ɪnstrʊmənt/
international /ˌɪntə'næʃnəl/
Internet /'ɪntəˌnet/
interpretation /ɪnˌtɜːprɪ'teɪʃn/
interview /'ɪntəˌvjuː/
IT /ˌaɪ 'tiː/
jazz /dʒæz/
jeans /dʒiːnz/
Jr. (= junior) /'dʒuːniə/
lacrosse /lə'krɒs/
land /lænd/
laptop /'læpˌtɒp/
layout /'leɪaʊt/
live /laɪv/

make-up /'meɪkˌʌp/
mama /'mæmə/
manager /'mænɪdʒə/
marketing /'mɑːkɪtɪŋ/
mast /mɑːst/
material /mə'tɪəriəl/
meme /miːm/
mild /maɪld/
million /'mɪljən/
mini (golf) /'mɪni gɒlf/
minute /'mɪnɪt/
modern /'mɒdən/
moment /'məʊmənt/
motto /'mɒtəʊ/
multiple-choice /ˌmʌltɪpl 'tʃɔɪs/
museum /mjuː'ziːəm/
musical /'mjuːzɪkl/
name /neɪm/
national /'næʃnəl/
nest /nest/
normal /'nɔːml/
offline /ˌɒf'laɪn/
OK, okay /ˌəʊ'keɪ/
online /'ɒnlaɪn/
outfit /'aʊtfɪt/
parade /pə'reɪd/
park /pɑːk/
partner /'pɑːtnə/
party /'pɑːti/
patient /'peɪʃnt/
person /'pɜːsn/
pier /pɪə/
pilot /'paɪlət/
pizza /'piːtsə/
plan /plæn/
planet /'plænɪt/
podcast /'pɒdˌkɑːst/
pogrom /'pɒgrəm/
pool /puːl/
pop /pɒp/
popcorn /'pɒpkɔːn/
post, poster /pəʊst, 'pəʊstə/
problem /'prɒbləm/
professor /prə'fesə/
quiz /kwɪz/
radar /'reɪdɑː/
radio /'reɪdiəʊ/
rap /ræp/
recycling /ˌriː'saɪklɪŋ/
reform /rɪ'fɔːm/

region(al) /'riːdʒn, 'riːdʒnəl/
reporter /rɪ'pɔːtə/
rest /rest/
restaurant /'restrɒnt/
revolution /ˌrevə'luːʃn/
routine /ruː'tiːn/
rugby /'rʌgbi/
sandwich /'sænwɪdʒ/
semester /sə'mestə/
service /'sɜːvɪs/
show /ʃəʊ/
sightseeing /'saɪtˌsiːɪŋ/
signal /'sɪgnl/
simulation /ˌsɪmjʊ'leɪʃn/
situation /ˌsɪtʃu'eɪʃn/
skyline /'skaɪlaɪn/
slogan /'sləʊgən/
smartphone /'smɑːtˌfəʊn/
so /səʊ/
software /'sɒfˌweə/
standard /'stændəd/
statue /'stætʃuː/
stunt /stʌnt/
super /'suːpə/
symbol /'sɪmbl/
system /'sɪstəm/
talent /'tælənt/
team(work) /tiːm, 'tiːmˌwɜːk/
teen(ager) /tiːn, 'tiːnˌeɪdʒə/
terrorist /'terərɪst/
test /test/
text, texting /tekst, 'tekstɪŋ/
ticket /'tɪkɪt/
toast /təʊst/
tornado /tɔː'neɪdəʊ/
tour, tourist /tʊə, 'tʊərɪst/
tradition /trə'dɪʃn/
training /'treɪnɪŋ/
trend /trend/
tuba /'tjuːbə/
tutorial /tjuː'tɔːriəl/
uniform /'juːnɪfɔːm/
verb /vɜːb/
video (call) /'vɪdiəʊ (kɔːl)/
vlog /vlɒg/
webcode /'webˌkəʊd/
website /'webˌsaɪt/
winter /'wɪntə/
workshop /'wɜːkˌʃɒp/
zone /zəʊn/
zoo /zuː/

Vocabulary

Quiz

p. 6	**state** /steɪt/	(der) Staat, (der) Bundesstaat	The **capital** is the most important city of a **state**.
	capital /ˈkæpɪtl/	(die) Hauptstadt	
	president /ˈprezɪdənt/	(der/die) Präsident/in	
	billion /ˈbɪljən/	(die) Milliarde	You can win an **award** for doing something great.
	award /əˈwɔːd/	(der) Preis, (die) Auszeichnung	
	America /əˈmerɪkə/	Amerika	
	(the) US (= the United States) /ðə ˌjuː_ˈes, ðə juːˌnaɪtɪd ˈsteɪts/	US, die Vereinigten Staaten (von Amerika); US-	
	(to) fight *(irr)* /faɪt/	kämpfen	
	equal /ˈiːkwəl/	gleich	**equal** = the same
	US-American /ˌjuː_ˌes_əˈmerɪkən/	(der/die) US-Amerikaner/in; US-amerikanisch	
	(to) make *(irr)* /meɪk/	*hier:* ergeben	
	the Oscars /ðiˈɒskəz/	*amerikanischer Filmpreis*	
	Thanksgiving /ˈθæŋksˌgɪvɪŋ/	Thanksgiving *(amerikanisches Erntedankfest)*	
	Independence Day /ˌɪndɪˈpendəns deɪ/	(der) Unabhängigkeitstag	
	Pancake Day /ˈpænkeɪk deɪ/	(der) Pfannkuchentag	
	the Statue of Liberty /ðə ˌstætʃuː_əv ˈlɪbəti/	(die) Freiheitsstatue	
	the very first /ðə ˌveri ˈfɜːst/	der/die/das allererste	**the Statue of Liberty**
	Antarctica /ænˈtɑːktɪkə/	(die) Antarktis	
	Asia /ˈeɪʒə/	Asien	
	Australia /ɒˈstreɪliə/	Australien	
	Olympic /əˈlɪmpɪk/	olympisch	
	medal /ˈmedl/	(die) Medaille	People who come from Europe are known as **Europeans**.
p. 7	**European** /ˌjʊərəˈpiːən/	(der/die) Europäer/in; europäisch	
	(to) shout /ʃaʊt/	rufen, schreien	
	Spanish /ˈspænɪʃ/	(das) Spanisch	
	moccasin /ˈmɒkəsɪn/	(der) Mokassin	
	kayak /ˈkaɪæk/	(der) Kajak	
	indigenous /ɪnˈdɪdʒənəs/	(ein)heimisch, indigen	
	Asian /ˈeɪʒn/	(der/die) Asiat/in; asiatisch	
	stadium *(pl stadiums or stadia)* /ˈsteɪdiəm, ˈsteɪdiəmz, ˈsteɪdiə/	(das) Stadion	
	(to) originate /əˈrɪdʒəneɪt/	entstehen, seinen Anfang nehmen	
	Super Bowl /ˈsuːpə bəʊl/	*(das) Finale der US-amerikanischen American Football-Profiliga*	
p. 8	**landscape** /ˈlænˌskeɪp/	(die) Landschaft	A **desert** is a large area of dry land. There are not many plants in a desert.
	desert /ˈdezət/	(die) Wüste	
	ride /raɪd/	(die) Fahrt	
	surfing /ˈsɜːfɪŋ/	(das) Surfen	
	dog sled /ˈdɒg sled/	(der) Hundeschlitten	
	farmland /ˈfɑːmˌlænd/	(das) Ackerland	

Unit 1 | Part A Impressions of the USA

p. 9	**impression** /ɪmˈpreʃn/	(der) Eindruck	
	travel guide /ˈtrævl ɡaɪd/	(der) Reiseführer *(Buch)*	**travel guide**
p. 10, 2	**east** /iːst/	(der) Osten	
	west /west/	(der) Westen	**west**

	wide /waɪd/	groß, breit, enorm
	variety /vəˈraɪəti/	(die) Vielfalt, (die) Auswahl
	climate /ˈklaɪmət/	(das) Klima
	island /ˈaɪlənd/	(die) Insel
	snow /snəʊ/	(der) Schnee
	innovation /ˌɪnəʊˈveɪʃn/	(die) Neuerung
	factory /ˈfæktri/	(die) Fabrik

A **factory** is a place where things are produced, mostly by machines.

	thus /ðʌs/	folglich; so, auf diese Weise
	(to) **extend** /ɪkˈstend/	sich erstrecken
	man (*pl* **men**) /mæn, men/	(der) Mensch
	(to) **contribute** /kənˈtrɪbjuːt/	beitragen
	(to) **develop** /dɪˈveləp/	erarbeiten, (sich) entwickeln
	artificial intelligence (= **AI**) /ˌɑːtɪˌfɪʃl ɪnˈtelɪdʒns, ˌeɪ ˈaɪ/	(die) künstliche Intelligenz

„Man" in der Bedeutung „Mensch" wird meist in der Literatur verwendet und gilt heute als veraltet. In der Bedeutung „Menschheit" hat es keine Pluralform.

	spotlight /ˈspɒtˌlaɪt/	(der) Scheinwerfer
	North America /ˌnɔːθ əˈmerɪkə/	Nordamerika
	area /ˈeəriə/	(die) Fläche
	square /ˈskweə/	quadratisch, Quadrat-
	noon /nuːn/	(der) Mittag
	eastern /ˈiːstən/	östlich, Ost-
	tropical /ˈtrɒpɪkl/	tropisch
	stretch /stretʃ/	*hier:* (der) Abschnitt
	California /ˌkæləˈfɔːniə/	Kalifornien
	peak /piːk/	(der) Gipfel, (die) Bergspitze
	all year round /ˌɔːl ˈjɪə raʊnd/	das ganze Jahr lang
	(to) **install** /ɪnˈstɔːl/	aufstellen, installieren
	assembly line /əˈsembli laɪn/	(das) Fließband
	significantly /sɪɡˈnɪfɪkəntli/	deutlich
	affordable /əˈfɔːdəbl/	erschwinglich
	outer space /ˌaʊtə ˈspeɪs/	(der) Weltraum

square kilometre (= km²) /ˌskweə ˈkɪləˌmiːtə/ (der) Quadratkilometer
square mile /ˌskweə ˈmaɪl/ (die) Quadratmeile

Astronauts often fly in **outer space**.

	(to) **set foot on** *(irr)* /ˌset ˈfʊt ɒn/	betreten
	groundbreaking /ˈɡraʊnˌbreɪkɪŋ/	bahnbrechend, wegweisend
	information technology (= IT) /ˌɪnfəˌmeɪʃn tekˈnɒlədʒi, ˌaɪ ˈtiː/	(die) Informationstechnologie, (die) IT
p. 11, 2	(to) **establish** /ɪˈstæblɪʃ/	gründen, einführen
	politician /ˌpɒləˈtɪʃn/	(der/die) Politiker/in
	(to) **preserve** /prɪˈzɜːv/	erhalten

A **politician** is someone whose job it is to work in politics, for example as a member of a parliament or in a local government.

Vocabulary

natural /ˈnætʃrəl/	natürlich	
beauty /ˈbjuːti/	(die) Schönheit	**diverse** = very different from something
diverse /daɪˈvɜːs/	vielfältig, unterschiedlich	
ecosystem /ˈiːkəʊˌsɪstəm/	(das) Ökosystem	
(to) **provide** /prəˈvaɪd/	zur Verfügung stellen	to **provide** = to give
(to) **influence** /ˈɪnfluəns/	beeinflussen	
(to) **put emphasis on** (irr) /ˌpʊt ˈemfəsɪs ɒn/	Wert legen auf	Part of a **director**'s job is to tell the actors and actresses in a film what to do.
director /dəˈrektə/	(der/die) Regisseur/in	
whose /huːz/	dessen, deren	
bill /bɪl/	(der) Gesetzentwurf, (die) Gesetzesvorlage	
geological /ˌdʒiːəˈlɒdʒɪkl/	geologisch	Vor einem Hauptwort schreibt man Adjektive, die aus zwei Wörtern bestehen, **mit** Bindestrich! She is a **well-known** author. Wenn dieses Adjektiv hinter dem Bezugswort steht, verwendet man **keinen** Bindestrich. Her books are **well known**.
wonder /ˈwʌndə/	(das) Wunder	
wetlands (pl) /ˈwetlændz/	(das) Sumpfgebiet	
eating habit /ˈiːtɪŋ ˌhæbɪt/	(die) Essgewohnheit	
organic /ɔːˈɡænɪk/	aus biologischem Anbau, Bio-	
eating /ˈiːtɪŋ/	(das) Essen	
(to) be well known (irr) /ˌbiː ˌwelˈnəʊn/	allgemein bekannt sein	
(to) inspire /ɪnˈspaɪə/	inspirieren	
country music /ˈkʌntri ˌmjuːzɪk/	(die) Countrymusik	
(to) evolve /ɪˈvɒlv/	sich entwickeln	
hotspot /ˈhɒtˌspɒt/	(der) angesagte Ort	
genre /ˈʒɒnrə/	(das) Genre, (die) Gattung	
youth culture /ˈjuːθ ˌkʌltʃə/	(die) Jugendkultur	
birthplace /ˈbɜːθˌpleɪs/	(der) Geburtsort	
p. 12, 3 — greetings (pl) /ˈɡriːtɪŋz/	Grüße	
p. 12, 4 — (to) unscramble /ʌnˈskræmbl/	ordnen, in die richtige Reihenfolge bringen	
p. 13, 6 — **destination** /ˌdestɪˈneɪʃn/	(das) Ziel, (das) Reiseziel	
trip /trɪp/	(die) Reise	
ultimate /ˈʌltɪmət/	höchste(r, s); stärkste(r, s)	
foot (pl **feet**) /fʊt, fiːt/	Fuß (Maßeinheit, 1 Fuß = 0,3048 Meter)	The glass is dangerously close to the **edge** of the table.
edge /edʒ/	(der) Rand	
(to) **experience** /ɪkˈspɪəriəns/	erleben, kennenlernen	
era /ˈɪərə/	(die) Epoche, (das) Zeitalter	
Civil War /ˌsɪvl ˈwɔː/	(der) Bürgerkrieg	
local /ˈləʊkl/	örtlich, hiesig	
independence /ˌɪndɪˈpendəns/	(die) Unabhängigkeit	
hall /hɔːl/	(die) Halle	A **hall** is a very large room.
breathtaking /ˈbreθˌteɪkɪŋ/	atemberaubend	
endless /ˈendləs/	endlos	
must-see /ˌmʌst ˈsiː/	etwas, das man unbedingt sehen muss	
lover /ˈlʌvə/	(der/die) Liebhaber/in	

	magnificent /mæɡˈnɪfɪsnt/	wunderbar, großartig
	thrill /θrɪl/	(der) Nervenkitzel, (der) Kick
	(to) step out /ˌstepˈaʊt/	heraustreten
	canyon /ˈkænjən/	(die) Schlucht
	stunning /ˈstʌnɪŋ/	toll, fantastisch
	northernmost /ˈnɔːðənˌməʊst/	nördlichste(r, s)
	charming /ˈtʃɑːmɪŋ/	charmant, reizend
	(to) step back in time /ˌstepˌbækˌɪn ˈtaɪm/	sich in die Vergangenheit zurückversetzen
	gold rush /ˈɡəʊld rʌʃ/	(der) Goldrausch
	adventurous /ədˈventʃrəs/	abenteuerlustig
	(to) take a ride (irr) /ˌteɪk ə ˈraɪd/	eine Fahrt machen
	magic /ˈmædʒɪk/	(die) Magie, (der) Zauber
	historic /hɪˈstɒrɪk/	historisch
p. 14, 7	(to) **suggest** /səˈdʒest/	hinweisen auf, andeuten
	(to) **claim** /kleɪm/	Anspruch erheben auf, behaupten
	(to) **settle** /ˈsetl/	sich niederlassen
	coast /kəʊst/	(die) Küste
	political /pəˈlɪtɪkl/	politisch
	economic /ˌiːkəˈnɒmɪk/	wirtschaftlich
	ship /ʃɪp/	(das) Schiff
	settler /ˈsetlə/	(der/die) Siedler/in
	Native American /ˌneɪtɪv əˈmerɪkən/	Native American (Selbstbezeichnung der ersten Bevölkerungen in den USA)
	nation /ˈneɪʃn/	(die) Nation, (das) Land; (das) Volk
	violence /ˈvaɪələns/	(die) Gewalt
	disease /dɪˈziːz/	(die) Krankheit
	familiar /fəˈmɪliə/	vertraut, bekannt
	tax /tæks/	(die) Steuer, (die) Abgabe
	(to) **declare** /dɪˈkleə/	verkünden; erklären
	glimpse /ɡlɪmps/	(der) flüchtige Blick
	archaeological /ˌɑːkiəˈlɒdʒɪkl/	archäologisch
	continent /ˈkɒntɪnənt/	(der) Kontinent
	Scandinavia /ˌskændɪˈneɪviə/	Skandinavien
	Canada /ˈkænədə/	Kanada
	settlement /ˈsetlmənt/	(die) Siedlung
	the Caribbean /ðə ˌkærɪˈbiən/	(die) Karibik, karibische Inseln
	Spain /speɪn/	Spanien
	colonization /ˌkɒlənaɪˈzeɪʃn/	(die) Kolonisierung
	suppression /səˈpreʃn/	(die) Unterdrückung
	pilgrim /ˈpɪlɡrɪm/	(der/die) Pilger/in
	way of living /ˌweɪ əv ˈlɪvɪŋ/	(die) Lebensweise
	(to) govern /ˈɡʌvən/	regieren

stunning = great, fantastic

The **coast** is very nice in this part of the country.

A **nation** is a country that has its own government and land.
The word can also refer to all the people in a country.

A **disease** is an illness.

to **declare** = to state

Spain is a country in south-west Europe.

Vocabulary

	Founding Fathers *(pl)* /ˌfaʊndɪŋ ˈfɑːðəz/	(die) Gründerväter
	War of Independence /ˌwɔːr əv ˌɪndɪˈpendəns/	(Amerikanischer) Unabhängigkeitskrieg
p. 15, 7	**institution** /ˌɪnstɪˈtjuːʃn/	(die) Einrichtung, (die) Institution
	(to) **force** /fɔːs/	zwingen, erzwingen
	condition /kənˈdɪʃn/	(die) Bedingung
	industrialized /ɪnˈdʌstriəlaɪzd/	industrialisiert
	freedom /ˈfriːdəm/	(die) Freiheit
	agricultural /ˌægrɪˈkʌltʃrəl/	landwirtschaftlich
	southern /ˈsʌðən/	südliche(r, s); Süd-
	in favour of /ɪn ˈfeɪvər əv/	für
	(to) **be involved in** *(irr)* /bɪ ɪnˈvɒlvd ɪn/	beteiligt sein an
	(to) **enter** /ˈentə/	eintreten in
	Pacific, Pacific Ocean /pəˈsɪfɪk, pəˌsɪfɪk ˈəʊʃn/	(der) Pazifik, (der) Pazifische Ozean
	presence /ˈprezns/	(die) Anwesenheit, (die) Präsenz
	(to) **lead** *(irr)* /liːd/	führen
	civil rights *(pl)* /ˌsɪvl ˈraɪts/	(die) Bürgerrechte
	movement /ˈmuːvmənt/	(die) Bewegung
	leader /ˈliːdə/	(der/die) Anführer/in
	attack /əˈtæk/	(der) Angriff
	(to) **serve** /sɜːv/	dienen; eine Amtszeit durchlaufen
	historical /hɪˈstɒrɪkl/	geschichtlich, historisch
	slavery /ˈsleɪvəri/	(die) Sklaverei
	slave /sleɪv/	(der/die) Sklave/Sklavin
	Africa /ˈæfrɪkə/	Afrika
	inhumane /ˌɪnhjuːˈmeɪn/	barbarisch, unmenschlich
	field of work /ˌfiːld əv ˈwɜːk/	(der) Arbeitsbereich
	fighting /ˈfaɪtɪŋ/	(die) Kämpfe, (die) Gefechte
	ally /ˈælaɪ/	(der/die) Verbündete, (der/die) Alliierte
	military /ˈmɪlɪtri/	militärisch
	mid- /mɪd/	Mitte
	racial segregation /ˌreɪʃl segrɪˈgeɪʃn/	(die) Rassentrennung
	(to) gain momentum /ˌgeɪn məʊˈmentəm/	in Schwung kommen
	(to) hijack /ˈhaɪdʒæk/	entführen
	(to) rebuild *(irr)* /ˌriːˈbɪld/	wieder aufbauen
	complex /ˈkɒmpleks/	(der) Komplex
	African American /ˌæfrɪkən əˈmerɪkən/	(der/die) Afroamerikaner/in; afroamerikanisch
	chronological /ˌkrɒnəˈlɒdʒɪkl/	chronologisch
	aboard /əˈbɔːd/	an Bord
People and Places 1	**tear** /tɪə/	(die) Träne
	arrival /əˈraɪvl/	(die) Ankunft

An **industrialized** country has lots of industries.

southern ≠ northern

Man verwendet „**historic**", wenn man ausdrücken will, dass etwas „historisch bedeutsam" ist, und „**historical**", wenn etwas „die Vergangenheit betreffend" ist.

The actors showed a **historical attack** and fought each other.

World War I (= **the First World War**) /ˌwɜːld wɔː ˈwʌn, ðə ˌfɜːst ˌwɜːld ˈwɔː/ (der) Erste Weltkrieg
World War II (= **the Second World War**) /ˌwɜːld wɔː ˈtuː, ðə ˌsekənd ˌwɜːld ˈwɔː/ (der) Zweite Weltkrieg

There are **tears** running down his face.

		poor /pɔː/	schlecht	
		southeast, south-east /ˌsaʊθˈiːst/	(der) Südosten	southeast
		route /ruːt/	(die) Strecke, (die) Route	
		trail /treɪl/	(der) Weg, (der) Pfad	
		estimated /ˈestɪmeɪtəd/	geschätzt	
		(to) drive away *(irr)* /ˌdraɪv əˈweɪ/	vertreiben	
		(to) murder /ˈmɜːdə/	ermorden, umbringen	to **murder** = to kill
		(to) resist /rɪˈzɪst/	sich wehren	
		reservation /ˌrezəˈveɪʃn/	(das) Reservat	
		far away /ˌfɑːr əˈweɪ/	weit weg	
		cotton /ˈkɒtn/	(die) Baumwolle	
		west /west/	westlich	
p. 16, 8		(to) commemorate /kəˈmeməreɪt/	*(einer Person oder Sache)* gedenken	A **one-minute** presentation
p. 16, 9		one-minute /ˌwʌnˈmɪnɪt/	einminütig	should last 60 seconds.
		sportsperson /ˈspɔːtsˌpɜːsn/	(der/die) Sportler/in	
		flag /flæg/	(die) Fahne, (die) Flagge	
p. 17, 10		**quote** /kwəʊt/	(das) Zitat	
		opportunity /ˌɒpəˈtjuːnəti/	(die) Chance, (die) Möglichkeit, (die) Gelegenheit	When you **give a reason**, you explain why you state a certain opinion.
		security /sɪˈkjʊərəti/	(die) Sicherheit	
		(to) **give a reason** *(irr)* /ˌɡɪv ə ˈriːzn/	einen Grund nennen	
		passage /ˈpæsɪdʒ/	(die) (Text)passage; (der) Gang; (die) Überfahrt	
		democracy /dɪˈmɒkrəsi/	(die) Demokratie	
		equality /ɪˈkwɒləti/	(die) Gleichberechtigung, (die) Gleichheit	
		regardless of /rɪˈɡɑːdləs əv/	trotz, ungeachtet	
		social /ˈsəʊʃl/	gesellschaftlich; sozial	
		origin /ˈɒrɪdʒɪn/	(der) Ursprung, (die) Herkunft	
		(to) **disagree** /ˌdɪsəˈɡriː/	nicht zustimmen	to **disagree** ≠ to agree
		born /bɔːn/	geboren	
		reality /riˈæləti/	(die) Realität, (die) Wirklichkeit	
		minimum wage /ˌmɪnɪməm ˈweɪdʒ/	(der) Mindestlohn	
		historian /hɪˈstɔːriən/	(der/die) Historiker/in	
		(to) rank /ræŋk/	einstufen, anordnen	
		tolerance /ˈtɒlərəns/	(die) Toleranz	
		set /set/	*hier:* (die) Reihe	
		greatness /ˈɡreɪtnəs/	(die) Bedeutsamkeit	
		(from) rags to riches /frəm ˌræɡz tə ˈrɪtʃɪz/	*(vom)* Tellerwäscher zum Millionär	
		were /wɜː/	*hier:* würde(st, n, t)	
		(to) maximize /ˈmæksɪmaɪz/	maximieren	
p. 18, 11		**themselves** /ðəmˈselvz/	sich; selbst	The village **is situated** between two mountains.
p. 18, 12		(to) **be situated** *(irr)* /ˌbiː ˈsɪtʃueɪtɪd/	liegen, gelegen sein	
		known /nəʊn/	bekannt	

200 two hundred

Vocabulary

	silver /ˈsɪlvə/	(das) Silber	
	bracket /ˈbrækɪt/	(die) Klammer	
	simple present /ˌsɪmpl ˈpreznt/	(die) einfache Gegenwart	
	simple past /ˌsɪmpl ˈpɑːst/	(die) einfache Vergangenheit	
	bean /biːn/	(die) Bohne	
p. 19, 13	economy /ɪˈkɒnəmi/	(die) Wirtschaft	This film is not **suitable** for children. = This film should not be seen by children.
	writer /ˈraɪtə/	(der/die) Schriftsteller/in	
	suitable /ˈsuːtəbl/	geeignet, passend	
	peer /ˈpɪə/	(der/die) Gleichaltrige	

Unit 1 | Part B New York City

p. 20, 1	noisy /ˈnɔɪzi/	laut	**noisy** = loud
	fascinating /ˈfæsɪneɪtɪŋ/	faszinierend	
	lively /ˈlaɪvli/	lebhaft, lebendig	
	sleepy /ˈsliːpi/	schläfrig, verschlafen	
	fabulous /ˈfæbjʊləs/	fabelhaft, toll	
p. 20, 2	at the back of /ˌæt ðə ˈbæk_əv/	am Ende von, hinten in	**at the back of** ≠ in the front
	awesome /ˈɔːsm/	beeindruckend; super	
	crown /kraʊn/	(die) Krone	
	ferry /ˈferi/	(die) Fähre	
	harbor (AE) = harbour (BE) /ˈhɑːbə/	(der) Hafen	
	across /əˈkrɒs/	über, quer durch	„Lady Liberty" ist ein Spitzname für die Freiheitsstatue in New York.
	apparently /əˈpærəntli/	offensichtlich	
	theater (AE) /ˈθɪətə/	(das) Theater	
	stop /stɒp/	(der) Halt	
	bike lane /ˈbaɪk leɪn/	(der) Fahrradweg	
	(to) tour /tʊə/	bereisen, erkunden	
p. 21, 2	lovely /ˈlʌvli/	schön, herrlich	
	calm /ˈkɑːm/	ruhig, friedlich	
	in the middle of /ˌɪn ðə ˈmɪdl_əv/	in der Mitte von, mitten in	
	(to) rent /rent/	mieten	
	(to) hit (irr) /hɪt/	treffen, stoßen gegen	
	since then /sɪns ˈðen/	seitdem, seither	
	skyscraper /ˈskaɪˌskreɪpə/	(der) Wolkenkratzer	There are often lots of **skyscrapers** in big cities.
	all around /ˌɔːl_əˈraʊnd/	rundherum, überall (in/auf)	
	moving /ˈmuːvɪŋ/	bewegend, ergreifend	
	(to) learn (irr) /lɜːn/	erfahren	
	borough /ˈbʌrə/	(der) Bezirk, (der) Stadtteil	
	(to) build a park (irr) /ˌbɪld_ə ˈpɑːk/	einen Park anlegen	
	all day long /ˌɔːl deɪ ˈlɒŋ/	den ganzen Tag lang	
	memorial /məˈmɔːriəl/	(das) Denkmal, (das) Ehrenmal	
	Twin Towers /ˌtwɪn ˈtaʊəz/	*Zwillingstürme in New York City*	
	footprint /ˈfʊtˌprɪnt/	(der) Fußabdruck, (die) Standfläche	

	man-made /ˌmæn ˈmeɪd/	künstlich	
	waterfall /ˈwɔːtəˌfɔːl/	(der) Wasserfall	
p. 22, 3	present perfect /ˌpreznt ˈpɜːfɪkt/	(das) Perfekt	
p. 22, 4	follow-up question /ˈfɒləʊ ˌʌp ˌkwestʃn/	(die) Folgefrage	Which **floor** do you want to go to?
p. 23, 5	**floor** /flɔː/	(das) Stockwerk	
	(to) **turn into** /ˌtɜːn ˈɪntʊ/	umwandeln in	
	railroad /ˈreɪlˌrəʊd/	*hier:* (das) Eisenbahngelände	Das Erdgeschoss ist in den USA „first floor", in Großbritannien „ground floor". Der erste Stock heißt in den USA „second floor", in Großbritannien „first floor".
p. 24, 6	(to) **make money** *(irr)* /ˌmeɪk ˈmʌni/	Geld verdienen	
	high school *(AE)* /ˈhaɪ skuːl/	(die) Highschool, (die) weiterführende Schule	
	(to) **be proud of** *(irr)* /ˌbiː ˈpraʊd əv/	stolz sein auf	
	cultural, culturally /ˈkʌltʃərəl, ˈkʌltʃərəli/	kulturell	
	reputation /ˌrepjʊˈteɪʃn/	(der) Ruf	„them" wird benutzt, wenn man vermeiden möchte, „him" oder „her" zu sagen. Man kann „they" sagen, wenn man vermeiden möchte, „he" oder „she" zu sagen.
	whenever /wenˈevə/	wann auch immer	
	Lebanon /ˈlebənən/	der Libanon	
	neighborhood *(AE)* /ˈneɪbəˌhʊd/	(das) Viertel, (die) Nachbarschaft	
	apartment *(AE)* /əˈpɑːtmənt/	(die) Wohnung	
	brownstone (house) /ˈbraʊnˌstəʊn haʊs/	(das) Haus aus rötlich braunem Sandstein	
	downtown *(AE)* /ˌdaʊnˈtaʊn/	in der Innenstadt, im Zentrum	
	sidewalk *(AE)* /ˈsaɪdˌwɔːk/	(der) Bürgersteig	
	store *(AE)* /stɔː/	(der) Laden	
	Hispanic /hɪˈspænɪk/	(der/die) Hispanoamerikaner/in; hispanisch	downtown *(AE)* = city (centre) *(BE)* store *(AE)* = shop *(BE)*
	crime rate /ˈkraɪm reɪt/	(die) Kriminalitätsrate	
p. 25, 7	**extract** /ˈekstrækt/	(der) Auszug, (das) Exzerpt	
	diversity /daɪˈvɜːsəti/	(die) Vielfalt	
	electric /ɪˈlektrɪk/	elektrisierend, spannungsgeladen	
	(to) **test** /test/	prüfen, testen	
	pretty /ˈprɪti/	hübsch	
	(to) **reject** /rɪˈdʒekt/	ablehnen, zurückweisen	
	(to) **accept** /əkˈsept/	anerkennen, akzeptieren	
	lyrics *(pl)* /ˈlɪrɪks/	(der) Liedtext	
	speaker /ˈspiːkə/	(der/die) Sprecher/in	The **speaker addresses** the people who are listening to him.
	(to) **address** /əˈdres/	ansprechen, adressieren	
	character /ˈkærəktə/	(das) Wesen, (der) Charakter	
	NYC (= New York City) /ˌen waɪ ˈsiː, ˌnjuː jɔːk ˈsɪti/	*die Stadt New York*	
	(to) **come to mind** *(irr)* /ˌkʌm tə ˈmaɪnd/	einfallen, in den Sinn kommen	
	the Battery /ðə ˈbætri/	*Park in New York*	
	Middle-Eastern /ˌmɪdl ˈiːstən/	(der) Mensch aus dem Nahen Osten; Nahost-, nahöstlich	"Latin" can relate to people that use a language such as Spanish or Portuguese in Mexico or Brazil.
	Latin /ˌlætɪn əˈmerɪkən/	(der/die) Lateinamerikaner/in; lateinamerikanisch	

Vocabulary

	Black /blæk/	politische Selbstbezeichnung Schwarzer Menschen in den USA	
	White /waɪt/	(der/die) Weiße	
	(to) make happen *(irr)* /ˌmeɪk ˈhæpən/	möglich machen	
	water tower /ˈwɔːtə ˌtaʊə/	(der) Wasserturm	
	prizefighter /ˈpraɪzˌfaɪtə/	(der/die) Preisboxer/in	
	Wall Street /ˌwɔːl striːt/	Straße in New York mit vielen Banken und der weltgrößten Wertpapierbörse	
	trader /ˈtreɪdə/	(der/die) Händler/in	The British English word for **"subway"** is "underground".
	subway *(AE)* /ˈsʌbˌweɪ/	(die) U-Bahn	
	car *(AE)* /kɑː/	(der) Waggon, (der) Wagen	
	unified /ˈjuːnɪfaɪd/	vereint	
	whoever /huːˈevə/	wer auch immer	
	(to) do well *(irr)* /ˌduː ˈwel/	erfolgreich sein	
	hell /hel/	(die) Hölle	
	(to) give thanks *(irr)* /ˌgɪv ˈθæŋks/	Dank sagen	to **give thanks** = to thank
	(to) pass /pɑːs/	*hier:* durchgehen	
	drove /drəʊv/	(die) Herde	
	love letter /ˈlʌv ˌletə/	(der) Liebesbrief	
	(to) bring together *(irr)* /ˌbrɪŋ təˈgeðə/	zusammenbringen	'cause (= because) /kɔːz, bɪˈkɒz/ weil, da
	lifelong /ˈlaɪfˌlɒŋ/	lebenslang	ain't (= am/are/is not) *(informal)* /eɪnt/ nicht sein
	(to) dedicate /ˈdedɪkeɪt/	widmen	
	(to) blend /blend/	vermischen	
	(to) mend /mend/	reparieren, in Ordnung bringen	
	9/11 /ˌnaɪn ɪˈlevn/	Terrorangriffe am 11. September 2001	
	gritty /ˈgrɪti/	grob; mutig, tapfer	
	peoples *(pl)* /ˈpiːplz/	(die) Völker	
	wherever /werˈevə/	wo(her) auch immer	
	landmark /ˈlænˌmɑːk/	(das) Wahrzeichen	
	home /həʊm/	(die) Heimat	
	birth /bɜːθ/	(die) Geburt	There **are** a lot of things **on display** at museums.
	(to) **be on display** *(irr)* /ˌbiː ɒn dɪˈspleɪ/	ausgestellt sein	
	at the moment /ˌæt ðə ˈməʊmənt/	im Moment	
	art gallery /ˈɑːt ˌgæləri/	(die) Kunstgalerie	
	world-class /ˌwɜːld ˈklɑːs/	Weltklasse-	
	leading /ˈliːdɪŋ/	führend	
	record /ˈrekɔːd/	(die) Schallplatte	
	musical /ˈmjuːzɪkl/	musikalisch	
	clothing /ˈkləʊðɪŋ/	(die) Kleidung	
	(to) **vary** /ˈveəri/	variieren, verschieden sein	to **vary** = to be different
	in advance /ɪn ədˈvɑːns/	im Voraus	
	admission /ədˈmɪʃn/	(der) Eintritt, (der) Eintrittspreis	
	above /əˈbʌv/	darüber	
	under /ˈʌndə/	darunter	

	within /wɪðˈɪn/	innerhalb, innen	
	including /ɪnˈkluːdɪŋ/	einschließlich	Painters or singers are **artists**.
	artist /ˈɑːtɪst/	(der/die) Künstler/in	
	electronic /ˌelekˈtrɒnɪk/	elektronisch	
	the media /ðə ˈmiːdiə/	die Medien	
	ID (card) (= identity card) /ˌaɪˈdiː (kɑːd), aɪˈdentəti kɑːd/	(der) Ausweis	
	due to /ˈdjuː tʊ/	wegen	**due to** = because of
	special offer /ˌspeʃl ˈɒfə/	(das) Sonderangebot	
	(to) take a tour *(irr)* /ˌteɪk ə ˈtʊə/	eine Tour machen	
	passionate /ˈpæʃnət/	leidenschaftlich	
	tour guide /ˈtʊə gaɪd/	(der/die) Reiseführer/in	
	senior /ˈsiːniə/	(der) ältere Mensch; ältere(r, s)	
	aged *(after noun)* /eɪdʒd/	im Alter von	
	architecture /ˈɑːkɪˌtektʃə/	(die) Architektur	
	sculpture /ˈskʌlptʃə/	(die) Bildhauerei	
	photography /fəˈtɒgrəfi/	(die) Fotografie	**Photography** is a popular hobby.
	print /prɪnt/	(der) Druck	
	illustrated /ˈɪləstreɪtɪd/	illustriert, bebildert	
	full-time /ˌfʊl ˈtaɪm/	Vollzeit-	
	renovation /ˌrenəˈveɪʃn/	(die) Renovierung, (die) Sanierung	
	monument /ˈmɒnjʊmənt/	(das) Denkmal	
p. 27, 9	**Grand Central Station** /ˌgrænd ˌsentrəl ˈsteɪʃn/	*Bahnhof in Manhattan*	When something is **essential**, it is extremely important and necessary.
p. 27, 10	**essential** /ɪˈsenʃl/	unbedingt erforderlich, unverzichtbar	
	(to) represent /ˌreprɪˈzent/	präsentieren, vertreten	
	nationality /ˌnæʃəˈnæləti/	(die) Nationalität	
	heritage /ˈherɪtɪdʒ/	(das) Erbe	
	(to) honor *(AE)* = **honour** *(BE)* /ˈɒnə/	ehren	
	legacy /ˈlegəsi/	(das) Vermächtnis, (das) Erbe	
	host /həʊst/	*hier:* (der/die) Podcast-Host	
	walking tour /ˈwɔːkɪŋ tʊə/	(die) Wanderung	
	Mexican /ˈmeksɪkən/	(der/die) Mexikaner/in; mexikanisch	
	amusement park /əˈmjuːzmənt pɑːk/	(der) Freizeitpark	There is an **amusement park** on Brighton Pier.
p. 27, 11	**acrostic** /əˈkrɒstɪk/	(das) Akrostichon, (der) Leistenvers	
	nickname /ˈnɪkˌneɪm/	(der) Spitzname, (der) Kosename	
p. 28, 12	**passive** /ˈpæsɪv/	(das) Passiv	
p. 28, 13	**curious** /ˈkjʊəriəs/	neugierig	
	(to) complete /kəmˈpliːt/	fertigstellen	**traveled** *(AE)* = **travelled** *(BE)*
p. 28, 14	**center** *(AE)* /ˈsentə/	(das) Zentrum	
	favorite *(AE)* /ˈfeɪvrət/	Liebling; Lieblings-	

Unit 2 | Part A Welcome to high school!

p. 33	**yearbook** /ˈjɪəˌbʊk/	(das) Jahrbuch	

Vocabulary

	after-school /ˌɑːftə ˈskuːl/	Nachmittags-
p. 34, 2	**exchange** /ɪksˈtʃeɪndʒ/	(der) Austausch; Austausch-
	stranger /ˈstreɪndʒə/	(der/die) Fremde
	(to) welcome /ˈwelkəm/	willkommen heißen
	host *(before nouns)* /həʊst/	Gast-
	keen /kiːn/	begeistert
	reader /ˈriːdə/	(der/die) Leser/in
	Congratulations! /kənˌɡrætʃʊˈleɪʃnz/	Glückwunsch!, Gratuliere!
	previous /ˈpriːviəs/	vorig, vorausgegangen
	election /ɪˈlekʃn/	(die) Wahl
	once /wʌns/	sobald; wenn; als
	football *(AE)* /ˈfʊtˌbɔːl/	American Football
	decade /ˈdekeɪd/	(das) Jahrzehnt
	support /səˈpɔːt/	(die) Unterstützung, (die) Hilfe
	championship /ˈtʃæmpiənʃɪp/	(die) Meisterschaft
	fall *(AE)* /fɔːl/	(der) Herbst
	past /pɑːst/	vergangen, frühere(r, s)
	program *(AE)* /ˈprəʊɡræm/	(das) Programm
	read /riːd/	(die) Lektüre
	vacation *(AE)* /vəˈkeɪʃn/	(die) Ferien, (der) Urlaub
	grade *(AE)* /ɡreɪd/	(die) Klasse
	in total /ˌɪn ˈtəʊtl/	insgesamt
	homecoming *(no pl, AE)* /ˈhəʊmˌkʌmɪŋ/	(das) Ehemaligentreffen
	(to) graduate *(AE)* /ˈɡrædʒueɪt/	die (Highschool-)Abschlussprüfung bestehen
	(to) crown /kraʊn/	krönen
	marching band /ˈmɑːtʃɪŋ bænd/	(die) Marschkapelle
	(to) come second *(irr)* /ˌkʌm ˈsekənd/	Zweite/r werden
	(to) be in full swing *(irr)* /ˌbiː ɪn ˌfʊl ˈswɪŋ/	in vollem Gang sein
p. 35, 2	**trial** /ˈtraɪəl/	(die) Probe, (der) Test
	(to) hold *(irr)* /həʊld/	veranstalten
	after /ˈɑːftə/	nachdem
	record /ˈrekɔːd/	(der) Rekord
	energy /ˈenədʒi/	(die) Energie, (die) Kraft
	(to) raise /reɪz/	beschaffen, sammeln
	cause /kɔːz/	(der) Grund, (die) Ursache; (die) Sache
	college /ˈkɒlɪdʒ/	(das) College *(Bildungseinrichtung)*
	suit /suːt/	(der) Anzug
	formal /ˈfɔːml/	formell; offiziell
	(to) continue /kənˈtɪnjuː/	andauern, weitergehen
	cheer team /ˈtʃɪə tiːm/	*(das) Cheerleading-Team*
	beginner /bɪˈɡɪnə/	(der/die) Anfänger/in
	freshman *(pl freshmen)* *(AE)* /ˈfreʃmən, ˈfreʃmən/	(der/die) *Schüler/in einer Highschool im ersten Jahr*

A **stranger** is a person that you do not know.

Die amerikanische Schreibweise für „programme" ist „program". Eine Ausnahme beim Hauptwort ist im britischen Englisch das Wort für „Computerprogramm", das auch „program" geschrieben wird. Ebenso schreibt man sowohl im amerikanischen als auch im britischen Englisch das Verb: „to program".

had travelled
war(en) gereist
had read
hatte(n) gelesen
had finished
hatte(n) beendet
had graduated
hatte(n) die Abschlussprüfung bestanden
had held
hatte(n) veranstaltet
had practised
hatte(n) geübt/trainiert
had trained
hatte(n) trainiert
had ended
hatte(n) geendet

The man is wearing a **suit**.

	demonstration /ˌdemənˈstreɪʃn/	(die) Vorführung, (die) Demonstration	
	tournament /ˈtʊənəmənt/	(das) Turnier	to practice (AE) =
	(to) practice (AE) /ˈpræktɪs/	üben, trainieren; praktizieren	to practise (BE)
	cheer basics (pl) /ˈtʃɪə ˌbeɪsɪks/	Grundkenntnisse beim Cheerleading	Im britischen Englisch ist „practice" mit „c" das
	(to) cheer for /ˈtʃɪə fə/	anfeuern	Hauptwort: die Übung,
	athlete /ˈæθliːt/	(der/die) Athlet/in	das Training.
	single /ˈsɪŋgl/	hier: (der) Einzelwettbewerb	
	thrilling /ˈθrɪlɪŋ/	aufregend	thrilling = exciting
	final /ˈfaɪnl/	(das) Endspiel, (das) Finale	
	competitor /kəmˈpetɪtə/	(der/die) Konkurrent/in	
	fundraising /ˈfʌndreɪzɪŋ/	(das) Spendensammeln	
	fundraiser /ˈfʌndˌreɪzə/	(der/die) Spendensammler/in	
	graduate /ˈgrædʒuət/	(der/die) Absolvent/in	
	prom (AE) /prɒm/	(der) Ball am Ende des Jahres in einer amerikanischen Highschool	
	glamorous /ˈglæmərəs/	glamourös	
	committee /kəˈmɪti/	(der) Ausschuss, (das) Komitee	
	graduation /ˌgrædʒuˈeɪʃn/	(der) Schulabschluss	
	(to) party /ˈpɑːti/	feiern	
	prom king (AE) /ˈprɒm kɪŋ/	(der) Ballkönig	
	prom queen (AE) /ˈprɒm kwiːn/	(die) Ballkönigin	
p. 36, 3	(to) **underline** /ˌʌndəˈlaɪn/	unterstreichen	
p. 36, 4	(to) **lie down** (irr) /ˌlaɪ ˈdaʊn/	sich hinlegen	
	(to) **fall asleep** (irr) /ˌfɔːl əˈsliːp/	einschlafen	She **has fallen asleep** in the park.
	(to) **dream** (irr) /driːm/	träumen	
People and Places 3	**credit** /ˈkredɪt/	(der) Schein, (der) Leistungsnachweis	
	foreign language /ˌfɒrɪn ˈlæŋgwɪdʒ/	(die) Fremdsprache	
	(to) **elect** /ɪˈlekt/	wählen	to **elect** = to choose
	obligatory /əˈblɪgətri/	verpflichtend	
	optional /ˈɒpʃnəl/	optional, fakultativ	
	elective /ɪˈlektɪv/	(das) Wahlpflichtfach	
	home economics (pl) /ˌhəʊm iːkəˈnɒmɪks/	(die) Hauswirtschaft(slehre)	
	ceremony /ˈserəməni/	(die) Zeremonie, (die) Feier	
	diploma /dɪˈpləʊmə/	(das) Diplom	
	cap /kæp/	hier: (die) Kappe	
	gown /gaʊn/	(die) Robe, (der) Talar	
p. 37, 5	(to) **call** /kɔːl/	nennen	
	difference /ˈdɪfrəns/	(der) Unterschied	
	pie /paɪ/	(die) Pastete, (der) Kuchen	
	dress code /ˈdres kəʊd/	(die) Bekleidungsvorschriften	
	French fries (AE, pl) /ˌfrentʃ ˈfraɪz/	(die) Pommes frites	
p. 38, 6	**cereal** /ˈsɪəriəl/	(die) Frühstücksflocken	The people are waiting at
	bus stop /ˈbʌs ˌstɒp/	(die) Bushaltestelle	the **bus stop**.

Vocabulary

hardly /ˈhɑːdli/	kaum	
over here /ˌəʊvə ˈhɪə/	hier (drüben)	
locker /ˈlɒkə/	(das) Schließfach, (der) Spind	
(to) **give out** *(irr)* /ˌgɪv ˈaʊt/	bekannt geben, verteilen	
republic /rɪˈpʌblɪk/	(die) Republik	
liberty /ˈlɪbəti/	(die) Freiheit	
justice /ˈdʒʌstɪs/	(die) Gerechtigkeit	
(to) **guess** /ges/	annehmen, vermuten	
rude /ruːd/	unhöflich	They **are staring at** each other through the glass.
(to) **stare at** /ˈsteər ˌæt/	anstarren	
(to) **feel uncomfortable** *(irr)* /ˌfiːl ʌnˈkʌmftəbl/	sich unwohl fühlen	
(to) blog /blɒg/	bloggen	
the ones /ðə ˈwʌnz/	diejenigen; diese	
schoolchild *(pl* schoolchildren*)* /ˈskuːl.tʃaɪld, ˈskuːl.tʃɪldrən/	(das) Schulkind	
luckily /ˈlʌkɪli/	zum Glück, glücklicherweise	
registrar's office /ˌredʒɪstrɑːz ˈɒfɪs/	(das) Sekretariat	
registrar /ˌredʒɪˈstrɑː/	(der/die) Sekretär/in	The British English word for **"schedule"** is "timetable".
schedule *(AE)* /ˈskedʒul, ˈʃedjuːl/	(der) Stundenplan	
homeroom /ˈhəʊmruːm/	(der) Klassenraum; (die) Klassenlehrkraftstunde	
attendance /əˈtendəns/	(die) Anwesenheit	
first thing *(informal)* /ˌfɜːst ˈθɪŋ/	als Erstes	
Pledge of Allegiance /ˌpledʒ əv əˈliːdʒ(ə)ns/	(der) Treueschwur	
(to) pledge /pledʒ/	versprechen, schwören	
allegiance /əˈliːdʒns/	(die) Loyalität, (die) Ergebenheit	
God /gɒd/	(der) Gott	
indivisible /ˌɪndɪˈvɪzəbl/	unteilbar	
strictly speaking /ˈstrɪkli ˌspiːkɪŋ/	streng genommen	An **elective** is a subject at school that you can choose to do but don't have to do.
p. 39, 6 **elective** /ɪˈlektɪv/	(das) Wahlpflichtfach	
hallway /ˈhɔːlˌweɪ/	(der) Korridor, (der) Flur	
(to) **carry** /ˈkæri/	tragen	
math *(AE, informal)* /mæθ/	Mathe (Schulfach)	
unlike /ʌnˈlaɪk/	anders als	**unlike** = not like
period *(AE)* /ˈpɪəriəd/	(die) Stunde	
gym *(AE)* /dʒɪm/	(der) Sportunterricht	
robotics /rəʊˈbɒtɪks/	(die) Robotertechnik	
study period /ˈstʌdi ˌpɪəriəd/	(die) Lernstunde, (die) Übungsstunde	
study hall /ˈstʌdi hɔːl/	(der) Lernraum, (der) Übungsraum	
lab /læb/	(das) Labor	
sophomore *(AE)* /ˈsɒfəˌmɔː/	(der/die) *Schüler/in einer Highschool im zweiten Jahr*	

p. 40, 7	junior *(AE)* /ˈdʒuːniə/	(der/die) Schüler/in einer Highschool im vorletzten Jahr	
	senior *(AE)* /ˈsiːniə/	(der/die) Schüler/in einer Highschool im letzten Jahr	
	locally /ˈləʊkli/	am Ort, vor Ort	
	robot /ˈrəʊbɒt/	(der) Roboter	**robot**
	(to) **program** /ˈprəʊɡræm/	programmieren	
	piece of paper /ˌpiːs əv ˈpeɪpə/	(das) Blatt Papier	
	(to) **involve** /ɪnˈvɒlv/	beinhalten, umfassen	
	literature /ˈlɪtrətʃə/	(die) Literatur	
	tough /tʌf/	schwierig	**tough** = hard, difficult
	motivation /ˌməʊtɪˈveɪʃn/	(der) Antrieb, (die) Motivation	I'm fine. Es geht mir gut. I'm doing OK. *(informal)* Es läuft ganz gut.
	(to) **videochat** /ˈvɪdiəʊtʃæt/	einen Videochat machen	
	(to) **be behind** *(irr, informal)* /ˌbiː bɪˈhaɪnd/	hinterher sein, zurückliegen	
	(to) **get to do something** *(irr)* /ˌɡet tə ˈduː ˌsʌmθɪŋ/	die Möglichkeit haben, etwas zu tun	„do" kann man auch verwenden, wenn man eine Aussage besonders betonen möchte: Do send me a video of your party!
	science fair /ˈsaɪəns feə/	(die) Naturwissenschaftsmesse	
	(to) wave a flag /ˌweɪv ə ˈflæɡ/	eine Fahne schwenken	
	business law /ˈbɪznəs lɔː/	(das) Wirtschaftsrecht	
	vocational /vəʊˈkeɪʃnəl/	beruflich	
	auto body repair /ˌɔːtəʊ ˌbɒdi rɪˈpeə/	(die) Karosseriereparatur	
	law /lɔː/	(die) Rechtswissenschaft	A **guidance counsellor**'s job is to listen to you and give you advice or help you when you've got problems.
	a different one /ə ˈdɪfrənt wʌn/	ein anderer/eine andere/ein anderes	
	guidance counsellor /ˈɡaɪdns ˌkaʊnslə/	(der/die) Beratungslehrer/in	
	plumbing /ˈplʌmɪŋ/	(das) Klempnern	
	women's studies /ˈwɪmɪnz ˌstʌdiz/	(das) Schulfach, das die Rolle der Frau in Geschichte, Gesellschaft und Literatur untersucht	
p. 41, 8	**finance** /ˈfaɪnæns/	(die) Finanzwirtschaft, (das) Geldwesen	A **tool** is something that you use in order to do a job.
	tool /tuːl/	(das) Mittel, (das) Instrument	
	(to) **manage** /ˈmænɪdʒ/	verwalten, organisieren	
	finances *(pl)* /ˈfaɪnænsɪz/	(die) Finanzen	
	(to) **cover** /ˈkʌvə/	abdecken, sich befassen mit	
	(to) **market** /ˈmɑːkɪt/	vermarkten	
	product /ˈprɒdʌkt/	(das) Produkt	
	movie *(AE)* /ˈmuːvi/	(der) Film	
	(to) **get to know** *(irr)* /ˌɡet tə ˈnəʊ/	kennenlernen	
	technique /tekˈniːk/	(die) Technik	
	skill /skɪl/	(die) Fertigkeit, (die) Kompetenz	
	preparation /ˌprepəˈreɪʃn/	(die) Vorbereitung; (die) Zubereitung	
	(to) **provide with** /prəˈvaɪd wɪθ/	versorgen mit, versehen mit	He **is providing** his daughter **with** food.
	ethics *(pl)* /ˈeθɪks/	(die) Ethik	
	maintenance /ˈmeɪntənəns/	(die) Pflege, (die) Wartung	
	repair /rɪˈpeə/	(die) Reparatur	

Vocabulary

	household /ˈhaʊsˌhəʊld/	(der) Haushalt	
	culinary art /ˌkʌlɪnri ˈɑːt/	(die) Kochkunst	
	hands-on /ˌhændzˈɒn/	aktiv, praktisch	**hands-on** = active, practical
	woodworking /ˈwʊdˌwɜːkɪŋ/	(das) Tischlern	
	processing /ˈprəʊsesɪŋ/	(das) Bearbeiten	
	safety precaution /ˈseɪfti prɪˌkɔːʃn/	(die) Sicherheitsvorkehrung	
p. 41, 9	(to) mill around /ˌmɪl əˈraʊnd/	umherlaufen	
p. 41, 10	commercial /kəˈmɜːʃl/	(der) Werbespot	
	(to) advertise /ˈædvətaɪz/	für etwas Werbung machen	
p. 42, 11	**whether** /ˈweðə/	ob	
p. 43, 14	**matching** /ˈmætʃɪŋ/	passend	A **headline** is the title of a newspaper story.
	headline /ˈhedˌlaɪn/	(die) Überschrift, (die) Schlagzeile	
	welding /ˈweldɪŋ/	(das) Schweißen	
	light technology /ˈlaɪt tekˌnɒlədʒi/	(die) Lichttechnik	
	sound technology /ˈsaʊnd tekˌnɒlədʒi/	(die) Tontechnik	
	gallery walk /ˈɡæləri wɔːk/	(die) Gruppendiskussion in Stationsarbeit	

Unit 2 | Part B After-school activities

p. 44, 2	(to) **spread** *(irr)* /spred/	verteilen, verbreiten	A **debate** is a special kind of discussion that follows certain rules.
	(to) **succeed** /səkˈsiːd/	erfolgreich sein	
	debate /dɪˈbeɪt/	(die) Debatte, (die) Diskussion	
	future /ˈfjuːtʃə/	zukünftig	
	career /kəˈrɪə/	(die) Karriere, (die) Laufbahn	
	academic /ˌækəˈdemɪk/	akademisch, wissenschaftlich	An **educational** game is fun to play but it also teaches you something.
	leadership /ˈliːdəʃɪp/	(die) Führung, (die) Leitung	
	educational /ˌedjʊˈkeɪʃnəl/	Bildungs-, pädagogisch	
	mathletics club *(informal)* /mæθˈletɪks klʌb/	(die) Mathe-AG	
	(to) stretch /stretʃ/	dehnen, spannen	
	mathematics /ˌmæθəˈmætɪks/	(die) Mathematik	
	pitcher /ˈpɪtʃə/	(der/die) Werfer/in	
	catcher /ˈkætʃə/	(der/die) Fänger/in	
	sports hall /ˈspɔːts hɔːl/	(die) Sporthalle	**sports hall** = gym
	glee club /ˈɡliː klʌb/	(die) Gesangs-AG	
	singing /ˈsɪŋɪŋ/	(das) Singen, (der) Gesang	
	joy /dʒɔɪ/	(die) Freude	
	congress /ˈkɒŋɡres/	(der) Kongress	
	role-playing /ˈrəʊlˌpleɪɪŋ/	(das) Rollenspiel	
	(to) debate /dɪˈbeɪt/	diskutieren, debattieren	
	(to) improvise /ˈɪmprəvaɪz/	improvisieren	
	auditorium *(AE)* /ˌɔːdɪˈtɔːriəm/	(der) Vortragssaal, (die) Festhalle	
	debating society /dɪˈbeɪtɪŋ səˌsaɪəti/	(die) Debattiergesellschaft	The boy has **fewer** apples than the girl.
p. 45, 2	**fewer** /ˈfjuːə/	weniger *(bei zählbaren Nomen)*	

	(to) be up to something *(irr)* /ˌbi ˌʌp tə ˈsʌmθɪŋ/	etwas vorhaben
	lunchtime /ˈlʌntʃtaɪm/	(die) Mittagszeit, (die) Mittagspause
	working /ˈwɜːkɪŋ/	arbeitend
	elementary school *(AE)* /elɪˈmentri skuːl/	(die) Grundschule
	primary school /ˈpraɪməri skuːl/	(die) Grundschule
	(to) drop out /ˌdrɒp ˈaʊt/	abbrechen
	chemistry /ˈkemɪstri/	(die) Chemie
p. 46, 4	**type** /taɪp/	(der) Typ
	conditional (clause) /kənˈdɪʃnəl klɔːz/	(das) Konditional, (der) Konditionalsatz
p. 47, 6	tailgate party *(AE)* /ˈteɪlˌgeɪt ˌpɑːti/	(das) *Picknick von der Ladefläche oder aus dem Kofferraum eines Autos während einer Sportveranstaltung oder eines Konzerts*
	parking lot *(AE)* /ˈpɑːkɪŋ lɒt/	(der) Parkplatz
	chilli *(pl* chillies*)* /ˈtʃɪli, ˈtʃɪliz/	(der) Chili, (die) Peperoni
	baked potatoes *(pl)* /ˌbeɪkt pəˈteɪtəʊz/	(die) Ofenkartoffeln
p. 48, 7	**car park** /ˈkɑː pɑːk/	(der) Parkplatz
	(to) **unpack** /ʌnˈpæk/	auspacken
	(to) **smell** *(irr)* /smel/	riechen
	seat /siːt/	(der) Sitz
	professional /prəˈfeʃnəl/	professionell, beruflich
	(to) **enjoy oneself** /ɪnˈdʒɔɪ wʌnˌself/	sich amüsieren
	incredible /ɪnˈkredəbl/	unglaublich
	spirit /ˈspɪrɪt/	(der) Geist, (die) Stimmung
	pattern /ˈpætən/	(das) Muster
	(to) hashtag /ˈhæʃˌtæg/	mit einem Hashtag versehen
	opening act /ˈəʊpənɪŋ ˌækt/	(die) Eröffnungsfeier
	tailgate *(AE)*	(die) Heckklappe, *hier:* (der) Kofferraum
	car boot /ˈkɑː ˌbuːt/	(der) Kofferraum
	trunk *(AE)* /trʌŋk/	(der) Kofferraum
	confusing /kənˈfjuːzɪŋ/	verwirrend
	chips *(pl, AE)* /tʃɪps/	(die) Chips
	crisps *(pl)* /krɪsps/	(die) Chips
	(to) barbecue /ˈbɑːbɪˌkjuː/	grillen
	second helping /ˌsekənd ˈhelpɪŋ/	(der) Nachschlag
	chilled *(informal)* /tʃɪld/	gechillt
	way *(informal)* /weɪ/	viel
	playing field /ˈpleɪɪŋ ˌfiːld/	(der) Sportplatz
	half-time /ˌhɑːf ˈtaɪm/	(die) Halbzeit
	beforehand /bɪˈfɔːhænd/	vorher
	athletic /æθˈletɪk/	athletisch, sportlich
	jump /dʒʌmp/	(der) Sprung
	flip /flɪp/	(der) Salto

In the United States, children start school at an **elementary school** when they are about 6 years old until they are about 12 years old. In Great Britain, a **primary school** is for children between about 4 or 5 and 11 years.

A **car park** is an area where people can leave their cars.

When something is **incredible** you can hardly believe it.

They love to **barbecue** at the weekends.

„Tailgating" bedeutet im britischen Englisch das zu dichte Auffahren, wenn man hinter einem anderen Auto fährt.

Vocabulary

p. 49, 7	(to) do one's best *(irr)* /ˌduː wʌnz ˈbest/	sein Bestes geben	You can have fun at **carnival**.
	carnival /ˈkɑːnɪvl/	(das) Volksfest, (der) Karneval	
	chant /tʃɑːnt/	(der) Sprechgesang	
	clap /klæp/	(das) Klatschen	
	(to) go crazy *(irr)* /ˌɡəʊ ˈkreɪzi/	verrückt werden; *hier:* ausrasten	**New Year's Day** is a holiday. Most people don't have to work.
People and Places 4	**New Year's Day** /ˌnjuː jɪəz ˈdeɪ/	(der) Neujahrstag	
	(to) animate /ˈænɪmeɪt/	animieren	
	spectator /spekˈteɪtə/	(der/die) Zuschauer/in	
	(to) cheer somebody on /ˌtʃɪə ˌsʌmbədi ˈɒn/	jemanden anfeuern	
	Opening Day /ˈəʊpənɪŋ deɪ/	(der) Eröffnungstag	When you take part in a competition and you want to win, your **aim** is to win.
p. 50, 8	**aim** /eɪm/	(das) Ziel	
	up (to) /ˈʌp tuː/	bis (zu)	
	full-contact sport /fʊl ˈkɒntækt spɔːt/	*(die)* Vollkontakt-Sportart	
	league /liːɡ/	(die) Liga	
p. 51, 11	**kind** /kaɪnd/	freundlich	A **kind** person is friendly.
	jam /dʒæm/	(die) Marmelade	**aside from** *(AE)* = apart from *(BE)*
	aside from *(AE)* /əˈsaɪd frəm/	abgesehen von	
p. 52, 12	**yourselves** /jɔːˈselvz/	euch; selbst	**myself** (ich) selbst **yourself** (du) selbst **himself** (er) selbst; sich **herself** (sie) selbst; sich **ourselves** (wir) selbst **yourselves** (ihr) selbst **themselves** (sie) selbst
	reflexive pronoun /rɪˌfleksɪv ˈprəʊnaʊn/	(das) Reflexivpronomen	
	pronoun /ˈprəʊnaʊn/	(das) Pronomen, (das) Fürwort	
p. 52, 13	(to) thank /θæŋk/	danken, sich bedanken	

Unit 3 | Part A Relationships

p. 57	**relationship** /rɪˈleɪʃnʃɪp/	(die) Beziehung	
	(to) make *(irr)* /meɪk/	*hier:* ausmachen	
	cyberbullying /ˈsaɪbəˌbʊliɪŋ/	(das) Cybermobbing	
p. 58, 2	**depressed** /dɪˈprest/	deprimiert	
	unhappy /ʌnˈhæpi/	unglücklich	**unhappy** ≠ happy
	helpless /ˈhelpləs/	hilflos	„(to) stand somebody" wird meistens negativ verwendet: I can't **stand** my new neighbours! I just don't like them! I couldn't **stand** the old ones either.
p. 58, 3	BFF (= best friend forever) *(informal)* /ˌbiː_efˈef, ˌbest ˌfrend fərˈevə/	*(der/die)* allerbeste Freund/in	
	that way /ˈðæt weɪ/	so, auf diese Weise	
	(to) stand somebody *(irr)* /ˈstænd ˌsʌmbədi/	jemanden leiden können	
p. 59, 3	**though** *(nachgestellt)* /ðəʊ/	jedoch	
	close /kləʊs/	nah(e); eng	Did you do it **by yourself**? Yes, I did it all **by myself**! Nobody helped me.
	lately /ˈleɪtli/	in letzter Zeit, kürzlich	
	by oneself /ˌbaɪ wʌnˈself/	allein	
	point of view /ˌpɔɪnt_əv_ˈvjuː/	(die) Ansicht, (die) Perspektive	
	mom *(AE)* /mɒm/	Mama	
	(to) be into *(informal, irr)* /ˌbi_ɪnˈtuː/	interessiert sein an	
	(to) stick with *(irr)* /ˈstɪk wɪð/	bleiben bei, festhalten an	
	for the time being /fə ðə ˌtaɪm ˈbiːɪŋ/	vorerst	

	(to) hang out *(informal, irr)* /ˌhæŋˈaʊt/	rumhängen, Zeit mit jemandem verbringen	To **report** means to give information about what you have seen or heard.
p. 60, 4	**report** (to) /rɪˈpɔːt/	berichten, wiedergeben	
	hopefully /ˈhəʊpfli/	hoffentlich	
p. 60, 5	reported speech /rɪˌpɔːtɪd ˈspiːtʃ/	(die) indirekte Rede	
p. 61, 6	**weakness** /ˈwiːknəs/	(die) Schwäche	
p. 61, 7	(to) **lie** /laɪ/	lügen	
	(to) **rely on** /rɪˈlaɪ ɒn/	sich verlassen auf	
	comment /ˈkɒment/	(der) Kommentar, (die) Bemerkung	
	conclusion /kənˈkluːʒn/	(die) Schlussfolgerung	
	(to) **sum up** /ˌsʌmˈʌp/	zusammenfassen	
	loyal /ˈlɔɪəl/	treu, loyal	
p. 62, 8	**research** /rɪˈsɜːtʃ/	(die) Forschung	They are doing **research**.
	out of /ˈaʊt əv/	von	
	rare /reə/	selten	**rare** = not often
	whom /huːm/	wem; wen; der/die/das	
	(to) **act** /ækt/	sich verhalten	A **mean** person is not very nice.
	mean /miːn/	gemein; bösartig	
	(to) **ignore** /ɪɡˈnɔː/	ignorieren	
	hurt /hɜːt/	verletzt, gekränkt	
	however /haʊˈevə/	aber, wie auch immer	
	(to) **remember** /rɪˈmembə/	bedenken, denken an	A **common** problem is a problem that many people have.
	common /ˈkɒmən/	üblich, weit verbreitet	
	period (of time) /ˌpɪəriəd əv ˈtaɪm/	(die) Zeitspanne, (der) Zeitraum	
	(to) **make sense** *(irr)* /ˌmeɪk ˈsens/	sinnvoll sein	
	(to) send in *(irr)* /ˌsendˈɪn/	einsenden	
	psychologist /saɪˈkɒlədʒɪst/	(der/die) Psychologe/Psychologin	
	based in /ˈbeɪst ɪn/	ansässig in	
	swim practice /ˈswɪm ˌpræktɪs/	(das) Schwimmtraining	
	next up *(informal)* /ˌnekstˈʌp/	(der/die/das) Nächste	
	for a long time /fər ə ˈlɒŋ taɪm/	lange	
	(to) **work out** /ˌwɜːkˈaʊt/	sich entwickeln	
	(to) walk away from /ˌwɔːk əˈweɪ frɒm/	aus dem Weg gehen	
	(to) pick up (on) /ˌpɪkˈʌp/	anknüpfen an	I don't think I'll remember the date. Would you please **remind** me about it?
p. 63, 8	(to) **remind somebody** /rɪˈmaɪnd ˌsʌmbədi/	jemanden erinnern	
	(to) **forgive** *(irr)* /fəˈɡɪv/	vergeben, verzeihen	
	(to) **be sorry** *(irr)* /ˌbiː ˈsɒri/	bedauern; sich entschuldigen	
	apart /əˈpɑːt/	getrennt	
	responsible /rɪˈspɒnsəbl/	verantwortungsbewusst, verantwortlich	
	(to) **behave** /bɪˈheɪv/	sich verhalten, sich benehmen	They don't **behave** well.
	qualified /ˈkwɒlɪfaɪd/	qualifiziert, ausgebildet	
	(to) **agree with** /əˈɡriː wɪð/	einer Meinung sein mit, übereinstimmen mit	

Vocabulary

	behavior *(AE)* /bɪˈheɪvjə/	(das) Benehmen, (das) Verhalten	
p. 64, 9	love /lʌv/	(die) Liebe	
	painfully /ˈpeɪnfli/	schmerzlich	
p. 64, 11	saying /ˈseɪɪŋ/	(das) Sprichwort	
p. 65, 12	empty /ˈempti/	leer	The cinema is nearly **empty**.
	(to) **keep from doing something** *(irr)* /ˌkiːp frəm ˈduːɪŋ ˌsʌmθɪŋ/	etwas unterlassen, sich etwas verkneifen	
	umbrella /ʌmˈbrelə/	(der) Regenschirm	
	hat /hæt/	(der) Hut	
	(to) **look away** /ˌlʊk_əˈweɪ/	wegsehen	
	shape /ʃeɪp/	(die) Form, (die) Gestalt	
	fat /fæt/	dick	
	(to) **fall in love** *(irr)* /ˌfɔːl_ɪn ˈlʌv/	sich verlieben	
	(to) **lie** *(irr)* /laɪ/	liegen	At night, you can see stars and the moon in the **sky**.
	sky /skaɪ/	(der) Himmel	
	cloud /klaʊd/	(die) Wolke	
	(to) **argue** /ˈɑːgjuː/	sich streiten	
	smile /smaɪl/	(das) Lächeln	
	connection /kəˈnekʃn/	(die) Verbindung	
	on /ɒn/	*hier:* über	
	discomfort /dɪsˈkʌmfət/	(das) Unbehagen	
	(to) **tell** *(irr)* /tel/	*hier:* bemerken	
	wallpaper /ˈwɔːlpeɪpə/	(die) Tapete	
	crack /kræk/	(der) Riss	
	ceiling /ˈsiːlɪŋ/	(die) Zimmerdecke	
	iced tea /ˌaɪst_ˈtiː/	(der) Eistee	
	light bulb /ˈlaɪt bʌlb/	(die) Glühbirne	
	standing lamp /ˈstændɪŋ læmp/	(die) Stehlampe	
	fan /fæn/	(der) Ventilator	
	whale /weɪl/	(der) Wal	
	elephant /ˈelɪfənt/	(der) Elefant	The **trunk** is the long nose of an **elephant**.
	trunk /trʌŋk/	(der) Rüssel	
	(to) **lower** /ˈləʊə/	senken	
	plaster /ˈplɑːstə/	(der) Verputz	
	(to) **daydream** /ˈdeɪˌdriːm/	vor sich hinträumen	
p. 66, 13	tense /tens/	(die) Zeitform	When you **are in love** you can **ask** the person you are in love with **on a date**.
	(to) **ask on a date** /ˌɑːsk_ɒn_ə ˈdeɪt/	um eine Verabredung bitten	
	(to) **be in love** *(irr)* /ˌbi_ɪn ˈlʌv/	verliebt sein	
	romantic /rəʊˈmæntɪk/	romantisch	
	comedy /ˈkɒmədi/	(die) Komödie	
	direct speech /daɪˌrekt ˈspiːtʃ/	(die) direkte Rede, (die) wörtliche Rede	
p. 66, 14	particular /pəˈtɪkjʊlə/	bestimmt; besondere(r, s)	With the help of the Internet you can **be connected to** people all around the world.
	(to) **be connected (to)** *(irr)* /ˌbi: kəˈnektɪd_tə/	verbunden sein (mit), in Verbindung stehen (mit)	

	distance /ˈdɪstəns/	(die) Distanz, (die) Entfernung	
	unknown /ʌnˈnəʊn/	unbekannt	
p. 67, 15	(to) **read out** *(irr)* /ˌriːd ˈaʊt/	(laut) vorlesen	

Unit 3 | Part B Digital communication

p. 68, 1	**channel** /ˈtʃænl/	(der) Kanal	
	voice message /ˈvɔɪs ˌmesɪdʒ/	(die) Sprachnachricht	
p. 68, 2	**virtual** /ˈvɜːtʃʊəl/	virtuell	
	easily /ˈiːzɪli/	leicht, mühelos	
	further /ˈfɜːðə/	weiter	The girl has **little** water. She has less water than the boy.
	little /ˈlɪtl/	wenig	
	compared to /kəmˈpeəd tʊ/	im Vergleich zu	
	since /sɪns/	da, weil	
	right away /ˌraɪt əˈweɪ/	sofort, gleich	
	(to) **access** /ˈækses/	zugreifen auf	
	recent /ˈriːsnt/	jüngste(r, s); letzte(r, s)	**recent** = not long ago
	study /ˈstʌdi/	(die) Studie	
	majority /məˈdʒɒrəti/	(die) Mehrheit	
	average /ˈævərɪdʒ/	durchschnittlich	When you **respond to** something, you answer or react to it.
	in fact /ɪn ˈfækt/	tatsächlich, in Wirklichkeit	
	(to) **respond to** /rɪˈspɒnd tə/	antworten auf, reagieren auf	
	(to) **receive** /rɪˈsiːv/	erhalten; empfangen	
	(to) **message** /ˈmesɪdʒ/	eine Nachricht schicken	
	mindlessly /ˈmaɪndləsli/	gedankenlos	
	self-confessed /ˌself kənˈfest/	selbsterklärt	
	addict /ˈædɪkt/	(der/die) Abhängige	
	pillow /ˈpɪləʊ/	(das) Kissen	
	(to) **glue** /gluː/	kleben	**cell phone** *(AE)* = mobile phone *(BE)*
	cell phone *(AE)* /ˈsel fəʊn/	(das) Handy	
	(to) **be far from reach** *(irr)* /ˌbiː ˌfɑː frəm ˈriːtʃ/	außer Reichweite sein	
p. 69, 2	(to) **bully** /ˈbʊli/	mobben	A **threat** is a situation or activity that could lead to danger.
	nasty /ˈnɑːsti/	böse, gemein	
	threat /θret/	(die) Bedrohung	
	rumor *(AE)* = **rumour** *(BE)* /ˈruːmə/	(das) Gerücht	
	social media /ˌsəʊʃl ˈmiːdiə/	soziale Medien	
	major /ˈmeɪdʒə/	bedeutend, wichtig; Haupt-	**major** = important
	proof /pruːf/	(der) Beweis	
	(to) **ban** /bæn/	verbieten; ausschließen	
	(to) **block** /blɒk/	blockieren	
	account /əˈkaʊnt/	(das) Benutzerkonto	
	age /eɪdʒ/	(das) Zeitalter	
	constantly /ˈkɒnstəntli/	ständig, dauernd	**constantly** = all the time

Vocabulary

	via /ˈvaɪə/	über	
	(to) **admit** (to) /ədˈmɪt/	zugeben, eingestehen	
	awkward /ˈɔːkwəd/	schwierig; unangenehm	
	shocked /ʃɒkt/	schockiert, entsetzt	You can do things …
	(to) harass /ˈhærəs/	belästigen	**more easily** leichter
	(to) humiliate /hjuːˈmɪlieɪt/	erniedrigen	**more happily** glücklicher
	bully /ˈbʊli/	(die) Person, die mobbt	**faster** schneller
	(to) expel /ɪkˈspel/	von der Schule verweisen	**more quickly** schneller
	unacceptable /ˌʌnəkˈseptəbl/	inakzeptabel	**more carefully** vorsichtiger
	(to) break up *(irr)* /ˌbreɪk ˈʌp/	Schluss machen	
	face-to-face /ˌfeɪs tə ˈfeɪs/	persönlich	
	harassment /ˈhærəsmənt/	(die) Belästigung, (die) Schikane	"Loudly", "badly" and
p. 70, 3	adverb of manner /ˌædvɜːb əv ˈmænə/	(das) Adverb der Art und Weise	"quickly" are **adverbs of manner**.
	comparative /kəmˈpærətɪv/	(der) Komparativ	
p. 70, 4	superlative /sʊˈpɜːlətɪv/	(der) Superlativ	
p. 71, 5	**nowadays** /ˈnaʊəˌdeɪz/	heutzutage	**nowadays** = today
	frequently /ˈfriːkwəntli/	häufig	
	emotion /ɪˈməʊʃn/	(das) Gefühl, (die) Emotion	
	character /ˈkærəktə/	(das) Zeichen, (das) Schriftzeichen	
	set /set/	(der) Satz, (die) Garnitur	
	understanding /ˌʌndəˈstændɪŋ/	(das) Verständnis	
	whereas /weərˈæz/	während; wohingegen	
	death /deθ/	(der) Tod	
	harmful /ˈhɑːmfl/	schädlich	
	translation /trænsˈleɪʃn/	(die) Übersetzung	
	agency /ˈeɪdʒənsi/	(die) Agentur	
	limit /ˈlɪmɪt/	(die) (Höchst)grenze, (das) Limit	
	(to) **replace** /rɪˈpleɪs/	ersetzen	
	(to) **lack** /læk/	nicht haben, fehlen	She **is aware of** the fact that
	(to) **be aware of** *(irr)* /ˌbi əˈweər əv/	sich bewusst sein	everybody is looking at her.
	(to) **intend** /ɪnˈtend/	beabsichtigen	
	misunderstanding /ˌmɪsʌndəˈstændɪŋ/	(das) Missverständnis	The langugage that people
	universal /ˌjuːnɪˈvɜːsl/	allgemein, universell	speak in Japan is called
	Japanese /ˌdʒæpəˈniːz/	Japaner/in; japanisch	**Japanese**.
	angel /ˈeɪndʒl/	(der) Engel	
	(to) portray /pɔːˈtreɪ/	porträtieren, darstellen	
	innocence /ˈɪnəsns/	(die) Unschuld	
	deed /diːd/	(die) Tat	
	threatening /ˈθretnɪŋ/	drohend, bedrohlich	
	insult /ˈɪnsʌlt/	(die) Beleidigung	**Brazil** is a country in South
	Brazil /brəˈzɪl/	Brasilien	America.
	folded hands /ˌfəʊldɪd ˈhændz/	betende Hände	
	gratitude /ˈɡrætɪtjuːd/	(die) Dankbarkeit	

	subtle /'sʌtl/	fein, subtil	
	translator /træns'leɪtə/	(der/die) Übersetzer/in	
	facial expression /ˌfeɪʃl ɪk'spreʃn/	(der) Gesichtsausdruck	
	tone of voice /ˌtəʊn əv 'vɔɪs/	(der) Ton	
	guarantee /ˌgærən'tiː/	(die) Garantie	
p. 72, 6	(to) feel comfortable *(irr)* /ˌfiːl 'kʌmftəbl/	sich wohl fühlen	to feel comfortable ≠ to feel uncomfortable
	advantage /əd'vɑːntɪdʒ/	(der) Vorteil	
	instead of /ɪn'sted əv/	anstatt	
	(to) represent /ˌreprɪ'zent/	darstellen, symbolisieren	
	interest /'ɪntrəst/	(das) Interesse, (das) Hobby	interest = hobby
	actually /'æktʃuəli/	wirklich	
	disadvantage /ˌdɪsəd'vɑːntɪdʒ/	(der) Nachteil	disadvantage ≠ advantage
	benefit /'benɪfɪt/	(der) Vorteil, (der) Nutzen	
	(to) affect /ə'fekt/	betreffen, beeinflussen	
	separate /'seprət/	separat, getrennt	
	(to) respond /rɪ'spɒnd/	antworten; reagieren	
	immediately /ɪ'miːdiətli/	sofort	immediately = right away
	(to) get connected *(irr)* /ˌget kə'nektɪd/	sich verbinden, in Kontakt treten	
	(to) impact /ɪm'pækt/	Einfluss haben auf	
	positive /'pɒzətɪv/	(der) Pluspunkt	
	sociologist /ˌsəʊsi'ɒlədʒɪst/	(der/die) Soziologe/Soziologin	
	loved ones *(pl)* /'lʌvd wʌnz/	(der/die) Angehörige, (die) nahestehenden Personen	loved ones: family, relatives and close friends
	phone call /'fəʊn kɔːl/	(der) Telefonanruf	
	time-saving /'taɪm seɪvɪŋ/	zeitsparend	
	isolated /'aɪsəˌleɪtɪd/	isoliert, einsam	
	plenty of /'plenti əv/	reichlich, genug	
	in person /ˌɪn 'pɜːsn/	persönlich	
	comfort /'kʌmfət/	(der) Komfort, (die) Bequemlichkeit	
	first of all /ˌfɜːst əv 'ɔːl/	zuallererst	
	expectation /ˌekspek'teɪʃn/	(die) Erwartung	
	boundary /'baʊndri/	(die) Grenze	
	physically /'fɪzɪkli/	physisch	
	blurred /blɜːd/	verschwommen, unscharf	
	at all times /æt ˌɔːl 'taɪmz/	jederzeit, immer	
p. 73, 6	likely /'laɪkli/	wahrscheinlich	
	(to) protect (from) /prə'tekt frəm/	schützen (vor)	
	offensive /ə'fensɪv/	beleidigend, ausfallend	
	(to) maintain /meɪn'teɪn/	erhalten, pflegen	
	carefully /'keəfli/	gründlich	
	aggressive /ə'gresɪv/	aggressiv, angriffslustig	The girl on the right seems to be quite **aggressive**.
	interaction /ˌɪntər'ækʃn/	(die) Interaktion, (die) Kommunikation	
	carelessly /'keələsli/	unvorsichtig, gedankenlos	

Vocabulary

	capital letter /ˌkæpɪtl ˈletə/	(der) Großbuchstabe
	exclamation point (AE) /ˌekskləˈmeɪʃn pɔɪnt/	(das) Ausrufezeichen
	question mark /ˈkwestʃn mɑːk/	(das) Fragezeichen
	authentic /ɔːˈθentɪk/	authentisch
	(to) enhance /ɪnˈhɑːns/	verbessern
	(to) harm /hɑːm/	schaden, Schaden zufügen
	(to) outweigh /ˌaʊtˈweɪ/	überwiegen
p. 74, 8	(to) be close to somebody's heart (irr) /ˌbiː ˌkləʊs tə ˌsʌmbədiz ˈhɑːt/	jemandem sehr wichtig sein
p. 75, 10	(to) **swap** /swɒp/	tauschen
	youth hostel /ˈjuːθ ˌhɒstl/	(die) Jugendherberge
	crib /krɪb/	(das) Gitterbett
	sleeping bag /ˈsliːpɪŋ bæɡ/	(der) Schlafsack
	choreographer /ˌkɒriˈɒɡrəfə/	(der/die) Choreograph/in
p. 75, 11	(to) translate /trænsˈleɪt/	übersetzen
p. 76, 12	non-stop /ˌnɒnˈstɒp/	ununterbrochen
p. 76, 13	prefix /ˈpriːfɪks/	(die) Vorsilbe, (das) Präfix
	acceptable /əkˈseptəbl/	akzeptabel
p. 77, 15	respectfully /rɪˈspektfəli/	respektvoll

The twins can always **swap** places, people never know who is who.

"Dis" is the **prefix** of "disagree".

Unit 4 | Part A The power of hope

p. 81	(to) **relate to** /rɪˈleɪt tʊ/	handeln von, zu tun haben mit
	hope /həʊp/	(die) Hoffnung
	power /ˈpaʊə/	(die) Macht, (der) Einfluss
	(to) **take action** (irr) /ˌteɪk ˈækʃn/	handeln, Maßnahmen ergreifen
	hard skill /ˌhɑːd ˈskɪl/	(die) berufstypische Qualifikation
	soft skill /ˌsɒft ˈskɪl/	(die) persönliche, soziale und methodische Kompetenz
	booklet /ˈbʊklət/	(die) Broschüre
p. 82, 2	**keyword** /ˈkiːˌwɜːd/	(das) Schlüsselwort, (das) Stichwort
	(to) **afford** /əˈfɔːd/	sich leisten
	qualification /ˌkwɒlɪfɪˈkeɪʃn/	(die) Qualifikation
	knowledge /ˈnɒlɪdʒ/	(die) Kenntnis, (das) Wissen
	dove /dʌv/	(die) Taube
	Navajo /ˈnævəhəʊ/	(die) Sprache der Navajo
	(to) motivate /ˈməʊtɪveɪt/	motivieren
	camerawork (no pl) /ˈkæmrəwɜːk/	(die) Kameraführung
	technical /ˈteknɪkl/	technisch
	making /ˈmeɪkɪŋ/	(die) Herstellung
	California Institute of the Arts /ˌkæləˌfɔːniə ˌɪnstɪˌtjuːt əv ði ˈɑːts/	private Kunsthochschule in Kalifornien
	(to) win a scholarship (irr) /ˌwɪn ə ˈskɒləʃɪp/	ein Stipendium bekommen

to **take action** = to act

If you are rich, you can **afford** to buy expensive things.

	Skills	Wordbanks	Grammar	**Words**

p. 83, 2	community college /kəˈmjuːnəti ˌkɒlɪdʒ/	(das) subventionierte zweijährige College	
	difficulty /ˈdɪfɪklti/	(die) Schwierigkeit, (das) Problem	
	disability /ˌdɪsəˈbɪləti/	(die) Behinderung, (die) Einschränkung	
	(to) make (it/something) (irr) /meɪk/	(es/etwas) schaffen	When you help someone, the person you help is certainly **grateful**.
	grateful /ˈgreɪtfl/	dankbar	
	goal /gəʊl/	(das) Ziel	
	(to) raise awareness /ˌreɪz əˈweənəz/	Bewusstsein schärfen	
	necessarily /ˈnesəsərəli/	notwendigerweise, unbedingt	
	climate change /ˈklaɪmət tʃeɪndʒ/	(die) Klimaveränderung, (der) Klimawandel	
	(to) train /treɪn/	eine Ausbildung machen	to **campaign** = to fight for something with a political aim
	sustainability /səˌsteɪnəˈbɪləti/	(die) Nachhaltigkeit	
	(to) campaign /kæmˈpeɪn/	kämpfen, sich engagieren	
	(to) take time (irr) /ˌteɪk ˈtaɪm/	Zeit beanspruchen; dauern	
	basically /ˈbeɪsɪkli/	im Wesentlichen	
	grown-up /ˌgrəʊn ˈʌp/	(der/die) Erwachsene	**grown-up** = adult
	concern /kənˈsɜːn/	(das) Anliegen, (die) Sorge	
	law /lɔː/	(das) Gesetz	
	paraclimber /ˈpærəˌklaɪmə/	(der/die) Kletterer/Kletterin mit Handicap	
	(to) overcome (irr) /ˌəʊvəˈkʌm/	bewältigen, überwinden	
	Paralympic /ˌpærəˈlɪmpɪk/	paralympisch	
	student council /ˈstjuːdnt ˌkaʊnsl/	(die) Schülervertretung	
p. 84, 3	(to) direct /daɪˈrekt/	Regie führen	
p. 85, 5	change /tʃeɪndʒ/	(die) Veränderung, (der) Wechsel	When you are able to create pictures in your mind you have **imagination**.
	imagination /ɪˌmædʒɪˈneɪʃn/	(die) Fantasie, (die) Vorstellungskraft	
	action /ˈækʃn/	(das) Handeln, (die) Maßnahmen	
	crisis (pl crises) /ˈkraɪsɪs, ˈkraɪsiːz/	(die) Krise	
	(to) make a difference (irr) /ˌmeɪk ə ˈdɪfrəns/	einen Unterschied machen, verändern	
	powerful /ˈpaʊəfl/	mächtig, stark	
	(to) get involved (irr) /ˌget ɪnˈvɒlvd/	sich engagieren	
	ecological footprint /ˌiːkəˌlɒdʒɪkl ˈfʊtprɪnt/	(der) ökologische Fußabdruck	
	direct /daɪˈrekt/	direkt	
	circle /ˈsɜːkl/	(der) Kreis, (die) Runde	
	public transport /ˌpʌblɪk ˈtrænspɔːt/	(das) öffentliche Verkehrsmittel	Buses are a kind of **public transport**.
	stamina /ˈstæmɪnə/	(das) Durchhaltevermögen, (die) Ausdauer	
	patience /ˈpeɪʃns/	(die) Geduld	
	(to) take a break (irr) /ˌteɪk ə ˈbreɪk/	eine Pause machen	
	(to) combat /ˈkɒmbæt/	bekämpfen	**combating** (AE) = **combatting** (BE)
	anxiety /æŋˈzaɪəti/	(die) Sorge, (die) Angst	
	in detail /ɪn ˈdiːteɪl/	im Einzelnen, ausführlich	
	livable (AE) = liveable (BE) /ˈlɪvəbl/	lebenswert	

Vocabulary

	(to) get going *(irr)* /ˌget ˈgəʊɪŋ/	in Gang bringen
	CO_2 (= carbon dioxide) /ˌsiː ˌəʊ ˈtuː, ˌkɑːbən daɪˈɒksaɪd/	(das) Kohlendioxid
	output /ˈaʊtpʊt/	(der) Ausstoß, (die) Produktion
	(to) adapt /əˈdæpt/	anpassen, bearbeiten
	systemic /sɪˈstiːmɪk/	systemisch
	as a whole /əz ə ˈhəʊl/	als Ganzes
	petition /pəˈtɪʃn/	(die) Petition, (die) Unterschriftenliste
	on a larger scale /ˌɒn ə ˌlɑːdʒə ˈskeɪl/	im größeren Rahmen
	short-distance flight /ˌʃɔːt ˌdɪstəns ˈflaɪt/	(der) Kurzstreckenflug
	burned-out *(AE)* = burnt-out *(BE)* /ˌbɜːnd ˈaʊt, ˌbɜːnt ˈaʊt/	ausgebrannt
p. 86, 6	**vision** /ˈvɪʒn/	(die) Vorstellung, (die) Vision
	(to) **purchase** /ˈpɜːtʃəs/	kaufen, erwerben
	(to) **power** /ˈpaʊə/	antreiben
	(to) **cause** /kɔːz/	verursachen
	worth /wɜːθ/	wert
	damage /ˈdæmɪdʒ/	(der) Schaden
	(to) **recycle** /riːˈsaɪkl/	recyceln, wiederaufbereiten
	garbage *(AE)* /ˈgɑːbɪdʒ/	(der) Abfall, (der) Müll
	pollution /pəˈluːʃn/	(die) Umweltverschmutzung
	valuable /ˈvæljʊbl/	wertvoll
	metal /ˈmetl/	(das) Metall
	point /pɔɪnt/	(die) Stelle
	eventually /ɪˈventʃuəli/	schließlich; irgendwann
	organization (= organisation) /ˌɔːgənaɪˈzeɪʃn/	(die) Organisation, (die) Vereinigung
	spark /spɑːk/	(der) Funke, (der) Auslöser
	battery /ˈbætri/	(die) Batterie
	potential /pəˈtenʃl/	potenziell, möglich
	(to) dispose of /dɪˈspəʊz əv/	entsorgen
	Californian /ˌkæləˈfɔːniən/	kalifornisch
	waste disposal plant /ˌweɪst dɪˈspəʊzl plɑːnt/	(die) Abfallentsorgungsanlage
	massive /ˈmæsɪv/	riesig, enorm
	harm /hɑːm/	(der) Schaden
	chemical /ˈkemɪkl/	(die) Chemikalie
	(to) end up /ˌend ˈʌp/	schließlich landen
	landfill /ˈlændfɪl/	(das) Deponiegelände
	recycling plant /riːˈsaɪklɪŋ plɑːnt/	(die) Recyclinganlage
	trash *(AE)* /træʃ/	(der) Müll, (der) Abfall
	globally /ˈgləʊbli/	weltweit
	non-profit /ˌnɒn ˈprɒfɪt/	nicht gewinnorientiert
p. 87, 6	(to) **run** *(irr)* /rʌn/	durchführen

In his dreams he has the **vision** that he can fly.

to **purchase** = to buy

Water **pollution** is a threat to nature.

Früher war die britische Schreibweise von Wörtern mit „-ise", „isation" oder „-iser" eindeutig die mit „s", nur im amerikanischen Englisch wurden alle diese Wörter mit „z" geschrieben. Mittlerweile werden kaum noch Unterschiede gemacht. Viele Briten schreiben „organize, organization, realize, …". In vielen Wörterbüchern wird sogar die Schreibweise mit „z" als die häufiger vorkommende gelistet.

	campaign /kæmˈpeɪn/	(die) Kampagne	A teacher **educates** children.
	(to) **educate** /ˈedjʊkeɪt/	unterrichten; aufklären	
	importance /ɪmˈpɔːtns/	(die) Bedeutung, (die) Wichtigkeit	
	among /əˈmʌŋ/	unter; zwischen	
	(to) **encourage** /ɪnˈkʌrɪdʒ/	ermutigen	
	(to) **turn out** /ˌtɜːnˈaʊt/	sich herausstellen	
	(to) **define** /dɪˈfaɪn/	definieren	Your **attitude** is the way you feel and think about something.
	attitude /ˈætɪˌtjuːd/	(die) Haltung, (die) Einstellung	
	starting point /ˈstɑːtɪŋ pɔɪnt/	(der) Ausgangspunkt	
	awareness /əˈweənəs/	(das) Bewusstsein	
	(to) spread the word *(irr)* /ˌspred ðə ˈwɜːd/	es allen mitteilen	
	inner circle /ˌɪnə ˈsɜːkl/	(der) engste Kreis	
	used /juːzd/	gebraucht	
	(to) recruit /rɪˈkruːt/	anwerben	You do not earn money for a **volunteer** job.
	volunteer /ˌvɒlənˈtɪə/	ehrenamtlich	
	commitment /kəˈmɪtmənt/	(das) Engagement	
	infectious /ɪnˈfekʃəs/	ansteckend	
	changemaker /ˈtʃeɪndʒˌmeɪkə/	*jemand, der sich aktiv bemüht, Dinge zu verändern*	
	(to) care about /ˈkeər əˌbaʊt/	sich aus etwas etwas machen	
	(to) take a step *(irr)* /ˌteɪk ə ˈstep/	einen Schritt machen	
	amazed /əˈmeɪzd/	erstaunt, verblüfft	
p. 88, 7	**environmentally friendly** /ɪnˌvaɪrənmentli ˈfrendli/	umweltfreundlich	to **enable** someone = to give someone the ability or opportunity to do something
People and Places 5	(to) **enable** /ɪnˈeɪbl/	ermöglichen	
	(to) **become involved in** *(irr)* /bɪˌkʌm ɪnˈvɒlvd ɪn/	sich beteiligen, sich engagieren	
	responsibility /rɪˌspɒnsəˈbɪləti/	(die) Verantwortung; (die) Pflicht	
	secondary school /ˈsekəndri skuːl/	(die) weiterführende Schule	
	affair /əˈfeə/	(die) Angelegenheit, (die) Sache	
	principal *(AE)* /ˈprɪnsəpl/	(der/die) Rektor/in	
	(to) raise funds /ˌreɪz ˈfʌndz/	Geld sammeln	
	in need /ɪnˈniːd/	bedürftig	
	food drive /ˈfuːd draɪv/	*(das) Sammeln von Lebensmitteln, um sie an bedürftige Menschen abzugeben*	
	fundraiser /ˈfʌndˌreɪzə/	(die) Spendensammelaktion	
	charity run /ˈtʃærəti rʌn/	(der) Wohltätigkeitslauf	
	(to) take on *(irr)* /ˌteɪkˈɒn/	übernehmen, auf sich nehmen	
p. 88, 8	(to) sponsor /ˈspɒnsə/	sponsern	
p. 89, 9	**speech** /spiːtʃ/	(die) Rede	He is giving a **speech**.
	citizen /ˈsɪtɪzn/	(der/die) Bürger/in	
	value /ˈvæljuː/	(der) Wert	
	force /fɔːs/	(die) Kraft	

Vocabulary

(to) **give up** *(irr)* /ˌgɪvˈʌp/	aufgeben		Your **belief** is what you believe in.
belief /bɪˈliːf/	(der) Glaube		
fundamental /ˌfʌndəˈmentl/	grundlegend		
doubt /daʊt/	(der) Zweifel		The girls **are facing** each other.
fear /fɪə/	(die) Angst		
(to) **face** /feɪs/	gegenüberstehen		
determined /dɪˈtɜːmɪnd/	entschlossen		
excerpt /ˈeksɜːpt/	(der) Auszug, (das) Exzerpt		
walk of life /ˌwɔːk_əvˈlaɪf/	(der) Lebensbereich, (die) Gesellschaftsschicht		
infusion /ɪnˈfjuːʒn/	(das) Einbringen, (der) Input		**folks** *(informal)* = guys *(informal)*
folks *(informal)* /fəʊks/	(die) Leute		
(to) start out /ˌstɑːtˈaʊt/	anfangen		
anything /ˈeniˌθɪŋ/	alles		
informed /ɪnˈfɔːmd/	informiert		
engaged /ɪnˈgeɪdʒd/	beschäftigt; *hier:* engagiert		
(to) stand up for *(irr)* /ˌstændˈʌp fɔː/	sich einsetzen für		
critically /ˈkrɪtɪkli/	kritisch		
(to) encounter /ɪnˈkaʊntə/	treffen, begegnen		to **encounter** = to meet
obstacle /ˈɒbstəkl/	(das) Hindernis, (die) Hürde		
(to) struggle /ˈstrʌgl/	sich abmühen, sich quälen		
(to) be willing to *(irr)* /ˌbiːˈwɪlɪŋ tə/	bereit sein		
(to) rise *(irr)* /raɪz/	aufgehen; steigen		
division /dɪˈvɪʒn/	(die) Teilung, (die) Meinungsverschiedenheit		**Anger** is the feeling that you have when you are angry about something.
anger /ˈæŋgə/	(der) Ärger, (die) Wut		
focused /ˈfəʊkəst/	fokussiert		
hopeful /ˈhəʊpfl/	zuversichtlich		
empowered /ɪmˈpaʊəd/	(mental) gestärkt		
(to) empower /ɪmˈpaʊə/	(mental) stärken, aufbauen		
(to) get out *(irr)* /ˌgetˈaʊt/	hinausgehen		
worthy /ˈwɜːði/	würdig		
boundless /ˈbaʊndləs/	grenzenlos, unbegrenzt		
promise /ˈprɒmɪs/	(das) Versprechen		
(to) lead by example *(irr)* /ˌliːd baɪ_ɪgˈzɑːmpl/	mit gutem Beispiel vorangehen		
(to) **combine** /kəmˈbaɪn/	verbinden	p. 90, 10	Ollie **is wishing for** a long holiday with lots of spaghetti to eat.
(to) **wish for** (something) /ˈwɪʃ fɔː/	sich (etwas) wünschen	p. 90, 11	
(to) sketch /sketʃ/	skizzieren	p. 91, 13	

Unit 4 | Part B The world of work

physiotherapist /ˌfɪziəʊˈθerəpɪst/	(der/die) Physiotherapeut/in	p. 92, 1	
electrician /ɪˌlekˈtrɪʃn/	(der/die) Elektriker/in		
gardener /ˈgɑːdnə/	(der/die) Gärtner/in		The **gardener** loves his job.

	Skills	Wordbanks	Grammar	**Words**

	nursery teacher /ˈnɜːsəri ˌtiːtʃə/	(der/die) Vorschullehrer/in; (der/die) Erzieher/in		
	construction worker /kənˈstrʌkʃn ˌwɜːkə/	(der/die) Bauarbeiter/in		An **accountant** works with numbers.
	accountant /əˈkaʊntənt/	(der/die) Buchhalter/in		
	lawyer /ˈlɔːjə/	(der/die) Rechtsanwalt/Rechtsanwältin		
	animal keeper /ˈænɪml ˌkiːpə/	(der/die) Tierpfleger/in		
p. 92, 2	(to) **do for a living** *(irr)* /ˌduː fərˌə ˈlɪvɪŋ/	seinen Lebensunterhalt verdienen		
	registered nurse /ˌredʒɪstəd ˈnɜːs/	(der/die) examinierte Krankenpfleger / examinierte Krankenschwester		A **registered nurse** is a qualified nurse.
	(to) **carry out** /ˌkæri ˈaʊt/	durchführen, betreiben		
	(to) **work shifts** /ˌwɜːk ˈʃɪfts/	Schichtdienst machen		Nurses have to **work shifts**.
	shift /ʃɪft/	(die) Schicht		
	ward /wɔːd/	(die) Station		
	blood sample /ˈblʌd ˌsɑːmpl/	(die) Blutprobe		
	wound dressing /ˈwuːnd ˌdresɪŋ/	(der) Verband		
	(to) take somebody's temperature *(irr)* /ˌteɪk ˌsʌmbədiz ˈtemprɪtʃə/	Fieber bei jemandem messen		
	(to) interpret /ɪnˈtɜːprɪt/	deuten, interpretieren		
	diagnostic /ˌdaɪəɡˈnɒstɪk/	diagnostisch		When you are ill and go to the doctor's, they often **prescribe** you **medication**.
	(to) prescribe /prɪˈskraɪb/	verschreiben		
	medication /ˌmedɪˈkeɪʃn/	(die) Medikamente *(pl)*		
p. 93, 2	**that's why** /ˈðæts ˌwaɪ/	deshalb		
	original /əˈrɪdʒnəl/	originell, außergewöhnlich		
	recently /ˈriːsntli/	vor Kurzem, neulich		**recently** = not long ago
	recycled /riːˈsaɪkld/	wiederverwertet, Recycling-		
	sustainable /səˈsteɪnəbl/	nachhaltig		A **sustainable** and **ecological** way of living tries not to harm the environment that much.
	worker /ˈwɜːkə/	(der/die) Arbeiter/in		
	ecological /ˌiːkəˈlɒdʒɪkl/	ökologisch		
	proper /ˈprɒpə/	richtig		
	(to) **start** /stɑːt/	gründen		
	duty /ˈdjuːti/	(die) Pflicht, (die) Aufgabe		
	accessory /əkˈsesəri/	(das) Accessoire		
	(to) host /həʊst/	ausrichten		
	(to) cut down *(irr)* /ˌkʌt ˈdaʊn/	abholzen, fällen		
	tractor /ˈtræktə/	(der) Traktor		**tractor**
	(to) drag /dræɡ/	ziehen, schleifen		
	truck *(AE)* /trʌk/	(der) Lastwagen		
	(to) operate /ˈɒpəreɪt/	bedienen		
	machinery /məˈʃiːnəri/	(die) Maschinen *(pl)*		
	log /lɒɡ/	(der) Baumstamm		
	firebreak /ˈfaɪəbreɪk/	(die) Brandschneise		
	surf instructor /ˈsɜːf ɪnˌstrʌktə/	(der/die) Surflehrer/in		
	swimmer /ˈswɪmə/	(der/die) Schwimmer/in		**swimmer**

Vocabulary

	life-saving skill /ˈlaɪfˌseɪvɪŋ skɪl/	(die) Kenntnis im Rettungsschwimmen	
	a number of /ə ˈnʌmbər əv/	einige, ein paar	
	certification /ˌsɜːtɪfɪˈkeɪʃn/	(die) Qualifizierung; (das) Zertifikat	At a **surf school** you can learn how to surf.
	surf school /ˈsɜːfskuːl/	(die) Surfschule	
	planning /ˈplænɪŋ/	(das) Planen	
	advertising /ˈædvəˌtaɪzɪŋ/	(die) Werbung	
	(to) be passionate about *(irr)* /ˌbiː ˈpæʃnət əˌbaʊt/	für etwas brennen	
	living /ˈlɪvɪŋ/	(der) Lebensunterhalt	
	inspiring /ɪnˈspaɪərɪŋ/	inspirierend, anregend	A **job** can be a task that you have to do or the work for which you are paid.
p. 93, 3	**working hours** *(pl)* /ˈwɜːkɪŋ ˌaʊəz/	(die) Arbeitszeiten	
p. 94, 4	**job** /dʒɒb/	(die) Stelle, (der) Job	
	modal verb /ˈməʊdl vɜːb/	(das) Modalverb	
p. 94, 6	**each** /iːtʃ/	je(weils)	
p. 95, 7	(to) **summarize** (= **summarise**) /ˈsʌməraɪz/	zusammenfassen	If you want a job, you have to **apply for** it.
	(to) **apply for** /əˈplaɪ fɔː/	sich bewerben um	
	employer /ɪmˈplɔɪə/	(der/die) Arbeitgeber/in	
	personality /ˌpɜːsəˈnæləti/	(die) Persönlichkeit	When you behave badly, you have no **manners**.
	manners *(pl)* /ˈmænəz/	(die) Manieren	
	politeness /pəˈlaɪtnəs/	(die) Höflichkeit	
	reliability /rɪˌlaɪəˈbɪlɪti/	(die) Zuverlässigkeit	
	ability /əˈbɪləti/	(die) Fähigkeit	
	(to) **recognize** (= **recognise**) /ˈrekəgnaɪz/	erkennen	
	reliable /rɪˈlaɪəbl/	verlässlich, zuverlässig	
	(to) **take a course** *(irr)* /ˌteɪk ə ˈkɔːs/	einen Kurs machen	
	bicycle /ˈbaɪsɪkl/	(das) Fahrrad	**bicycle**
	programming /ˈprəʊˌɡræmɪŋ/	(das) Programmieren	
	program /ˈprəʊɡræm/	(das) Computerprogramm	
	volunteering /ˌvɒlənˈtɪərɪŋ/	(das) Verrichten von Freiwilligendienst	
	(to) babysit /ˈbeɪbiˌsɪt/	babysitten	
	neighbor *(AE)* /ˈneɪbə/	(der/die) Nachbar/in	
p. 96, 8	**specific** /spəˈsɪfɪk/	genau, bestimmte(r, s); spezifisch	
	(to) **complain (to)** /kəmˈpleɪn/	sich beklagen (bei)	
	due /djuː/	fällig	An **assignment** is a kind of task that you have to do.
	assignment /əˈsaɪnmənt/	(die) Aufgabe, (der) Auftrag	
	(to) **volunteer** /ˌvɒlənˈtɪə/	sich freiwillig melden	
	(to) **listen carefully** /ˌlɪsn ˈkeəfli/	aufmerksam zuhören	
	organizational (= **organisational**) /ˌɔːɡənaɪˈzeɪʃnəl/	organisatorisch	
	(to) **take the initiative** *(irr)* /ˌteɪk ði ɪˈnɪʃətɪv/	die Initiative ergreifen	
	(to) **work on** /ˈwɜːk ɒn/	arbeiten an	You can get a lot of food at a **supermarket**.
p. 97, 9	**supermarket** /ˈsuːpəˌmɑːkɪt/	(der) Supermarkt	

	(to) **consider** /kənˈsɪdə/	nachdenken über, denken an; halten für	to **consider** = to think about
	pay /peɪ/	(der) Lohn	
	patient /ˈpeɪʃnt/	geduldig	
	progress /ˈprəʊgres/	(der) Fortschritt	
	auntie *(informal)* /ˈɑːnti/	(die) Tante	
	(to) add to /ˈæd tʊ/	beitragen	
	on the weekends *(AE)* /ˌɒn ðə ˈwiːkendz/	an den Wochenenden	**on** the weekends *(AE)* = **at** the weekends *(BE)*
	cash register *(AE)* /ˈkæʃ ˌredʒɪstə/	(die) Kasse	
	(to) mow /məʊ/	mähen	
	lawn /lɔːn/	(der) Rasen	
	paper boy /ˈpeɪpə bɔɪ/	(der) Zeitungsjunge	Something that **tires** you **out** makes you tired.
	(to) tire out /ˌtaɪərˈaʊt/	müde machen	
	busboy *(AE)* /ˈbʌsbɔɪ/	(der) Abräumer, (der) Hilfskellner	
	dog walking /ˈdɒg ˌwɔːkɪŋ/	(das) Ausführen von Hunden	
	tuition /tjuːˈɪʃn/	*hier:* (die) Nachhilfe	
	job opening /ˈdʒɒb ˌəʊpənɪŋ/	(die) freie Stelle	
	(to) update /ˌʌpˈdeɪt/	auf den neuesten Stand bringen	When you want to get a job, you have to write an **application**.
	job hunt /ˈdʒɒb hʌnt/	(die) Jobsuche	
p. 98, 10	**application** /ˌæplɪˈkeɪʃn/	(die) Bewerbung	
	form /fɔːm/	(das) Formular	
	grade /greɪd/	(die) Note	
	current /ˈkʌrənt/	gegenwärtig, aktuell	**current** = happening now
	reference /ˈrefrəns/	(die) Referenz, (das) Zeugnis	
	tutoring /ˈtjuːtərɪŋ/	(die) Nachhilfe	
	Rd (= road) /rəʊd/	(die) Straße	
	(to) tutor /ˈtjuːtə/	Nachhilfe geben	
	report /rɪˈpɔːt/	(das) Zeugnis	
	A /eɪ/	*etwa:* Note 1, sehr gut	
	relevant /ˈreləvnt/	relevant; wichtig	
	boy scout /ˌbɔɪ ˈskaʊt/	(der) Pfadfinder	
	counselor *(AE)* = counsellor *(BE)* /ˈkaʊnslə/	*hier:* (der/die) Betreuer/in	
	tutor /ˈtjuːtə/	(der/die) Nachhilfelehrer/in	In a **job interview**, a future employer talks to someone who is applying for a job.
p. 98, 11	**job interview** (= interview) /ˈdʒɒb ˌɪntəvjuː, ˈɪntəˌvjuː/	(das) Bewerbungsgespräch, (das) Vorstellungsgespräch	
	(to) **follow** /ˈfɒləʊ/	befolgen	
People and Places 6	**employment** /ɪmˈplɔɪmənt/	(die) Beschäftigung, (die) Anstellung	During an **apprenticeship** you learn how to do a job.
	apprenticeship /əˈprentɪʃɪp/	(die) Ausbildung, (die) Lehre	
	on-the-job training /ˌɒn ðə ˌdʒɒb ˈtreɪnɪŋ/	(die) Ausbildung am Arbeitsplatz	
	career and technical education (CTE) /kəˌrɪər ən ˌteknɪkl ˌedjʊˈkeɪʃn, ˌsiː ˌtiː ˈiː/	*etwa:* (die) Berufsbildung	
	auto shop *(AE)* /ˈɔːtəʊ ʃɒp/	(die) Werkstatt	
	dual /ˈdjuːəl/	doppelte(r, s)	

Vocabulary

	fixed /fɪkst/	festgelegt	
p. 99, 13	**profession** /prəˈfeʃn/	(der) Beruf	
p. 100, 15	**appropriate** /əˈprəʊpriət/	angemessen, passend	**appropriate** = right for a particular situation
p. 100, 16	(to) **suit** /suːt/	passen (zu)	
	(to) sit still *(irr)* /ˌsɪt ˈstɪl/	stillsitzen	

Unit 5 | Part A Immigration

p. 105	**immigration** /ˌɪmɪˈɡreɪʃn/	(die) Einwanderung, (die) Immigration	
	statistics *(pl)* /stəˈtɪstɪks/	(die) Statistik	
	the Republic of Ireland /ðə rɪˌpʌblɪk əv ˈaɪələnd/	(die Republik) Irland	to **flee** = to leave a place very quickly, especially because of a dangerous situation
	horizon /həˈraɪzn/	(der) Horizont	
p. 106, 1	(to) **flee** *(irr)* /fliː/	fliehen	
p. 106, 2	**harvest** /ˈhɑːvɪst/	(die) Ernte	
	farmer /ˈfɑːmə/	(der/die) Bauer/Bäuerin	
	desperate /ˈdesprət/	verzweifelt	
	soil /sɔɪl/	(der) Boden, (die) Erde	
	(to) **starve** /stɑːv/	verhungern	
	rent /rent/	(die) Miete, (die) Pacht	
	(to) **threaten** /ˈθretn/	bedrohen	
	air /eə/	(die) Luft	
	tiny /ˈtaɪni/	winzig	
	(to) **board a ship** /ˌbɔːd ə ˈʃɪp/	ein Schiff besteigen	The people **are boarding the ship**.
	potato blight /pəˈteɪtəʊ blaɪt/	(die) Kartoffelfäule	
	(to) rot /rɒt/	verrotten, verfaulen	
	staple food /ˈsteɪpl fuːd/	(das) Grundnahrungsmittel	
	literally /ˈlɪtrəli/	buchstäblich, wirklich	
	landlord/landlady /ˈlændlɔːd, ˈlændleɪdi/	(der/die) Vermieter/in	
	(to) throw out *(irr)* /ˌθrəʊ ˈaʊt/	hinauswerfen	
	prepaid /ˌpriːˈpeɪd/	im Voraus bezahlt	
	sailing ship /ˈseɪlɪŋ ʃɪp/	(das) Segelschiff	**sailing ship**
	stormy /ˈstɔːmi/	stürmisch	
	overcrowded /ˌəʊvəˈkraʊdɪd/	überfüllt	
	seasick /ˈsiːˌsɪk/	seekrank	
	cabin /ˈkæbɪn/	(die) Kabine	
	visa /ˈviːzə/	(das) Visum	
	emigrant /ˈemɪɡrənt/	(der/die) Auswanderer/Auswanderin	The **unemployment rate** tells you what per cent of a country's population are without jobs.
p. 107, 2	**unemployment rate** /ˌʌnɪmˈplɔɪmənt reɪt/	(die) Arbeitslosenrate	
	financial /faɪˈnænʃl/	finanziell	
	grandson /ˈɡrænˌsʌn/	(der) Enkel	
	granddaughter /ˈɡrænˌdɔːtə/	(die) Enkelin	
	South Korea /ˌsaʊθ kəˈrɪə/	Südkorea	

	at that time /æt‿ˈðæt‿taɪm/	zu jener Zeit	
	thanks to /ˈθæŋks tʊ/	dank, wegen	
	then /ðen/	damals	A **Korean** is a person from Korea.
	Korean /kəˈriːən/	(der/die) Koreaner/in; koreanisch	
	by then /ˌbaɪ ˈðen/	bis dahin	
	consultant /kənˈsʌltənt/	(der/die) Berater/in	
	(to) retire /rɪˈtaɪə/	in den Ruhestand treten	
p. 108, 3	**suitcase** /ˈsuːtˌkeɪs/	(der) Koffer	**suitcase**
	storm /stɔːm/	(der) Sturm	
	overboard /ˈəʊvəbɔːd/	über Bord	
	(to) start a fire /ˌstɑːt‿ə ˈfaɪə/	Feuer machen	
p. 108, 4	**emigration** /ˌemɪˈgreɪʃn/	(die) Auswanderung, (die) Emigration	
p. 109, 5	**graph** /grɑːf/	(das) Diagramm, (der) Graph	
	increase /ˈɪŋkriːs/	(der) Anstieg, (das) Wachstum	
	decrease /ˈdiːkriːs/	(der) Rückgang	
	wave /weɪv/	(die) Welle	
	eastern /ˈiːstən/	östlich, Ost-	to **increase** = to go up in number
	(to) **increase** /ɪnˈkriːs/	ansteigen	
	quota /ˈkwəʊtə/	(die) Quote	
	(to) **peak** /piːk/	den Höhepunkt erreichen	
	per cent (BE), **percent** (AE) /pəˈsent/	(das) Prozent	
	(to) **decrease** /diːˈkriːs/	abnehmen, zurückgehen	to **decrease** ≠ to **increase**
	(to) **immigrate** /ˈɪmɪgreɪt/	einwandern	
p. 110, 6	(to) **question** /ˈkwestʃn/	befragen, verhören	
	(to) **return** /rɪˈtɜːn/	zurückkehren, zurückkommen	to **return** = to come back
	southwest /ˌsaʊθˈwest/	in den Südwesten, nach Südwesten	
	territory /ˈterətri/	(das) Gebiet, (das) Territorium	
	official /əˈfɪʃl/	(die) Amtsperson	
	medical /ˈmedɪkl/	medizinisch	
	inspection /ɪnˈspekʃn/	(die) Untersuchung	
	Russian /ˈrʌʃn/	(der/die) Russe/Russin; russisch	
	tuberculosis /tjuːˌbɜːkjʊˈləʊsɪs/	(die) Tuberkulose	
	thank God /ˌθæŋk ˈgɒd/	Gott sei Dank	
	steamboat /ˈstiːmbəʊt/	(das) Dampfschiff	
	humid /ˈhjuːmɪd/	feucht	
	poisonous /ˈpɔɪznəs/	giftig	
	snake /sneɪk/	(die) Schlange	Many **snakes** are **poisonous**.
	wagon train /ˈwægən treɪn/	(der) Planwagenzug	
	advertisement /ədˈvɜːtɪsmənt/	(die) Werbung, (die) Anzeige	
	wagon /ˈwægən/	(der) Planwagen	
	ox (pl oxen) /ɒks, ˈɒksn/	(der) Ochse	
	gun /gʌn/	(die) Waffe	
	record /ˈrekɔːd/	(die) Aufzeichnungen	

Vocabulary

p. 111, 7	**nowhere** /ˈnəʊweə/	nirgends, nirgendwo	**nowhere** = not anywhere
	unnecessary /ʌnˈnesəsəri/	unnötig	**unnecessary** ≠ necessary
	east /iːst/	nach Osten	
	(to) **fix** /fɪks/	reparieren	
	(to) **survive** /səˈvaɪv/	überleben	
	the Great Plains /ðə ˌgreɪt ˈpleɪnz/	(die) Great Plains *(Kurzgras-Prärien)*	
	bison *(pl* bison*)* /ˈbaɪsn, ˈbaɪsn/	(das) Bison, (das) Wisent	
	deer *(pl* deer*)* /dɪə, dɪə/	(der) Hirsch, (das) Reh	
	thunderstorm /ˈθʌndəstɔːm/	(das) Gewitter	
	thunder /ˈθʌndə/	(der) Donner	Even if it is dark at night, you can see well when there is **lightning**.
	lightning /ˈlaɪtnɪŋ/	(der) Blitz	
	plains *(pl)* /pleɪnz/	(die) Ebene, (das) Flachland	
	wolf *(pl* wolves*)* /wʊlf, wʊlvz/	(der) Wolf	
	coyote /kaɪˈəʊti/	(der) Kojote	
	(to) howl /haʊl/	brüllen, heulen	
	by /baɪ/	*hier:* an … vorbei	
	buffalo chips *(pl)* /ˈbʌfələʊ tʃɪps/	(der) getrocknete Büffeldung	
	(to) milk /mɪlk/	melken	He **is milking** the cow.
	(to) make camp *(irr)* /ˌmeɪk ˈkæmp/	das Lager aufschlagen	
	wooden /ˈwʊdn/	Holz-, hölzern	
	stake /steɪk/	(der) Pfahl, (der) Pflock	
	barn /bɑːn/	(die) Scheune	
	(to) plant /plɑːnt/	pflanzen	
	farming /ˈfɑːmɪŋ/	(der) Ackerbau, (die) Viehzucht	When the opening times of a shop are from 9 to 5, the shop is open **from** 9 o'clock **onwards**.
ople and Places 7	**directly** /dəˈrektli, daɪˈrektli/	direkt	
	from … onwards /ˌfrəm … ˈɒnwədz/	von … an	
	examination /ɪgˌzæmɪˈneɪʃn/	(die) Untersuchung	
	(to) **fail** /feɪl/	durchfallen	to **fail** = to not be successful
	(to) **pass** /pɑːs/	bestehen	
	sight /saɪt/	(der) Anblick, (die) Sicht	
	(to) face /feɪs/	blicken nach	
	(to) pass through /ˌpɑːs ˈθruː/	durchreisen, durchlaufen	When an exact number is not known, it has to **be estimated**.
	station /ˈsteɪʃn/	*hier:* (die) Station	
	(to) be estimated *(irr)* /bi ˈestɪmeɪtəd/	geschätzt werden	
	officer /ˈɒfɪsə/	(der/die) Beamte/Beamtin	
p. 112, 8	splendid /ˈsplendɪd/	großartig	
p. 113, 9	on the move /ˌɒn ðə ˈmuːv/	unterwegs	A **secretary** is a person who works in an office.
p. 113, 10	**secretary** /ˈsekrətri/	(der/die) Sekretär/in	
	scholarship /ˈskɒləʃɪp/	(das) Stipendium	
	studies *(pl)* /ˈstʌdiz/	(das) Studium	
	(to) get homesick *(irr)* /ˌget ˈhəʊmsɪk/	Heimweh bekommen	
p. 114, 11	past progressive /ˌpɑːst prəʊˈgresɪv/	(die) Verlaufsform der Vergangenheit	**Irish** = connected with Ireland or of Ireland
p. 114, 13	**Irish** /ˈaɪrɪʃ/	irisch	

p. 115, 14	(to) keep in mind *(irr)* /ˌkiːp ɪn ˈmaɪnd/	im Gedächtnis behalten	
	worksheet /ˈwɜːkʃiːt/	(das) Arbeitsblatt	

Unit 5 | Part B The Republic of Ireland

p. 116, 1	Gaelic football /ˌɡeɪlɪk ˈfʊtbɔːl/	Ballsportart mit zwei Teams zu je 15 Spielern/Spielerinnen	
	ruin /ˈruːɪn/	(die) Ruine	
	fisherman *(pl* fishermen*)* /ˈfɪʃəmən/	(der) Fischer, (der) Angler	
	county /ˈkaʊnti/	(der) (Verwaltungs)bezirk; (die) Grafschaft	
	the docklands *(pl)* /ðə ˈdɒkləndz/	(das) Hafenviertel	
p. 117, 2	**tonight** /təˈnaɪt/	heute Abend	**tonight** = in the evening of today
	goalkeeper /ˈɡəʊlˌkiːpə/	(der/die) Tormann/Torfrau	Gruppenbezeichnungen wie „team", „family" oder „police" werden von einem Verb in der Pluralform gefolgt, wenn man beschreiben will, was die einzelnen Mitglieder der Gruppe tun. Will man die Einheit der Gruppe betonen, benutzt man ein Verb in der Singularform.
	one day /ˌwʌn ˈdeɪ/	eines Tages	
	great-great-grandparents *(pl)* /ˌɡreɪt ˌɡreɪt ˈɡrænˌpeərənts/	(die) Ururgroßeltern	
	fiddle /ˈfɪdl/	(die) Geige	
	Polish /ˈpəʊlɪʃ/	(das) Polnisch; polnisch	
	non- /nɒn/	nicht	
p. 118, 3	present perfect progressive /ˌpreznt ˌpɜːfɪkt prəʊˈɡresɪv/	(die) Verlaufsform des Perfekt	
p. 119, 5	**Atlantic, Atlantic Ocean** /ətˈlæntɪk, ətˌlæntɪk ˈəʊʃn/	(der) Atlantik, (der) Atlantische Ozean	
	lighthouse /ˈlaɪtˌhaʊs/	(der) Leuchtturm	
	peninsula /pəˈnɪnsjələ/	(die) Halbinsel	
	mystical /ˈmɪstɪkl/	mystisch	
	(to) kiss /kɪs/	küssen	
	hiking trail /ˈhaɪkɪŋ treɪl/	(der) Wanderweg	
	dolphin /ˈdɒlfɪn/	(der) Delfin	**dolphin**
	seal /siːl/	(der) Seehund, (die) Robbe	
p. 120, 6	**roughly** /ˈrʌfli/	grob, ungefähr	
	(to) **date back** /ˌdeɪt ˈbæk/	zurückgehen auf, stammen aus	
	sweater /ˈswetə/	(der) Pullover	**sweater**
	spot /spɒt/	(die) Stelle	
	campus /ˈkæmpəs/	(die) Universität, (der) Campus	
	manuscript /ˈmænjuskrɪpt/	(das) Manuskript	
	bible /ˈbaɪbl/	(die) Bibel	
	hip /hɪp/	hip, cool	
	countless /ˈkaʊntləs/	zahllos, unzählig	
	nightlife /ˈnaɪtlaɪf/	(das) Nachtleben	
p. 121, 6	(to) **take a journey** *(irr)* /ˌteɪk ə ˈdʒɜːni/	eine Reise machen	to **take a journey** = to travel
	living conditions *(pl)* /ˈlɪvɪŋ kənˌdɪʃnz/	(die) Lebensbedingungen	
	(to) make one's mark *(irr)* /ˌmeɪk wʌnz ˈmɑːk/	seine Spuren hinterlassen	
	sword /sɔːd/	(das) Schwert	

Vocabulary

shield /ʃiːld/	(der) Schild	
Viking /ˈvaɪkɪŋ/	(der/die) Wikinger/in; Wikinger-	
warrior /ˈwɒriə/	(der/die) Krieger/in	
medieval /ˌmediˈiːvl/	mittelalterlich	
(to) follow in somebody's footsteps /ˌfɒləʊ ɪn ˌsʌmbədiz ˈfʊtsteps/	in jemandes Fußstapfen treten	
the potato famine /ðə pəˈteɪtəʊ ˌfæmɪn/	Hungersnot in Irland zwischen 1845 und 1849	When people lack food in a certain region over a period of time, it is a **famine**.
famine /ˈfæmɪn/	(die) Hungersnot	
(to) sail /seɪl/	segeln	
nightmare /ˈnaɪtˌmeə/	(der) Albtraum	A long journey, especially by ship, is called a **voyage**.
voyage /ˈvɔɪdʒ/	(die) Reise, (die) Seereise	
on board /ˌɒn ˈbɔːd/	an Bord	
starvation /stɑːˈveɪʃn/	(der) Hungertod	
(to) **divide** /dɪˈvaɪd/	teilen, aufteilen	
Northern Ireland /ˌnɔːðən ˈaɪələnd/	Nordirland	
rule /ruːl/	(die) Herrschaft	
(to) **want somebody to do something** /wɒnt ˌsʌmbədi tə ˈduː ˌsʌmθɪŋ/	wollen, dass jemand etwas tut	The father **wants** his son **to** tidy his room.
minority /maɪˈnɒrəti/	(die) Minderheit	
(to) **remain** /rɪˈmeɪn/	bleiben	
European Union /ˌjʊərəˌpiːən ˈjuːnjən/	(die) Europäische Union	
besides /bɪˈsaɪdz/	außer, abgesehen von	**besides** = apart from
protestant /ˈprɒtɪstənt/	(der/die) Protestant/in	
unrest /ʌnˈrest/	(die) Unruhen, (die) Spannungen	
Denmark /ˈdenmɑːk/	Dänemark	
Brexit /ˈbreksɪt/	(der) Brexit *(Ausstieg Großbritanniens aus der EU)*	
western /ˈwestən/	West-, westlich	You can tell **jokes** to make people laugh.
joke /dʒəʊk/	(der) Witz	
falcon /ˈfɔːlkən/	(der) Falke	
silver /ˈsɪlvə/	silbern	
winged /wɪŋd/	mit Flügeln, geflügelt	A bird is a **winged** animal.
call of freedom /ˌkɔːl əv ˈfriːdəm/	(der) Ruf der Freiheit	
breast /brest/	(die) Brust	
(to) soar /sɔː/	aufsteigen, sich erheben	
twisted /ˈtwɪstɪd/	verdreht, verschlungen	
shore /ʃɔː/	(die) Küste, (das) Ufer	**shore**
sunset /ˈsʌnˌset/	(der) Sonnenuntergang	
(to) stand by /ˌstænd ˈbaɪ/	dabeistehen	
(to) pass away /ˌpɑːs əˈweɪ/	verbringen	
salmon /ˈsæmən/	(der) Lachs	
(to) dart /dɑːt/	flitzen, sausen	

	(to) evoke /ɪˈvəʊk/	hervorrufen	You need a ball and a **basket** to play basketball.
p. 123, 8	**basket** /ˈbɑːskɪt/	(der) Korb	
	(to) punch /pʌntʃ/	schlagen	
	epic *(informal)* /ˈepɪk/	super, klasse	
p. 123, 9	itinerary /aɪˈtɪnərəri/	(die) Reiseroute	
p. 123, 10	(to) **advertise** /ˈædvətaɪz/	für etwas Werbung machen	

Results for the soft skill check on page 96:

	a	b	c
1	1 point	2 points	3 points
2	2 points	3 points	1 point
3	2 points	3 points	1 point
4	3 points	1 point	2 points
5	1 point	3 points	2 points
6	3 points	2 points	1 point

15–18: You have very good soft skills. You are a very responsible, polite and patient person who can work and communicate well with other people.

10–14: There is room to improve your soft skills, but in general you are a good team player.

6–9: You should work on your soft skills!

Dictionary

Hier findest du alphabetisch sortiert alle Wörter aus dem vorliegenden Buch mit der Angabe der Seite *(p.)*, auf der das Wort das erste Mal vorkommt oder auf der es zum Lernwort gemacht wird. Die Zahl hinter dem Komma bezeichnet die Aufgabe auf der Seite.
Lernwörter aus den vorigen Bänden sind mit „NHG 5", „NHG 6" oder „NHG 7" markiert.
Die **fett** gedruckten Lernwörter solltest du dir merken.
(informal) bedeutet: Dieses Wort oder dieser Ausdruck ist umgangssprachlich.
Folgende Abkürzungen werden verwendet: *(pl)* = (unregelmäßige) Mehrzahlform, *(no pl)* = keine Mehrzahlform, *(irr)* = unregelmäßiges Verb, *(AE)* = amerikanisches Englisch, P&P = People and Places

A

a, an /ə/eɪ, ən/ ein(e) NHG 5
a /ə/ pro NHG 6
A /eɪ/ *etwa:* Note 1, sehr gut p. 98, 10
ability /əˈbɪləti/ Fähigkeit p. 95, 7
(to) **be able to do something** *(irr)* /ˌbiːˌeɪbl tə ˈduː ˌsʌmθɪŋ/ etwas tun können NHG 6
aboard /əˈbɔːd/ an Bord p. 15, 7
about /əˈbaʊt/ über; an NHG 5; ungefähr NHG 6
(to) **be about** *(irr)* /ˌbiːˌəˈbaʊt/ gehen um; handeln von NHG 5
above /əˈbʌv/ über NHG 5; oben, oberhalb NHG 7; darüber p. 26, 8
(to) **go abroad** *(irr)* /ˌɡəʊˌəˈbrɔːd/ ins Ausland gehen / fahren NHG 6
absolutely /ˈæbsəluːtli/ absolut NHG 7
academic /ˌækəˈdemɪk/ akademisch; wissenschaftlich p. 44, 2
accent /ˈæksnt/ Akzent NHG 7
(to) **accept** /əkˈsept/ anerkennen; akzeptieren p. 25, 7
acceptable /əkˈseptəbl/ akzeptabel p. 76, 13
(to) **access** /ˈækses/ zugreifen auf p. 68, 2
accessory /əkˈsesəri/ Accessoire p. 93, 2
accident /ˈæksɪdnt/ Unfall NHG 7
by accident /ˌbaɪˈæksɪdnt/ zufällig; aus Versehen NHG 7
accidentally /ˌæksɪˈdentli/ versehentlich; zufällig NHG 7
according to /əˈkɔːdɪŋ ˌtuː/ nach; gemäß NHG 7
account /əˈkaʊnt/ Benutzerkonto p. 69, 2
accountant /əˈkaʊntənt/ Buchhalter/in p. 92, 1
(to) **achieve** /əˈtʃiːv/ erreichen NHG 7

across /əˈkrɒs/ über, quer durch p. 20, 2
acrostic /əˈkrɒstɪk/ Akrostichon; Leistenvers p. 27, 11
(to) **act** /ækt/ handeln; spielen NHG 6; sich verhalten p. 62, 8
(to) **act out** /ˌæktˈaʊt/ nachspielen; vorspielen NHG 5
acting /ˈæktɪŋ/ Schauspielern p. 149
action /ˈækʃn/ Handlung NHG 5; Handeln; Maßnahmen p. 85, 5
(to) **take action** *(irr)* /ˌteɪkˈækʃn/ handeln, Maßnahmen ergreifen p. 81
(to) activate /ˈæktɪveɪt/ aktivieren p. 10, 2
active /ˈæktɪv/ aktiv NHG 7
activist /ˈæktɪvɪst/ Aktivist/in p. 15, 7
activity /ækˈtɪvəti/ Aktivität NHG 5
actor/actress /ˈæktə, ˈæktrəs/ Schauspieler/in NHG 6
actually /ˈæktʃuəli/ eigentlich; tatsächlich NHG 6; wirklich p. 72, 6
AD (= Anno Domini) /ˌeɪˈdiː, ˌænəʊˈdɒmɪnaɪ/ n. Chr. (= nach Christus) NHG 7
(to) adapt /əˈdæpt/ anpassen, bearbeiten p. 85, 5
(to) **add** /æd/ hinzufügen NHG 5
(to) add to /ˈædˌtuː/ beitragen p. 97, 9
addict /ˈædɪkt/ Abhängige/r p. 68, 2
address /əˈdres/ Adresse NHG 5
(to) **address** /əˈdres/ ansprechen; adressieren p. 25, 7
adjective /ˈædʒɪktɪv/ Adjektiv NHG 6
admission /ədˈmɪʃn/ Eintritt; Eintrittspreis p. 26, 8
(to) **admit (to)** /ədˈmɪt/ zugeben, eingestehen p. 69, 2
(to) **adopt** /əˈdɒpt/ annehmen, übernehmen NHG 7

adult /ˈædʌlt/ Erwachsene/r NHG 6
in advance /ˌɪnˌədˈvɑːns/ im Voraus p. 26, 8
advantage /ədˈvɑːntɪdʒ/ Vorteil p. 72, 6
adventure /ədˈventʃə/ Abenteuer NHG 6
adventurous /ədˈventʃrəs/ abenteuerlustig p. 13, 6
adverb of manner /ˌædvɜːb əv ˈmænə/ Adverb der Art und Weise p. 70
advert (= ad) /ˈædvɜːt, æd/ Werbung; Anzeige NHG 7
(to) **advertise** /ˈædvətaɪz/ für etwas Werbung machen p. 123, 10
advertisement /ədˈvɜːtɪsmənt/ Werbung; Anzeige p. 110, 6
advertising /ˈædvəˌtaɪzɪŋ/ Werbung p. 93, 2
advice /ədˈvaɪs/ Rat; Ratschlag NHG 7
(to) **ask for advice** /ˌɑːsk fərˌədˈvaɪs/ um Rat bitten NHG 7
(to) **give advice** *(irr)* /ˌɡɪvˌədˈvaɪs/ Rat geben NHG 7
piece of advice /ˌpiːs əvˌədˈvaɪs/ Rat(schlag) NHG 7
(to) **seek advice** *(irr)* /ˌsiːkˌədˈvaɪs/ Rat suchen NHG 7
(to) **advise** /ədˈvaɪz/ raten, beraten NHG 7
affair /əˈfeə/ Angelegenheit; Sache P&P 5
(to) **affect** /əˈfekt/ betreffen; beeinflussen p. 72, 6
(to) **afford** /əˈfɔːd/ sich leisten p. 82, 2
affordable /əˈfɔːdəbl/ erschwinglich p. 10, 2
(to) **be afraid of** *(irr)* /ˌbiːˌəˈfreɪdˌəv/ Angst haben vor NHG 6

| Skills | Wordbanks | Grammar | **Words** |

Africa /ˈæfrɪkə/ Afrika p. 15, 7
African American /ˌæfrɪkən əˈmerɪkən/ Afroamerikaner/in; afroamerikanisch p. 15, 7
after /ˈɑːftə/ nach NHG 5; nachdem p. 35, 2
after that /ˌɑːftə ˈðæt/ danach NHG 7
after-school /ˌɑːftə ˈskuːl/ Nachmittags- p. 33
afternoon /ˌɑːftəˈnuːn/ Nachmittag NHG 5
afterwards /ˈɑːftəwədz/ anschließend; später NHG 6
again /əˈgen/ wieder; noch einmal NHG 5
against /əˈgenst/ gegen NHG 6
age /eɪdʒ/ Alter NHG 7; Zeitalter p. 69, 2
aged *(after noun)* /eɪdʒd/ im Alter von p. 26, 8
agency /ˈeɪdʒənsi/ Agentur p. 71, 5
aggressive /əˈgresɪv/ aggressiv, angriffslustig p. 73, 6
… ago /əˈgəʊ/ vor … NHG 6
(to) **agree** /əˈgriː/ zustimmen NHG 7
(to) **agree on** /əˈgriː ɒn/ sich einigen auf NHG 7
(to) **agree with** /əˈgriː wɪð/ einer Meinung sein mit, übereinstimmen mit p. 63, 8
agricultural /ˌægrɪˈkʌltʃrəl/ landwirtschaftlich p. 15, 7
aim /eɪm/ Ziel p. 50, 8
ain't (= am/are/is not) *(informal)* /eɪnt/ nicht sein p. 25, 7
air /eə/ Luft p. 106, 2
airplane *(AE)* /ˈeəpleɪn/ Flugzeug p. 165
airport /ˈeəpɔːt/ Flughafen NHG 6
alive /əˈlaɪv/ lebendig; am Leben NHG 7
all /ɔːl/ alle; alles; ganz; völlig NHG 5
all around /ˌɔːl əˈraʊnd/ rundherum; überall (in/auf) p. 21, 2
all day long /ˌɔːl deɪ ˈlɒŋ/ den ganzen Tag lang p. 21, 2
all kinds of /ˌɔːl ˈkaɪndz əv/ alle möglichen NHG 6
all over /ˌɔːl ˈəʊvə/ überall NHG 6
all over the world /ˌɔːl ˌəʊvə ðə ˈwɜːld/ auf der ganzen Welt NHG 6
all right /ˌɔːl ˈraɪt/ in Ordnung NHG 7
All the best! /ˌɔːl ðə ˈbest/ Alles Gute! NHG 7

all the time /ˌɔːl ðə ˈtaɪm/ die ganze Zeit NHG 6
all year round /ˌɔːl ˈjɪə raʊnd/ das ganze Jahr lang p. 10, 2
allegiance /əˈliːdʒns/ Loyalität; Ergebenheit p. 38, 6
to be allergic to *(irr)* /ˌbiː əˈlɜːdʒɪk tʊ/ allergisch sein auf NHG 7
(to) **allow** /əˈlaʊ/ erlauben NHG 7
allowed /əˈlaʊd/ erlaubt NHG 7
(to) **be allowed (to)** *(irr)* /ˌbiː əˈlaʊd tə/ erlaubt sein, dürfen NHG 6
ally /ˈælaɪ/ Verbündete/r; Alliierte/r p. 15, 7
almost /ˈɔːlməʊst/ fast; beinahe NHG 6
alone /əˈləʊn/ allein NHG 5
along /əˈlɒŋ/ entlang NHG 6
already /ɔːlˈredi/ schon; bereits NHG 5
also /ˈɔːlsəʊ/ auch NHG 5
although /ɔːlˈðəʊ/ obwohl NHG 6
always /ˈɔːlweɪz/ immer NHG 5
am (= ante meridiem) /ˌeɪ ˈem, ˌænti məˈrɪdiəm/ morgens, vormittags *(hinter Uhrzeit zwischen Mitternacht und 12 Uhr mittags)* NHG 5
amazed /əˈmeɪzd/ erstaunt, verblüfft p. 87, 6
amazing *(informal)* /əˈmeɪzɪŋ/ toll NHG 6
(to) **call an ambulance** /ˌkɔːl ən ˈæmbjʊləns/ einen Krankenwagen rufen NHG 7
America /əˈmerɪkə/ Amerika p. 6
American /əˈmerɪkən/ Amerikaner/in; amerikanisch NHG 7
among /əˈmʌŋ/ unter; zwischen p. 87, 6
amusement park /əˈmjuːzmənt pɑːk/ Freizeitpark p. 27, 10
ancient /ˈeɪnʃnt/ alt; antik NHG 6
and /ænd/ und NHG 5
and so on /ˌænd ˈsəʊ ɒn/ und so weiter NHG 6
angel /ˈeɪndʒl/ Engel p. 71, 5
anger /ˈæŋgə/ Ärger; Wut p. 89, 9
angry /ˈæŋgri/ zornig, wütend NHG 6
animal /ˈænɪml/ Tier NHG 5
animal keeper /ˈænɪml ˌkiːpə/ Tierpfleger/in p. 92, 1

(to) **animate** /ˈænɪmeɪt/ animieren P&P 4
ankle /ˈæŋkl/ (Fuß)knöchel NHG 7
announcement /əˈnaʊnsmənt/ Mitteilung; Durchsage NHG 6
annoyed /əˈnɔɪd/ genervt NHG 6
annoying /əˈnɔɪɪŋ/ ärgerlich NHG 7
another /əˈnʌðə/ noch ein/e; ein anderer/ein anderes/eine andere NHG 5
answer /ˈɑːnsə/ Antwort NHG 5
(to) **answer** /ˈɑːnsə/ (be)antworten NHG 5
Antarctica /ænˈtɑːktɪkə/ die Antarktis p. 6
anxiety /æŋˈzaɪəti/ Sorge; Angst p. 85, 5
any /ˈeni/ (irgend)ein(e) NHG 5; jede(r, s); alle NHG 7
any more /ˌeni ˈmɔː/ noch mehr NHG 7
anybody /ˈenibɒdi/ irgendjemand; jede(r, s) NHG 7
anyone /ˈeniwʌn/ jede(r, s); (irgend)jemand NHG 7
anything /ˈeniθɪŋ/ irgendetwas NHG 5
anything /ˈeniθɪŋ/ alles p. 89, 9
anyway /ˈeniweɪ/ jedenfalls NHG 6; sowieso NHG 7
anywhere /ˈeniweə/ überall; irgendwo NHG 7
apart /əˈpɑːt/ auseinander NHG 6; getrennt p. 63, 8
apart from /əˈpɑːt frəm/ abgesehen von NHG 7
apartment *(AE)* /əˈpɑːtmənt/ Wohnung p. 24, 6
(to) **apologize** (= apologise) /əˈpɒlədʒaɪz/ sich entschuldigen NHG 7
apparently /əˈpærəntli/ anscheinend NHG 7; offensichtlich p. 20, 2
(to) **appeal to** /əˈpiːl tʊ/ appellieren an, bitten um NHG 7
(to) **appear** /əˈpɪə/ erscheinen, auftauchen NHG 7
apple /ˈæpl/ Apfel NHG 5
application /ˌæplɪˈkeɪʃn/ Bewerbung p. 98, 10
(to) **apply** /əˈplaɪ/ anwenden p. 10, 2
(to) **apply for** /əˈplaɪ fɔː/ sich bewerben um p. 95, 7

Dictionary

appointment /əˈpɔɪntmənt/ Termin NHG 7
apprenticeship /əˈprentɪʃɪp/ Ausbildung; Lehre P&P 6
appropriate /əˈprəʊpriət/ angemessen; passend p. 100, 15
April /ˈeɪprəl/ April NHG 5
archaeological /ˌɑːkiəˈlɒdʒɪkl/ archäologisch p. 14, 7
architecture /ˈɑːkɪˌtektʃə/ Architektur p. 26, 8
area /ˈeəriə/ Gebiet; Region NHG 5
area /ˈeəriə/ Fläche p. 10, 2
(to) **argue** /ˈɑːgjuː/ sich streiten p. 65, 12
argument /ˈɑːgjəmənt/ Argument; Streit NHG 7
around /əˈraʊnd/ um; herum; umher NHG 6; ungefähr NHG 7
from (all) around the world /frəm ˌɔːl ə ˌraʊnd ðə ˈwɜːld/ aus der (ganzen) Welt NHG 7
arrival /əˈraɪvl/ Ankunft P&P 1
(to) **arrive** /əˈraɪv/ ankommen NHG 5
art /ɑːt/ Kunst NHG 5
art gallery /ˈɑːt ˌgæləri/ Kunstgalerie P&P 2
article /ˈɑːtɪkl/ Artikel NHG 5
artificial intelligence (= AI) /ˌɑːtɪfɪʃl ɪnˈtelɪdʒns, ˌeɪ ˈaɪ/ künstliche Intelligenz p. 10, 2
artist /ˈɑːtɪst/ Künstler/in p. 26, 8
as /əz/ als; wie; während NHG 5
as … as /əz əz/ so … wie NHG 6
as a whole /əz ə ˈhəʊl/ als Ganzes p. 85, 5
as well /ˌəz ˈwel/ auch NHG 6
Asia /ˈeɪʒə/ Asien p. 6
Asian /ˈeɪʒn/ Asiat/in; asiatisch p. 7
aside from (AE) /əˈsaɪd frəm/ abgesehen von p. 51, 11
(to) **ask** /ɑːsk/ fragen; bitten NHG 5
(to) **ask for advice** /ˌɑːsk fər ədˈvaɪs/ um Rat bitten NHG 7
(to) **ask on a date** /ˌɑːsk ɒn ə ˈdeɪt/ um eine Verabredung bitten p. 66, 13
(to) **ask questions** /ˌɑːsk ˈkwestʃnz/ Fragen stellen NHG 5
aspect /ˈæspekt/ Aspekt; Gesichtspunkt NHG 7
assembly /əˈsembli/ (Schüler)versammlung NHG 5
assembly hall /əˈsembli hɔːl/ Aula p. 165
assembly line /əˈsembli laɪn/ Fließband p. 10, 2
assignment /əˈsaɪnmənt/ Aufgabe; Auftrag p. 96, 8
association /əˌsəʊsiˈeɪʃn/ Vereinigung NHG 7
at /æt/ an; in; bei; um NHG 5
at all /ˌæt ˈɔːl/ überhaupt NHG 7
at all times /ˌæt ˌɔːl ˈtaɪmz/ jederzeit, immer p. 72, 6
at first /ˌæt ˈfɜːst/ zuerst NHG 6
at home /ˌæt ˈhəʊm/ zu Hause NHG 5
at least /ˌæt ˈliːst/ mindestens; wenigstens NHG 6
at that time /ˌæt ˈðæt ˌtaɪm/ zu jener Zeit p. 107, 2
at the back /ˌæt ðə ˈbæk/ hinten NHG 5
at the back of /ˌæt ðə ˈbæk əv/ am Ende von; hinten in p. 20, 2
at the doctor's /ˌæt ðə ˈdɒktəz/ beim Arzt/bei der Ärztin NHG 7
at the front /ˌæt ðə ˈfrʌnt/ vorne NHG 5
at the moment /ˌæt ðə ˈməʊmənt/ im Moment P&P 2
at the same time /ˌæt ðə ˌseɪm ˈtaɪm/ gleichzeitig; zur gleichen Zeit NHG 7
at the weekend /ˌæt ðə ˈwiːkend/ am Wochenende p. 135
athlete /ˈæθliːt/ Athlet/in p. 35, 2
athletic /æθˈletɪk/ athletisch; sportlich p. 48, 7
(to) **do athletics** (irr) /ˌduː æθˈletɪks/ Leichtathletik machen NHG 5
Atlantic, Atlantic Ocean /ətˈlæntɪk, ətˌlæntɪk ˈəʊʃn/ Atlantik, Atlantischer Ozean p. 119, 5
atmosphere /ˈætməsˌfɪə/ Atmosphäre NHG 7
attack /əˈtæk/ Angriff p. 15, 7
(to) **attempt** /əˈtempt/ versuchen p. 138
(to) **attend** /əˈtend/ besuchen NHG 7
attendance /əˈtendəns/ Anwesenheit p. 38, 6
(to) **draw attention to** (irr) /ˌdrɔː əˈtenʃn tə/ Aufmerksamkeit lenken auf NHG 7
(to) **pay attention (to)** (irr) /ˌpeɪ əˈtenʃn tə/ aufpassen; achten auf NHG 6
attitude /ˈætɪˌtjuːd/ Haltung; Einstellung p. 87, 6
(to) **attract** /əˈtrækt/ anziehen p. 148
attraction /əˈtrækʃn/ Attraktion NHG 6
auto body repair /ˌɔːtəʊ ˌbɒdi rɪˈpeə/ Karosseriereparatur p. 40, 7
auditorium (AE) /ˌɔːdɪˈtɔːriəm/ Vortragssaal; Festhalle p. 41, 10
August /ˈɔːgəst/ August NHG 5
auk /ɔːk/ Alk p. 138
aunt /ɑːnt/ Tante NHG 5
auntie (informal) /ˈɑːnti/ Tante p. 97, 9
auto shop (AE) /ˈɔːtəʊ ʃɒp/ Werkstatt P&P 6
Australia /ɒˈstreɪliə/ Australien p. 6
authentic /ɔːˈθentɪk/ authentisch p. 73, 6
author /ˈɔːθə/ Autor/in NHG 7
autumn /ˈɔːtəm/ Herbst NHG 6
average /ˈævərɪdʒ/ durchschnittlich p. 68, 2
(to) **avoid** /əˈvɔɪd/ (ver)meiden NHG 7
award /əˈwɔːd/ Preis; Auszeichnung p. 6
(to) **be aware of** (irr) /bi əˈweər əv/ sich bewusst sein p. 71, 5
awareness /əˈweənəs/ Bewusstsein p. 87, 6
(to) **raise awareness** /ˌreɪz əˈweənəz/ Bewusstsein schärfen p. 83, 2
away /əˈweɪ/ weg NHG 5
(to) **go away** (irr) /ˌgəʊ əˈweɪ/ weggehen; verschwinden NHG 6
awesome /ˈɔːsm/ beeindruckend; super p. 20, 2
awkward /ˈɔːkwəd/ schwierig; unangenehm p. 69, 2

B

(to) **babysit** /ˈbeɪbiˌsɪt/ babysitten p. 95, 7
back /bæk/ zurück NHG 5; Rücken NHG 7
at the back /ˌæt ðə ˈbæk/ hinten NHG 5
at the back of /ˌæt ðə ˈbæk əv/ am Ende von; hinten in p. 20, 2

in the back /ˌɪn ðə ˈbæk/ hinten NHG 5
background /ˈbækˌɡraʊnd/ Hintergrund NHG 6
bad /bæd/ schlecht; schlimm NHG 5
bag /bæɡ/ Tasche; Tüte NHG 5
(to) **bake** /beɪk/ backen NHG 5
baked potatoes (pl) /ˌbeɪkt pəˈteɪtəʊz/ Ofenkartoffeln p. 47, 6
baker /ˈbeɪkə/ Bäcker/in NHG 6
balloon /bəˈluːn/ Luftballon NHG 5
(to) **ban** /bæn/ verbieten p. 69, 2
banana /bəˈnɑːnə/ Banane NHG 5
bandage /ˈbændɪdʒ/ Verband NHG 7
bar chart /ˈbɑː tʃɑːt/ Säulendiagramm p. 171
(to) **barbecue** /ˈbɑːbɪˌkjuː/ grillen p. 48, 7
bargain /ˈbɑːɡɪn/ Schnäppchen NHG 7
barn /bɑːn/ Scheune p. 111, 7
based in /ˈbeɪst ɪn/ ansässig in p. 62, 8
basic /ˈbeɪsɪk/ grundlegend; wesentlich NHG 7
basically /ˈbeɪsɪkli/ im Wesentlichen p. 83, 2
basket /ˈbɑːskɪt/ Korb p. 123, 8
bathroom /ˈbɑːθˌruːm/ Badezimmer NHG 5
battery /ˈbætri/ Batterie p. 86, 6
the Battery /ðə ˈbætri/ Park in New York p. 25, 7
battle /ˈbætl/ Kampf NHG 7
BC (= before Christ) /ˌbiː ˈsiː, bɪˌfɔː ˈkraɪst/ v. Chr. (= vor Christus) NHG 7
(to) **be** (irr) /biː/ sein NHG 5
(to) **be a shame** (irr) /ˌbi ə ˈʃeɪm/ schade sein NHG 7
(to) **be able to do something** (irr) /ˌbi ˌeɪbl tə ˈduː ˌsʌmθɪŋ/ etwas tun können NHG 6
(to) **be about** (irr) /ˌbi əˈbaʊt/ gehen um; handeln von NHG 5
(to) **be afraid of** (irr) /ˌbi əˈfreɪd əv/ Angst haben vor NHG 6
(to) **be allergic to** (irr) /ˌbi əˈlɜːdʒɪk tʊ/ allergisch sein auf NHG 7
(to) **be allowed (to)** (irr) /ˌbi əˈlaʊd tə/ erlaubt sein, dürfen NHG 6
(to) **be aware of** (irr) /ˌbi əˈweər əv/ sich bewusst sein p. 71, 5

(to) **be behind** (irr, informal) /ˌbi bɪˈhaɪnd/ hinterher sein p. 40, 7
(to) **be born** (irr) /ˌbi ˈbɔːn/ geboren werden NHG 7
(to) **be close to somebody's heart** /ˌbi ˌkləʊs tə ˌsʌmbədiz ˈhɑːt/ jemandem sehr wichtig sein p. 74, 8
(to) **be connected (to)** (irr) /ˌbi kəˈnektɪd tə/ verbunden sein (mit), in Verbindung stehen (mit) p. 66, 14
(to) **be estimated** (irr) /ˌbiˈestɪmeɪtəd/ geschätzt werden P&P 7
(to) **be far from reach** (irr) /ˌbi ˌfɑː frəm ˈriːtʃ/ außer Reichweite sein p. 68, 2
(to) **be good at doing something** (irr) /ˌbi ˌɡʊd ət ˈduːɪŋ ˌsʌmθɪŋ/ gut darin sein, etwas zu tun NHG 5
(to) **be good at something** (irr) /ˌbi ˌɡʊd æt ˌsʌmθɪŋ/ gut in etwas sein NHG 6
(to) **be (good/great) fun** (irr) /ˌbi ˌɡʊd/ˌɡreɪt ˈfʌn/ (viel/großen) Spaß machen NHG 5
(to) **be in love** (irr) /ˌbi ɪn ˈlʌv/ verliebt sein p. 66, 13
(to) **be into** (irr, informal) /ˌbi ɪnˈtuː/ interessiert sein an p. 59, 3
(to) **be interested in** (irr) /ˌbi ˈɪntrəstɪd ɪn/ interessiert sein an NHG 7
(to) **be involved in** (irr) /ˌbi ɪnˈvɒlvd ɪn/ beteiligt sein an p. 15, 7
(to) **be located** (irr) /ˌbi ləʊˈkeɪtɪd/ gelegen sein NHG 7
(to) **be lucky** (irr) /ˌbi ˈlʌki/ Glück haben NHG 7
(to) **be on display** (irr) /ˌbi ɒn dɪˈspleɪ/ ausgestellt sein P&P 2
(to) **be one's turn** (irr) /ˌbi wʌnz ˈtɜːn/ an der Reihe sein NHG 5
(to) **be passionate about** (irr) /ˌbi ˈpæʃnət əˌbaʊt/ für etwas brennen p. 93, 2
(to) **be proud of** (irr) /ˌbi ˈpraʊd əv/ stolz sein auf p. 24, 6
(to) **be right** (irr) /ˌbi ˈraɪt/ recht haben NHG 5
(to) **be situated** (irr) /ˌbi ˈsɪtʃueɪtɪd/ liegen, gelegen sein p. 18, 12
(to) **be sorry** (irr) /ˌbi ˈsɒri/ bedauern; sich entschuldigen p. 63, 8

(to) **be up to something** (irr) /ˌbi ˌʌp tə ˈsʌmθɪŋ/ etwas vorhaben p. 45, 2
(to) **be well known** (irr) /ˌbi ˌwel ˈnəʊn/ allgemein bekannt sein p. 11, 2
(to) **be willing to** (irr) /ˌbi ˈwɪlɪŋ tʊ/ bereit sein p. 89, 9
(to) **be worth** (irr) /ˌbi ˈwɜːθ/ (sich) lohnen; wert sein NHG 7
(to) **be wrong** (irr) /ˌbi ˈrɒŋ/ im Unrecht sein NHG 7
(to) **be wrong (with)** (irr) /ˌbi ˈrɒŋ wɪθ/ nicht in Ordnung sein (mit) NHG 7
beach /biːtʃ/ Strand NHG 5
bean /biːn/ Bohne p. 18, 12
beard /bɪəd/ Bart NHG 7
beautiful /ˈbjuːtəfl/ schön NHG 5
beauty /ˈbjuːti/ Schönheit p. 11, 2
because /bɪˈkɒz/ weil; da NHG 5
because of /bɪˈkɒz əv/ wegen NHG 7
(to) **become involved in** (irr) /bɪˌkʌm ɪnˈvɒlvd ɪn/ sich beteiligen, sich engagieren P&P 5
(to) **become** (irr) /bɪˈkʌm/ werden NHG 6
bed /bed/ Bett NHG 5
bedroom /ˈbedruːm/ Schlafzimmer NHG 5
bee /biː/ Biene NHG 6
before /bɪˈfɔː/ bevor; zuvor, vorher; vor NHG 5
beforehand /bɪˈfɔːhænd/ vorher p. 48, 7
(to) **begin** (irr) /bɪˈɡɪn/ anfangen; beginnen NHG 5
beginner /bɪˈɡɪnə/ Anfänger/in p. 35, 2
beginning /bɪˈɡɪnɪŋ/ Anfang; Beginn NHG 6
(to) **behave** /bɪˈheɪv/ sich verhalten, sich benehmen p. 63, 8
behavior (AE) /bɪˈheɪvjə/ Benehmen; Verhalten p. 63, 8
behaviour /bɪˈheɪvjə/ Benehmen; Verhalten NHG 7
behind /bɪˈhaɪnd/ hinter NHG 5
(to) **be behind** (irr, informal) /ˌbi bɪˈhaɪnd/ hinterher sein p. 40, 7
belief /bɪˈliːf/ Glaube p. 89, 9
(to) **believe (in)** /bɪˈliːv ɪn/ glauben (an) NHG 6
bell /bel/ Glocke NHG 6

Dictionary

(to) **belong (to)** /bɪˈlɒŋ/ gehören (zu) NHG 7
below /bɪˈləʊ/ unten, unter NHG 6
benefit /ˈbenɪfɪt/ Vorteil; Nutzen p. 72, 6
besides /bɪˈsaɪdz/ außer, abgesehen von P&P 8
best /best/ beste(r, s) NHG 5
All the best! /ˌɔːl ðə ˈbest/ Alles Gute! NHG 7
the best /ðə ˈbest/ der/die/das beste NHG 5; am besten NHG 6
(to) **like best** /ˌlaɪk ˈbest/ am liebsten mögen NHG 5
(to) **do one's best** *(irr)* /ˌduː wʌnz ˈbest/ sein Bestes geben p. 48, 7
best wishes /ˌbest ˈwɪʃɪz/ viele Grüße p. 167
better /ˈbetə/ besser NHG 6
(to) **get better** *(irr)* /ˌget ˈbetə/ besser werden; gesund werden NHG 7
between /bɪˈtwiːn/ zwischen NHG 5
BFF (= best friend forever) *(informal)* /ˌbiː_ef_ˈef, ˌbest ˌfrend fərˈevə/ *allerbeste/r Freund/in* p. 58, 3
bible /ˈbaɪbl/ Bibel p. 120, 6
bicycle /ˈbaɪsɪkl/ Fahrrad p. 95, 7
big /bɪg/ groß NHG 5
bike /baɪk/ Fahrrad NHG 5
(to) **ride a bike** *(irr)* /ˌraɪd_ə ˈbaɪk/ Fahrrad fahren NHG 5
bike lane /ˈbaɪk leɪn/ Fahrradweg p. 20, 2
biking /ˈbaɪkɪŋ/ Radfahren p. 140
bill /bɪl/ Rechnung NHG 7
bill /bɪl/ Gesetzentwurf; Gesetzesvorlage p. 11, 2
billion /ˈbɪljən/ Milliarde p. 6
bin /bɪn/ Abfalleimer NHG 5
bird /bɜːd/ Vogel NHG 6
birth /bɜːθ/ Geburt P&P 2
birthday /ˈbɜːθdeɪ/ Geburtstag NHG 5
Happy birthday (to you)! /ˌhæpi ˈbɜːθdeɪ tʊ juː/ Herzlichen Glückwunsch zum Geburtstag! NHG 5
birthplace /ˈbɜːθˌpleɪs/ Geburtsort p. 11, 2
biscuit /ˈbɪskɪt/ Keks NHG 5
bison *(pl* bison*)* /ˈbaɪsn, ˈbaɪsn/ Bison; Wisent p. 111, 7
a bit /ə ˈbɪt/ ein bisschen NHG 5
black /blæk/ schwarz NHG 5
Black /blæk/ *politische Selbstbezeichnung Schwarzer Menschen in den USA* p. 25, 7
(to) **bleed** *(irr)* /bliːd/ bluten NHG 7
(to) **blend** /blend/ vermischen p. 25, 7
(to) **block** /blɒk/ blockieren p. 69, 2
(to) **blog** /blɒg/ bloggen p. 38, 6
blood /blʌd/ Blut NHG 6
blood sample /ˈblʌd ˌsɑːmpl/ Blutprobe p. 92, 2
blue /bluː/ blau NHG 5
blurred /blɜːd/ verschwommen, unscharf p. 72, 6
board /bɔːd/ Tafel; Brett NHG 5
(to) **board a ship** /ˌbɔːd_ə ˈʃɪp/ ein Schiff besteigen p. 106, 2
board game /ˈbɔːd geɪm/ Brettspiel NHG 6
on board /ˌɒn ˈbɔːd/ an Bord p. 121, 6
boat /bəʊt/ Boot NHG 5
body /ˈbɒdi/ Körper NHG 5
book /bʊk/ Buch NHG 5
(to) **book** /bʊk/ buchen, reservieren NHG 6
booklet /ˈbʊklət/ Broschüre p. 81
bookshelf *(pl* bookshelves*)* /ˈbʊkʃelf, ˈbʊkʃelvz/ Bücherregal NHG 5
boot /buːt/ Kofferraum p. 165
bored /bɔːd/ gelangweilt NHG 6
boring /ˈbɔːrɪŋ/ langweilig NHG 5
born /bɔːn/ geboren p. 17, 10
(to) **be born** *(irr)* /ˌbiː ˈbɔːn/ geboren werden NHG 7
borough /ˈbʌrə/ Bezirk; Stadtteil p. 21, 2
(to) **borrow** /ˈbɒrəʊ/ (aus)leihen NHG 5
both /bəʊθ/ beide NHG 7
both … and … /ˈbəʊθ ænd/ sowohl … als auch … NHG 7
(to) **bother** /ˈbɒðə/ stören; belästigen NHG 7
bottle /ˈbɒtl/ Flasche NHG 5
bottlenose dolphin /ˈbɒtlnəʊz ˌdɒlfɪn/ Tümmler p. 141
boundary /ˈbaʊndri/ Grenze p. 72, 6
boundless /ˈbaʊndləs/ grenzenlos, unbegrenzt p. 89, 9
bowl /bəʊl/ Schüssel; Schale NHG 5
box /bɒks/ Kasten; Kiste NHG 5
boy /bɔɪ/ Junge NHG 5

boy scout /ˌbɔɪ ˈskaʊt/ Pfadfinder p. 98, 10
bracket /ˈbrækɪt/ Klammer p. 18, 12
brain /breɪn/ Gehirn NHG 7
Brazil /brəˈzɪl/ Brasilien p. 71, 5
bread /bred/ Brot NHG 7
break /breɪk/ Pause NHG 5
(to) **break** *(irr)* /breɪk/ brechen; zerbrechen; kaputt machen NHG 6
(to) **take a break** *(irr)* /ˌteɪk ə ˈbreɪk/ eine Pause machen p. 85, 5
(to) **break up** *(irr)* /ˌbreɪk_ˈʌp/ Schluss machen p. 69, 2
breakfast /ˈbrekfəst/ Frühstück NHG 5
breast /brest/ Brust p. 122, 7
breathtaking /ˈbreθˌteɪkɪŋ/ atemberaubend p. 13, 6
Brexit /ˈbreksɪt/ Brexit *(Ausstieg Großbritanniens aus der EU)* P&P 8
bridge /brɪdʒ/ Brücke NHG 6
bright, brightly /braɪt, ˈbraɪtli/ hell; strahlend NHG 6
brilliant /ˈbrɪljənt/ genial, klasse NHG 5
(to) **bring** *(irr)* /brɪŋ/ mitbringen NHG 5
(to) **bring over** *(irr)* /ˌbrɪŋ ˈəʊvə/ herbeibringen NHG 7
(to) **bring together** *(irr)* /ˌbrɪŋ təˈgeðə/ zusammenbringen p. 25, 7
Britain /ˈbrɪtn/ Großbritannien NHG 6
British /ˈbrɪtɪʃ/ britisch NHG 6
brochure /ˈbrəʊʃə/ Broschüre NHG 7
broken /ˈbrəʊkən/ gebrochen; zerbrochen; kaputt NHG 7
brother /ˈbrʌðə/ Bruder NHG 5
brown /braʊn/ braun NHG 5
brownstone (house) /ˈbraʊnˌstəʊn haʊs/ *Haus aus rötlich braunem Sandstein* p. 24, 6
(to) **brush one's teeth** /ˌbrʌʃ wʌnz ˈtiːθ/ sich die Zähne putzen NHG 5
buffalo chips *(pl)* /ˈbʌfələʊ tʃɪps/ getrockneter Büffeldung p. 111, 7
(to) **build** *(irr)* /bɪld/ bauen NHG 5
(to) **build a park** *(irr)* /ˌbɪld_ə ˈpɑːk/ einen Park anlegen p. 21, 2
building /ˈbɪldɪŋ/ Gebäude NHG 6
(to) **bully** /ˈbʊli/ mobben p. 69, 2
bully /ˈbʊli/ *Person, die mobbt* p. 69, 2

burned-out *(AE)* = burnt-out *(BE)* /bɜːndˈaʊt, ˌbɜːntˈaʊt,/ ausgebrannt p. 85, 5
bus stop /ˈbʌsˌstɒp/ Bushaltestelle p. 38, 6
busboy *(AE)* /ˈbʌsbɔɪ/ Abräumer; Hilfskellner p. 97, 9
business /ˈbɪznəs/ Geschäft; Handel NHG 7
business law /ˈbɪznəs lɔː/ Wirtschaftsrecht p. 40, 7
business trip /ˈbɪznəs trɪp/ Geschäftsreise p. 147
busy /ˈbɪzi/ beschäftigt NHG 5; bewegt, ereignisreich; belebt; verkehrsreich NHG 6
but /bʌt/ aber NHG 5; außer NHG 6
(to) **buy** *(irr)* /baɪ/ kaufen NHG 5
by /baɪ/ von; mit NHG 5; bei, an; *hier:* (spätestens) bis NHG 6
by *(+ Verbform mit -ing)* /baɪ/ indem NHG 6
by /baɪ/ *hier:* an ... vorbei p. 111, 7
by accident /ˌbaɪˈæksɪdnt/ zufällig; aus Versehen NHG 7
by heart /ˌbaɪˈhɑːt/ auswendig NHG 7
by oneself /ˌbaɪ wʌnˈself/ allein p. 59, 3
by then /ˌbaɪˈðen/ bis dahin p. 107, 2
bye /baɪ/ tschüs(s) NHG 5

C
cabin /ˈkæbɪn/ Kabine p. 106, 2
cage /keɪdʒ/ Käfig NHG 5
cake /keɪk/ Kuchen NHG 5
calculator /ˈkælkjʊˌleɪtə/ Taschenrechner NHG 5
calendar /ˈkælɪndə/ Kalender NHG 5
calf *(pl calves)* /kɑːf, kɑːvz/ Jungtier p. 141
California /ˌkæləˈfɔːniə/ Kalifornien p. 10, 2
California Institute of the Arts /ˌkæləˌfɔːniəˌɪnstɪˌtjuːt əv ðiˈɑːts/ *private Kunsthochschule in Kalifornien* p. 82, 2
Californian /ˌkæləˈfɔːniən/ kalifornisch p. 86, 6
call /kɔːl/ Anruf; Gespräch NHG 7
(to) **give somebody a call** *(irr)* /ˌɡɪv ˌsʌmbədi əˈkɔːl/ jemanden anrufen NHG 7

call of freedom /ˌkɔːl əvˈfriːdəm/ Ruf der Freiheit p. 122, 7
(to) call /kɔːl/ anrufen NHG 6; nennen p. 37, 5
(to) **call an ambulance** /ˌkɔːl ənˈæmbjʊləns/ einen Krankenwagen rufen NHG 7
(to) be called /ˌbiːˈkɔːld/ heißen, genannt werden NHG 5
calm /kɑːm/ ruhig; friedlich p. 21, 2
(to) **calm down** /ˌkɑːmˈdaʊn/ (sich) beruhigen NHG 7
camera /ˈkæmrə/ Kamera; Fotoapparat NHG 6
camerawork *(no pl)* /ˈkæmrəwɜːk/ Kameraführung p. 82, 2
camp /kæmp/ (Zelt)lager NHG 6
(to) **make camp** *(irr)* /ˌmeɪkˈkæmp/ das Lager aufschlagen p. 111, 7
campaign /kæmˈpeɪn/ Kampagne p. 87, 6
(to) campaign /kæmˈpeɪn/ kämpfen; sich engagieren p. 83, 2
campus /ˈkæmpəs/ Universität; Campus p. 120, 6
can /kæn/ können NHG 5
can /kæn/ Dose; Büchse NHG 7
can't (= cannot) /kɑːnt, ˈkænɒt/ nicht können NHG 5
Canada /ˈkænədə/ Kanada p. 14, 7
(to) **cancel** /ˈkænsl/ absagen, streichen NHG 7
candle /ˈkændl/ Kerze NHG 5
canyon /ˈkænjən/ Schlucht p. 13, 6
cap /kæp/ Mütze NHG 6
cap /kæp/ *hier:* Kappe P&P 3
capital /ˈkæpɪtl/ Hauptstadt p. 6
capital letter /ˌkæpɪtlˈletə/ Großbuchstabe p. 73, 6
caption /ˈkæpʃn/ Bildunterschrift NHG 7
car /kɑː/ Auto NHG 5
car *(AE)* /kɑː/ Waggon; Wagen p. 25, 7
car boot /ˈkɑːˌbuːt/ Kofferraum p. 48, 7
car boot sale /ˌkɑːˈbuːt seɪl/ Kofferraum-Flohmarkt NHG 7
car park /ˈkɑː pɑːk/ Parkplatz p. 48, 7
card /kɑːd/ Karte NHG 5
(to) **take care (of)** *(irr)* /ˌteɪkˈkeər əv/ sich kümmern um NHG 6

(to) **care about** /ˈkeər əˌbaʊt/ sich aus etwas etwas machen p. 87, 6
career /kəˈrɪə/ Karriere; Laufbahn p. 44, 2
career and technical education (CTE) /kəˌrɪər ənˌteknɪklˌedjʊˈkeɪʃn, ˌsiːˌtiːˈiː/ *etwa:* Berufsbildung P&P 6
careful /ˈkeəfl/ vorsichtig NHG 6
carefully /ˈkeəfli/ vorsichtig NHG 6; gründlich p. 73, 6
(to) **listen carefully** /ˌlɪsnˈkeəfli/ aufmerksam zuhören p. 96, 8
carelessly /ˈkeələsli/ unvorsichtig, gedankenlos p. 73, 6
the Caribbean /ðəˌkærɪˈbiən/ Karibik, karibische Inseln p. 14, 7
caring /ˈkeərɪŋ/ Kümmern p. 151
carnival /ˈkɑːnɪvl/ Volksfest; Karneval p. 49, 7
carpet /ˈkɑːpɪt/ Teppich p. 148
carrot /ˈkærət/ Möhre; Karotte NHG 5
(to) **carry** /ˈkæri/ tragen p. 39, 6
(to) **carry out** /ˌkæriˈaʊt/ durchführen, betreiben p. 92, 2
case /keɪs/ Fall NHG 6
cash /kæʃ/ Geld; Bargeld NHG 7
cash register *(AE)* /ˈkæʃˌredʒɪstə/ Kasse p. 97, 9
cast /kɑːst/ Gips NHG 7
cast /kɑːst/ Besetzung p. 149
castle /ˈkɑːsl/ Burg; Schloss NHG 6
cat /kæt/ Katze NHG 5
(to) **catch** *(irr)* /kætʃ/ fangen NHG 5
(to) **catch a cold** *(irr)* /ˌkætʃ əˈkəʊld/ sich erkälten NHG 7
catcher /ˈkætʃə/ Fänger/in p. 44, 2
category /ˈkætəɡri/ Kategorie NHG 6
cause /kɔːz/ Grund, Ursache; Sache p. 35, 2
(to) cause /kɔːz/ verursachen p. 86, 6
'cause (= because) /kɔːz, bɪˈkɒz/ weil, da p. 25, 7
cave /keɪv/ Höhle p. 135
ceiling /ˈsiːlɪŋ/ Zimmerdecke p. 65, 12
(to) **celebrate** /ˈseləˌbreɪt/ feiern NHG 6
celebration /ˌseləˈbreɪʃn/ Feier NHG 6
cell phone *(AE)* /ˈsel fəʊn/ Handy p. 68, 2
cellar /ˈselə/ Keller NHG 7
center *(AE)* /ˈsentə/ Zentrum p. 28, 14
centre /ˈsentə/ Zentrum NHG 6

Dictionary

shopping centre /ˈʃɒpɪŋ ˌsentə/ Einkaufszentrum NHG 5
century /ˈsentʃəri/ Jahrhundert NHG 6
cereal /ˈsɪəriəl/ Frühstücksflocken p. 38, 6
ceremony /ˈserəməni/ Zeremonie; Feier P&P 3
certain /ˈsɜːtn/ bestimmt; gewiss NHG 7
certainly /ˈsɜːtnli/ sicher; gerne NHG 7
certification /ˌsɜːtɪfɪˈkeɪʃn/ Qualifizierung; Zertifikat p. 93, 2
chain /tʃeɪn/ Kette NHG 6
chair /tʃeə/ Stuhl NHG 5
challenge /ˈtʃæləndʒ/ Herausforderung NHG 5
championship /ˈtʃæmpiənʃɪp/ Meisterschaft p. 34, 2
chance /tʃɑːns/ Möglichkeit; Gelegenheit NHG 7
change /tʃeɪndʒ/ Wechselgeld NHG 5; Veränderung; Wechsel p. 85, 5
(to) change /tʃeɪndʒ/ (sich) ändern; verändern NHG 6
(to) change lines /ˌtʃeɪndʒ ˈlaɪnz/ umsteigen NHG 6
(to) change one's mind /ˌtʃeɪndʒ wʌnz ˈmaɪnd/ seine Meinung ändern NHG 6
changemaker /ˈtʃeɪndʒ ˌmeɪkə/ jemand, der sich aktiv bemüht, Dinge zu verändern p. 87, 6
channel /ˈtʃænl/ Kanal p. 68, 1
chant /tʃɑːnt/ Sprechgesang p. 49, 7
character /ˈkærəktə/ Figur; Charakter NHG 6; Wesen p. 25, 7; Zeichen; Schriftzeichen p. 71, 5
charity /ˈtʃærəti/ Wohltätigkeitsorganisation NHG 7
charity run /ˈtʃærəti rʌn/ Wohltätigkeitslauf P&P 5
charming /ˈtʃɑːmɪŋ/ charmant; reizend p. 13, 6
(to) chat /tʃæt/ plaudern; chatten NHG 7
cheap /tʃiːp/ billig NHG 7
check /tʃek/ Überprüfung; Kontrolle NHG 7
(to) check /tʃek/ überprüfen; kontrollieren NHG 7
(to) check out (informal) /ˌtʃek ˈaʊt/ sich ansehen; ausprobieren NHG 7

(to) check out /ˌtʃek ˈaʊt/ auschecken p. 29, 15
cheer basics (pl) /ˈtʃɪə ˌbeɪsɪks/ Grundkenntnisse beim Cheerleading p. 35, 2
(to) cheer for /ˈtʃɪə fə/ anfeuern p. 35, 2
(to) cheer somebody on /ˌtʃɪə ˌsʌmbədi ˈɒn/ anfeuern P&P 4
cheer team /ˈtʃɪə tiːm/ Cheerleading-Team p. 35, 2
cheerful /ˈtʃɪəfl/ fröhlich, vergnügt NHG 7
cheese /tʃiːz/ Käse NHG 5
chemical /ˈkemɪkl/ Chemikalie p. 86, 6
chemistry /ˈkemɪstri/ Chemie p. 45, 2
chess /tʃes/ Schach NHG 7
chicken /ˈtʃɪkɪn/ Huhn NHG 6
child (pl **children**) /tʃaɪld, ˈtʃɪldrən/ Kind NHG 5
(to) chill (informal) /tʃɪl/ relaxen, chillen p. 140
chilled (informal) /tʃɪld/ gechillt p. 48, 7
chilli (pl chillies) /ˈtʃɪli, ˈtʃɪliz/ Chili; Peperoni p. 47, 6
Chinese /ˌtʃaɪˈniːz/ Chinese/Chinesin; chinesisch NHG 6
chips (pl) /tʃɪps/ Pommes frites NHG 5
chips (AE, pl) /tʃɪps/ Chips p. 48, 7
chocolate /ˈtʃɒklət/ Schokolade NHG 5
choice /tʃɔɪs/ Auswahl; Wahl NHG 7
(to) choose (irr) /tʃuːz/ wählen; sich entscheiden NHG 5
(to) chop /tʃɒp/ hacken NHG 7
chore /tʃɔː/ lästige Aufgabe; Hausarbeit NHG 5
choreographer /ˌkɒriˈɒɡrəfə/ Choreograph/in p. 75, 10
Christian /ˈkrɪstʃən/ Christ/in; christlich NHG 6
Christmas /ˈkrɪsməs/ Weihnachten NHG 6
chronological /ˌkrɒnəˈlɒdʒɪkl/ chronologisch p. 15, 7
church /tʃɜːtʃ/ Kirche NHG 6
cinema /ˈsɪnəmə/ Kino NHG 5
circle /ˈsɜːkl/ Kreis; Runde p. 85, 5
inner circle /ˌɪnə ˈsɜːkl/ engster Kreis p. 87, 6
citizen /ˈsɪtɪzn/ Bürger/in p. 89, 9

city /ˈsɪti/ Stadt; Innenstadt NHG 5
civil rights (pl) /ˌsɪvl ˈraɪts/ Bürgerrechte p. 15, 7
Civil War /ˌsɪvl ˈwɔː/ Bürgerkrieg p. 13, 6
(to) claim /kleɪm/ Anspruch erheben auf; behaupten p. 14, 7
clap /klæp/ Klatschen p. 49, 7
(to) clap /klæp/ klatschen p. 50, 9
class /klɑːs/ Klasse; Unterrichtsstunde NHG 5
classmate /ˈklɑːsˌmeɪt/ Klassenkamerad/in; Mitschüler/in NHG 5
classroom /ˈklɑːsˌruːm/ Klassenzimmer NHG 5
clause /klɔːz/ Satzglied; Satzteil p. 46
clean /kliːn/ sauber NHG 5
(to) clean (up) /kliːn, ˌkliːn ˈʌp/ sauber machen NHG 5
clear /klɪə/ klar; deutlich NHG 6
clearly /ˈklɪəli/ klar; deutlich NHG 6
(to) click on /ˈklɪk ɒn/ anklicken NHG 7
climate /ˈklaɪmət/ Klima p. 10, 2
climate change /ˈklaɪmət tʃeɪndʒ/ Klimaveränderung; Klimawandel p. 83, 2
(to) climb /klaɪm/ auf etwas (hinauf)steigen; klettern NHG 5
clock /klɒk/ Uhr NHG 5
(to) close /kləʊz/ zumachen; schließen NHG 5
close /kləʊs/ nah(e); eng p. 59, 3
(to) be close to somebody's heart (irr) /ˌbiː ˌkləʊs tə ˌsʌmbədiz ˈhɑːt/ jemandem sehr wichtig sein p. 74, 8
closed /kləʊzd/ geschlossen NHG 6
(to) take a closer look at (irr) /ˌteɪk ə ˌkləʊsə ˈlʊk ət/ sich genauer ansehen p. 148
clothes (pl) /kləʊðz/ Kleider; Kleidung NHG 5
clothing /ˈkləʊðɪŋ/ Kleidung P&P 2
cloud /klaʊd/ Wolke p. 65, 12
club /klʌb/ AG; Klub NHG 5
CO_2 (= carbon dioxide) /ˌsiː ˌəʊ ˈtuː, ˌkɑːbən daɪˈɒksaɪd/ Kohlendioxid p. 85, 5
coach /kəʊtʃ/ Trainer/in NHG 7
coast /kəʊst/ Küste p. 14, 7
coffee /ˈkɒfi/ Kaffee NHG 5

| Skills | Wordbanks | Grammar | **Words** |

cold /kəʊld/ kalt NHG 5; Erkältung NHG 7
(to) **catch a cold** (irr) /ˌkætʃ_ə ˈkəʊld/ sich erkälten NHG 7
(to) **collect** /kəˈlekt/ sammeln NHG 5
collection /kəˈlekʃn/ Sammlung NHG 6
college /ˈkɒlɪdʒ/ College (Bildungseinrichtung, die zu einem eher praxisorientierten Bachelor-Abschluss hinführt) p. 35, 2
community college /kəˈmjuːnəti ˌkɒlɪdʒ/ subventioniertes zweijähriges College p. 82, 2
colonization /ˌkɒlənaɪˈzeɪʃn/ Kolonisierung p. 14, 7
colony /ˈkɒləni/ Kolonie NHG 7
color (AE) /ˈkʌlə/ Farbe p. 165
colour /ˈkʌlə/ Farbe NHG 5
colourful /ˈkʌləfl/ farbenfroh; bunt NHG 7
(to) **combat** /ˈkɒmbæt/ bekämpfen p. 85, 5
combination /ˌkɒmbɪˈneɪʃn/ Kombination; Mischung NHG 6
(to) **combine** /kəmˈbaɪn/ verbinden p. 90, 10
(to) **come** (irr) /kʌm/ kommen NHG 5
(to) **come back** (irr) /ˌkʌm ˈbæk/ zurückkommen NHG 5
(to) **come in** (irr) /ˌkʌm_ˈɪn/ hereinkommen NHG 7
(to) **come to mind** (irr) /ˌkʌm tə ˈmaɪnd/ einfallen, in den Sinn kommen p. 25, 7
(to) **come second** (irr) /ˌkʌm ˈsekənd/ Zweite/r werden p. 34, 2
(to) **come up with** (irr) /ˌkʌm_ˈʌp wɪð/ sich einfallen lassen p. 43, 14
(to) **make one's dream come true** (irr) /ˌmeɪk wʌnz ˈdriːm kʌm ˌtruː/ seinen Traum wahr werden lassen p. 149
comedy /ˈkɒmədi/ Komödie p. 66, 13
comfort /ˈkʌmfət/ Komfort; Bequemlichkeit p. 72, 6
comfortable /ˈkʌmftəbl/ bequem NHG 7
(to) **feel comfortable** (irr) /ˌfiːl ˈkʌmftəbl/ sich wohl fühlen p. 72, 6
command /kəˈmɑːnd/ Befehl NHG 5
reported command /ˌrɪ pɔːtɪd kəˈmɑːnd/ indirekter Befehl p. 108

(to) **commemorate** /kəˈmeməreɪt/ (einer Person oder Sache) gedenken p. 16, 8
comment /ˈkɒment/ Kommentar; Bemerkung p. 61, 7
(to) **comment on** /ˈkɒment_ɒn/ kommentieren NHG 6
commercial /kəˈmɜːʃl/ kommerziell, profitorientiert NHG 6
commercial /kəˈmɜːʃl/ Werbespot p. 41, 10
commitment /kəˈmɪtmənt/ Engagement p. 87, 6
committee /kəˈmɪti/ Ausschuss; Komitee p. 35, 2
common /ˈkɒmən/ üblich; weit verbreitet p. 62, 8
(to) **have in common** (irr) /ˌhæv_ɪn ˈkɒmən/ gemeinsam haben NHG 6
communal /ˈkɒmjənl/ Gemeinschafts- p. 150
(to) **communicate** /kəˈmjuːnɪkeɪt/ kommunizieren, sprechen NHG 7
communication /kəˌmjuːnɪˈkeɪʃn/ Verständigung; Kommunikation NHG 7
community /kəˈmjuːnəti/ Gemeinschaft; Gemeinde NHG 7
community college /kəˈmjuːnəti ˌkɒlɪdʒ/ subventioniertes zweijähriges College p. 82, 2
company /ˈkʌmpni/ Firma; Unternehmen NHG 7
comparative /kəmˈpærətɪv/ Komparativ p. 70, 3
(to) **compare** /kəmˈpeə/ vergleichen NHG 6
compared to /kəmˈpeəd_tʊ/ im Vergleich zu p. 68, 2
comparison /kəmˈpærɪsn/ Vergleich NHG 6
(to) **compete** /kəmˈpiːt/ an einem Wettkampf teilnehmen; kämpfen NHG 7
(to) **compete in** /kəmˈpiːt_ɪn/ teilnehmen an NHG 7
competition /ˌkɒmpəˈtɪʃn/ Wettbewerb NHG 5
competitor /kəmˈpetɪtə/ Konkurrent/in p. 35, 2
(to) **complain (to)** /kəmˈpleɪn/ sich beklagen (bei) p. 96, 8

complete /kəmˈpliːt/ vollständig, komplett NHG 7
(to) **complete** /kəmˈpliːt/ vervollständigen NHG 5; fertigstellen p. 28, 13
completely /kəmˈpliːtli/ völlig, absolut NHG 6
complex /ˈkɒmpleks/ Komplex p. 15, 7
complicated /ˈkɒmplɪˌkeɪtɪd/ kompliziert NHG 7
composer /kəmˈpəʊzə/ Komponist/in p. 148
compromise /ˈkɒmprəmaɪz/ Kompromiss NHG 6
con /kɒn/ Nachteil; Kontra NHG 6
(to) **concentrate** /ˈkɒnsnˌtreɪt/ sich konzentrieren NHG 7
concept /ˈkɒnsept/ Entwurf; Konzept NHG 6
concern /kənˈsɜːn/ Anliegen; Sorge p. 83, 2
concert /ˈkɒnsət/ Konzert NHG 6
conclusion /kənˈkluːʒn/ Schlussfolgerung p. 61, 7
condition /kənˈdɪʃn/ Zustand NHG 7; Bedingung p. 15, 7
conditional (clause) /kənˈdɪʃnəl klɔːz/ Konditional; Konditionalsatz p. 46
conflict /ˈkɒnflɪkt/ Konflikt NHG 6
confusing /kənˈfjuːzɪŋ/ verwirrend p. 48, 7
Congratulations! /kənˌgrætʃəˈleɪʃnz/ Glückwunsch!; Gratuliere! p. 34, 2
congress /ˈkɒŋgres/ Kongress p. 44, 2
(to) **connect** /kəˈnekt/ verbinden NHG 7
(to) **be connected (to)** (irr) /ˌbiː kəˈnektɪd_tə/ verbunden sein (mit), in Verbindung stehen (mit) p. 66, 14
(to) **get connected** (irr) /ˌget kəˈnektɪd/ sich verbinden, in Kontakt treten p. 72, 6
connection /kəˈnekʃn/ Verbindung p. 65, 12
consequence /ˈkɒnsɪkwəns/ Konsequenz; Folge NHG 7
(to) **consider** /kənˈsɪdə/ nachdenken über, denken an; halten für p. 97, 9
constantly /ˈkɒnstəntli/ ständig; dauernd p. 62, 8

Dictionary

construction /kənˈstrʌkʃn/ Bau NHG 7
construction worker /kənˈstrʌkʃn ˌwɜːkə/ Bauarbeiter/in p. 92, 1
consultant /kənˈsʌltənt/ Berater/in p. 107, 2
(to) contact /ˈkɒntækt/ sich in Verbindung setzen mit NHG 6
(to) contain /kənˈteɪn/ enthalten NHG 7
content /ˈkɒntent/ Inhalt NHG 7
continent /ˈkɒntɪnənt/ Kontinent p. 14, 7
(to) continue /kənˈtɪnjuː/ andauern, weitergehen p. 35, 2
(to) continue to do /kənˌtɪnjuː tə ˈduː/ weiter(hin) tun, nach wie vor tun p. 148
(to) contribute /kənˈtrɪbjuːt/ beitragen p. 10, 2
conversation /ˌkɒnvəˈseɪʃn/ Gespräch; Unterhaltung NHG 7
(to) cook /kʊk/ kochen NHG 5; braten, backen NHG 6
cooking /ˈkʊkɪŋ/ Kochen; Koch- NHG 5
(to) do the cooking (irr) /ˌduː ðə ˈkʊkɪŋ/ kochen NHG 5
cool /kuːl/ kühl; kalt NHG 7
(to) cool /kuːl/ kühlen NHG 7
(to) copy /ˈkɒpi/ abschreiben NHG 5; kopieren NHG 7
corner /ˈkɔːnə/ Ecke NHG 6
correct /kəˈrekt/ richtig, korrekt NHG 5
(to) correct /kəˈrekt/ korrigieren NHG 5
(to) cost (irr) /kɒst/ kosten NHG 5
costume /ˈkɒstjuːm/ Kostüm NHG 6
cotton /ˈkɒtn/ Baumwolle P&P 1
cough /kɒf/ Husten NHG 7
could /kʊd/ könnte(st, n, t) NHG 5; Vergangenheitsform von can NHG 6
counselor (AE) = counsellor (BE) /ˈkaʊnslə/ hier: Betreuer/in p. 98, 10
(to) count /kaʊnt/ zählen NHG 7
countless /ˈkaʊntləs/ zahllos; unzählig p. 120, 6
country /ˈkʌntri/ Land NHG 6
country music /ˈkʌntri ˌmjuːzɪk/ Countrymusik p. 11, 2
countryside /ˈkʌntrisaɪd/ Land; Landschaft NHG 6

county /ˈkaʊnti/ (Verwaltungs)bezirk; Grafschaft p. 116, 1
a couple of /ə ˈkʌpl əv/ einige, ein paar NHG 6
couple /ˈkʌpl/ Paar p. 149
course /kɔːs/ Kurs NHG 6
(to) take a course (irr) /ˌteɪk ə ˈkɔːs/ einen Kurs machen p. 95, 7
court /kɔːt/ Platz NHG 5
cousin /ˈkʌzn/ Cousin/e NHG 5
(to) cover /ˈkʌvə/ bedecken NHG 6; abdecken; sich befassen mit p. 41, 8
cow /kaʊ/ Kuh NHG 6
coyote /kaɪˈəʊti/ Kojote p. 111, 7
crack /kræk/ Riss p. 65, 12
(to) create /kriˈeɪt/ erschaffen; erzeugen NHG 5
creative /kriˈeɪtɪv/ kreativ NHG 5
credit /ˈkredɪt/ Schein; Leistungsnachweis P&P 3
crib /krɪb/ Gitterbett p. 75, 10
crime rate /ˈkraɪm reɪt/ Kriminalitätsrate p. 24, 6
crisis (pl crises) /ˈkraɪsɪs, ˈkraɪsiːz/ Krise p. 85, 5
crisps (pl) /krɪsps/ Chips p. 48, 7
critically /ˈkrɪtɪkli/ kritisch p. 89, 9
(to) cross /krɒs/ überqueren NHG 6
crowd /kraʊd/ Menschenmenge NHG 7
crowded /ˈkraʊdɪd/ überfüllt NHG 7
crown /kraʊn/ Krone p. 20, 2
(to) crown /kraʊn/ krönen p. 34, 2
(to) cry /kraɪ/ weinen; schreien NHG 6
cue card /ˈkjuː kɑːd/ *Stichwortkarte* NHG 6
culinary art /ˌkʌlɪnri ˈɑːt/ Kochkunst p. 41, 8
cultural, culturally /ˈkʌltʃərəl, ˈkʌltʃərəli/ kulturell p. 24, 6
culture /ˈkʌltʃə/ Kultur NHG 6
cup /kʌp/ Tasse NHG 5; Pokal NHG 7
cupboard /ˈkʌbəd/ Schrank NHG 7
curious /ˈkjʊəriəs/ neugierig p. 28, 13
current /ˈkʌrənt/ gegenwärtig; aktuell p. 98, 10
currently /ˈkʌrəntli/ zurzeit, momentan NHG 7
curry /ˈkʌri/ Curry(gericht) NHG 7
customer /ˈkʌstəmə/ Kunde/Kundin NHG 6

(to) cut (irr) /kʌt/ schneiden NHG 6
(to) cut down (irr) /ˌkʌt ˈdaʊn/ abholzen, fällen p. 93, 2
cyberbullying /ˈsaɪbəˌbʊliɪŋ/ Cybermobbing p. 57
(to) cycle /ˈsaɪkl/ Rad fahren, radeln NHG 6
(to) go cycling (irr) /ˌgəʊ ˈsaɪklɪŋ/ Rad fahren gehen NHG 6

D

dad /dæd/ Papa; Vati NHG 5
daily /ˈdeɪli/ täglich NHG 5
damage /ˈdæmɪdʒ/ Schaden p. 86, 6
dance /dɑːns/ Tanz NHG 7
(to) dance /dɑːns/ tanzen NHG 5
dancer /ˈdɑːnsə/ Tänzer/in NHG 6
dancing /ˈdɑːnsɪŋ/ Tanzen NHG 5
danger /ˈdeɪndʒə/ Gefahr NHG 6
dangerous /ˈdeɪndʒərəs/ gefährlich NHG 6
dark /dɑːk/ dunkel; Dunkelheit NHG 6
darkness /ˈdɑːknəs/ Dunkelheit NHG 6
(to) dart /dɑːt/ flitzen, sausen p. 122, 7
date /deɪt/ Datum NHG 5
(to) ask on a date /ˌɑːsk ɒn ə ˈdeɪt/ um eine Verabredung bitten p. 66, 13
(to) date back /ˌdeɪt ˈbæk/ zurückgehen auf, stammen aus p. 120, 6
daughter /ˈdɔːtə/ Tochter NHG 5
day /deɪ/ Tag NHG 5
some day /ˈsʌmˌdeɪ/ eines Tages NHG 7
all day long /ˌɔːl deɪ ˈlɒŋ/ den ganzen Tag lang p. 21, 2
day out /ˌdeɪ ˈaʊt/ *Ausflugstag* NHG 6
(to) daydream /ˈdeɪdriːm/ vor sich hinträumen p. 65, 12
(to) deal with (irr) /ˈdiːl wɪð/ sich befassen mit; umgehen mit NHG 7
dear /dɪə/ liebe/r (Anrede) NHG 5
death /deθ/ Tod p. 71, 5
debate /dɪˈbeɪt/ Debatte; Diskussion p. 44, 2
(to) debate /dɪˈbeɪt/ diskutieren, debattieren p. 44, 2
debating society /dɪˈbeɪtɪŋ səˌsaɪəti/ Debattiergesellschaft p. 44, 2
decade /ˈdekeɪd/ Jahrzehnt p. 34, 2

| Skills | Wordbanks | Grammar | **Words** |

December /dɪˈsembə/ Dezember NHG 5
(to) **decide** /dɪˈsaɪd/ entscheiden; sich entscheiden NHG 5
(to) **declare** /dɪˈkleə/ verkünden; erklären p. 14, 7
(to) **decorate** /ˈdekəreɪt/ schmücken; dekorieren NHG 5
decoration /ˌdekəˈreɪʃn/ Dekoration; Schmuck NHG 6
decrease /ˈdiːkriːs/ Rückgang p. 109, 5
(to) **decrease** /diːˈkriːs/ abnehmen, zurückgehen p. 109, 5
(to) **dedicate** /ˈdedɪkeɪt/ widmen p. 25, 7
deed /diːd/ Tat p. 71, 5
deep /diːp/ tief p. 171
deer (pl deer) /dɪə, dɪə/ Hirsch; Reh p. 111, 7
(to) **define** /dɪˈfaɪn/ definieren p. 87, 6
definitely /ˈdefnətli/ eindeutig, definitiv NHG 6
(to) **delete** /dɪˈliːt/ löschen NHG 7
delicious /dɪˈlɪʃəs/ köstlich, lecker NHG 6
democracy /dɪˈmɒkrəsi/ Demokratie p. 17, 10
demonstration /ˌdemənˈstreɪʃn/ Vorführung; Demonstration p. 35, 2
Denmark /ˈdenmɑːk/ Dänemark P&P 8
dentist /ˈdentɪst/ Zahnarzt/Zahnärztin NHG 7
(to) **depend on** /dɪˈpend ɒn/ abhängen von NHG 6
depressed /dɪˈprest/ deprimiert p. 58, 2
(to) **describe** /dɪˈskraɪb/ beschreiben NHG 5
description /dɪˈskrɪpʃn/ Beschreibung NHG 6
desert /ˈdezət/ Wüste p. 8
design /dɪˈzaɪn/ Entwurf; Design NHG 6
(to) **design** /dɪˈzaɪn/ entwerfen NHG 5
desk /desk/ Schreibtisch NHG 5
desperate /ˈdesprət/ verzweifelt p. 106, 2
dessert /dɪˈzɜːt/ Nachtisch NHG 7
destination /ˌdestɪˈneɪʃn/ Ziel; Reiseziel p. 13, 6

(to) **destroy** /dɪˈstrɔɪ/ zerstören NHG 6
detail /ˈdiːteɪl/ Detail; Einzelheit NHG 5
in detail /ɪn ˈdiːteɪl/ im Einzelnen, ausführlich p. 85, 5
detailed /ˈdiːteɪld/ detailliert, genau p. 149
determined /dɪˈtɜːmɪnd/ entschlossen p. 89, 9
(to) **develop** /dɪˈveləp/ erarbeiten; (sich) entwickeln p. 10, 2
development /dɪˈveləpmənt/ Entwicklung NHG 7
device /dɪˈvaɪs/ Gerät; Apparat NHG 7
diagnostic /ˌdaɪəɡˈnɒstɪk/ diagnostisch p. 92, 2
dialogue /ˈdaɪəlɒɡ/ Gespräch; Dialog NHG 5
diary /ˈdaɪəri/ Tagebuch NHG 6
diary entry /ˈdaɪəriˌentri/ Tagebucheintrag NHG 6
dictionary /ˈdɪkʃənri/ Lexikon; Wörterbuch NHG 6
(to) **die** /daɪ/ sterben NHG 7
diet /ˈdaɪət/ Ernährung; Diät NHG 7
difference /ˈdɪfrəns/ Unterschied p. 37, 5
(to) **make a difference** (irr) /ˌmeɪk ə ˈdɪfrəns/ einen Unterschied machen; verändern p. 85, 5
different /ˈdɪfrənt/ anders; andere(r, s); verschiedene(r, s) NHG 5
difficult /ˈdɪfɪklt/ schwierig; schwer NHG 6
difficulty /ˈdɪfɪklti/ Schwierigkeit; Problem p. 83, 2
dinner /ˈdɪnə/ Abendessen NHG 5
diploma /dɪˈpləʊmə/ Diplom P&P 3
direct /daɪˈrekt/ direkt p. 85, 5
(to) **direct** /daɪˈrekt/ Regie führen p. 84, 3
direct speech /daɪˌrekt ˈspiːtʃ/ direkte / wörtliche Rede p. 66, 13
directions (pl) /daɪˈrekʃnz/ hier: Wegbeschreibungen NHG 6
(to) **give directions** (irr) /ˌɡɪv daɪˈrekʃnz/ den Weg beschreiben NHG 6
directly /dəˈrektli, daɪˈrektli/ direkt P&P 7

director /dəˈrektə/ Regisseur/in p. 11, 2
dirty /ˈdɜːti/ dreckig; schmutzig NHG 5
disability /ˌdɪsəˈbɪləti/ Behinderung; Einschränkung p. 83, 2
disadvantage /ˌdɪsədˈvɑːntɪdʒ/ Nachteil p. 72, 6
(to) **disagree** /ˌdɪsəˈɡriː/ nicht zustimmen p. 17, 10
(to) **disappear** /ˌdɪsəˈpɪə/ verschwinden NHG 6
disappointed /ˌdɪsəˈpɔɪntɪd/ enttäuscht NHG 6
disappointing /ˌdɪsəˈpɔɪntɪŋ/ enttäuschend NHG 7
discipline /ˈdɪsəplɪn/ Disziplin NHG 7
discomfort /dɪsˈkʌmfət/ Unbehagen p. 65, 12
(to) **discover** /dɪˈskʌvə/ entdecken NHG 6
discovery /dɪˈskʌvri/ Entdeckung NHG 7
(to) **discuss** /dɪˈskʌs/ besprechen; diskutieren NHG 6
discussion /dɪˈskʌʃn/ Diskussion NHG 6
disease /dɪˈziːz/ Krankheit p. 14, 7
disgusting /dɪsˈɡʌstɪŋ/ widerlich NHG 7
dish (pl **dishes**) /dɪʃ, ˈdɪʃɪz/ Gericht; Speise NHG 7
dishwasher /ˈdɪʃˌwɒʃə/ Spülmaschine NHG 5
(to) **dislike** /dɪsˈlaɪk/ nicht mögen NHG 7
display /dɪˈspleɪ/ Auslage; Ausstellung NHG 7
(to) **display** /dɪˈspleɪ/ aushängen; zeigen NHG 5
(to) **be on display** (irr) /ˌbi ɒn dɪˈspleɪ/ ausgestellt sein P&P 2
(to) **put on display** (irr) /ˌpʊt ɒn dɪˈspleɪ/ ausstellen NHG 6
(to) **dispose of** /dɪˈspəʊz əv/ entsorgen p. 86, 6
distance /ˈdɪstəns/ Distanz; Entfernung p. 66, 14
(to) **dive** /daɪv/ tauchen NHG 7
diverse /daɪˈvɜːs/ vielfältig, unterschiedlich p. 11, 2
diversity /daɪˈvɜːsəti/ Vielfalt p. 25, 7

Dictionary

(to) **divide** /dɪˈvaɪd/ teilen, aufteilen P&P 8
diving /ˈdaɪvɪŋ/ Tauchen NHG 7
division /dɪˈvɪʒn/ Teilung; Meinungsverschiedenheit p. 89, 9
(to) **do** *(irr)* /duː/ tun; machen NHG 5
do /duː/ *hier als Verstärkung benutzt* p. 40, 7
(to) **do athletics** *(irr)* /ˌduː_æθˈletɪks/ Leichtathletik machen NHG 5
(to) **do for a living** *(irr)* /ˌduː fər ə ˈlɪvɪŋ/ seinen Lebensunterhalt verdienen p. 92, 2
(to) **do gymnastics** *(irr)* /ˌduː dʒɪmˈnæstɪks/ turnen NHG 5
(to) **do one's best** *(irr)* /ˌduː wʌnz ˈbest/ sein Bestes geben p. 48, 7
(to) **do research** *(irr)* /ˌduː rɪˈsɜːtʃ/ recherchieren NHG 5
(to) **do sports** *(irr)* /ˌduː ˈspɔːts/ Sport treiben NHG 6
(to) **do the cooking** *(irr)* /ˌduː ðə ˈkʊkɪŋ/ kochen NHG 5
(to) **do the shopping** *(irr)* /ˌduː ðə ˈʃɒpɪŋ/ einkaufen NHG 5
(to) **do well** *(irr)* /ˌduː ˈwel/ erfolgreich sein p. 25, 7
the docklands *(pl)* /ðə ˈdɒkləndz/ Hafenviertel p. 116, 1
doctor /ˈdɒktə/ Arzt/Ärztin NHG 7
at the doctor's /ˌæt ðə ˈdɒktəz/ beim Arzt/bei der Ärztin NHG 7
(to) **see a doctor** *(irr)* /ˌsiː ə ˈdɒktə/ einen Arzt/eine Ärztin aufsuchen NHG 7
document /ˈdɒkjəmənt/ Dokument NHG 7
dog /dɒɡ/ Hund NHG 5
(to) **take a dog for a walk** *(irr)* /ˌteɪk ə ˌdɒɡ fər ə ˈwɔːk/ mit einem Hund Gassi gehen p. 141
dog sled /ˈdɒɡ sled/ Hundeschlitten p. 8
dog walking /ˈdɒɡ ˌwɔːkɪŋ/ Ausführen von Hunden p. 97, 9
dogsitter /ˈdɒɡsɪtə/ Hundesitter/in p. 135
dolphin /ˈdɒlfɪn/ Delfin p. 119, 5
door /dɔː/ Tür NHG 5
dos and don'ts /ˌduːz ən ˈdəʊnts/ was man tun und was man nicht tun sollte NHG 7

double /ˈdʌbl/ doppelt, Doppel- NHG 5
doubt /daʊt/ Zweifel p. 89, 9
dove /dʌv/ Taube p. 82, 2
down /daʊn/ hinunter; (nach) unten NHG 6
(to) **download** /ˌdaʊnˈləʊd/ herunterladen NHG 7
downtown *(AE)* /ˌdaʊnˈtaʊn/ in der Innenstadt; im Zentrum p. 24, 6
Dr (= Doctor) /ˈdɒktə/ Dr. (= Doktor) NHG 6
draft /drɑːft/ Entwurf NHG 6
(to) **drag** /dræɡ/ ziehen, schleifen p. 93, 2
dragon /ˈdræɡən/ Drache NHG 6
drama /ˈdrɑːmə/ Theater-; Schauspiel- NHG 6
dramatic /drəˈmætɪk/ dramatisch NHG 7
(to) **draw** *(irr)* /drɔː/ zeichnen NHG 5
(to) **draw attention to** *(irr)* /ˌdrɔː əˈtenʃn tə/ Aufmerksamkeit lenken auf NHG 7
drawing /ˈdrɔːɪŋ/ Zeichnung NHG 6
dreadful /ˈdredfl/ schrecklich; furchtbar p. 121, 6
dream /driːm/ Traum NHG 5
(to) **dream** *(irr)* /driːm/ träumen p. 36, 4
(to) **make one's dream come true** *(irr)* /ˌmeɪk wʌnz ˈdriːm kʌm ˌtruː/ seinen Traum wahr werden lassen p. 149
dress /dres/ Kleid; Kleidung NHG 7
(to) **dress** /dres/ sich anziehen; sich kleiden NHG 7
dress code /ˈdres kəʊd/ Bekleidungsvorschriften p. 37, 5
drink /drɪŋk/ Trinken; Getränk NHG 5
(to) **drink** /drɪŋk/ trinken NHG 5
(to) **drive** *(irr)* /draɪv/ fahren NHG 6
(to) **drive away** *(irr)* /ˌdraɪv əˈweɪ/ vertreiben P&P 1
(to) **drop out** /ˌdrɒp ˈaʊt/ abbrechen p. 45, 2
drove /drəʊv/ Herde p. 25, 7
dry /draɪ/ trocken NHG 6
dual /ˈdjuːəl/ doppelte(r, s) P&P 6
due /djuː/ fällig p. 96, 8
due to /ˈdjuː tə/ wegen p. 26, 8
during /ˈdjʊərɪŋ/ während NHG 6
duty /ˈdjuːti/ Pflicht; Aufgabe p. 93, 2

E

each /iːtʃ/ jede(r, s) NHG 5; je(weils) p. 94, 6
each other /ˌiːtʃ ˈʌðə/ einander NHG 5
ear /ɪə/ Ohr NHG 5
earlier /ˈɜːliə/ vorhin, früher NHG 6
early /ˈɜːli/ früh NHG 6
(to) **earn** /ɜːn/ verdienen NHG 6
earth /ɜːθ/ Erde NHG 6
easily /ˈiːzɪli/ leicht; mühelos p. 68, 2
East /iːst/ östlich, Ost- NHG 7
east /iːst/ Osten p. 10, 2; nach Osten p. 111, 7
Easter /ˈiːstə/ Ostern NHG 6
eastern /ˈiːstən/ östlich, Ost- p. 109, 5
easy /ˈiːzi/ leicht; einfach NHG 5
(to) **eat** *(irr)* /iːt/ essen NHG 5
(to) **eat out** *(irr)* /ˌiːt ˈaʊt/ auswärts essen; im Restaurant essen NHG 7
eating /ˈiːtɪŋ/ Essen p. 11, 2
eating habit /ˈiːtɪŋ ˌhæbɪt/ Essgewohnheit p. 11, 2
ecological /ˌiːkəˈlɒdʒɪkl/ ökologisch p. 93, 2
ecological footprint /ˌiːkəˌlɒdʒɪkl ˈfʊtprɪnt/ ökologischer Fußabdruck p. 85, 5
economic /ˌiːkəˈnɒmɪk/ wirtschaftlich p. 14, 7
economy /ɪˈkɒnəmi/ Wirtschaft p. 19, 13
ecosystem /ˈiːkəʊˌsɪstəm/ Ökosystem p. 11, 2
edge /edʒ/ Rand p. 13, 6
edible /ˈedɪbəl/ essbar; genießbar p. 151
(to) **edit** /ˈedɪt/ bearbeiten NHG 5
(to) **educate** /ˈedjʊkeɪt/ unterrichten; aufklären p. 87, 6
education /ˌedjʊˈkeɪʃn/ Bildung; Ausbildung; Erziehung NHG 7
educational /ˌedjʊˈkeɪʃnəl/ Bildungs-; pädagogisch p. 44, 2
egg /eɡ/ Ei NHG 5
either ... or ... /ˌaɪðə ˈɔː/ entweder ... oder ... NHG 6
not ... either /ˌnɒt ˈaɪðə/ auch nicht NHG 7
(to) **elect** /ɪˈlekt/ wählen P&P 3
election /ɪˈlekʃn/ Wahl p. 34, 2
elective /ɪˈlektɪv/ Wahlpflichtfach p. 39, 6

electric /ɪˈlektrɪk/ elektrisch; Elektro- NHG 7; elektrisierend, spannungsgeladen p. 25, 7
electrician /ɪˌlekˈtrɪʃn/ Elektriker/in p. 92, 1
electricity /ɪˌlekˈtrɪsəti/ Elektrizität; Strom NHG 7
electronic /ˌelekˈtrɒnɪk/ elektronisch p. 26, 8
elementary school *(AE)* /elɪˈmentri skuːl/ Grundschule p. 45, 2
elephant /ˈelɪfənt/ Elefant p. 65, 12
else /els/ anders; sonst NHG 5
(to) **email** /ˈiːmeɪl/ mailen p. 167
emergency /ɪˈmɜːdʒnsi/ Notfall NHG 7
emigrant /ˈemɪgrənt/ Auswanderer/Auswanderin p. 106, 2
(to) **emigrate** /ˈemɪgreɪt/ auswandern NHG 7
emigration /ˌemɪˈgreɪʃn/ Auswanderung; Emigration p. 108, 4
emotion /ɪˈməʊʃn/ Gefühl; Emotion p. 71, 5
(to) **put emphasis on** *(irr)* /ˌpʊt_ˈemfəsɪs_ɒn/ Wert legen auf p. 11, 2
employer /ɪmˈplɔɪə/ Arbeitgeber/in p. 95, 7
employment /ɪmˈplɔɪmənt/ Beschäftigung; Anstellung P&P 6
(to) **empower** /ɪmˈpaʊə/ (mental) stärken; aufbauen p. 89, 9
empowered /ɪmˈpaʊəd/ (mental) gestärkt p. 89, 9
empty /ˈempti/ leer p. 65, 12
(to) **empty** /ˈempti/ ausleeren; ausräumen NHG 5
(to) **enable** /ɪnˈeɪbl/ ermöglichen P&P 5
(to) **encounter** /ɪnˈkaʊntə/ treffen; begegnen p. 89, 9
(to) **encourage** /ɪnˈkʌrɪdʒ/ ermutigen p. 87, 6
end /end/ Ende; Schluss NHG 5
(to) **end** /end/ enden; beenden NHG 6
in the end /ˌɪn ðɪ_ˈend/ am Ende, schließlich NHG 5
(to) **end up** /ˌend_ˈʌp/ schließlich landen p. 86, 6
ending /ˈendɪŋ/ Ende; Schluss NHG 5
endless /ˈendləs/ endlos p. 13, 6
energy /ˈenədʒi/ Energie; Kraft p. 35, 2

engaged /ɪnˈgeɪdʒd/ beschäftigt; *hier:* engagiert p. 89, 9
engine /ˈendʒɪn/ Maschine; Motor NHG 7
engineer /ˌendʒɪˈnɪə/ Ingenieur/in NHG 6
English /ˈɪŋglɪʃ/ Englisch; englisch NHG 5
English-speaking /ˈɪŋglɪʃ_ˌspiːkɪŋ/ englischsprachig NHG 7
(to) **enhance** /ɪnˈhɑːns/ verbessern p. 73, 6
(to) **enjoy** /ɪnˈdʒɔɪ/ genießen NHG 5
(to) **enjoy oneself** /ɪnˈdʒɔɪ wʌnˌself/ sich amüsieren p. 48, 7
enough /ɪˈnʌf/ genug NHG 5
(to) **enter** /ˈentə/ eingeben; betreten NHG 6; eintreten in p. 15, 7
entertainment /ˌentəˈteɪnmənt/ Unterhaltung NHG 6
enthusiasm /ɪnˈθjuːziˌæzəm/ Enthusiasmus p. 50, 9
entrance /ˈentrəns/ Eingang; Eintritt NHG 6
entry /ˈentri/ Eintritt NHG 6; Eintrag NHG 7
diary entry /ˈdaɪəriˌentri/ Tagebucheintrag NHG 6
environment /ɪnˈvaɪrənmənt/ Umwelt; Umgebung NHG 6
environmentally friendly /ɪnˌvaɪrənmentli ˈfrendli/ umweltfreundlich p. 88, 7
epic *(informal)* /ˈepɪk/ super, klasse p. 123, 8
equal /ˈiːkwəl/ gleich p. 6
equality /iˈkwɒləti/ Gleichberechtigung; Gleichheit p. 17, 10
equipment /ɪˈkwɪpmənt/ Ausrüstung; Ausstattung NHG 5
era /ˈɪərə/ Epoche; Zeitalter p. 13, 6
eraser /ɪˈreɪzə/ Radiergummi NHG 5
(to) **escape** /ɪˈskeɪp/ fliehen; entkommen NHG 5
especially /ɪˈspeʃli/ besonders; vor allem NHG 6
essential /ɪˈsenʃl/ unbedingt erforderlich; unverzichtbar p. 27, 10
(to) **establish** /ɪˈstæblɪʃ/ gründen; einführen p. 11, 2
estimated /ˈestɪmeɪtəd/ geschätzt P&P 1

(to) **be estimated** *(irr)* /ˌbi_ˈestɪmeɪtəd/ geschätzt werden P&P 7
ethics *(pl)* /ˈeθɪks/ Ethik p. 41, 8
Europe /ˈjʊərəp/ Europa NHG 6
European /ˌjʊərəˈpiːən/ Europäer/in; europäisch p. 7
European Union /ˌjʊərəˌpiːən ˈjuːnjən/ Europäische Union P&P 8
even /ˈiːvn/ selbst; sogar NHG 5
evening /ˈiːvnɪŋ/ Abend NHG 5
evening dress /ˈiːvnɪŋ dres/ Abendgarderobe p. 41, 10
event /ɪˈvent/ Ereignis; Veranstaltung NHG 5
eventually /ɪˈventʃuəli/ schließlich; irgendwann p. 86, 6
ever /ˈevə/ jemals NHG 6
every /ˈevri/ jede(r, s) NHG 5
everybody /ˈevriˌbɒdi/ alle; jeder NHG 5
everyday /ˈevriˌdeɪ/ alltäglich, Alltags- NHG 6
everyone /ˈevriwʌn/ alle; jeder NHG 5
everything /ˈevriθɪŋ/ alles NHG 5
everywhere /ˈevriweə/ überall NHG 5
(to) **evoke** /ɪˈvəʊk/ hervorrufen p. 122, 7
(to) **evolve** /ɪˈvɒlv/ sich entwickeln p. 11, 2
exactly /ɪgˈzæklɪ/ genau NHG 6
examination /ɪgˌzæmɪˈneɪʃn/ Untersuchung P&P 7
(to) **examine** /ɪgˈzæmɪn/ untersuchen NHG 7
example /ɪgˈzɑːmpl/ Beispiel NHG 5
for example /fərˌɪgˈzɑːmpl/ zum Beispiel NHG 5
(to) **lead by example** *(irr)* /ˌliːd baɪ_ɪgˈzɑːmpl/ mit gutem Beispiel vorangehen p. 89, 9
excellent /ˈeksələnt/ ausgezeichnet NHG 5
except /ɪkˈsept/ außer NHG 6
excerpt /ˈeksɜːpt/ Auszug; Exzerpt p. 89, 9
exchange /ɪksˈtʃeɪndʒ/ Austausch; Austausch- p. 34, 2
exchange student /ɪksˈtʃeɪndʒ ˌstjuːdnt/ Austauschschüler/in NHG 7

Dictionary

excited /ɪkˈsaɪtɪd/ aufgeregt NHG 6
exciting /ɪkˈsaɪtɪŋ/ aufregend NHG 5
exclamation point *(AE)* /ˌekskləˈmeɪʃn pɔɪnt/ Ausrufezeichen p. 73, 6
Excuse me! /ɪkˈskjuːz ˌmi/ Entschuldigung! NHG 5
exercise /ˈeksəsaɪz/ Übung NHG 6
exercise book /ˈeksəsaɪz ˌbʊk/ Heft NHG 5
exhausting /ɪgˈzɔːstɪŋ/ anstrengend NHG 7
exhibit /ɪgˈzɪbɪt/ Ausstellungsstück p. 138
exhibition /ˌeksɪˈbɪʃn/ Ausstellung NHG 6
(to) **exist** /ɪgˈzɪst/ existieren NHG 6
(to) **expect** /ɪkˈspekt/ erwarten NHG 6
expectation /ˌekspekˈteɪʃn/ Erwartung p. 72, 6
(to) **expel** /ɪkˈspel/ von der Schule verweisen p. 69, 2
expensive /ɪkˈspensɪv/ teuer NHG 6
experience /ɪkˈspɪəriəns/ Erfahrung NHG 5
(to) **experience** /ɪkˈspɪəriəns/ erleben, kennenlernen p. 13, 6
experiment /ɪkˈsperɪmənt/ Experiment; Versuch NHG 5
expert /ˈekspɜːt/ Experte/Expertin NHG 6
(to) **explain** /ɪkˈspleɪn/ erklären NHG 5
(to) **explore** /ɪkˈsplɔː/ erforschen; untersuchen NHG 6
(to) **express** /ɪkˈspres/ ausdrücken NHG 6
expression /ɪkˈspreʃn/ Ausdruck NHG 7
facial expression /ˌfeɪʃl ɪkˈspreʃn/ Gesichtsausdruck p. 71, 5
(to) **extend** /ɪkˈstend/ sich erstrecken p. 10, 2
extinct /ɪkˈstɪŋkt/ ausgestorben p. 138
extra /ˈekstrə/ zusätzlich NHG 5
extract /ˈekstrækt/ Auszug; Exzerpt p. 25, 7
extremely /ɪkˈstriːmli/ äußerst, höchst; außerordentlich NHG 7
eye /aɪ/ Auge NHG 5

F

fabulous /ˈfæbjələs/ fabelhaft; toll p. 20, 1
face /feɪs/ Gesicht NHG 5
(to) **face** /feɪs/ gegenüberstehen p. 89, 9
(to) **face** /feɪs/ blicken nach P&P 7
face-to-face /ˌfeɪs tə ˈfeɪs/ persönlich p. 69, 2
facial expression /ˌfeɪʃl ɪkˈspreʃn/ Gesichtsausdruck p. 71, 5
fact /fækt/ Tatsache; Fakt NHG 5
in fact /ɪn ˈfækt/ tatsächlich; in Wirklichkeit p. 68, 2
fact file /ˈfækt faɪl/ Steckbrief NHG 5
factory /ˈfæktri/ Fabrik p. 10, 2
(to) **fail** /feɪl/ durchfallen P&P 7
science fair /ˈsaɪəns feə/ Naturwissenschaftsmesse p. 40, 7
falcon /ˈfɔːlkən/ Falke p. 122, 7
(to) **fall** *(irr)* /fɔːl/ fallen NHG 7
fall *(AE)* /fɔːl/ Herbst p. 34, 2
(to) **fall asleep** *(irr)* /ˌfɔːl əˈsliːp/ einschlafen p. 36, 4
(to) **fall in love** *(irr)* /ˌfɔːl ɪn ˈlʌv/ sich verlieben p. 65, 12
(to) **fall off** *(irr)* /ˌfɔːl ˈɒf/ (herunter)fallen NHG 7
false /fɔːls/ falsch NHG 5
familiar /fəˈmɪliə/ vertraut, bekannt p. 14, 7
family /ˈfæmli/ Familie NHG 5
famine /ˈfæmɪn/ Hungersnot p. 121, 6
famous /ˈfeɪməs/ berühmt NHG 5
fan /fæn/ Ventilator p. 65, 12
fantastic /fænˈtæstɪk/ fantastisch; super NHG 5
far /fɑː/ weit NHG 5
far away /ˌfɑːr əˈweɪ/ weit weg P&P 1
(to) **be far from reach** *(irr)* /ˌbiː ˌfɑː frəm ˈriːtʃ/ außer Reichweite sein p. 68, 2
farm /fɑːm/ Bauernhof NHG 6
farmer /ˈfɑːmə/ Bauer/Bäuerin p. 106, 2
farming /ˈfɑːmɪŋ/ Ackerbau; Viehzucht p. 111, 7
farmland /ˈfɑːmlænd/ Ackerland p. 8
fascinating /ˈfæsɪneɪtɪŋ/ faszinierend p. 20, 1
fashion /ˈfæʃn/ Mode NHG 6
fast /fɑːst/ schnell NHG 5
fat /fæt/ dick p. 65, 12

father /ˈfɑːðə/ Vater NHG 5
fault /fɔːlt/ Schuld; Fehler NHG 7
favorite *(AE)* /ˈfeɪvrət/ Liebling; Lieblings- p. 28, 14
in favour of /ɪn ˈfeɪvər əv/ für p. 15, 7
favourite /ˈfeɪvrət/ Liebling; Lieblings- NHG 5
fear /fɪə/ Angst p. 89, 9
February /ˈfebruəri/ Februar NHG 5
fee /fiː/ Gebühr; Geld NHG 7
(to) **feed** *(irr)* /fiːd/ füttern NHG 6
feedback /ˈfiːdbæk/ Feedback; Rückmeldung NHG 5
(to) **feel** *(irr)* /fiːl/ fühlen, sich fühlen NHG 6
(to) **feel comfortable** *(irr)* /ˌfiːl ˈkʌmftəbl/ sich wohl fühlen p. 72, 6
(to) **feel uncomfortable** *(irr)* /ˌfiːl ʌnˈkʌmftəbl/ sich unwohl fühlen p. 38, 6
feeling /ˈfiːlɪŋ/ Gefühl NHG 6
felt-tip /ˈfelt tɪp/ Filzstift NHG 5
ferry /ˈferi/ Fähre p. 20, 2
festival /ˈfestɪvl/ Fest; Festival NHG 6
fever /ˈfiːvə/ Fieber NHG 7
a few /ə ˈfjuː/ einige; wenige NHG 6
fewer /ˈfjuːə/ weniger *(bei zählbaren Nomen)* p. 45, 2
fiddle /ˈfɪdl/ Geige p. 117, 2
field /fiːld/ Feld NHG 5
field of work /ˌfiːld əv ˈwɜːk/ Arbeitsbereich p. 15, 7
fight /faɪt/ Kampf; Streit NHG 7
(to) **fight** *(irr)* /faɪt/ bekämpfen; ankämpfen gegen NHG 6; kämpfen p. 6
fighting /ˈfaɪtɪŋ/ Kämpfe; Gefechte p. 15, 7
(to) **fill** /fɪl/ füllen NHG 6
(to) **fill in** /ˌfɪl ˈɪn/ eintragen, ausfüllen NHG 5
(to) **film** /fɪlm/ drehen, filmen NHG 6
final /ˈfaɪnl/ letzte(r, s); endgültig NHG 5
final /ˈfaɪnl/ Endspiel; Finale p. 35, 2
finally /ˈfaɪnli/ schließlich; endlich NHG 7
finance /ˈfaɪnæns/ Finanzwirtschaft; Geldwesen p. 41, 8
finances *(pl)* /ˈfaɪnænsɪz/ Finanzen p. 41, 8

two hundred and forty-three 243

financial /faɪˈnænʃl/ finanziell p. 107, 2
(to) find *(irr)* /faɪnd/ finden NHG 5
(to) find out *(irr)* /ˌfaɪnd ˈaʊt/ herausfinden NHG 5
finding /ˈfaɪndɪŋ/ Entdeckung; Ergebnis NHG 7
fine /faɪn/ in Ordnung, gut NHG 5
I'm fine. /aɪm ˈfaɪn/ Es geht mir gut. p. 40, 7
(to) finish /ˈfɪnɪʃ/ beenden; enden; fertigstellen NHG 6; aufessen NHG 7
fire /ˈfaɪə/ Feuer NHG 6
(to) start a fire /ˌstɑːt ə ˈfaɪə/ Feuer machen p. 108, 3
firebreak /ˈfaɪəbreɪk/ Brandschneise p. 93, 2
firefighter /ˈfaɪəˌfaɪtə/ Feuerwehrmann/-frau NHG 6
fireworks *(pl)* /ˈfaɪəˌwɜːks/ Feuerwerk NHG 6
first /fɜːst/ erste(r, s); zuerst NHG 5
at first /ˌæt ˈfɜːst/ zuerst NHG 6
first of all /ˌfɜːst əv ˈɔːl/ zuallererst p. 72, 6
first thing *(informal)* /ˌfɜːst ˈθɪŋ/ als Erstes p. 38, 6
the very first /ðə ˌveri ˈfɜːst/ der/die/das allererste p. 6
fish *(pl fish or fishes)* /fɪʃ, fɪʃ, ˈfɪʃɪz/ Fisch NHG 5
fisherman *(pl fishermen)* /ˈfɪʃəmən/ Fischer; Angler p. 116, 1
(to) fit /fɪt/ passen NHG 5
(to) keep fit *(irr)* /ˌkiːp ˈfɪt/ fit bleiben, (sich) fit halten NHG 7
(to) fix /fɪks/ reparieren p. 111, 7
fixed /fɪkst/ festgelegt P&P 6
flag /flæg/ Fahne; Flagge p. 16, 9
(to) wave a flag /ˌweɪv ə ˈflæg/ eine Fahne schwenken p. 40, 7
flat /flæt/ Wohnung NHG 6
flea market /ˈfliː ˌmɑːkɪt/ Flohmarkt NHG 7
(to) flee *(irr)* /fliː/ fliehen p. 106, 1
flexible /ˈfleksəbl/ biegsam, gelenkig NHG 7
short-distance flight /ˌʃɔːt ˌdɪstəns ˈflaɪt/ Kurzstreckenflug p. 85, 5
flip /flɪp/ Salto p. 48, 7
floor /flɔː/ Fußboden NHG 5; Stockwerk p. 23, 5

(to) flow /fləʊ/ fließen, strömen p. 141
flower /ˈflaʊə/ Blume NHG 6
(to) fly *(irr)* /flaɪ/ fliegen NHG 6
(to) focus on /ˈfəʊkəs ɒn/ sich konzentrieren auf NHG 5
focused /ˈfəʊkəst/ fokussiert p. 89, 9
folded hands /ˌfəʊldɪd ˈhændz/ betende Hände p. 71, 5
folder /ˈfəʊldə/ Mappe; Ordner NHG 5
folks *(informal)* /fəʊks/ Leute p. 89, 9
(to) follow /ˈfɒləʊ/ folgen; verfolgen NHG 6; befolgen p. 98, 11
(to) follow in somebody's footsteps /ˌfɒləʊ ɪn ˌsʌmbədiz ˈfʊtsteps/ in jemandes Fußstapfen treten p. 121, 6
follow-up question /ˈfɒləʊ ʌp ˌkwestʃn/ Folgefrage p. 22, 4
following /ˈfɒləʊɪŋ/ folgende(r,s) NHG 6
food /fuːd/ Essen NHG 5
food drive /ˈfuːd draɪv/ Sammeln von Lebensmitteln, um sie an bedürftige Menschen abzugeben P&P 5
foot *(pl feet)* /fʊt, fiːt/ Fuß NHG 5; Fuß (Maßeinheit, 1 Fuß = 0,3048 Meter) p. 13, 6
(to) set foot on *(irr)* /ˌset ˈfʊt ɒn/ betreten p. 10, 2
football /ˈfʊtbɔːl/ Fußball NHG 5
football *(AE)* /ˈfʊtbɔːl/ American Football p. 34, 2
footprint /ˈfʊtprɪnt/ Fußabdruck; Standfläche p. 21, 2
ecological footprint /ˌiːkəˌlɒdʒɪkl ˈfʊtprɪnt/ ökologischer Fußabdruck p. 85, 5
(to) follow in somebody's footsteps /ˌfɒləʊ ɪn ˌsʌmbədiz ˈfʊtsteps/ in jemandes Fußstapfen treten p. 121, 6
for /fɔː/ für NHG 5
for *(+ Zeitraum)* /fɔː/ ... lang NHG 6
for a long time /fər ə ˈlɒŋ taɪm/ lange p. 62, 8
for a while /fər ə ˈwaɪl/ eine Weile NHG 7
for example /fər ɪgˈzɑːmpl/ zum Beispiel NHG 5
for free /fə ˈfriː/ gratis NHG 6
for the first time /fə ðə ˈfɜːst taɪm/ zum ersten Mal NHG 6

for the time being /fə ðə ˌtaɪm ˈbiːɪŋ/ vorerst p. 59, 3
force /fɔːs/ Kraft p. 89, 9
(to) force /fɔːs/ (er)zwingen p. 15, 7
foreign /ˈfɒrɪn/ ausländisch; fremd NHG 7
foreign language /ˌfɒrɪn ˈlæŋgwɪdʒ/ Fremdsprache P&P 3
forest /ˈfɒrɪst/ Wald NHG 6
forever /fərˈevə/ ewig, für immer p. 67, 15
(to) forget *(irr)* /fəˈget/ vergessen NHG 5
(to) forgive *(irr)* /fəˈgɪv/ vergeben; verzeihen p. 63, 8
fork /fɔːk/ Gabel NHG 5
form /fɔːm/ Klasse NHG 5; Formular p. 98, 10
(to) form /fɔːm/ formen, bilden, gründen p. 149
formal /ˈfɔːml/ formell; offiziell p. 35, 2
former /ˈfɔːmə/ ehemalige(r, s); frühere(r, s) NHG 7
Founding Fathers *(pl)* /ˌfaʊndɪŋ ˈfɑːðəz/ Gründerväter p. 14, 7
France /frɑːns/ Frankreich NHG 5
free /friː/ frei; kostenlos NHG 6
for free /fə ˈfriː/ gratis NHG 6
free time /ˌfriː ˈtaɪm/ Freizeit NHG 5
freedom /ˈfriːdəm/ Freiheit p. 15, 7
call of freedom /ˌkɔːl əv ˈfriːdəm/ Ruf der Freiheit p. 122, 7
French /frentʃ/ Französisch NHG 5
French /frentʃ/ Franzose/Französin; französisch p. 162
French fries *(AE, pl)* /ˌfrentʃ ˈfraɪz/ Pommes frites p. 37, 5
frequently /ˈfriːkwəntli/ häufig p. 71, 5
fresh /freʃ/ frisch; neu NHG 6
freshman *(pl freshmen)* *(AE)* /ˈfreʃmən, ˈfreʃmən/ Schüler/in einer Highschool im ersten Jahr p. 35, 2
Friday /ˈfraɪdeɪ/ Freitag NHG 5
(on) Fridays /ˈfraɪdeɪz/ freitags NHG 5
fridge /frɪdʒ/ Kühlschrank NHG 7
friend /frend/ Freund/in NHG 5
friendly /ˈfrendli/ freundlich NHG 6
(to) make friends (with) *(irr)* /ˌmeɪk ˈfrendz/ sich anfreunden (mit) NHG 6

Dictionary

friendship /ˈfrenʃɪp/ Freundschaft NHG 6
from /frɒm/ von; aus NHG 5
from abroad /frəm_əˈbrɔːd/ aus dem Ausland p. 135
from (all) around the world /frəm_ˌɔːl_əˌraʊnd ðə ˈwɜːld/ aus der (ganzen) Welt NHG 7
from all over the world /frəm_ˌɔːl_ˌəʊvə ðə ˈwɜːld/ aus der ganzen Welt NHG 5
from ... onwards /frəm ...ˈɒnwədz/ von ... an P&P 7
at the front /ˌæt ðə ˈfrʌnt/ vorne NHG 5
in front of /ˌɪn ˈfrʌnt_əv/ vor NHG 5
in the front /ˌɪn ðə ˈfrʌnt/ vorne NHG 5
fruit /fruːt/ Frucht; Obst NHG 5
frustrated /frʌˈstreɪtɪd/ frustriert NHG 6
full /fʊl/ voll, vollständig NHG 6; satt NHG 7
(to) **be in full swing** *(irr)* /ˌbiː_ɪn ˌfʊl ˈswɪŋ/ in vollem Gang sein p. 34, 2
full-contact sport /ˌfʊl ˈkɒntækt spɔːt/ Vollkontakt-Sportart p. 50, 8
full-time /ˌfʊl ˈtaɪm/ Vollzeit- p. 26, 8
fun /fʌn/ Spaß NHG 5; lustig; witzig NHG 6
(to) **be (good/great) fun** *(irr)* /ˌbiː_ˌgʊd/ˌgreɪt ˈfʌn/ (viel/großen) Spaß machen NHG 5
(to) **have (a lot of) fun** *(irr)* /ˌhæv_ə ˌlɒt_əv_ˈfʌn/ (viel) Spaß haben NHG 6
function /ˈfʌŋkʃn/ Aufgabe; Funktion NHG 7
fundamental /ˌfʌndəˈmentl/ grundlegend p. 89, 9
fundraiser /ˈfʌndˌreɪzə/ Spendensammler/in p. 35, 2; Spendensammelaktion P&P 5
fundraising /ˈfʌndreɪzɪŋ/ Spendensammeln p. 35, 2
(to) **raise funds** /ˌreɪz ˈfʌndz/ Geld sammeln P&P 5
funny /ˈfʌni/ lustig; komisch NHG 5
furniture /ˈfɜːnɪtʃə/ Möbel(stück) NHG 5
further /ˈfɜːðə/ weiter p. 68, 2
future /ˈfjuːtʃə/ Zukunft NHG 6; zukünftig p. 44, 2

G

Gaelic football /ˌgeɪlɪk ˈfʊtbɔːl/ Ballsportart mit zwei Teams zu je 15 Spielern/Spielerinnen p. 116, 1
(to) **gain momentum** /ˌgeɪn məʊˈmentəm/ in Schwung kommen p. 15, 7
gallery walk /ˈgæləri wɔːk/ Gruppendiskussion in Stationsarbeit p. 43, 14
game /geɪm/ Spiel NHG 5
board game /ˈbɔːd geɪm/ Brettspiel NHG 6
gap /gæp/ Lücke NHG 5
garbage *(AE)* /ˈgɑːbɪdʒ/ Abfall; Müll p. 86, 6
garden /ˈgɑːdn/ Garten NHG 5
gardener /ˈgɑːdnə/ Gärtner/in p. 92, 1
gardening /ˈgɑːdnɪŋ/ Gärtnern p. 150
gate /geɪt/ Tor NHG 6
general /ˈdʒenrəl/ allgemein NHG 7
in general /ˌɪn ˈdʒenrəl/ im Allgemeinen NHG 7
genre /ˈʒɒnrə/ Genre; Gattung p. 11, 2
geography /dʒiːˈɒgrəfi/ Erdkunde NHG 5
geological /ˌdʒiːəˈlɒdʒɪkl/ geologisch p. 11, 2
German /ˈdʒɜːmən/ Deutsch; deutsch NHG 5
Germany /ˈdʒɜːməni/ Deutschland NHG 5
(to) **get** *(irr)* /get/ bekommen; holen; kaufen NHG 5; kommen; gelangen; werden NHG 6; bringen NHG 7
(to) **get along** *(irr)* /ˌget_əˈlɒŋ/ sich verstehen NHG 6
(to) **get better** *(irr)* /ˌget ˈbetə/ besser werden; gesund werden NHG 7
(to) **get connected** *(irr)* /ˌget kəˈnektɪd/ sich verbinden, in Kontakt treten p. 72, 6
(to) **get to do something** *(irr)* /ˌget_tə ˈduː_ˌsʌmθɪŋ/ die Möglichkeit haben, etwas zu tun p. 40, 7
(to) **get going** *(irr)* /ˌget ˈgəʊɪŋ/ in Gang bringen p. 85, 5
(to) **get involved** *(irr)* /ˌget_ɪnˈvɒlvd/ sich engagieren p. 85, 5
(to) **get to know** *(irr)* /ˌget tə_ˈnəʊ/ kennenlernen p. 41, 8
(to) **get married** *(irr)* /ˌget ˈmærɪd/ heiraten NHG 7
(to) get out *(irr)* /ˌget_ˈaʊt/ hinausgehen p. 89, 9
(to) **get rid of** *(irr)* /ˌget ˈrɪd_əv/ loswerden NHG 7
(to) **get together** *(irr)* /ˌget_təˈgeðə/ zusammenkommen NHG 5
(to) **get up** *(irr)* /ˌget_ˈʌp/ aufstehen NHG 6
(to) **get well** *(irr)* /ˌget ˈwel/ gesund werden NHG 7
Get well soon! /ˌget ˌwel ˈsuːn/ Gute Besserung! NHG 7
ghost /gəʊst/ Geist; Gespenst NHG 6
girl /gɜːl/ Mädchen NHG 5
(to) **give** *(irr)* /gɪv/ geben NHG 5; angeben, mitteilen NHG 6
(to) **give a presentation** *(irr)* /ˌgɪv_ə ˌpreznˈteɪʃn/ eine Präsentation halten NHG 7
(to) **give a reason** *(irr)* /ˌgɪv_ə ˈriːzn/ einen Grund nennen p. 17, 10
(to) **give a talk** *(irr)* /ˌgɪv_ə ˈtɔːk/ einen Vortrag halten NHG 7
(to) **give advice** *(irr)* /ˌgɪv_ədˈvaɪs/ Rat geben NHG 7
(to) **give directions** *(irr)* /ˌgɪv daɪˈrekʃnz/ den Weg beschreiben NHG 6
(to) **give out** *(irr)* /ˌgɪv_ˈaʊt/ bekannt geben; verteilen p. 38, 6
(to) **give somebody a call** *(irr)* /ˌgɪv ˌsʌmbədi_ə ˈkɔːl/ jemanden anrufen NHG 7
(to) give thanks *(irr)* /ˌgɪv ˈθæŋks/ Dank sagen p. 25, 7
(to) **give up** *(irr)* /ˌgɪv_ˈʌp/ aufgeben p. 89, 9
glad /glæd/ glücklich, froh NHG 7
glamorous /ˈglæmərəs/ glamourös p. 35, 2
glass /glɑːs/ Glas NHG 6
glee club /ˈgliː klʌb/ Gesangs-AG p. 44, 2
glimpse /glɪmps/ flüchtiger Blick p. 14, 7
glitz /glɪts/ Glanz p. 148
globally /ˈgləʊbli/ weltweit p. 86, 6
the globe /ðə ˈgləʊb/ die Erde p. 150
glue /gluː/ Klebstoff NHG 5
(to) **glue** /gluː/ kleben p. 68, 2

(to) **go** *(irr)* /gəʊ/ gehen; fahren NHG 5
(to) **go abroad** *(irr)* /ˌgəʊ ə'brɔːd/ ins Ausland gehen / fahren NHG 6
(to) **go away** *(irr)* /ˌgəʊ ə'weɪ/ weggehen; verschwinden NHG 6
(to) **go crazy** *(irr)* /ˌgəʊ 'kreɪzi/ verrückt werden; *hier:* ausrasten p. 49, 7
(to) **go cycling** *(irr)* /ˌgəʊ 'saɪklɪŋ/ Rad fahren gehen NHG 6
(to) **go hiking** *(irr)* /ˌgəʊ 'haɪkɪŋ/ wandern gehen NHG 6
(to) **go on** *(irr)* /ˌgəʊ 'ɒn/ passieren; weitergehen, weiterreden NHG 7
(to) **go out** *(irr)* /ˌgəʊ 'aʊt/ (hinaus) gehen; ausgehen NHG 6
(to) **go riding** *(irr)* /ˌgəʊ 'raɪdɪŋ/ reiten gehen NHG 6
(to) **go shopping** *(irr)* /ˌgəʊ 'ʃɒpɪŋ/ einkaufen gehen NHG 6
(to) **go swimming** *(irr)* /ˌgəʊ 'swɪmɪŋ/ schwimmen gehen NHG 6
(to) **go with** *(irr)* /ˌgəʊ 'wɪθ/ gehören zu; passen zu NHG 6
goal /gəʊl/ Tor NHG 5; Ziel p. 83, 2
goalkeeper /'gəʊlˌkiːpə/ Tormann/Torfrau p. 117, 2
God /gɒd/ Gott p. 38, 6
thank God /ˌθæŋk 'gɒd/ Gott sei Dank p. 110, 6
(to) be going to *(irr)* /ˌbi: 'gəʊɪŋ tʊ/ werden NHG 5
(to) **get going** *(irr)* /ˌget 'gəʊɪŋ/ in Gang bringen p. 85, 5
gold rush /'gəʊld rʌʃ/ Goldrausch p. 13, 6
goldfish *(pl goldfish)* /'gəʊldˌfɪʃ/ Goldfisch p. 75, 11
gone /gɒn/ weg NHG 6
good /gʊd/ gut NHG 5
(to) **be good at doing something** *(irr)* /ˌbi: gʊd ət 'duːɪŋ ˌsʌmθɪŋ/ gut darin sein, etwas zu tun NHG 5
(to) **be good at something** *(irr)* /ˌbi: 'gʊd æt ˌsʌmθɪŋ/ gut in etwas sein NHG 6
I'm good, thanks. /aɪm 'gʊd ˌθæŋks/ Es geht mir gut, danke. NHG 5
Good luck! /ˌgʊd 'lʌk/ Viel Glück! NHG 7
Good morning! /ˌgʊd 'mɔːnɪŋ/ Guten Morgen! NHG 5

goodbye /ˌgʊd'baɪ/ auf Wiedersehen NHG 5
(to) **govern** /'gʌvən/ regieren p. 14, 7
government /'gʌvənmənt/ Regierung NHG 7
gown /gaʊn/ Robe; Talar P&P 3
grade /greɪd/ Note p. 98, 10
grade *(AE)* /greɪd/ Klasse p. 34, 2
graduate /'grædʒuət/ Absolvent/in p. 35, 2
(to) **graduate** *(AE)* /'grædʒueɪt/ die (Highschool-)Abschlussprüfung bestehen p. 34, 2
graduation /ˌgrædʒu'eɪʃn/ Schulabschluss p. 35, 2
grammar /'græmə/ Grammatik p. 12
Grand Central Station /ˌgrænd ˌsentrəl 'steɪʃn/ Bahnhof in Manhattan p. 27, 9
grandad *(informal)* /'grænˌdæd/ Opa NHG 7
granddaughter /'grænˌdɔːtə/ Enkelin p. 107, 2
grandfather /'grænˌfɑːðə/ Großvater NHG 5
grandma *(informal)* /'grænˌmɑː/ Oma NHG 7
grandmother /'grænˌmʌðə/ Großmutter NHG 5
grandpa *(informal)* /'grænˌpɑː/ Opa NHG 7
grandparents *(pl)* /'grænˌpeərənts/ Großeltern NHG 6
grandson /'grænˌsʌn/ Enkel p. 107, 2
grape /greɪp/ (Wein)traube NHG 6
graph /grɑːf/ Diagramm; Graph p. 109, 5
grass /grɑːs/ Gras NHG 6
grateful /'greɪtfl/ dankbar p. 83, 2
gratitude /'grætɪtjuːd/ Dankbarkeit p. 71, 5
great /greɪt/ groß; großartig NHG 5
Great Britain /ˌgreɪt 'brɪtn/ Großbritannien NHG 7
the Great Plains /ðə ˌgreɪt 'pleɪnz/ Kurzgras-Prärien p. 111, 7
great-great-grandparents *(pl)* /ˌgreɪt ˌgreɪt 'grænˌpeərənts/ Ururgroßeltern p. 117, 2
greatness /'greɪtnəs/ Bedeutsamkeit p. 17, 10
green /griːn/ grün NHG 5; umweltfreundlich, ökologisch NHG 7

greetings *(pl)* /'griːtɪŋz/ Grüße p. 12, 3
grey /greɪ/ grau NHG 5
gritty /'grɪti/ grob; mutig, tapfer p. 25, 7
ground /graʊnd/ Boden NHG 6
groundbreaking /'graʊnˌbreɪkɪŋ/ bahnbrechend, wegweisend p. 10, 2
group /gruːp/ Gruppe NHG 5
(to) **grow** *(irr)* /grəʊ/ anbauen NHG 6; wachsen NHG 7
(to) **grow up** *(irr)* /ˌgrəʊ 'ʌp/ erwachsen sein, erwachsen werden NHG 6; aufwachsen NHG 7
grown-up /ˌgrəʊn 'ʌp/ Erwachsene/r p. 83, 2
guarantee /ˌgærən'tiː/ Garantie p. 71, 5
(to) **guess** /ges/ (er)raten NHG 5; annehmen; vermuten p. 38, 6
guest /gest/ Gast NHG 5
guidance counsellor /'gaɪdns ˌkaʊnslə/ Beratungslehrer/in p. 40, 7
(tour) guide /'tʊə gaɪd/ Reiseführer/in p. 26, 8
guitar /gɪ'tɑː/ Gitarre NHG 5
gun /gʌn/ Waffe p. 110, 6
(you) guys *(pl, informal)* /gaɪz/ Leute *(umgangssprachl.)* NHG 6
gym (= gymnasium) /dʒɪm, dʒɪm'neɪziəm/ Turnhalle NHG 5
gym *(AE)* /dʒɪm/ Sportunterricht p. 39, 6
(to) **do gymnastics** *(irr)* /ˌduː dʒɪm'næstɪks/ turnen NHG 5

H

habit /'hæbɪt/ Gewohnheit; Angewohnheit NHG 7
hair /heə/ Haar; Haare NHG 5
hairdresser /'heəˌdresə/ Friseur/in NHG 6
half /hɑːf/ halb NHG 5
half *(pl halves)* /hɑːf, hɑːvz/ Hälfte NHG 6
half-time /ˌhɑːf'taɪm/ Halbzeit p. 48, 7
hall /hɔːl/ Halle p. 13, 6
hallway /'hɔːlˌweɪ/ Korridor; Flur p. 39, 6
on the one hand, ... /ˌɒn ðə 'wʌn hænd/ einerseits ... NHG 7

Dictionary

on the other hand, ... /ˌɒn ðiˈʌðə hænd/ andererseits ... NHG 7
(to) hand in /ˌhændˈɪn/ einreichen; abgeben NHG 6
handful /ˈhænfʊl/ Handvoll p. 138
(to) handle /ˈhændl/ anfassen, berühren p. 138
folded hands /ˌfəʊldɪd ˈhændz/ betende Hände p. 71, 5
hands-on /ˌhændzˈɒn/ aktiv; praktisch p. 41, 8
(to) hang out (informal, irr) /ˌhæŋˈaʊt/ rumhängen; Zeit mit jemandem verbringen p. 59, 3
(to) hang (up) (irr) /ˌhæŋˈʌp/ hängen, aufhängen NHG 6
(to) happen /ˈhæpən/ geschehen; passieren NHG 5
(to) make happen (irr) /ˌmeɪk ˈhæpən/ möglich machen p. 25, 7
happy /ˈhæpi/ glücklich NHG 5; zufrieden NHG 7
Happy birthday (to you)! /ˌhæpi ˈbɜːθdeɪ tə juː/ Herzlichen Glückwunsch zum Geburtstag! NHG 5
(to) harass /ˈhærəs/ belästigen p. 69, 2
harassment /ˈhærəsmənt/ Belästigung; Schikane p. 69, 2
harbor (AE) = **harbour** (BE) /ˈhɑːbə/ Hafen p. 20, 2
hard /hɑːd/ hart, schwierig NHG 6; fest; kräftig NHG 7
hard skill /ˌhɑːd ˈskɪl/ berufstypische Qualifikation p. 81
hardly /ˈhɑːdli/ kaum p. 38, 6
harm /hɑːm/ Schaden p. 86, 6
(to) harm /hɑːm/ schaden, Schaden zufügen p. 73, 6
harmful /ˈhɑːmfl/ schädlich p. 71, 5
harvest /ˈhɑːvɪst/ Ernte p. 106, 2
(to) hashtag /ˈhæʃˌtæg/ mit einem Hashtag versehen p. 48, 7
hat /hæt/ Hut p. 65, 12
(to) hate /heɪt/ hassen; nicht ausstehen können NHG 5
(to) have (irr) /hæv/ haben; essen; trinken NHG 5
(to) have a look at (irr) /ˌhæv ə ˈlʊk ət/ sich ansehen NHG 6
(to) have (a lot of) fun (irr) /ˌhæv ə ˌlɒt əv ˈfʌn/ (viel) Spaß haben NHG 6

(to) have got (irr) /ˌhæv ˈgɒt/ haben NHG 5
(to) have in common (irr) /ˌhæv ɪn ˈkɒmən/ gemeinsam haben NHG 6
(to) have to (irr) /ˈhæv tə/ müssen NHG 5
(to) have one's photograph taken (irr) /ˌhæv wʌnz ˈfəʊtəˌgrɑːf ˌteɪkən/ sich fotografieren lassen p. 132
he /hiː/ er NHG 5
head /hed/ Kopf NHG 6
headache /ˈhedeɪk/ Kopfschmerzen NHG 7
heading /ˈhedɪŋ/ Überschrift; Titel NHG 6
headline /ˈhedˌlaɪn/ Überschrift; Schlagzeile p. 43, 14
headteacher /ˌhedˈtiːtʃə/ Schulleiter/in, Rektor/in p. 165
health /helθ/ Gesundheit NHG 7
healthy /ˈhelθi/ gesund NHG 6
(to) hear (irr) /hɪə/ hören NHG 5
heart /hɑːt/ Herz NHG 6
by heart /ˌbaɪ ˈhɑːt/ auswendig NHG 7
(to) be close to somebody's heart (irr) /ˌbiː ˌkləʊs tə ˌsʌmbədiz ˈhɑːt/ jemandem sehr wichtig sein p. 74, 8
(to) heat /hiːt/ erhitzen NHG 7
heavy /ˈhevi/ schwer NHG 5
hedgehog /ˈhedʒˌhɒg/ Igel NHG 6
height /haɪt/ Höhe NHG 6
hell /hel/ Hölle p. 25, 7
hello /həˈləʊ/ hallo NHG 5
helmet /ˈhelmɪt/ Helm NHG 7
help /help/ Hilfe NHG 5
(to) help /help/ helfen NHG 5
(to) help out /ˌhelpˈaʊt/ aushelfen NHG 7
helpful /ˈhelpfl/ hilfreich; nützlich NHG 7
second helping /ˌsekənd ˈhelpɪŋ/ Nachschlag p. 48, 7
helpless /ˈhelpləs/ hilflos p. 58, 2
her /hɜː/ ihr/ihre; sie NHG 5
herb /hɜːb/ (Gewürz)kraut NHG 7
here /hɪə/ hier; hierher NHG 5
Here you are! /ˌhɪə juˈɑː/ Hier, bitte! NHG 5
heritage /ˈherɪtɪdʒ/ Erbe p. 27, 10
hers /hɜːz/ ihre(r, s) NHG 7
herself /həˈself/ sich; (sie) selbst NHG 7

(to) hide (irr) /haɪd/ verstecken, sich verstecken NHG 6
high /haɪ/ hoch NHG 5
high school (AE) /ˈhaɪ skuːl/ Highschool p. 24, 6
highlight /ˈhaɪˌlaɪt/ Höhepunkt NHG 7
highly /ˈhaɪli/ äußerst; stark p. 138
(to) hijack /ˈhaɪdʒæk/ entführen p. 15, 7
(to) go hiking (irr) /ˌgəʊ ˈhaɪkɪŋ/ wandern gehen NHG 6
hiking trail /ˈhaɪkɪŋ treɪl/ Wanderweg p. 119, 5
hill /hɪl/ Hügel NHG 6
him /hɪm/ ihm, ihn NHG 5
himself /hɪmˈself/ selbst; sich (selbst) NHG 6
Hinduism /ˈhɪnduˌɪzm/ Hinduismus NHG 6
hip /hɪp/ hip, cool p. 120, 6
(to) hire /ˈhaɪə/ mieten NHG 6
his /hɪz/ sein; seine(r, s) NHG 5
Hispanic /hɪˈspænɪk/ Hispanoamerikaner/in; hispanisch p. 24, 6
historian /hɪˈstɔːriən/ Historiker/in p. 17, 10
historic /hɪˈstɒrɪk/ historisch p. 13, 6
historical /hɪˈstɒrɪkl/ geschichtlich; historisch p. 15, 7
history /ˈhɪstri/ Geschichte NHG 5
(to) hit (irr) /hɪt/ schlagen NHG 5; treffen; stoßen gegen p. 21, 2
(to) hold (irr) /həʊld/ (fest)halten NHG 5; veranstalten p. 35, 2
hole /həʊl/ Loch NHG 5
holiday /ˈhɒlɪdeɪ/ Feiertag NHG 6
holiday(s) /ˈhɒlɪdeɪ(z)/ Ferien; Urlaub NHG 5
home /həʊm/ nach Hause; zu Hause; daheim NHG 5; Zuhause; Haus NHG 6; Heimat P&P 2
at home /ˌæt ˈhəʊm/ zu Hause NHG 5
home economics (pl) /ˌhəʊm ˌiːkəˈnɒmɪks/ Hauswirtschaft(slehre) P&P 3
home town /ˈhəʊm ˌtaʊn/ Heimatstadt NHG 5
home-made /ˌhəʊmˈmeɪd/ hausgemacht, selbst gemacht NHG 7
homecoming (no pl, AE) /ˈhəʊmˌkʌmɪŋ/ Ehemaligentreffen p. 34, 2

homeroom /ˈhəʊmruːm/ Klassenlehrkraftstunde; Klassenraum p. 38, 6
(to) be homesick *(irr)* /ˌbiː ˈhəʊmˌsɪk/ Heimweh haben NHG 7
(to) get homesick *(irr)* /ˌget ˈhəʊmˌsɪk/ Heimweh bekommen p. 113, 10
homework /ˈhəʊmwɜːk/ Hausaufgaben NHG 5
honest /ˈɒnɪst/ ehrlich NHG 6
(to) **honor** *(AE)* = honour *(BE)* /ˈɒnə/ ehren p. 27, 10
hope /həʊp/ Hoffnung p. 81
(to) **hope** /həʊp/ hoffen NHG 5
hopeful /ˈhəʊpfl/ zuversichtlich p. 89, 9; hoffnungsvoll p. 149
hopefully /ˈhəʊpfli/ hoffentlich p. 60, 4
horizon /həˈraɪzn/ Horizont p. 105
horrible /ˈhɒrəbl/ schrecklich; gemein NHG 6
horse /hɔːs/ Pferd NHG 6
(to) **ride a horse** *(irr)* /ˌraɪd ə ˈhɔːs/ reiten NHG 5
hospital /ˈhɒspɪtl/ Krankenhaus NHG 6
host *(before nouns)* /həʊst/ Gast- p. 34, 2
host /həʊst/ *hier:* Podcast-Host p. 27, 10
(to) **host** /həʊst/ ausrichten p. 93, 2
hot /hɒt/ heiß NHG 6; scharf NHG 7
hotspot /ˈhɒtˌspɒt/ *angesagter Ort* p. 11, 2
hour /aʊə/ Stunde NHG 5
house /haʊs/ Haus NHG 5
household /ˈhaʊsˌhəʊld/ Haushalt p. 41, 8
how /haʊ/ wie NHG 5
How about …? /ˈhaʊ ə ˌbaʊt/ Wie wäre es / Was ist mit …? NHG 7
How are you? /ˌhaʊ ˈɑː jə/ Wie geht es dir / euch / Ihnen? NHG 5
How much is it? /ˌhaʊ mʌtʃ ˈɪz ɪt/ Wie viel kostet es? NHG 5
however /haʊˈevə/ aber; wie auch immer p. 62, 8
(to) **howl** /haʊl/ brüllen; heulen p. 111, 7
huge /hjuːdʒ/ riesig NHG 6
humid /ˈhjuːmɪd/ feucht p. 110, 6
(to) **humiliate** /hjuːˈmɪlieɪt/ erniedrigen p. 69, 2

hundred /ˈhʌndrəd/ Hundert NHG 6
hungry /ˈhʌŋɡri/ hungrig NHG 5
(to) **hurry (up)** /ˌhʌri ˈʌp/ sich beeilen NHG 5
hurt /hɜːt/ verletzt; gekränkt p. 62, 8
(to) **hurt** *(irr)* /hɜːt/ wehtun; schmerzen; verletzen NHG 7
husband /ˈhʌzbənd/ Ehemann NHG 5

I

I /aɪ/ ich NHG 5
ice /aɪs/ Eis NHG 6
ice cream /ˌaɪs ˈkriːm/ Eis NHG 5
(to) **ice-skate** /ˈaɪsˌskeɪt/ Schlittschuh laufen NHG 5
iced tea /ˌaɪst ˈtiː/ Eistee p. 65, 12
ICT (= Information and Communication Technology) /ˌaɪsiːˈtiː, ˌɪnfəˈmeɪʃn ən kəˌmjuːnɪˈkeɪʃn tekˌnɒlədʒi/ Informatik *(Schulfach)* NHG 5
ID (card) (= identity card) /ˌaɪˈdiː kɑːd, aɪˈdentəti kɑːd/ Ausweis p. 26, 8
idea /aɪˈdɪə/ Idee; Vorstellung NHG 5
if /ɪf/ wenn; falls; ob NHG 5
(to) **ignore** /ɪɡˈnɔː/ ignorieren p. 62, 8
ill /ɪl/ krank NHG 6
illness /ˈɪlnəs/ Krankheit NHG 7
illustrated /ˈɪləstreɪtɪd/ illustriert, bebildert p. 26, 8
imagination /ɪˌmædʒɪˈneɪʃn/ Fantasie; Vorstellungskraft p. 85, 5
(to) **imagine** /ɪˈmædʒɪn/ sich etwas vorstellen NHG 5
immediate /ɪˈmiːdiət/ umgehend; unmittelbar NHG 7
immediately /ɪˈmiːdiətli/ sofort p. 72, 6
immigrant /ˈɪmɪɡrənt/ Einwanderer/in; Immigrant/in NHG 7
(to) **immigrate** /ˈɪmɪɡreɪt/ einwandern p. 109, 5
immigration /ˌɪmɪˈɡreɪʃn/ Einwanderung; Immigration p. 105
impact /ˈɪmpækt/ Auswirkung; Einfluss NHG 7
(to) **impact** /ɪmˈpækt/ Einfluss haben auf p. 72, 6
importance /ɪmˈpɔːtns/ Bedeutung; Wichtigkeit p. 87, 6
important /ɪmˈpɔːtnt/ wichtig NHG 5

impossible /ɪmˈpɒsəbl/ unmöglich NHG 6
impression /ɪmˈpreʃn/ Eindruck p. 9
impressive /ɪmˈpresɪv/ beeindruckend NHG 7
(to) **improve** /ɪmˈpruːv/ verbessern; besser werden NHG 6
(to) **improvise** /ˈɪmprəvaɪz/ improvisieren p. 44, 2
in /ɪn/ in; auf NHG 5
in advance /ɪn ədˈvɑːns/ im Voraus p. 26, 8
in fact /ɪn ˈfækt/ tatsächlich; in Wirklichkeit p. 68, 2
in favour of /ɪn ˈfeɪvər əv/ für p. 15, 7
in front of /ɪn ˈfrʌnt əv/ vor NHG 5
in general /ɪn ˈdʒenrəl/ im Allgemeinen NHG 7
in my opinion /ɪn ˈmaɪ əˌpɪnjən/ meiner Meinung nach NHG 6
in need /ɪn ˈniːd/ bedürftig P&P 5
in order to /ɪn ˈɔːdə tʊ/ um zu NHG 7
in person /ɪn ˈpɜːsn/ persönlich p. 72, 6
in the back /ɪn ðə ˈbæk/ hinten NHG 5
in the end /ɪn ðɪ ˈend/ am Ende, schließlich NHG 6
in the front /ɪn ðə ˈfrʌnt/ vorne NHG 5
in the middle of /ɪn ðə ˈmɪdl əv/ in der Mitte von; mitten in p. 21, 2
in total /ɪn ˈtəʊtl/ insgesamt p. 34, 2
(to) **include** /ɪnˈkluːd/ beinhalten; einbeziehen NHG 6
including /ɪnˈkluːdɪŋ/ einschließlich p. 26, 8
increase /ˈɪŋkriːs/ Anstieg, Wachstum p. 109, 5
(to) **increase** /ɪnˈkriːs/ ansteigen p. 109, 5
incredible /ɪnˈkredəbl/ unglaublich p. 48, 7
independence /ˌɪndɪˈpendəns/ Unabhängigkeit p. 13, 6
Independence Day /ˌɪndɪˈpendəns deɪ/ Unabhängigkeitstag p. 6
independent /ˌɪndɪˈpendənt/ unabhängig NHG 7
indigenous /ɪnˈdɪdʒənəs/ (ein)heimisch, indigen p. 7
individual /ˌɪndɪˈvɪdʒuəl/ individuell; einzeln NHG 7

Dictionary

indivisible /ˌɪndɪˈvɪzəbl/ unteilbar p. 38, 6
indoor /ˈɪnˌdɔː/ Hallen- NHG 7
indoors /ˌɪnˈdɔːz/ drinnen, im Haus NHG 7
industrial /ɪnˈdʌstriəl/ industriell NHG 7
industrialized /ɪnˈdʌstriəlaɪzd/ industrialisiert p. 15, 7
industry /ˈɪndəstri/ Industrie NHG 7
infection /ɪnˈfekʃn/ Infektion NHG 7
infectious /ɪnˈfekʃəs/ ansteckend p. 87, 6
influence /ˈɪnfluəns/ Einfluss NHG 7
(to) **influence** /ˈɪnfluəns/ beeinflussen p. 11, 2
influential /ˌɪnfluˈenʃl/ einflussreich p. 148
(to) **inform** /ɪnˈfɔːm/ informieren NHG 6
information *(no pl)* /ˌɪnfəˈmeɪʃn/ Informationen NHG 5
information technology (= IT) /ˌɪnfəˌmeɪʃn tekˈnɒlədʒi, ˌaɪ ˈtiː/ Informationstechnologie, IT p. 10, 2
informed /ɪnˈfɔːmd/ informiert p. 89, 9
infusion /ɪnˈfjuːʒn/ Einbringen, Input p. 89, 9
ingredient /ɪnˈɡriːdiənt/ Zutat NHG 7
inhumane /ˌɪnhjuːˈmeɪn/ barbarisch; unmenschlich p. 15, 7
(to) **take the initiative** *(irr)* /ˌteɪk ðɪ ɪˈnɪʃətɪv/ die Initiative ergreifen p. 96, 8
injury /ˈɪndʒəri/ Verletzung NHG 7
inner circle /ˌɪnə ˈsɜːkl/ engster Kreis p. 87, 6
innocence /ˈɪnəsns/ Unschuld p. 71, 5
innovation /ˌɪnəʊˈveɪʃn/ Neuerung p. 10, 2
inside /ˈɪnˌsaɪd/ innerhalb NHG 5; innen; drinnen; hinein NHG 6
inspection /ɪnˈspekʃn/ Untersuchung p. 110, 6
(to) **inspire** /ɪnˈspaɪə/ inspirieren p. 11, 2
inspiring /ɪnˈspaɪərɪŋ/ inspirierend, anregend p. 93, 2
(to) **install** /ɪnˈstɔːl/ aufstellen, installieren p. 10, 2
instead of /ɪnˈsted əv/ anstatt p. 72, 6

institution /ˌɪnstɪˈtjuːʃn/ Einrichtung; Institution p. 15, 7
instruction /ɪnˈstrʌkʃn/ Anweisung; Instruktion NHG 6
insult /ˈɪnsʌlt/ Beleidigung p. 71, 5
artificial intelligence (= AI) /ˌɑːtɪfɪʃl ɪnˈtelɪdʒns, ˌeɪ ˈaɪ/ künstliche Intelligenz p. 10, 2
(to) **intend** /ɪnˈtend/ beabsichtigen p. 71, 5
interaction /ˌɪntərˈækʃn/ Interaktion; Kommunikation p. 73, 6
interactive /ˌɪntərˈæktɪv/ interaktiv p. 135
interest /ˈɪntrəst/ Interesse; Hobby p. 72, 6
interested /ˈɪntrəstɪd/ interessiert NHG 6
(to) **be interested in** *(irr)* /ˌbi ˈɪntrəstɪd ɪn/ interessiert sein an NHG 7
interesting /ˈɪntrəstɪŋ/ interessant NHG 5
(to) **interpret** /ɪnˈtɜːprɪt/ deuten, interpretieren p. 92, 2
job interview (= **interview**) /ˈdʒɒbˌɪntəvjuː, ˈɪntəˌvjuː/ Bewerbungsgespräch; Vorstellungsgespräch p. 98, 11
(to) **interview** /ˈɪntəvjuː/ interviewen, befragen NHG 5
into /ˈɪntuː/ in NHG 5
(to) **introduce** /ˌɪntrəˈdjuːs/ einführen; vorstellen NHG 5
introduction /ˌɪntrəˈdʌkʃn/ Einleitung NHG 5
(to) **invent** /ɪnˈvent/ erfinden NHG 6
invented /ɪnˈventɪd/ erfunden NHG 7
invention /ɪnˈvenʃn/ Erfindung NHG 6
invitation /ˌɪnvɪˈteɪʃn/ Einladung NHG 5
(to) **invite** /ɪnˈvaɪt/ einladen NHG 5
(to) **involve** /ɪnˈvɒlv/ beinhalten; umfassen p. 40, 7
(to) **be involved in** /ˌbi ɪnˈvɒlvd ɪn/ beteiligt sein an p. 15, 7
(to) **become involved in** *(irr)* /bɪˌkʌm ɪnˈvɒlvd ɪn/ sich beteiligen, sich engagieren P&P 5
(to) **get involved** *(irr)* /ˌɡet ɪnˈvɒlvd ɪn/ sich engagieren p. 85, 5
Ireland /ˈaɪələnd/ Irland NHG 6
Irish /ˈaɪrɪʃ/ irisch p. 114, 13

the Iron Age /ðɪ ˈaɪən eɪdʒ/ die Eisenzeit p. 135
island /ˈaɪlənd/ Insel p. 10, 2
isolated /ˈaɪsəˌleɪtɪd/ isoliert, einsam p. 72, 6
issue /ˈɪʃuː/ Frage; Thema NHG 7
it /ɪt/ es NHG 5
it's (= **it is**) /ɪts, ˈɪt ɪz/ *hier:* es kostet NHG 5
Italian /ɪˈtæljən/ Italiener/in; italienisch p. 162
Italy /ˈɪtəli/ Italien NHG 5
item /ˈaɪtəm/ Gegenstand NHG 7
itinerary /aɪˈtɪnərəri/ Reiseroute p. 123, 9
its /ɪts/ sein(e), ihr(e) *(sächlich)* NHG 5
itself /ɪtˈself/ selbst, sich selbst NHG 7

J

jacket /ˈdʒækɪt/ Jacke NHG 6
jam /dʒæm/ Marmelade p. 51, 11
January /ˈdʒænjuəri/ Januar NHG 5
Japanese /ˌdʒæpəˈniːz/ Japaner/in; japanisch p. 71, 5
jaw /dʒɔː/ Kiefer p. 135
jewellery *(no pl)* /ˈdʒuːəlri/ Schmuck NHG 6
Jewish /ˈdʒuːɪʃ/ jüdisch NHG 6
job /dʒɒb/ Aufgabe; Beruf NHG 6; Stelle; Job p. 94, 4
job hunt /ˈdʒɒb hʌnt/ Jobsuche p. 97, 9
job interview (= **interview**) /ˈdʒɒbˌɪntəvjuː, ˈɪntəˌvjuː/ Bewerbungsgespräch; Vorstellungsgespräch p. 98, 11
job opening /ˈdʒɒbˌəʊpənɪŋ/ freie Stelle p. 97, 9
(to) **join** /dʒɔɪn/ mitmachen (bei) NHG 5; sich zu jemandem gesellen; Mitglied werden NHG 7
(to) **join in** /ˌdʒɔɪn ˈɪn/ sich beteiligen an; mitmachen bei NHG 6
joke /dʒəʊk/ Witz p. 122, 7
journey /ˈdʒɜːni/ Reise; Fahrt NHG 6
(to) **take a journey** *(irr)* /ˌteɪk ə ˈdʒɜːni/ eine Reise machen p. 121, 6
joy /dʒɔɪ/ Freude p. 44, 2
(to) **judge** /dʒʌdʒ/ urteilen; beurteilen NHG 7
juice /dʒuːs/ Saft NHG 5
July /dʒʊˈlaɪ/ Juli NHG 5

(to) **jump** /dʒʌmp/ springen NHG 5
jump /dʒʌmp/ Sprung p. 48, 7
June /dʒuːn/ Juni NHG 5
junior *(AE)* /ˈdʒuːniə/ Schüler/in einer Highschool im vorletzten Jahr p. 39, 6
just /dʒʌst/ nur; bloß NHG 5; einfach; wirklich; gerade NHG 6
justice /ˈdʒʌstɪs/ Gerechtigkeit p. 38, 6

K
kayak /ˈkaɪæk/ Kajak p. 7
keen /kiːn/ begeistert p. 34, 2
(to) **keep** *(irr)* /kiːp/ halten; behalten; aufbewahren NHG 5
(to) **keep doing something** *(irr)* /ˌkiːp ˈduːɪŋ sʌmθɪŋ/ etwas weiter tun NHG 7
(to) **keep fit** *(irr)* /ˌkiːp ˈfɪt/ fit bleiben, (sich) fit halten NHG 7
(to) **keep from doing something** *(irr)* /ˌkiːp frəm ˈduːɪŋ ˌsʌmθɪŋ/ etwas unterlassen, sich etwas verkneifen p. 65, 12
(to) **keep in mind** *(irr)* /ˌkiːp ɪn ˈmaɪnd/ im Gedächtnis behalten p. 115, 14
(to) **keep in touch** *(irr)* /ˌkiːp ɪn ˈtʌtʃ/ Kontakt halten; in Verbindung bleiben NHG 7
keyword /ˈkiːˌwɜːd/ Schlüsselwort; Stichwort p. 82, 2
kg (= **kilogram**) /ˈkɪləˌɡræm/ Kilogramm NHG 6
(to) **kick** /kɪk/ treten NHG 5
kid /kɪd/ Kind NHG 5
(to) **kill** /kɪl/ töten NHG 7
kind /kaɪnd/ Art; Sorte NHG 5; freundlich p. 51, 11
all kinds of /ˌɔːl ˈkaɪndz əv/ alle möglichen NHG 6
king /kɪŋ/ König NHG 6
(to) **kiss** /kɪs/ küssen p. 119, 5
kitchen /ˈkɪtʃən/ Küche NHG 5
km (= **kilometre**) /ˈkɪləˌmiːtə/ Kilometer NHG 7
knee /niː/ Knie NHG 6
knife (*pl* **knives**) /naɪf, naɪvz/ Messer NHG 5
(to) **knock** /nɒk/ klopfen NHG 6
(to) **know** *(irr)* /nəʊ/ wissen; kennen NHG 5

(to) **get to know** *(irr)* /ˌɡet tə ˈnəʊ/ kennenlernen p. 41, 8
knowledge /ˈnɒlɪdʒ/ Kenntnis; Wissen p. 82, 2
known /nəʊn/ bekannt p. 18, 12
Korean /kəˈriːən/ Koreaner/in; koreanisch p. 107, 2

L
lab /læb/ Labor p. 39, 6
label /ˈleɪbl/ Etikett NHG 7
(to) **label** /ˈleɪbl/ beschriften NHG 5
(to) **lack** /læk/ nicht haben, fehlen p. 71, 5
lady /ˈleɪdi/ Frau; Dame NHG 7
Lady Liberty /ˌleɪdi ˈlɪbəti/ Freiheitsstatue in New York p. 20, 2
lake /leɪk/ See NHG 5
standing lamp /ˈstændɪŋ læmp/ Stehlampe p. 65, 12
(to) **land** /lænd/ landen NHG 7
landfill /ˈlændˌfɪl/ Deponiegelände p. 86, 6
landlord / landlady /ˈlændlɔːd/ Vermieter/in p. 106, 2
landmark /ˈlænˌmɑːk/ Wahrzeichen p. 25, 7
landscape /ˈlænˌskeɪp/ Landschaft p. 8
lane /leɪn/ Spur p. 150
language /ˈlæŋɡwɪdʒ/ Sprache NHG 5
foreign language /ˌfɒrɪn ˈlæŋɡwɪdʒ/ Fremdsprache P&P 3
lantern /ˈlæntən/ Laterne NHG 6
large /lɑːdʒ/ groß NHG 6
last /lɑːst/ letzte(r, s) NHG 5
(to) **last** /lɑːst/ (an)dauern NHG 6
late /leɪt/ (zu) spät NHG 5
(to) **stay up (late)** /ˌsteɪ ˌʌp ˈleɪt/ lange aufbleiben NHG 7
lately /ˈleɪtli/ in letzter Zeit, kürzlich p. 59, 3
later /ˈleɪtə/ später NHG 5
latest /ˈleɪtɪst/ neueste(r, s) NHG 7
Latin /ˌlætɪn əˈmerɪkən/ Lateinamerikaner/in; lateinamerikanisch p. 25, 7
(to) **laugh** /lɑːf/ lachen NHG 6
law /lɔː/ Gesetz p. 83, 2
law /lɔː/ Rechtswissenschaft p. 40, 7
business law /ˈbɪznəs lɔː/ Wirtschaftsrecht p. 40, 7

lawn /lɔːn/ Rasen p. 97, 9
lawyer /ˈlɔːjə/ Rechtsanwalt/ Rechtsanwältin p. 92, 1
lazy /ˈleɪzi/ faul NHG 6
lead /liːd/ Leine NHG 6
(to) **lead** *(irr)* /liːd/ führen p. 15, 7
(to) **lead by example** *(irr)* /ˌliːd baɪ ɪɡˈzɑːmpl/ mit gutem Beispiel vorangehen p. 89, 9
leader /ˈliːdə/ Leiter/in NHG 6; Anführer/in p. 15, 7
leadership /ˈliːdəʃɪp/ Führung; Leitung p. 44, 2
leading /ˈliːdɪŋ/ führend P&P 2
leaf (*pl* **leaves**) /liːf, liːvz/ Blatt NHG 6
league /liːɡ/ Liga p. 50, 8
(to) **learn** *(irr)* /lɜːn/ lernen NHG 6; erfahren p. 21, 2
least /liːst/ am wenigsten NHG 7
at least /ˌæt ˈliːst/ mindestens; wenigstens NHG 6
(to) **leave** *(irr)* /liːv/ weggehen NHG 5; verlassen, abfahren; (übrig) lassen; zurücklassen; hinterlassen NHG 6
Lebanon /ˈlebənən/ der Libanon p. 24, 6
left /left/ links, nach links NHG 6; übrig NHG 7
on the left /ˌɒn ðə ˈleft/ links, auf der linken Seite NHG 5
leg /leɡ/ Bein NHG 6
legacy /ˈleɡəsi/ Vermächtnis; Erbe p. 27, 10
lemon /ˈlemən/ Zitrone NHG 5
lemonade /ˌleməˈneɪd/ Limonade NHG 7
less /les/ weniger NHG 6
lesson /ˈlesn/ Stunde; Unterricht NHG 5
(to) **let** *(irr)* /let/ lassen NHG 5
letter /ˈletə/ Buchstabe NHG 5; Brief NHG 6
level /ˈlevl/ Stufe; Level NHG 5
liberty /ˈlɪbəti/ Freiheit p. 38, 6
library /ˈlaɪbrəri/ Bücherei NHG 5
(to) **lie** /laɪ/ lügen p. 61, 7
(to) **lie** *(irr)* /laɪ/ liegen p. 65, 12
(to) **lie down** *(irr)* /ˌlaɪ ˈdaʊn/ sich hinlegen p. 36, 4
life (*pl* **lives**) /laɪf, laɪvz/ Leben NHG 5

Dictionary

life-saving skill /ˈlaɪfˌseɪvɪŋ skɪl/ *Kenntnis im Rettungsschwimmen* p. 93, 2
walk of life /ˌwɔːk_əv_ˈlaɪf/ Lebensbereich; Gesellschaftsschicht p. 89, 9
lifelong /ˈlaɪfˌlɒŋ/ lebenslang p. 25, 7
lifestyle /ˈlaɪfˌstaɪl/ Lebensstil NHG 7
(to) lift /lɪft/ (hoch)heben NHG 7
light /laɪt/ Licht NHG 5
(to) light (irr) /laɪt/ anzünden NHG 6
light bulb /ˈlaɪt bʌlb/ Glühbirne p. 65, 12
light technology /ˈlaɪt tekˌnɒlədʒi/ Lichttechnik p. 43, 14
lighthouse /ˈlaɪtˌhaʊs/ Leuchtturm p. 119, 5
lightning /ˈlaɪtnɪŋ/ Blitz p. 111, 7
like /laɪk/ wie NHG 5
(to) like /laɪk/ mögen NHG 5
(to) like best /ˌlaɪk ˈbest/ am liebsten mögen NHG 5
(to) like doing something /laɪk ˈduːɪŋ ˌsʌmθɪŋ/ etwas gern tun NHG 6
like that /ˌlaɪk ˈðæt/ so NHG 7
likely /ˈlaɪkli/ wahrscheinlich p. 73, 6
limit /ˈlɪmɪt/ (Höchst)grenze; Limit p. 71, 5
line /laɪn/ Linie; Zeile NHG 5
list /lɪst/ Liste NHG 5
(to) list /lɪst/ auflisten NHG 5
(to) listen (to) /ˈlɪsn/ zuhören, anhören NHG 5
(to) listen carefully /ˌlɪsn ˈkeəfli/ aufmerksam zuhören p. 96, 8
listening /ˈlɪsnɪŋ/ Hören p. 37, 5
literally /ˈlɪtrəli/ buchstäblich, wirklich p. 106, 2
literature /ˈlɪtrətʃə/ Literatur p. 40, 7
little /ˈlɪtl/ klein NHG 5; wenig p. 68, 2
a little /ə ˈlɪtl/ ein bisschen NHG 6
livable (AE) = liveable (BE) /ˈlɪvəbl/ lebenswert p. 85, 5
(to) live /lɪv/ leben; wohnen NHG 5
lively /ˈlaɪvli/ lebhaft, lebendig p. 20, 1
living /ˈlɪvɪŋ/ Lebensstil NHG 7
living /ˈlɪvɪŋ/ Lebensunterhalt p. 93, 2
(to) do for a living (irr) /ˌduː fər_ə ˈlɪvɪŋ/ seinen Lebensunterhalt verdienen p. 92, 2

way of living /ˌweɪ_əv ˈlɪvɪŋ/ Lebensweise p. 14, 7
living conditions (pl) /ˈlɪvɪŋ kənˌdɪʃnz/ Lebensbedingungen p. 121, 6
living room /ˈlɪvɪŋ ˌruːm/ Wohnzimmer NHG 5
'll (= will) /l, wɪl/ werden NHG 6
(to) load /ləʊd/ laden NHG 5
local /ˈləʊkl/ örtlich; hiesig p. 13, 6
locally /ˈləʊkli/ am Ort; vor Ort p. 39, 6
(to) be located (irr) /ˌbiː ləʊˈkeɪtɪd/ gelegen sein NHG 7
locker /ˈlɒkə/ Schließfach; Spind p. 38, 6
log /lɒɡ/ Baumstamm p. 93, 2
lonely /ˈləʊnli/ einsam NHG 6
long /lɒŋ/ lang NHG 5
all day long /ˌɔːl deɪ ˈlɒŋ/ den ganzen Tag lang p. 21, 2
for a long time /fər_ə ˈlɒŋ taɪm/ lange p. 62, 8
look /lʊk/ Aussehen; Look NHG 7
(to) look /lʊk/ aussehen NHG 5
(to) have a look at (irr) /ˌhæv_ə ˈlʊk_ət/ sich ansehen NHG 6
(to) take a closer look at (irr) /ˌteɪk_ə ˌkləʊsə ˈlʊk_ət/ sich genauer ansehen p. 148
(to) look after /ˌlʊk_ˈɑːftə/ aufpassen auf; sich kümmern um NHG 5
(to) look (at) /ˌlʊk_ət/ (an)sehen, (an)schauen NHG 5
(to) look away /ˌlʊk_əˈweɪ/ wegsehen p. 65, 12
(to) look for /ˈlʊk fə/ suchen nach NHG 5
(to) look forward to /ˌlʊk ˈfɔːwəd_tə/ sich freuen auf NHG 6
(to) look up /ˌlʊk_ˈʌp/ hochschauen; nachschlagen NHG 7
lorry /ˈlɒri/ Lastwagen p. 165
(to) lose (irr) /luːz/ verlieren NHG 7
a lot /ə ˈlɒt/ viel, sehr NHG 5
a lot (of) /ə ˈlɒt/ viel(e), jede Menge NHG 5
thanks a lot /ˌθæŋks_ə ˈlɒt/ vielen Dank NHG 5
lots of /ˈlɒts_əv/ viel(e) NHG 5
loud /laʊd/ laut NHG 5
love /lʌv/ viele Grüße; alles Liebe (in Briefen) NHG 6; Liebe p. 64, 9

(to) love /lʌv/ lieben, sehr mögen NHG 5
(to) love doing something /lʌv ˈduːɪŋ ˌsʌmθɪŋ/ etwas sehr gern tun NHG 5
(to) be in love (irr) /ˌbiː_ɪn ˈlʌv/ verliebt sein p. 66, 13
(to) fall in love (irr) /ˌfɔːl_ɪn ˈlʌv/ sich verlieben p. 65, 12
love letter /ˈlʌv ˌletə/ Liebesbrief p. 25, 7
loved ones (pl) /ˈlʌvd wʌnz/ Angehörige; nahestehende Personen p. 72, 6
lovely /ˈlʌvli/ schön; herrlich p. 21, 2
lover /ˈlʌvə/ Liebhaber/in p. 13, 6
(to) lower /ˈləʊə/ senken p. 65, 12
loyal /ˈlɔɪəl/ treu; loyal p. 61, 7
(good) luck /lʌk/ Glück NHG 6
Good luck! /ˌɡʊd ˈlʌk/ Viel Glück! NHG 7
luckily /ˈlʌkɪli/ zum Glück; glücklicherweise p. 38, 6
(to) be lucky (irr) /ˌbiː ˈlʌki/ Glück haben NHG 7
lunch /lʌntʃ/ Mittagessen NHG 5
lunchtime /ˈlʌntʃtaɪm/ Mittagszeit; Mittagspause p. 45, 2
lyrics (pl) /ˈlɪrɪks/ Liedtext p. 25, 7

M

machine /məˈʃiːn/ Maschine; Apparat NHG 6
machinery /məˈʃiːnəri/ Maschinen (pl) p. 93, 2
(is) made /ˌɪz ˈmeɪd/ (wird) gemacht, (wird) hergestellt NHG 7
magazine /ˌmæɡəˈziːn/ Zeitschrift NHG 7
magic /ˈmædʒɪk/ Magie; Zauber p. 13, 6
magnificent /mæɡˈnɪfɪsnt/ wunderbar; großartig p. 13, 6
main /meɪn/ Haupt- NHG 5
main (course) /ˈmeɪn kɔːs/ Hauptgericht NHG 7
mainly /ˈmeɪnli/ hauptsächlich NHG 7
(to) maintain /meɪnˈteɪn/ erhalten; pflegen p. 73, 6
maintenance /ˈmeɪntənəns/ Pflege; Wartung p. 41, 8
major /ˈmeɪdʒə/ bedeutend, wichtig; Haupt- p. 69, 2

majority /məˈdʒɒrəti/ Mehrheit p. 68, 2
(to) **make** *(irr)* /meɪk/ machen NHG 5
(to) **make** (it/something) *(irr)* /meɪk/ (es/etwas) schaffen p. 83, 2
(to) make *(irr)* /meɪk/ *hier:* ergeben p. 6; *hier:* ausmachen p. 57
(to) **make a difference** *(irr)* /ˌmeɪk ə ˈdɪfrəns/ einen Unterschied machen; verändern p. 85, 5
(to) **make camp** *(irr)* /ˌmeɪk ˈkæmp/ das Lager aufschlagen p. 111, 7
(to) **make friends (with)** *(irr)* /ˌmeɪk ˈfrendz/ sich anfreunden (mit) NHG 6
(to) **make happen** *(irr)* /ˌmeɪk ˈhæpən/ möglich machen p. 25, 7
(to) **make money** *(irr)* /ˌmeɪk ˈmʌni/ Geld verdienen p. 24, 6
(to) **make notes** *(irr)* /ˌmeɪk ˈnəʊts/ sich Notizen machen NHG 5
(to) **make one's dream come true** *(irr)* /ˌmeɪk wʌnz ˈdriːm kʌm ˌtruː/ seinen Traum wahr werden lassen p. 149
(to) **make one's mark** *(irr)* /ˌmeɪk wʌnz ˈmɑːk/ seine Spuren hinterlassen p. 121, 6
(to) **make sense** *(irr)* /ˌmeɪk ˈsens/ sinnvoll sein p. 62, 8
(to) **make somebody do something** *(irr)* /ˌmeɪk ˌsʌmbədi ˈduː ˌsʌmθɪŋ/ jemanden dazu bringen, etwas zu tun NHG 7
(to) **make sure** *(irr)* /ˌmeɪk ˈʃɔː/ darauf achten, dass … NHG 6
(to) **make up** *(irr)* /ˌmeɪk ˈʌp/ erfinden, sich ausdenken NHG 6
making /ˈmeɪkɪŋ/ Herstellung p. 82, 2
man *(pl* **men*)* /mæn, men/ Mann NHG 5; Mensch p. 10, 2
man-made /ˌmæn ˈmeɪd/ künstlich p. 21, 2
(to) **manage** /ˈmænɪdʒ/ zurechtkommen, es schaffen NHG 7; verwalten; organisieren p. 41, 8
manners *(pl)* /ˈmænə/ Manieren p. 95, 7
adverb of manner /ˌædvɜːb əv ˈmænə/ Adverb der Art und Weise p. 70
manuscript /ˈmænjuskrɪpt/ Manuskript p. 120, 6
many /ˈmeni/ viele NHG 5

map /mæp/ Karte NHG 5
March /mɑːtʃ/ März NHG 5
marching band /ˈmɑːtʃɪŋ bænd/ Marschkapelle p. 34, 2
mark /mɑːk/ Note; Zensur NHG 6
(to) **mark** /mɑːk/ markieren, kennzeichnen NHG 7
(to) **make one's mark** *(irr)* /ˌmeɪk wʌnz ˈmɑːk/ seine Spuren hinterlassen p. 121, 6
market /ˈmɑːkɪt/ Markt NHG 5
(to) **market** /ˈmɑːkɪt/ vermarkten p. 41, 8
(to) **be married** *(irr)* /bi ˈmærid/ verheiratet sein NHG 6
(to) **get married** *(irr)* /ˌget ˈmærid/ heiraten NHG 7
(to) **marry** /ˈmæri/ heiraten NHG 7
massive /ˈmæsɪv/ riesig; enorm p. 86, 6
match /mætʃ/ Spiel NHG 5
(to) **match** /mætʃ/ passen zu NHG 6
(to) **match (with/to)** /mætʃ/ zuordnen NHG 5
matching /ˈmætʃɪŋ/ passend p. 43, 14
math *(AE, informal)* /mæθ/ Mathe (Schulfach) p. 39, 6
mathematics /ˌmæθəˈmætɪks/ Mathematik p. 44, 2
mathletics club *(informal)* /mæθˈletɪks klʌb/ Mathe-AG p. 44, 2
maths *(informal)* /mæθ/ Mathe (Schulfach) NHG 5
matter /ˈmætə/ Angelegenheit NHG 7
What's the matter? /ˌwɒts ðə ˈmætə/ Was ist los? NHG 7
(to) **maximize** /ˈmæksɪmaɪz/ maximieren p. 17, 10
May /meɪ/ Mai NHG 5
may /meɪ/ können; dürfen NHG 6
maybe /ˈmeɪbi/ vielleicht NHG 5
me, to me /miː/ mir; mich; ich NHG 5
meal /miːl/ Mahlzeit; Essen NHG 5
mean /miːn/ gemein; bösartig p. 62, 8
(to) **mean** *(irr)* /miːn/ meinen; bedeuten NHG 6
meaning /ˈmiːnɪŋ/ Bedeutung NHG 7
(to) **take measures** *(irr)* /ˌteɪk ˈmeʒəz/ Maßnahmen ergreifen p. 150
meat /miːt/ Fleisch NHG 7
mechanic /mɪˈkænɪk/ Mechaniker/in NHG 6

medal /ˈmedl/ Medaille p. 6
the media /ðə ˈmiːdiə/ die Medien p. 26, 8
social media /ˌsəʊʃl ˈmiːdiə/ soziale Medien p. 69, 2
mediation /ˌmiːdiˈeɪʃn/ Sprachmittlung; Mediation p. 16, 8
medical /ˈmedɪkl/ medizinisch p. 110, 6
medication /ˌmedɪˈkeɪʃn/ Medikamente *(pl)* p. 92, 2
medicine /ˈmedsn/ Medizin; Medikamente NHG 7
medieval /ˌmediˈiːvl/ mittelalterlich p. 121, 6
medium /ˈmiːdiəm/ mittel(groß) NHG 7
(to) **meet** *(irr)* /miːt/ treffen; sich treffen NHG 5; kennenlernen NHG 6
meeting /ˈmiːtɪŋ/ Versammlung; Treffen NHG 6
member /ˈmembə/ Mitglied NHG 5
memorial /məˈmɔːriəl/ Denkmal; Ehrenmal p. 21, 2
memory /ˈmemri/ Erinnerung NHG 7
(to) **mend** /mend/ reparieren; in Ordnung bringen p. 25, 7
(to) **mention** /ˈmenʃn/ erwähnen NHG 7
menu /ˈmenjuː/ Speisekarte; Menü NHG 5
message /ˈmesɪdʒ/ Nachricht; Botschaft NHG 5
(to) **message** /ˈmesɪdʒ/ eine Nachricht schicken p. 68, 2
metal /ˈmetl/ Metall p. 86, 6
method /ˈmeθəd/ Methode NHG 7
metre /ˈmiːtə/ Meter NHG 6
Mexican /ˈmeksɪkən/ Mexikaner/in; mexikanisch p. 27, 10
mid- /mɪd/ Mitte p. 15, 7
middle /ˈmɪdl/ Mitte NHG 5
in the middle of /ˌɪn ðə ˈmɪdl əv/ in der Mitte von; mitten in p. 21, 2
Middle-Eastern /ˌmɪdl ˈiːstən/ Mensch aus dem Nahen Osten; Nahost-; nahöstlich p. 25, 7
might /maɪt/ könnte(st, n, t) NHG 6
mile /maɪl/ Meile NHG 6
military /ˈmɪlɪtri/ militärisch p. 15, 7
milk /mɪlk/ Milch NHG 5
(to) **milk** /mɪlk/ melken p. 111, 7

Dictionary

(to) **mill around** /ˌmɪl_əˈraʊnd/ umherlaufen p. 41, 9
mind /maɪnd/ Geist; Verstand NHG 7
(to) **change one's mind** /ˌtʃeɪndʒ wʌnz ˈmaɪnd/ seine Meinung ändern NHG 6
(to) **come to mind** (irr) /ˌkʌm tə ˈmaɪnd/ einfallen, in den Sinn kommen p. 25, 7
mindlessly /ˈmaɪndləsli/ gedankenlos p. 68, 2
mine /maɪn/ meine(r, s) NHG 7
mineral water /ˈmɪnrəl ˌwɔːtə/ Mineralwasser NHG 7
minimum wage /ˌmɪnɪməm ˈweɪdʒ/ Mindestlohn p. 17, 10
minority /maɪˈnɒrəti/ Minderheit P&P 8
(to) **miss** /mɪs/ vermissen; verpassen NHG 5
(to) **miss out (on)** /ˌmɪs_ˈaʊt_ ɒn/ verpassen, sich entgehen lassen p. 163
missing /ˈmɪsɪŋ/ fehlend NHG 5
mistake /mɪˈsteɪk/ Fehler NHG 7
misunderstanding /ˌmɪsʌndəˈstændɪŋ/ Missverständnis p. 71, 5
(to) **mix** /mɪks/ sich (ver)mischen NHG 6
mixture /ˈmɪkstʃə/ Mischung NHG 7
mobile (phone) /ˈməʊbaɪl/ Handy NHG 6
moccasin /ˈmɒkəsɪn/ Mokassin p. 7
modal verb /ˈməʊdl vɜːb/ Modalverb p. 94
model /ˈmɒdl/ Modell NHG 6
mom (AE) /mɒm/ Mama p. 59, 3
at the moment /ˌæt_ðə ˈməʊmənt/ im Moment P&P 2
(to) **gain momentum** /ˌgeɪn məʊˈmentəm/ in Schwung kommen p. 15, 7
Monday /ˈmʌndeɪ/ Montag NHG 5
(on) Mondays /ˈmʌndeɪz/ montags NHG 5
money /ˈmʌni/ Geld NHG 5
(to) **make money** (irr) /ˌmeɪk ˈmʌni/ Geld verdienen p. 24, 6
pocket money /ˈpɒkɪt ˌmʌni/ Taschengeld NHG 7
month /mʌnθ/ Monat NHG 5
monument /ˈmɒnjəmənt/ Denkmal p. 26, 8

mood /muːd/ Laune; Stimmung NHG 6
moon /muːn/ Mond NHG 5
more /mɔː/ mehr; weitere NHG 5
morning /ˈmɔːnɪŋ/ Morgen NHG 5
mosque /mɒsk/ Moschee NHG 6
most /məʊst/ die meisten; am meisten NHG 7
most of the time /ˌməʊst_əv ðə ˌtaɪm/ meistens NHG 7
mostly /ˈməʊstli/ meistens, größtenteils NHG 7
mother /ˈmʌðə/ Mutter NHG 5
(to) **motivate** /ˈməʊtɪveɪt/ motivieren p. 82, 2
motivation /ˌməʊtɪˈveɪʃn/ Antrieb, Motivation p. 40, 7
mountain /ˈmaʊntɪn/ Berg NHG 5
move /muːv/ Bewegung NHG 5
(to) **move** /muːv/ umziehen NHG 6; (sich) bewegen NHG 7
(to) **move something** /ˈmuːv ˌsʌmθɪŋ/ etwas wegräumen, etwas woanders hinstellen NHG 6
on the move /ˌɒn ðə ˈmuːv/ unterwegs p. 113, 9
movement /ˈmuːvmənt/ Bewegung p. 15, 7
movie (AE) /ˈmuːvi/ Film p. 41, 8
movie theater (AE) /ˈmuːvi ˌθɪətə/ Kino p. 165
moving /ˈmuːvɪŋ/ beweglich NHG 6; bewegend; ergreifend p. 21, 2
(to) **mow** /məʊ/ mähen p. 97, 9
Mr /ˈmɪstə/ Herr (Anrede) NHG 5
Mrs /ˈmɪsɪz/ Frau (Anrede) NHG 5
much /mʌtʃ/ viel NHG 5; sehr NHG 7
multicultural /ˌmʌltiˈkʌltʃərəl/ multikulturell NHG 7
mum /mʌm/ Mama; Mutti NHG 5
(to) **murder** /ˈmɜːdə/ ermorden; umbringen P&P 1
muscle /ˈmʌsl/ Muskel NHG 7
music /ˈmjuːzɪk/ Musik NHG 5
musical /ˈmjuːzɪkl/ musikalisch P&P 2
musician /mjuˈzɪʃn/ Musiker/in NHG 6
Muslim /ˈmʊzləm/ Muslim/in; muslimisch NHG 6
must /mʌst/ müssen NHG 6
must-see /ˌmʌst ˈsiː/ etwas, das man unbedingt sehen muss p. 13, 6
mustn't (= must not) /ˈmʌsnt, ˌmʌst ˈnɒt/ nicht dürfen NHG 6

my /maɪ/ mein(e) NHG 5
myself /maɪˈself/ mir / mich / ich (selbst) NHG 7
mystical /ˈmɪstɪkl/ mystisch p. 119, 5

N

(to) **name** /neɪm/ (be)nennen NHG 5
nasty /ˈnɑːsti/ böse, gemein p. 69, 2
nation /ˈneɪʃn/ Nation; Land; Volk p. 14, 7
national park /ˌnæʃnl ˈpɑːk/ Nationalpark NHG 6
nationality /ˌnæʃəˈnæləti/ Nationalität p. 27, 10
Native American /ˌneɪtɪv_əˈmerɪkən/ Native American (Selbstbezeichnung der ersten Bevölkerungen in den USA) p. 14, 7
natural /ˈnætʃrəl/ natürlich p. 11, 2
nature /ˈneɪtʃə/ Natur NHG 5
Navajo /ˈnævəhəʊ/ Sprache der Navajo p. 82, 2
near /nɪə/ nahe, in der Nähe von NHG 5
nearby /ˌnɪəˈbaɪ/ in der Nähe (gelegen) NHG 7
nearly /ˈnɪəli/ fast; beinahe NHG 7
necessarily /ˈnesəsərəli/ notwendigerweise; unbedingt p. 83, 2
necessary /ˈnesəsri/ notwendig, erforderlich NHG 5
(to) **need** /niːd/ brauchen NHG 5
(to) **need to** /ˈniːd_tʊ/ müssen NHG 5
negative /ˈnegətɪv/ negativ NHG 6
neighbor (AE) /ˈneɪbə/ Nachbar/in p. 95, 7
neighborhood (AE) /ˈneɪbəˌhʊd/ Viertel; Nachbarschaft p. 24, 6
neighbour /ˈneɪbə/ Nachbar/in NHG 7
neighbourhood /ˈneɪbəˌhʊd/ Viertel; Nachbarschaft NHG 5
neither /ˈnaɪðə, ˈniːðə/ auch nicht NHG 7
nervous /ˈnɜːvəs/ nervös NHG 5
net /net/ Netz NHG 5
network /ˈnetwɜːk/ Netzwerk NHG 7
never /ˈnevə/ nie, niemals NHG 5
new /njuː/ neu NHG 5
New Year /ˌnjuːˈjɪə/ Neujahr NHG 6
New Year's Day /ˌnjuː jɪəz ˈdeɪ/ Neujahrstag P&P 4

news *(no pl)* /njuːz/ Neuigkeit; Nachrichten NHG 7
newspaper /ˈnjuːzˌpeɪpə/ Zeitung NHG 6
next /nekst/ nächste(r, s) NHG 5; dann, als Nächstes NHG 6
next to /ˈnekstˌtə/ neben NHG 5
next up *(informal)* /ˌnekstˌˈʌp/ Nächste/r p. 62, 8
nice /naɪs/ schön; nett NHG 5
nickname /ˈnɪkˌneɪm/ Spitzname; Kosename p. 27, 11
night /naɪt/ Nacht; Abend NHG 6
nightlife /ˈnaɪtlaɪf/ Nachtleben p. 120, 6
nightmare /ˈnaɪtˌmeə/ Albtraum p. 121, 6
9 / 11 /ˌnaɪnˌɪˈlevn/ *Terrorangriffe am 11. September 2001* p. 25, 7
no /nəʊ/ kein(e); nein NHG 5
no longer /ˌnəʊ ˈlɒŋgə/ nicht mehr NHG 7
no one /ˈnəʊ wʌn/ keiner NHG 6
nobody /ˈnəʊbədi/ niemand; keiner NHG 7
noise /nɔɪz/ Geräusch; Lärm NHG 6
noisy /ˈnɔɪzi/ laut p. 20, 1
non- /nɒn/ nicht p. 117, 2
non-profit /ˌnɒn ˈprɒfɪt/ nicht gewinnorientiert p. 86, 6
non-stop /ˌnɒn ˈstɒp/ ununterbrochen p. 76, 12
noon /nuːn/ Mittag p. 10, 2
normally /ˈnɔːmli/ normalerweise NHG 7
north /nɔːθ/ Norden; Nord- NHG 7
North America /ˌnɔːθ əˈmerɪkə/ Nordamerika p. 10, 2
northern /ˈnɔːðən/ nördlich, Nord- NHG 6
Northern Ireland /ˌnɔːðənˈaɪələnd/ Nordirland P&P 8
northernmost /ˈnɔːðənˌməʊst/ nördlichste(r, s) p. 13, 6
nose /nəʊz/ Nase NHG 5
not /nɒt/ nicht NHG 5
not any /ˌnɒtˌˈeni/ kein(e) NHG 5
not anymore /ˌnɒtˌeni ˈmɔː/ nicht mehr NHG 6
not anyone /ˌnɒtˌˈeniwʌn/ niemand NHG 7
not anything /ˌnɒtˌˈeniθɪŋ/ nichts NHG 6

not anywhere /ˌnɒtˌˈeniˌweə/ nirgendwo NHG 6
not at all /ˌnɒtˌətˌˈɔːl/ überhaupt nicht NHG 7
not ... either /ˌnɒtˌˈaɪðə/ auch nicht NHG 7
not yet /nɒt ˈjet/ noch nicht NHG 6
note /nəʊt/ Nachricht; Notiz NHG 5
(to) note /nəʊt/ beachten, zur Kenntnis nehmen NHG 6
notepad /ˈnəʊtˌpæd/ Notizblock NHG 5
(to) make notes *(irr)* /ˌmeɪk ˈnəʊts/ sich Notizen machen NHG 5
nothing /ˈnʌθɪŋ/ nichts NHG 6
(to) notice /ˈnəʊtɪs/ bemerken; wahrnehmen NHG 6
noticeboard /ˈnəʊtɪsˌbɔːd/ Schwarzes Brett NHG 5
notorious /nəʊˈtɔːriəs/ berüchtigt p. 121, 6
noun /naʊn/ Hauptwort; Substantiv; Nomen NHG 5
November /nəʊˈvembə/ November NHG 5
now /naʊ/ jetzt NHG 5
nowadays /ˈnaʊəˌdeɪz/ heutzutage p. 71, 5
nowhere /ˈnəʊweə/ nirgends; nirgendwo p. 111, 7
number /ˈnʌmbə/ Zahl; Nummer; Anzahl NHG 5
phone number /ˈfəʊn ˌnʌmbə/ Telefonnummer NHG 5
a number of /ə ˈnʌmbərˌəv/ einige, ein paar p. 93, 2
nurse /nɜːs/ Krankenschwester; Krankenpfleger NHG 6
registered nurse /ˌredʒɪstəd ˈnɜːs/ examinierte Krankenschwester/ examinierter Krankenpfleger p. 92, 2
nursery teacher /ˈnɜːsəri ˌtiːtʃə/ Vorschullehrer/in; Erzieher/in p. 92, 1
NYC (= New York City) /ˌen waɪ ˈsiː, ˌnjuː jɔːk ˈsɪti/ *die Stadt New York* p. 25, 7

O

o'clock /əˈklɒk/ Uhr *(bei Nennung einer Uhrzeit)* NHG 5

object /ˈɒbdʒekt/ Gegenstand NHG 6
obligatory /əˈblɪgətri/ verpflichtend P&P 3
obstacle /ˈɒbstəkl/ Hindernis; Hürde p. 89, 9
occasion /əˈkeɪʒn/ Gelegenheit; Anlass NHG 7
October /ɒkˈtəʊbə/ Oktober NHG 5
of /əv/ von; aus NHG 5
Of course! /əv ˈkɔːs/ Natürlich! NHG 5
off /ɒf/ von; hinunter, herunter NHG 6
offensive /əˈfensɪv/ beleidigend, ausfallend p. 73, 6
(to) offer /ˈɒfə/ anbieten NHG 6
special offer /ˌspeʃlˈɒfə/ Sonderangebot p. 26, 8
offer /ˈɒfə/ Angebot p. 115, 14
office /ˈɒfɪs/ Büro NHG 5
office manager /ˈɒfɪs ˌmænɪdʒə/ Sekretär/in NHG 7
officer /ˈɒfɪsə/ Beamter/Beamtin P&P 7
official /əˈfɪʃl/ Amtsperson p. 110, 6
official, officially /əˈfɪʃl, əˈfɪʃli/ offiziell NHG 7
often /ˈɒfn/ oft; häufig NHG 5
oil /ɔɪl/ Öl NHG 7
old /əʊld/ alt NHG 5
Olympic /əˈlɪmpɪk/ olympisch p. 6
on /ɒn/ auf; an; in NHG 5
on /ɒn/ *hier:* über p. 65, 12
on a larger scale /ˌɒnˌə ˌlɑːdʒə ˈskeɪl/ im größeren Rahmen p. 85, 5
on board /ˌɒn ˈbɔːd/ an Bord p. 121, 6
on one's own /ˌɒnˌwʌnzˌˈəʊn/ allein NHG 5
on the left /ˌɒn ðə ˈleft/ links, auf der linken Seite NHG 5
on the move /ˌɒn ðə ˈmuːv/ unterwegs p. 113, 9
on the one hand, ... /ˌɒn ðə ˈwʌn hænd/ einerseits ... NHG 7
on the other hand, ... /ˌɒn ðiˌˈʌðə hænd/ andererseits ... NHG 7
on the right /ˌɒn ðə ˈraɪt/ rechts, auf der rechten Seite NHG 5
on the weekends *(AE)* /ˌɒn ðə ˈwiːkendz/ an den Wochenenden p. 97, 9
on time /ˌɒn ˈtaɪm/ pünktlich NHG 5
on-the-job training /ˌɒn ðə ˌdʒɒb ˈtreɪnɪŋ/ Ausbildung am Arbeitsplatz P&P 6

Dictionary

once /wʌns/ einmal NHG 7; sobald; wenn, als p. 34, 2
one /wʌn/ ein(e); eins NHG 5; eine(r, s) NHG 7
a different one /ə ˈdɪfrənt wʌn/ ein anderer/eine andere/ein anderes p. 40, 7
one day /ˌwʌn ˈdeɪ/ eines Tages p. 117, 2
one-minute /ˌwʌnˈmɪnɪt/ einminütig p. 16, 9
the ones /ðə ˈwʌnz/ diejenigen; diese p. 38, 6
onion /ˈʌnjən/ Zwiebel NHG 7
only /ˈəʊnli/ nur, bloß; erst; einzige(r, s) NHG 5
onto /ˈɒntə/ auf, in NHG 6
from … onwards /ˌfrəm …ˈɒnwədz/ von … an P&P 7
open /ˈəʊpən/ offen; geöffnet NHG 5
(to) open /ˈəʊpən/ öffnen; aufmachen NHG 5; sich öffnen, aufgehen; eröffnen NHG 6
job opening /ˈdʒɒbˌəʊpənɪŋ/ freie Stelle p. 97, 9
opening act /ˈəʊpənɪŋ ˌækt/ Eröffnungsfeier p. 48, 7
Opening Day /ˈəʊpənɪŋ deɪ/ Eröffnungstag P&P 4
opening times *(pl)* /ˈəʊpənɪŋ taɪmz/ Öffnungszeiten NHG 6
(to) operate /ˈɒpəreɪt/ bedienen p. 93, 2
opinion /əˈpɪnjən/ Meinung; Ansicht NHG 6
in my opinion /ɪn ˈmaɪˌəˌpɪnjən/ meiner Meinung nach NHG 6
opportunity /ˌɒpəˈtjuːnəti/ Chance; Möglichkeit; Gelegenheit p. 17, 10
opposite /ˈɒpəzɪt/ Gegenteil NHG 5
option /ˈɒpʃn/ Wahlmöglichkeit NHG 7
optional /ˈɒpʃnəl/ optional, fakultativ P&P 3
or /ɔː/ oder NHG 5
orange /ˈɒrɪndʒ/ Orange; Apfelsine; orange NHG 5
order /ˈɔːdə/ Reihenfolge; Ordnung NHG 6
in order to /ɪnˈɔːdə tʊ/ um zu NHG 7
(to) take an order *(irr)* /ˌteɪk ən ˈɔːdə/ eine Bestellung aufnehmen NHG 7

(to) order (in) /ˈɔːdə, ˈɔːdərˌɪn/ bestellen NHG 7
organic /ɔːˈɡænɪk/ aus biologischem Anbau, Bio- p. 11, 2
organization (= organisation) /ˌɔːɡənaɪˈzeɪʃn/ Organisation; Vereinigung p. 86, 6
organizational (= organisational) /ˌɔːɡənaɪˈzeɪʃnəl/ organisatorisch p. 96, 8
(to) organize (= organise) /ˈɔːɡənaɪz/ organisieren NHG 6
origin /ˈɒrɪdʒɪn/ Ursprung; Herkunft p. 17, 10
original /əˈrɪdʒnəl/ originell, außergewöhnlich p. 93, 2
original, originally /əˈrɪdʒnəl, əˈrɪdʒnəli/ ursprünglich NHG 7
(to) originate /əˈrɪdʒəneɪt/ entstehen, seinen Anfang nehmen p. 7
the Oscars /ðɪ ˈɒskəz/ amerikanischer Filmpreis p. 6
other /ˈʌðə/ andere(r, s) NHG 5
otherwise /ˈʌðəwaɪz/ sonst, im Übrigen NHG 7
our /aʊə/ unser(e) NHG 5
ours /aʊəz/ unsere(r, s) NHG 7
ourselves /aʊəˈselvz/ uns; wir selbst NHG 7
out /aʊt/ heraus, hinaus; aus NHG 5; draußen NHG 6
out of /ˈaʊt ˌəv/ aus NHG 6; von p. 62, 8
outdoor /ˌaʊtˈdɔː/ Outdoor-, im Freien NHG 7
outdoors /ˌaʊtˈdɔːz/ draußen; im Freien NHG 7
outer space /ˌaʊtə ˈspeɪs/ Weltraum p. 10, 2
output /ˈaʊtpʊt/ Ausstoß; Produktion p. 85, 5
outside /ˌaʊtˈsaɪd/ außen; (nach) draußen NHG 5
(to) outweigh /ˌaʊtˈweɪ/ überwiegen p. 73, 6
over /ˈəʊvə/ über, hinüber; vorbei NHG 5
all over the world /ˌɔːl ˌəʊvə ðə ˈwɜːld/ auf der ganzen Welt NHG 6
over here /ˌəʊvə ˈhɪə/ hier (drüben) p. 38, 6
over there /ˌəʊvə ˈðeə/ dort (drüben) NHG 5

overboard /ˈəʊvəbɔːd/ über Bord p. 108, 3
(to) overcome *(irr)* /ˌəʊvəˈkʌm/ bewältigen; überwinden p. 83, 2
overcrowded /ˌəʊvəˈkraʊdɪd/ überfüllt p. 106, 2
(to) overload /ˌəʊvəˈləʊd/ überladen p. 101, 17
overnight /ˌəʊvəˈnaɪt/ über Nacht p. 147
own /əʊn/ eigene(r, s) NHG 5
(to) own /əʊn/ besitzen NHG 7
on one's own /ˌɒn ˌwʌnz ˈəʊn/ allein NHG 5
owner /ˈəʊnə/ Besitzer/in NHG 7
ox *(pl* oxen*)* /ɒks, ˈɒksn/ Ochse p. 110, 6

P

p. (= page) /peɪdʒ/ Seite p. 10, 1
p (= penny, *pl* **pence)** /piː, ˈpeni, pens/ Penny *(brit. Währung)* NHG 5
Pacific, Pacific Ocean /pəˈsɪfɪk, pəˌsɪfɪk ˈəʊʃn/ Pazifik, Pazifischer Ozean p. 15, 7
(to) pack /pæk/ packen NHG 5
packaging /ˈpækɪdʒɪŋ/ Verpackung NHG 7
packet /ˈpækɪt/ Packung NHG 5
page /peɪdʒ/ Seite NHG 5
painfully /ˈpeɪnfli/ schmerzlich p. 64, 9
(to) paint /peɪnt/ (an)malen NHG 5
painting /ˈpeɪntɪŋ/ Bild; Gemälde NHG 5
pair /peə/ Paar NHG 6
(a pair of) trousers /əˌpeər ˌəv ˈtraʊzəz/ Hose NHG 5
pajama day *(AE)* /pəˈdʒɑːmə deɪ/ *Schlafanzugtag* p. 43, 14
pajamas *(AE)* = pyjamas *(BE)* /pəˈdʒɑːməz/ *Schlafanzug* p. 43, 14
palace /ˈpæləs/ Palast NHG 6
Pancake Day /ˈpænkeɪk deɪ/ Pfannkuchentag p. 6
paper /ˈpeɪpə/ Papier NHG 6
piece of paper /ˌpiːs ˌəv ˈpeɪpə/ Blatt Papier p. 40, 7
paper boy /ˈpeɪpə bɔɪ/ Zeitungsjunge p. 97, 9
paraclimber /ˈpærəˌklaɪmə/ *Kletterer / Kletterin mit Handicap* p. 83, 2

paragraph /ˈpærəˌgrɑːf/ Absatz; Abschnitt NHG 6
Paraguayan /ˌpærəˈgwaɪən/ Paraguayaner/in; paraguayisch p. 162
Paralympic /ˌpærəˈlɪmpɪk/ paralympisch p. 83, 2
parent /ˈpeərənt/ Elternteil NHG 7
parents *(pl)* /ˈpeərənts/ Eltern NHG 5
(to) **build a park** *(irr)* /ˌbɪld ə ˈpɑːk/ einen Park anlegen p. 21, 2
parking lot *(AE)* /ˈpɑːkɪŋ lɒt/ Parkplatz p. 47, 6
parliament /ˈpɑːləmənt/ Parlament NHG 6
part /pɑːt/ Teil NHG 5; Rolle NHG 7
particular /pəˈtɪkjʊlə/ bestimmt; besondere(r, s) p. 66, 14
particularly /pəˈtɪkjʊləli/ besonders; vor allem NHG 7
(to) **party** /ˈpɑːti/ feiern p. 35, 2
(to) **pass** /pɑːs/ geben, herüberreichen NHG 5; bestehen P&P 7
(to) **pass** /pɑːs/ *hier:* durchgehen p. 25, 7
(to) **pass away** /ˌpɑːs əˈweɪ/ verbringen p. 122, 7
(to) **pass through** /ˌpɑːs ˈθruː/ durchreisen; durchlaufen P&P 7
passage /ˈpæsɪdʒ/ (Text)passage; Gang; Überfahrt p. 17, 10
passenger /ˈpæsɪndʒə/ Passagier/in NHG 7
passionate /ˈpæʃnət/ leidenschaftlich p. 26, 8
(to) **be passionate about** *(irr)* /ˌbi ˈpæʃnət əˌbaʊt/ für etwas brennen p. 93, 2
passive /ˈpæsɪv/ Passiv p. 28, 12
password /ˈpɑːsˌwɜːd/ Passwort NHG 7
past /pɑːst/ nach; Vergangenheit NHG 5; vorbei; vorüber NHG 6; vergangen; frühere(r, s) p. 34, 2
past perfect /ˌpɑːst ˈpɜːfɪkt/ Plusquamperfekt; Vorvergangenheit p. 36
past progressive /ˌpɑːst prəʊˈgresɪv/ Verlaufsform der Vergangenheit p. 114, 11
pasta /ˈpæstə/ Nudeln NHG 7
path /pɑːθ/ Weg; Pfad NHG 5
patience /ˈpeɪʃns/ Geduld p. 85, 5
patient /ˈpeɪʃnt/ geduldig p. 97, 9

pattern /ˈpætən/ Muster p. 48, 7
pay /peɪ/ Lohn p. 97, 9
(to) **pay** /peɪ/ (be)zahlen NHG 5
(to) **pay attention (to)** *(irr)* /ˌpeɪ əˈtenʃn tʊ/ aufpassen; achten auf NHG 6
payment /ˈpeɪmənt/ Bezahlung NHG 6
PE (= Physical Education) /ˌpiː ˈiː, ˌfɪzɪkl ˌedjʊˈkeɪʃn/ Sport *(Schulfach)* NHG 5
peace /piːs/ Frieden NHG 7
peaceful /ˈpiːsfl/ friedlich; friedfertig NHG 7
(to) **peak** /piːk/ den Höhepunkt erreichen p. 109, 5
peak /piːk/ Gipfel; Bergspitze p. 10, 2
peer /pɪə/ Gleichaltrige/r p. 19, 13
pen /pen/ Stift NHG 5
pencil /ˈpensl/ Bleistift NHG 5
pencil case /ˈpensl ˌkeɪs/ Federmäppchen NHG 5
pencil sharpener /ˈpensl ˌʃɑːpnə/ Bleistiftspitzer NHG 5
peninsula /pəˈnɪnsjələ/ Halbinsel p. 119, 5
people /ˈpiːpl/ Leute; Menschen NHG 5
peoples *(pl)* /ˈpiːplz/ Völker p. 25, 7
pepper /ˈpepə/ Paprika; Pfeffer NHG 7
per /pɜː/ pro NHG 5
per cent *(BE)*, **percent** *(AE)* /pəˈsent/ Prozent p. 109, 5
perfect /ˈpɜːfɪkt/ perfekt NHG 5
(to) **perform** /pəˈfɔːm/ aufführen; durchführen NHG 6
performance /pəˈfɔːməns/ Aufführung; Leistung NHG 6
period *(AE)* /ˈpɪəriəd/ Stunde p. 39, 6
period (of time) /ˌpɪəriəd əv ˈtaɪm/ Zeitspanne; Zeitraum p. 62, 8
permission /pəˈmɪʃn/ Erlaubnis; Genehmigung NHG 6
in person /ˌɪn ˈpɜːsn/ persönlich p. 72, 6
personal /ˈpɜːsnəl/ persönlich NHG 5
personality /ˌpɜːsəˈnæləti/ Persönlichkeit p. 95, 7
pet /pet/ Haustier NHG 5
petition /pəˈtɪʃn/ Petition; Unterschriftenliste p. 85, 5
phone /fəʊn/ Telefon NHG 5

cell phone *(AE)* /ˈsel fəʊn/ Handy p. 68, 2
phone call /ˈfəʊn kɔːl/ Telefonanruf p. 72, 6
phone number /ˈfəʊn ˌnʌmbə/ Telefonnummer NHG 5
photo /ˈfəʊtəʊ/ Foto NHG 5
(to) **take a photo** *(irr)* /ˌteɪk ə ˈfəʊtəʊ/ ein Foto machen NHG 5
photograph /ˈfəʊtəˌgrɑːf/ Fotografie; Foto NHG 6
photographer /fəˈtɒgrəfə/ Fotograf/in NHG 6
photography /fəˈtɒgrəfi/ Fotografie p. 26, 8
phrase /freɪz/ Satz; Ausdruck NHG 5
physical /ˈfɪzɪkl/ körperlich NHG 7
physically /ˈfɪzɪkli/ physisch p. 72, 6
physiotherapist /ˌfɪziəʊˈθerəpɪst/ Physiotherapeut/in p. 92, 1
piano /piˈænəʊ/ Klavier NHG 5
(to) **pick up** /ˌpɪk ˈʌp/ aufheben; abholen NHG 5
(to) **pick up (on)** /ˌpɪk ˈʌp/ anknüpfen an p. 62, 8
picture /ˈpɪktʃə/ Bild NHG 5
(to) **take a picture** *(irr)* /ˌteɪk ə ˈpɪktʃə/ ein Foto machen NHG 5
pie /paɪ/ Pastete; Kuchen p. 37, 5
pie chart /ˈpaɪ tʃɑːt/ Tortendiagramm, Kuchendiagramm p. 171
piece /piːs/ Stück; Teil NHG 6
piece of advice /ˌpiːs əv ədˈvaɪs/ Rat(schlag) NHG 7
piece of paper /ˌpiːs əv ˈpeɪpə/ Blatt Papier p. 40, 7
pilgrim /ˈpɪlgrɪm/ Pilger/in p. 14, 7
pillow /ˈpɪləʊ/ Kissen p. 68, 2
pitcher /ˈpɪtʃə/ Werfer/in p. 44, 2
place /pleɪs/ Ort; Platz; Haus, Zuhause NHG 5
(to) **place** /pleɪs/ platzieren; stellen NHG 5
(to) **take place** *(irr)* /ˌteɪk ˈpleɪs/ stattfinden NHG 6
plains *(pl)* /pleɪnz/ Ebene; Flachland p. 111, 7
(to) **plan** /plæn/ planen NHG 5
plane /pleɪn/ Flugzeug NHG 6
planning /ˈplænɪŋ/ Planen p. 93, 2
plant /plɑːnt/ Pflanze NHG 6
(to) **plant** /plɑːnt/ pflanzen p. 111, 7

Dictionary

recycling plant /riːˈsaɪklɪŋ plɑːnt/ Recyclinganlage p. 86, 6
plaster /ˈplɑːstə/ Gips; Pflaster NHG 7
plaster /ˈplɑːstə/ Verputz p. 65, 12
plastic /ˈplæstɪk/ Plastik NHG 6
plate /pleɪt/ Teller NHG 5
platform /ˈplætˌfɔːm/ Bahnsteig; Plattform NHG 6
play /pleɪ/ Spiel; (Theater)stück NHG 6
(to) play /pleɪ/ spielen NHG 5
player /ˈpleɪə/ Spieler/in NHG 5
playground /ˈpleɪˌɡraʊnd/ Spielplatz NHG 5
playing /ˈpleɪɪŋ/ Spielen NHG 5
playing field /ˈpleɪɪŋ ˌfiːld/ Sportplatz p. 48, 7
please /pliːz/ bitte NHG 5
(to) pledge /pledʒ/ versprechen; schwören p. 38, 6
Pledge of Allegiance /ˌpledʒ ˌəv əˈliːdʒns/ Treueschwur p. 38, 6
plenty of /ˈplentɪ ˌəv/ reichlich; genug p. 72, 6
plumbing /ˈplʌmɪŋ/ Klempnern p. 40, 7
pm (= post meridiem) /ˌpiː ˈem, ˌpəʊst məˈrɪdiəm/ nachmittags; abends (hinter Uhrzeit zwischen 12 Uhr mittags und Mitternacht) NHG 5
pocket /ˈpɒkɪt/ (Hosen)tasche NHG 7
pocket money /ˈpɒkɪt ˌmʌni/ Taschengeld NHG 7
poem /ˈpəʊɪm/ Gedicht NHG 5
poet /ˈpəʊɪt/ Dichter/in NHG 7
point /pɔɪnt/ Punkt NHG 5; Stelle p. 86, 6
(to) point (at/to) /pɔɪnt/ deuten (auf); zeigen (auf) NHG 5
point of view /ˌpɔɪnt ˌəv ˈvjuː/ Ansicht; Perspektive p. 59, 3
poisonous /ˈpɔɪznəs/ giftig p. 110, 6
Poland /ˈpəʊlənd/ Polen NHG 5
police officer /pəˈliːs ˌɒfɪsə/ Polizeibeamter/Polizeibeamtin NHG 6
Polish /ˈpəʊlɪʃ/ Polnisch; polnisch p. 117, 2
polite /pəˈlaɪt/ höflich NHG 6
politeness /pəˈlaɪtnəs/ Höflichkeit p. 95, 7
political /pəˈlɪtɪkl/ politisch p. 14, 7

politician /ˌpɒləˈtɪʃn/ Politiker/in p. 11, 2
pollution /pəˈluːʃn/ Umweltverschmutzung p. 86, 6
poor /pɔː/ arm NHG 6; schlecht P&P 1
popular /ˈpɒpjʊlə/ beliebt NHG 6
population /ˌpɒpjʊˈleɪʃn/ Bevölkerung NHG 7
(to) portray /pɔːˈtreɪ/ porträtieren, darstellen p. 71, 5
positive /ˈpɒzətɪv/ positiv NHG 6
positive /ˈpɒzətɪv/ Pluspunkt p. 72, 6
possibility /ˌpɒsəˈbɪləti/ Möglichkeit NHG 6
possible /ˈpɒsəbl/ möglich NHG 7
(to) post /pəʊst/ posten; bekannt geben NHG 6
postcard /ˈpəʊstˌkɑːd/ Postkarte NHG 5
pot /pɒt/ Topf NHG 7
potato blight /pəˈteɪtəʊ blaɪt/ Kartoffelfäule p. 106, 2
the potato famine /ðə pəˈteɪtəʊ ˌfæmɪn/ Hungersnot in Irland zwischen 1845 und 1849 p. 121, 6
potato (pl potatoes) /pəˈteɪtəʊ, pəˈteɪtəʊz/ Kartoffel NHG 7
potential /pəˈtenʃl/ potenziell, möglich p. 86, 6
pound (= £) /paʊnd/ Pfund (britische Währung) NHG 5
power /ˈpaʊə/ Kraft NHG 7; Macht; Einfluss p. 81
(to) power /ˈpaʊə/ antreiben p. 86, 6
powerful /ˈpaʊəfl/ mächtig, stark p. 85, 5
practical /ˈpræktɪkl/ praktisch NHG 7
practice /ˈpræktɪs/ Übung; Training NHG 6; Praxis NHG 7
(to) practice (AE) /ˈpræktɪs/ üben; trainieren; praktizieren p. 35, 2
(to) practise /ˈpræktɪs/ üben; trainieren NHG 5
prayer /preə/ Gebet NHG 6
precise /prɪˈsaɪs/ genau; präzise p. 101, 17
(to) prefer /prɪˈfɜː/ vorziehen; bevorzugen NHG 7
prefix /ˈpriːfɪks/ Vorsilbe; Präfix p. 76, 13
prepaid /ˌpriːˈpeɪd/ im Voraus bezahlt p. 106, 2
preparation /ˌprepəˈreɪʃn/ Vorbereitung; Zubereitung p. 41, 8

(to) prepare /prɪˈpeə/ vorbereiten NHG 5; zubereiten NHG 7
(to) prepare for /prɪˈpeə fɔː/ sich vorbereiten auf NHG 7
(to) prescribe /prɪˈskraɪb/ verschreiben p. 92, 2
presence /ˈprezns/ Anwesenheit; Präsenz p. 15, 7
present /ˈpreznt/ Geschenk NHG 5; Gegenwart NHG 6
present perfect /ˌpreznt ˈpɜːfɪkt/ Perfekt p. 22
present perfect progressive /ˌpreznt ˌpɜːfɪkt prəˈɡresɪv/ Verlaufsform des Perfekt p. 118
(to) present (to) /prɪˈzent/ präsentieren, vorstellen NHG 5
presentation /ˌpreznˈteɪʃn/ Präsentation; Vortrag NHG 5
(to) give a presentation (irr) /ˌɡɪv ˌə ˌpreznˈteɪʃn/ eine Präsentation halten NHG 7
(to) preserve /prɪˈzɜːv/ erhalten p. 11, 2
president /ˈprezɪdənt/ Präsident/in p. 6
pressure /ˈpreʃə/ Druck NHG 7
pretty /ˈprɪti/ ziemlich NHG 5; hübsch p. 25, 7
(to) prevent /prɪˈvent/ verhindern, vorbeugen NHG 7
previous /ˈpriːviəs/ vorig, vorausgegangen p. 34, 2
price /praɪs/ Preis (Kosten) NHG 7
primary school /ˈpraɪməri skuːl/ Grundschule p. 45, 2
principal (AE) /ˈprɪnsəpl/ Rektor/in P&P 5
(to) print /prɪnt/ drucken NHG 7
print /prɪnt/ Druck p. 26, 8
prize /praɪz/ Preis; Gewinn NHG 7
prizefighter /ˈpraɪzˌfaɪtə/ Preisboxer/in p. 25, 7
pro /prəʊ/ Vorteil; Pro NHG 6
probably /ˈprɒbəbli/ wahrscheinlich NHG 6
process /ˈprəʊses/ Prozess; Verfahren NHG 7
processing /ˈprəʊsesɪŋ/ Bearbeiten p. 41, 8
(to) produce /prəˈdjuːs/ herstellen NHG 6; produzieren NHG 7

produce /ˈprɒdjuːs/ Obst und Gemüse p. 151
producer /prəˈdjuːsə/ Produzent/in p. 148
product /ˈprɒdʌkt/ Produkt p. 41, 8
production /prəˈdʌkʃn/ Produktion NHG 7
profession /prəˈfeʃn/ Beruf p. 99, 13
professional /prəˈfeʃnəl/ professionell; beruflich p. 48, 7
profile /ˈprəʊfaɪl/ Profil; Porträt NHG 7
(to) **program** /ˈprəʊɡræm/ programmieren p. 40, 7
program /ˈprəʊɡræm/ Computerprogramm p. 95, 7
program (AE) /ˈprəʊɡræm/ Programm p. 34, 2
programme /ˈprəʊɡræm/ Programm NHG 6
programming /ˈprəʊˌɡræmɪŋ/ Programmieren p. 95, 7
progress /ˈprəʊɡres/ Fortschritt p. 97, 9
project /ˈprɒdʒekt/ Projekt NHG 6
prom (AE) /prɒm/ Ball am Ende des Jahres in einer amerikanischen Highschool p. 35, 2
prom king (AE) /ˈprɒm kɪŋ/ Ballkönig p. 35, 2
prom queen (AE) /ˈprɒm kwiːn/ Ballkönigin p. 35, 2
(to) **promise** /ˈprɒmɪs/ versprechen NHG 7
promise /ˈprɒmɪs/ Versprechen p. 89, 9
pronoun /ˈprəʊnaʊn/ Pronomen, Fürwort p. 52, 12
reflexive pronoun /rɪˌfleksɪv ˈprəʊnaʊn/ Reflexivpronomen p. 52, 12
(to) **pronounce** /prəˈnaʊns/ aussprechen NHG 6
proof /pruːf/ Beweis p. 69, 2
prop /prɒp/ Requisite NHG 7
proper /ˈprɒpə/ richtig p. 93, 2
properly /ˈprɒpəli/ richtig NHG 7
(to) **protect** /prəˈtekt/ beschützen NHG 6
(to) **protect (from)** /prəˈtekt frəm/ schützen (vor) p. 73, 6
protestant /ˈprɒtɪstənt/ Protestant/in P&P 8
proud, proudly /praʊd, ˈpraʊdli/ stolz NHG 6

(to) **be proud of** (irr) /ˌbiː ˈpraʊd əv/ stolz sein auf p. 24, 6
(to) **prove** (irr) /pruːv/ beweisen NHG 7
(to) **provide** /prəˈvaɪd/ zur Verfügung stellen p. 11, 2
(to) **provide with** /prəˈvaɪd wɪð/ versorgen mit; versehen mit p. 41, 8
psychologist /saɪˈkɒlədʒɪst/ Psychologe/Psychologin p. 62, 8
pub /pʌb/ Kneipe NHG 7
public /ˈpʌblɪk/ öffentlich NHG 6
the public /ðə ˈpʌblɪk/ die Öffentlichkeit NHG 6
public transport /ˌpʌblɪk ˈtrænspɔːt/ öffentliche Verkehrsmittel p. 85, 5
(to) **publish** /ˈpʌblɪʃ/ veröffentlichen; herausgeben NHG 6
(to) **pull** /pʊl/ ziehen NHG 7
pumpkin /ˈpʌmpkɪn/ Kürbis NHG 6
(to) **punch** /pʌntʃ/ schlagen p. 123, 8
pupil /ˈpjuːpl/ Schüler/in NHG 7
(to) **purchase** /ˈpɜːtʃəs/ kaufen; erwerben p. 86, 6
purple /ˈpɜːpl/ violett; lila NHG 5
(to) **push** /pʊʃ/ schieben; stoßen NHG 6
(to) **put** (irr) /pʊt/ setzen; stellen; legen NHG 5
(to) **put emphasis on** (irr) /ˌpʊt ˈemfəsɪs ɒn/ Wert legen auf p. 11, 2
(to) **put in** (irr) /ˌpʊt ˈɪn/ hineintun, hinzufügen NHG 7
(to) **put on** (irr) /ˌpʊt ˈɒn/ anlegen; auftragen; anziehen (Kleidung) NHG 7
(to) **put on display** (irr) /ˌpʊt ɒn dɪˈspleɪ/ ausstellen NHG 6
(to) **put together** (irr) /ˌpʊt təˈɡeðə/ zusammenstellen; zusammensetzen NHG 6
(to) **put up** (irr) /ˌpʊt ˈʌp/ aufhängen; aufstellen NHG 6

Q

qualification /ˌkwɒlɪfɪˈkeɪʃn/ Qualifikation p. 82, 2
qualified /ˈkwɒlɪfaɪd/ qualifiziert; ausgebildet p. 63, 8
quality /ˈkwɒləti/ Qualität NHG 7
quarter /ˈkwɔːtə/ Viertel NHG 5
queen /kwiːn/ Königin NHG 6
question /ˈkwestʃn/ Frage NHG 5

(to) **question** /ˈkwestʃn/ befragen; verhören p. 110, 6
follow-up question /ˈfɒləʊ ʌp ˌkwestʃn/ Folgefrage p. 22, 4
question mark /ˈkwestʃn mɑːk/ Fragezeichen p. 73, 6
quick /kwɪk/ schnell, kurz NHG 7
quickly /ˈkwɪkli/ schnell NHG 6
quiet /ˈkwaɪət/ leise; ruhig NHG 5
quite /kwaɪt/ ziemlich NHG 6
quota /ˈkwəʊtə/ Quote p. 109, 5
quote /kwəʊt/ Zitat p. 17, 10
(to) **quote** /kwəʊt/ zitieren NHG 7

R

rabbit /ˈræbɪt/ Kaninchen NHG 5
race /reɪs/ Rennen NHG 7
racial segregation /ˌreɪʃl seɡrɪˈɡeɪʃn/ Rassentrennung p. 15, 7
(from) **rags to riches** /frəm ˌræɡz tə ˈrɪtʃɪz/ (vom) Tellerwäscher zum Millionär p. 17, 10
railroad /ˈreɪlˌrəʊd/ hier: Eisenbahngelände p. 23, 5
rain /reɪn/ Regen NHG 6
(to) **rain** /reɪn/ regnen NHG 5
rainy /ˈreɪni/ regnerisch NHG 5
(to) **raise** /reɪz/ beschaffen; sammeln p. 35, 2
(to) **raise awareness** /ˌreɪz əˈweənəz/ Bewusstsein schärfen p. 83, 2
(to) **raise funds** /ˌreɪz ˈfʌndz/ Geld sammeln P&P 5
(to) **rank** /ræŋk/ einstufen; anordnen p. 17, 10
rare /reə/ selten p. 62, 8
(to) **rate** /reɪt/ einschätzen; bewerten NHG 7
rather /ˈrɑːðə/ eher, lieber NHG 6
rather than /ˈrɑːðə ðæn/ anstatt NHG 6
Rd (= road) /rəʊd/ Straße p. 98, 10
RE (= Religious Education) /ˌɑːr ˈiː, reˌlɪdʒəs ˌedjʊˈkeɪʃn/ Religion (Schulfach) NHG 5
(to) **reach** /riːtʃ/ erreichen NHG 7
(to) **be far from reach** (irr) /ˌbiː ˌfɑː frəm ˈriːtʃ/ außer Reichweite sein p. 68, 2
(to) **react (to)** /riˈækt/ reagieren (auf) NHG 6
reaction /riˈækʃn/ Reaktion NHG 6

Dictionary

(to) **read** *(irr)* /riːd/ lesen NHG 5
read /riːd/ Lektüre p. 34, 2
(to) **read along** *(irr)* /ˌriːd_əˈlɒŋ/ mitlesen NHG 5
(to) **read out** *(irr)* /ˌriːd_ˈaʊt/ (laut) vorlesen p. 67, 15
reader /ˈriːdə/ Leser/in p. 34, 2
reading /ˈriːdɪŋ/ Lesen NHG 5; Lesung NHG 7
ready /ˈredi/ fertig, bereit NHG 5
real /rɪəl/ wirklich; echt NHG 6
realistic /ˌrɪəˈlɪstɪk/ realistisch p. 149
reality /riˈæləti/ Realität; Wirklichkeit p. 17, 10
(to) **realize (= realise)** /ˈrɪəlaɪz/ sich bewusst sein, erkennen NHG 6
really /ˈrɪəli/ wirklich NHG 5
reason /ˈriːzn/ Grund NHG 6
(to) **give a reason** *(irr)* /ˌgɪv_ə ˈriːzn/ einen Grund nennen p. 17, 10
(to) **rebuild** *(irr)* /ˌriːˈbɪld/ wieder aufbauen p. 15, 7
(to) **receive** /rɪˈsiːv/ erhalten; empfangen p. 68, 2
recent /ˈriːsnt/ jüngste(r, s); letzte(r, s) p. 68, 2
recently /ˈriːsntli/ vor Kurzem; neulich p. 93, 2
recipe /ˈresəpi/ Rezept NHG 7
(to) **recognize (= recognise)** /ˈrekəgnaɪz/ erkennen p. 95, 7
(to) **recommend** /ˌrekəˈmend/ empfehlen NHG 6
recommendation /ˌrekəmenˈdeɪʃn/ Empfehlung NHG 7
record /ˈrekɔːd/ Rekord p. 35, 2
(to) **record** /rɪˈkɔːd/ aufnehmen NHG 5
record /ˈrekɔːd/ Schallplatte P&P 2; Aufzeichnungen p. 110, 6
recording /rɪˈkɔːdɪŋ/ Aufnahme NHG 5
(to) **recreate** /ˌriːkriˈeɪt/ wieder schaffen, nachschaffen p. 135
(to) **recruit** /rɪˈkruːt/ anwerben p. 87, 6
(to) **recycle** /ˌriːˈsaɪkl/ recyceln; wiederaufbereiten p. 86, 6
recycled /ˌriːˈsaɪkld/ wiederverwertet; Recycling- p. 93, 2
recycling plant /riːˈsaɪklɪŋ plɑːnt/ Recyclinganlage p. 86, 6
red /red/ rot NHG 5

(to) **reduce** /rɪˈdjuːs/ reduzieren NHG 7
(to) **refer to** /rɪˈfɜː tu/ hinweisen auf, gelten für NHG 7
reference /ˈrefrəns/ Referenz; Zeugnis p. 98, 10
reflexive pronoun /rɪˌfleksɪv ˈprəʊnaʊn/ Reflexivpronomen p. 52, 12
regardless of /rɪˈgɑːdləs_əv/ trotz, ungeachtet p. 17, 10
registered nurse /ˌredʒɪstəd ˈnɜːs/ examinierte Krankenschwester/ examinierter Krankenpfleger p. 92, 2
registrar /ˌredʒɪˈstrɑː/ Sekretär/in p. 38, 6
registrar's office /ˌredʒɪstrɑːz_ˈɒfɪs/ Sekretariat p. 38, 6
registration /ˌredʒɪˈstreɪʃn/ Überprüfung der Anwesenheit NHG 5
regular /ˈregjələ/ üblich, normal NHG 6
regularly /ˈregjələli/ regelmäßig NHG 7
(to) **reject** /rɪˈdʒekt/ ablehnen, zurückweisen p. 25, 7
(to) **relate to** /rɪˈleɪt_tʊ/ handeln von; zu tun haben mit p. 81
relationship /rɪˈleɪʃnʃɪp/ Beziehung p. 57
relative /ˈrelətɪv/ Verwandte NHG 6
(to) **relax** /rɪˈlæks/ entspannen NHG 5
relaxed /rɪˈlækst/ entspannt NHG 6
relaxing /rɪˈlæksɪŋ/ entspannend NHG 7
relevant /ˈreləvnt/ relevant; wichtig p. 98, 10
reliability /rɪˌlaɪəˈbɪliti/ Zuverlässigkeit p. 95, 7
reliable /rɪˈlaɪəbl/ verlässlich; zuverlässig p. 95, 7
religious /rəˈlɪdʒəs/ religiöse(r, s) NHG 6
(to) **rely on** /rɪˈlaɪ_ɒn/ sich verlassen auf p. 61, 7
(to) **remain** /rɪˈmeɪn/ bleiben P&P 8
remember /rɪˈmembə/ sich erinnern an NHG 5; bedenken, denken an p. 62, 8
(to) **remind somebody** /rɪˈmaɪnd ˌsʌmbədi/ jemanden erinnern p. 63, 8

(to) **remove** /rɪˈmuːv/ entfernen NHG 6
renewable /rɪˈnjuːəbl/ erneuerbar p. 150
renovation /ˌrenəˈveɪʃn/ Renovierung; Sanierung p. 26, 8
rent /rent/ Miete; Pacht p. 106, 2
(to) **rent** /rent/ mieten p. 21, 2
(to) **repair** /rɪˈpeə/ reparieren NHG 6
repair /rɪˈpeə/ Reparatur p. 41, 8
auto body repair /ˌɔːtəʊ ˌbɒdi rɪˈpeə/ Karosseriereparatur p. 40, 7
(to) **repeat** /rɪˈpiːt/ wiederholen NHG 5
(to) **replace** /rɪˈpleɪs/ ersetzen p. 71, 5
(to) **reply** /rɪˈplaɪ/ antworten; erwidern NHG 6
report /rɪˈpɔːt/ Zeugnis p. 98, 10
(to) **report** /rɪˈpɔːt/ sich melden NHG 6
report (to) /rɪˈpɔːt/ berichten; wiedergeben p. 60, 4
reported command /rɪˌpɔːtɪd kəˈmɑːnd/ indirekter Befehl p. 108
reported speech /rɪˌpɔːtɪd ˈspiːtʃ/ indirekte Rede p. 60
(to) **represent** /ˌreprɪˈzent/ präsentieren, vertreten p. 27, 10; darstellen; symbolisieren p. 72, 6
republic /rɪˈpʌblɪk/ Republik p. 38, 6
the Republic of Ireland /ðə rɪˌpʌblɪk_əv_ˈaɪələnd/ (die Republik) Irland p. 105
reputation /ˌrepjʊˈteɪʃn/ Ruf p. 24, 6
research /rɪˈsɜːtʃ/ Forschung p. 62, 8
(to) **research** /rɪˈsɜːtʃ/ recherchieren NHG 6
(to) **do research** *(irr)* /ˌduː rɪˈsɜːtʃ/ recherchieren NHG 5
reservation /ˌrezəˈveɪʃn/ Reservierung NHG 7
reservation /ˌrezəˈveɪʃn/ Reservat P&P 1
resident /ˈrezɪdnt/ Bewohner/in NHG 7
resident /ˈrezɪdnt/ *hier:* heimisch p. 144
(to) **resist** /rɪˈzɪst/ sich wehren P&P 1
respect /rɪˈspekt/ Respekt NHG 6
(to) **respect** /rɪˈspekt/ respektieren NHG 6
respectfully /rɪˈspektfəli/ respektvoll p. 77, 15

(to) **respond** /rɪˈspɒnd/ antworten; reagieren p. 72, 6
(to) **respond to** /rɪˈspɒnd tə/ antworten auf, reagieren auf p. 68, 2
responsibility /rɪˌspɒnsəˈbɪləti/ Verantwortung; Pflicht P&P 5
responsible /rɪˈspɒnsəbl/ verantwortungsbewusst, verantwortlich p. 63, 8
(to) **rest** /rest/ ausruhen NHG 7
result /rɪˈzʌlt/ Ergebnis NHG 7
(to) **retire** /rɪˈtaɪə/ in den Ruhestand treten p. 107, 2
(to) **return** /rɪˈtɜːn/ zurückgeben NHG 6; zurückkehren, zurückkommen p. 110, 6
return ticket /rɪˌtɜːn ˈtɪkɪt/ Hin- und Rückfahrkarte p. 130
(to) **reuse** /riːˈjuːz/ wiederverwenden NHG 7
review /rɪˈvjuː/ Kritik; Rezension NHG 7
rhyming word /ˈraɪmɪŋ wɜːd/ Reimwort NHG 7
rice /raɪs/ Reis NHG 5
rich /rɪtʃ/ reich NHG 7
(to) **get rid of** (irr) /ˌget ˈrɪd əv/ loswerden NHG 7
ride /raɪd/ Fahrt p. 8
(to) **ride** (irr) /raɪd/ fahren; reiten NHG 5
(to) **ride a bike** (irr) /ˌraɪd ə ˈbaɪk/ Fahrrad fahren NHG 5
(to) **ride a horse** (irr) /ˌraɪd ə ˈhɔːs/ reiten NHG 5
(to) **go riding** (irr) /ˌgəʊ ˈraɪdɪŋ/ reiten gehen NHG 6
(to) **take a ride** (irr) /ˌteɪk ə ˈraɪd/ eine Fahrt machen p. 13, 6
right /raɪt/ richtig NHG 5; rechts, nach rechts; genau; direkt NHG 6; Recht NHG 7
(to) **be right** (irr) /ˌbiː ˈraɪt/ recht haben NHG 5
on the right /ˌɒn ðə ˈraɪt/ rechts, auf der rechten Seite NHG 5
right away /ˌraɪt əˈweɪ/ sofort, gleich p. 68, 2
right now /ˌraɪt ˈnaʊ/ jetzt; im Moment NHG 7
ringfort /ˈrɪŋfɔːt/ Ringfestung p. 135
rise /raɪz/ Aufstieg NHG 7
rise /raɪz/ Anstieg p. 171

(to) **rise** (irr) /raɪz/ aufgehen; steigen p. 89, 9
river /ˈrɪvə/ Fluss NHG 6
road /rəʊd/ Straße NHG 5
robot /ˈrəʊbɒt/ Roboter p. 40, 7
robotics /rəʊˈbɒtɪks/ Robotertechnik p. 39, 6
rock /rɒk/ Stein; Fels NHG 7
role /rəʊl/ Rolle NHG 6
role play /ˈrəʊl pleɪ/ Rollenspiel NHG 6
role-playing /ˈrəʊl ˌpleɪɪŋ/ Rollenspiel p. 44, 2
(to) **roll** /rəʊl/ rollen NHG 7
Roman /ˈrəʊmən/ Römer/in; römisch NHG 6
romance /rəʊˈmæns/ Romanze p. 149
romantic /rəʊˈmæntɪk/ romantisch p. 66, 13
rooftop /ˈruːfˌtɒp/ Dach p. 150
room /ruːm/ Platz; Raum; Zimmer NHG 5
waiting room /ˈweɪtɪŋ ˌruːm/ Wartezimmer NHG 7
root /ruːt/ Wurzel NHG 7
(to) **rot** /rɒt/ verrotten, verfaulen p. 106, 2
roughly /ˈrʌfli/ grob, ungefähr p. 120, 6
round /raʊnd/ rund NHG 5; (um ...) herum NHG 6
all year round /ˌɔːl ˌjɪə raʊnd/ das ganze Jahr lang p. 10, 2
round trip /ˌraʊnd ˈtrɪp/ Rundreise p. 138
route /ruːt/ Strecke; Route P&P 1
royal /ˈrɔɪəl/ königlich NHG 6
rubbish /ˈrʌbɪʃ/ Müll NHG 5
rude /ruːd/ unhöflich p. 38, 6
ruin /ˈruːɪn/ Ruine p. 116, 1
rule /ruːl/ Regel NHG 5; Herrschaft P&P 8
(to) **rule** /ruːl/ herrschen, regieren NHG 6
ruler /ˈruːlə/ Lineal NHG 5
rumor (AE) = **rumour** (BE) /ˈruːmə/ Gerücht p. 69, 2
run /rʌn/ Lauf NHG 7
(to) **run** (irr) /rʌn/ laufen; rennen NHG 6; leiten, betreiben NHG 7; durchführen p. 87, 6
runner /ˈrʌnə/ Läufer/in NHG 6
running time /ˈrʌnɪŋ taɪm/ Laufzeit p. 149

Russian /ˈrʌʃn/ Russe, Russin; russisch p. 110, 6

S

sad /sæd/ traurig NHG 6
safe /seɪf/ sicher; ungefährlich NHG 6
safety /ˈseɪfti/ Sicherheit NHG 6
safety precaution /ˈseɪfti prɪˌkɔːʃn/ Sicherheitsvorkehrung p. 41, 8
(to) **sail** /seɪl/ segeln p. 121, 6
sailing ship /ˈseɪlɪŋ ʃɪp/ Segelschiff p. 106, 2
salad /ˈsæləd/ Salat NHG 7
salmon /ˈsæmən/ Lachs p. 122, 7
salt /sɔːlt/ Salz NHG 5
the same /ðə ˈseɪm/ der/die/das Gleiche; der-/die-/dasselbe NHG 5
at the same time /ˌæt ðə ˌseɪm ˈtaɪm/ gleichzeitig; zur gleichen Zeit NHG 7
Saturday /ˈsætədeɪ/ Samstag NHG 5
(on) Saturdays /ˈsætədeɪz/ samstags NHG 5
sauce /sɔːs/ Soße NHG 7
(to) **save** /seɪv/ aufheben; sichern; sparen; retten NHG 7
savoury /ˈseɪvəri/ pikant; salzig NHG 7
(to) **say** (irr) /seɪ/ sagen NHG 5
saying /ˈseɪɪŋ/ Sprichwort p. 64, 11
on a larger scale /ˌɒn ə ˌlɑːdʒə ˈskeɪl/ im größeren Rahmen p. 85, 5
(to) **scan** /skæn/ absuchen, überfliegen NHG 7
Scandinavia /ˌskændɪˈneɪviə/ Skandinavien p. 14, 7
scared /skeəd/ verängstigt, ängstlich NHG 6
(to) **be scared (of)** /ˌbiː ˈskeəd əv/ Angst haben (vor) NHG 5
scary /ˈskeəri/ Furcht erregend NHG 6
scene /siːn/ Szene NHG 5
scenery /ˈsiːnəri/ Landschaft p. 138
schedule (AE) /ˈskedʒul, ˈʃedjuːl/ Stundenplan p. 38, 6
scholarship /ˈskɒləʃɪp/ Stipendium p. 113, 10
(to) **win a scholarship** (irr) /ˌwɪn ə ˈskɒləʃɪp/ ein Stipendium bekommen p. 82, 2
school /skuːl/ Schule NHG 5
school counsellor /ˌskuːl ˈkaʊnslə/ Beratungslehrer/in p. 131

Dictionary

school grounds *(pl)* /ˈskuːl ˌɡraʊndz/ Schulgelände NHG 6
schoolbag /ˈskuːl.bæɡ/ Schultasche NHG 5
schoolchild (*pl* schoolchildren) /ˈskuːl.tʃaɪld, ˈskuːl.tʃɪldrən/ Schulkind p. 38, 6
science /ˈsaɪəns/ Naturwissenschaft NHG 5
science fair /ˈsaɪəns feə/ Naturwissenschaftsmesse p. 40, 7
scientist /ˈsaɪəntɪst/ Wissenschaftler/in NHG 7
(a pair of) scissors /ˈsɪzəz/ Schere NHG 5
Scotland /ˈskɒtlənd/ Schottland NHG 5
Scottish /ˈskɒtɪʃ/ schottisch p. 162
(to) **scream** /skriːm/ schreien NHG 7
screen /skriːn/ Bildschirm NHG 6
script /skrɪpt/ Drehbuch; Skript NHG 6
sculpture /ˈskʌlptʃə/ Bildhauerei p. 26, 8
seal /siːl/ Seehund; Robbe p. 119, 5
search /sɜːtʃ/ Suche NHG 5
search engine /ˈsɜːtʃ ˌendʒɪn/ Suchmaschine NHG 7
(to) search /sɜːtʃ/ suchen NHG 5
(to) **search the Internet** /ˌsɜːtʃ ðɪ ˈɪntənet/ im Internet suchen NHG 5
seasick /ˈsiːˌsɪk/ seekrank p. 106, 2
seaside /ˈsiːˌsaɪd/ (Meeres)küste; Meer NHG 6
season /ˈsiːzn/ Saison NHG 7
seat /siːt/ Sitz p. 48, 7
(to) **take a seat** *(irr)* /ˌteɪk ə ˈsiːt/ sich setzen NHG 7
second /ˈsekənd/ Sekunde; zweite(r, s) NHG 5
(to) **come second** *(irr)* /ˌkʌm ˈsekənd/ Zweite/r werden p. 34, 2
second helping /ˌsekənd ˈhelpɪŋ/ Nachschlag p. 48, 7
the Second World War /ðə ˌsekənd ˌwɜːld ˈwɔː/ Zweiter Weltkrieg p. 15, 7
second-hand /ˌsekənd ˈhænd/ gebraucht NHG 7
secondary school /ˈsekəndri skuːl/ weiterführende Schule P&P 5
secretary /ˈsekrətri/ Sekretär/in p. 113, 10

section /ˈsekʃn/ Teil; Stück; Abschnitt; Abteilung NHG 7
security /sɪˈkjʊərəti/ Sicherheit p. 17, 10
(to) **see** *(irr)* /siː/ sehen NHG 5; empfangen, drannehmen NHG 7
(to) **see a doctor** *(irr)* /ˌsiː ə ˈdɒktə/ einen Arzt/eine Ärztin aufsuchen NHG 7
See you (soon)! /ˌsiː juː ˈsuːn/ Bis bald! NHG 6
(to) **seek** *(irr)* /siːk/ suchen, streben nach NHG 7
(to) **seek advice** *(irr)* /ˌsiːk ədˈvaɪs/ Rat suchen NHG 7
(to) **seem** /siːm/ scheinen NHG 7
racial segregation /ˌreɪʃl segrɪˈɡeɪʃn/ Rassentrennung p. 15, 7
selection /sɪˈlekʃn/ Auswahl NHG 7
self-confessed /ˌself kənˈfest/ selbsterklärt p. 68, 2
self-esteem /ˌself ɪˈstiːm/ Selbstwertgefühl NHG 7
(to) **sell** *(irr)* /sel/ verkaufen NHG 7
seller /ˈselə/ Verkäufer/in NHG 7
(to) **send** *(irr)* /send/ schicken NHG 5
(to) **send in** *(irr)* /ˌsend ˈɪn/ einsenden p. 62, 8
senior /ˈsiːniə/ älterer Mensch; ältere(r, s) p. 26, 8
senior *(AE)* /ˈsiːniə/ Schüler/in einer Highschool im letzten Jahr p. 39, 6
(to) **make sense** *(irr)* /ˌmeɪk ˈsens/ sinnvoll sein p. 62, 8
sentence /ˈsentəns/ Satz NHG 5
separate /ˈseprət/ separat; getrennt p. 72, 6
September /sepˈtembə/ September NHG 5
series /ˈsɪəriːz/ Folge; Serie NHG 7
serious /ˈsɪəriəs/ ernst NHG 7
(to) **serve** /sɜːv/ servieren; reichen für NHG 7; dienen; eine Amtszeit durchlaufen p. 15, 7
session /ˈseʃn/ Stunde; Session NHG 5
set /set/ Satz; Garnitur p. 71, 5
set /set/ *hier:* Reihe p. 17, 10
(to) **set foot on** *(irr)* /ˌset ˈfʊt ˌɒn/ betreten p. 10, 2
(to) **set the table** *(irr)* /ˌset ðə ˈteɪbl/ den Tisch decken NHG 5
(to) **set up** *(irr)* /ˌset ˈʌp/ aufbauen NHG 7

(to) **settle** /ˈsetl/ sich niederlassen p. 14, 7
settlement /ˈsetlmənt/ Siedlung p. 14, 7
settler /ˈsetlə/ Siedler/in p. 14, 7
several /ˈsevrəl/ einige; verschiedene NHG 7
shall /ʃæl/ sollen; werden NHG 7
(to) **be a shame** *(irr)* /ˌbi ə ˈʃeɪm/ schade sein NHG 7
shape /ʃeɪp/ Form; Gestalt p. 65, 12
(to) **share** /ʃeə/ teilen NHG 5
sharing /ˈʃeərɪŋ/ Teilen p. 151
shark /ʃɑːk/ Hai p. 135
she /ʃiː/ sie NHG 5
sheet /ʃiːt/ Blatt; Bogen NHG 6
shelf (*pl* shelves) /ʃelf, ʃelvz/ Regal NHG 5
shield /ʃiːld/ Schild p. 121, 6
shift /ʃɪft/ Schicht p. 92, 2
(to) **work shifts** /ˌwɜːk ˈʃɪfts/ Schichtdienst machen p. 92, 2
ship /ʃɪp/ Schiff p. 14, 7
(to) **board a ship** /ˌbɔːd ə ˈʃɪp/ ein Schiff besteigen p. 106, 2
shirt /ʃɜːt/ Hemd NHG 5
shocked /ʃɒkt/ schockiert, entsetzt p. 69, 2
shoe /ʃuː/ Schuh NHG 6
(to) **shoot** *(irr)* /ʃuːt/ schießen NHG 7
shop /ʃɒp/ Geschäft; Laden NHG 5
shop assistant /ˈʃɒp əˌsɪstnt/ Verkäufer/in NHG 6
shopping /ˈʃɒpɪŋ/ Einkaufen; Einkaufs- NHG 5
(to) **do the shopping** *(irr)* /ˌduː ðə ˈʃɒpɪŋ/ einkaufen NHG 5
(to) **go shopping** *(irr)* /ˌɡəʊ ˈʃɒpɪŋ/ einkaufen gehen NHG 6
shopping centre /ˈʃɒpɪŋ ˌsentə/ Einkaufszentrum NHG 5
shore /ʃɔː/ Küste; Ufer p. 122, 7
short /ʃɔːt/ kurz NHG 5
short-distance flight /ˌʃɔːt ˌdɪstəns ˈflaɪt/ Kurzstreckenflug p. 85, 5
should /ʃʊd/ sollte(st, n, t) NHG 6
shoulder /ˈʃəʊldə/ Schulter NHG 7
(to) **shout** /ʃaʊt/ rufen; schreien p. 7
(to) **shout at somebody** /ˈʃaʊt ət ˌsʌmbədi/ jemanden anschreien NHG 6
(to) **show** *(irr)* /ʃəʊ/ zeigen NHG 5

shy /ʃaɪ/ schüchtern NHG 7
sick /sɪk/ krank NHG 6
side /saɪd/ Seite NHG 6
side (dish) /ˈsaɪd ˌdɪʃ/ Beilage NHG 7
on the side /ˌɒn ðə ˈsaɪd/ als Beilage NHG 7
sidewalk (AE) /ˈsaɪdˌwɔːk/ Bürgersteig p. 24, 6
sight /saɪt/ Sehenswürdigkeit NHG 5
sight /saɪt/ Anblick; Sicht P&P 7
sign /saɪn/ Zeichen; Schild NHG 6
(to) sign /saɪn/ unterschreiben NHG 7
(to) sign up (for) /ˌsaɪn ˈʌp/ sich anmelden NHG 7
significantly /sɪɡˈnɪfɪkəntli/ deutlich p. 10, 2
silly /ˈsɪli/ albern; dumm NHG 7
silver /ˈsɪlvə/ Silber p. 18, 12; silbern p. 122, 7
similar /ˈsɪmɪlə/ ähnlich NHG 6
simple /ˈsɪmpl/ einfach; simpel NHG 7
simple past /ˌsɪmpl ˈpɑːst/ einfache Vergangenheit p. 12
simple present /ˌsɪmpl ˈpreznt/ einfache Gegenwart p. 18, 12
simply /ˈsɪmpli/ einfach NHG 6
since /sɪns/ seit NHG 6; da; weil p. 68, 2
since then /sɪns ˈðen/ seitdem, seither p. 21, 2
(to) sing (irr) /sɪŋ/ singen NHG 5
(to) sing along (irr) /ˌsɪŋ əˈlɒŋ/ mitsingen NHG 5
singer /ˈsɪŋə/ Sänger/in NHG 6
singing /ˈsɪŋɪŋ/ Singen; Gesang p. 44, 2
single /ˈsɪŋɡl/ einzelne(r, s) NHG 6
single /ˈsɪŋɡl/ hier: Einzelwettbewerb p. 35, 2
single ticket /ˌsɪŋɡl ˈtɪkɪt/ einfache Fahrkarte, Einzelfahrkarte p. 163
sir/Sir /sɜː/ Sir; Herr *(Anrede vor Vornamen)* NHG 7
sister /ˈsɪstə/ Schwester NHG 5
(to) sit (irr) /sɪt/ sitzen NHG 7
(to) sit down (irr) /ˌsɪt ˈdaʊn/ sich hinsetzen NHG 5
(to) sit still (irr) /ˌsɪt ˈstɪl/ stillsitzen p. 100, 16
site /saɪt/ Stelle; Platz NHG 7
(to) be situated (irr) /ˌbiː ˈsɪtʃueɪtɪd/ liegen, gelegen sein p. 18, 12

size /saɪz/ Größe NHG 5
skateboarding /ˈskeɪtbɔːdɪŋ/ Skateboardfahren NHG 5
(to) sketch /sketʃ/ skizzieren p. 91, 13
skill /skɪl/ Fähigkeit; Geschick NHG 7; Fertigkeit; Kompetenz p. 41, 8
(to) skim /skɪm/ überfliegen NHG 7
skirt /skɜːt/ Rock NHG 5
sky /skaɪ/ Himmel p. 65, 12
skyscraper /ˈskaɪˌskreɪpə/ Wolkenkratzer p. 21, 2
slave /sleɪv/ Sklave/Sklavin p. 15, 7
slavery /ˈsleɪvəri/ Sklaverei p. 15, 7
dog sled /ˈdɒɡ sled/ Hundeschlitten p. 13, 6
sleep /sliːp/ Schlaf NHG 7
(to) sleep /sliːp/ schlafen NHG 5
sleeping bag /ˈsliːpɪŋ bæɡ/ Schlafsack p. 75, 10
sleepy /ˈsliːpi/ schläfrig; verschlafen p. 20, 1
(to) slice /slaɪs/ in Scheiben schneiden NHG 7
slide /slaɪd/ Folie NHG 7
slow, slowly /sləʊ, ˈsləʊli/ langsam NHG 6
small /smɔːl/ klein NHG 5
smart /smɑːt/ schlau, clever NHG 6
(to) smell (irr) /smel/ riechen p. 48, 7
(to) smile /smaɪl/ lächeln NHG 6
smile /smaɪl/ Lächeln p. 65, 12
snake /sneɪk/ Schlange p. 110, 6
snow /snəʊ/ Schnee p. 10, 2
so /səʊ/ also; deshalb; daher NHG 5
so far /ˌsəʊ ˈfɑː/ bisher NHG 6
so that /ˌsəʊ ˈðæt/ damit NHG 6
(to) soar /sɔː/ aufsteigen, sich erheben p. 122, 7
soccer (AE) /ˈsɒkə/ Fußball p. 165
social /ˈsəʊʃl/ gesellschaftlich; sozial p. 17, 10
social media /ˌsəʊʃl ˈmiːdiə/ soziale Medien p. 69, 2
sociologist /ˌsəʊsiˈɒlədʒɪst/ Soziologe/Soziologin p. 72, 6
sock /sɒk/ Socke NHG 7
soft /sɒft/ weich NHG 7
soft skill /ˌsɒft ˈskɪl/ *persönliche, soziale und methodische Kompetenz* p. 81
soil /sɔɪl/ Boden; Erde p. 106, 2
solution /səˈluːʃn/ Lösung NHG 6

(to) solve /sɒlv/ lösen NHG 6
some /sʌm/ einige, ein paar; etwas NHG 5
some day /ˈsʌmˌdeɪ/ eines Tages NHG 7
somebody /ˈsʌmbədi/ jemand; irgendwer NHG 6
someone /ˈsʌmwʌn/ jemand; irgendwer NHG 5
something /ˈsʌmθɪŋ/ etwas NHG 5
sometimes /ˈsʌmtaɪmz/ manchmal NHG 5
somewhere /ˈsʌmweə/ irgendwo NHG 6
son /sʌn/ Sohn NHG 5
song /sɒŋ/ Lied NHG 5
soon /suːn/ bald NHG 7
Get well soon! /ˌɡet ˌwel ˈsuːn/ Gute Besserung! NHG 7
See you (soon)! /ˌsiː juː ˈsuːn/ Bis bald! NHG 6
sophomore (AE) /ˈsɒfəˌmɔː/ Schüler/Schülerin einer Highschool im zweiten Jahr p. 39, 6
sore throat /ˌsɔː ˈθrəʊt/ Halsschmerzen NHG 7
sorry /ˈsɒri/ es tut mir leid, Entschuldigung NHG 5
(to) be sorry (irr) /ˌbiː ˈsɒri/ bedauern; sich entschuldigen p. 63, 8
sort /sɔːt/ Sorte; Art NHG 6
(to) sort /sɔːt/ sortieren NHG 5
sound /saʊnd/ Geräusch; Klang NHG 6
(to) sound /saʊnd/ klingen, sich anhören NHG 5
sound technology /ˈsaʊnd tekˌnɒlədʒi/ Tontechnik p. 43, 14
soup /suːp/ Suppe NHG 7
source /sɔːs/ Quelle NHG 7
south /saʊθ/ Süden; Süd- NHG 7
South Korea /ˌsaʊθ kəˈrɪə/ Südkorea p. 107, 2
southeast, south-east /ˌsaʊθˈiːst/ Südosten P&P 1
southern /ˈsʌðən/ südliche(r, s); Süd- p. 15, 7
southwest /ˌsaʊθˈwest/ in den Südwesten, nach Südwesten p. 110, 6
space /speɪs/ Raum; Platz NHG 6; Weltall NHG 7
Spain /speɪn/ Spanien p. 14, 7
Spanish /ˈspænɪʃ/ Spanisch p. 7

Dictionary

spark /spɑːk/ Funke; Auslöser p. 86, 6
(to) **speak** *(irr)* /spiːk/ sprechen; reden NHG 5
speaker /ˈspiːkə/ Sprecher/in p. 25, 7
This is ... speaking. /ðɪs ɪz ... ˈspiːkɪŋ/ Hier spricht ... NHG 7
strictly speaking /ˈstrɪkli ˌspiːkɪŋ/ streng genommen p. 38, 6
special /ˈspeʃl/ besondere(r, s); besonders NHG 5
special offer /ˌspeʃl ˈɒfə/ Sonderangebot p. 26, 8
speciality /ˌspeʃiˈæləti/ Spezialität NHG 7
species *(pl* **species)** /ˈspiːʃiːz, ˈspiːʃiːz/ Art; Spezies NHG 6
specific /spəˈsɪfɪk/ genau, bestimmte(r, s); spezifisch p. 96, 8
spectacular /spekˈtækjələ/ atemberaubend; spektakulär NHG 7
spectator /spekˈteɪtə/ Zuschauer/in P&P 4
speech /spiːtʃ/ Rede p. 89, 9
direct speech /ˌdaɪrekt ˈspiːtʃ/ direkte / wörtliche Rede p. 66, 13
speech bubble /ˈspiːtʃ ˌbʌbl/ Sprechblase NHG 7
(to) **spell** *(irr)* /spel/ buchstabieren NHG 5
spelling /ˈspelɪŋ/ Buchstabieren; Rechtschreibung NHG 6
(to) **spend** *(irr)* /spend/ verbringen *(Zeit)*; ausgeben *(Geld)* NHG 6
spice /spaɪs/ Gewürz NHG 7
spicy /ˈspaɪsi/ würzig; scharf NHG 7
spirit /ˈspɪrɪt/ Geist; Stimmung p. 48, 7
splendid /ˈsplendɪd/ großartig p. 112, 8
(to) **sponsor** /ˈspɒnsə/ sponsern; als Sponsor/in finanzieren p. 88, 8
spoon /spuːn/ Löffel NHG 5
sport /spɔːt/ Sport; Sportart NHG 5
full-contact sport /ˌfʊl ˈkɒntækt spɔːt/ Vollkontakt-Sportart p. 50, 8
sports hall /ˈspɔːts hɔːl/ Sporthalle p. 44, 2
sportsperson /ˈspɔːtsˌpɜːsn/ Sportler/in p. 16, 9
spot /spɒt/ Stelle p. 120, 6
spotlight /ˈspɒtˌlaɪt/ Scheinwerfer p. 10, 2

sprained /spreɪnd/ verstaucht NHG 7
(to) **spread** *(irr)* /spred/ verteilen; verbreiten p. 44, 2
(to) **spread the word** *(irr)* /ˌspred ðə ˈwɜːd/ es allen mitteilen p. 87, 6
spring /sprɪŋ/ Frühling NHG 6
square /ˈskweə/ Quadrat- p. 10, 2
stadium *(pl* stadiums or stadia) /ˈsteɪdiəm, ˈsteɪdiəmz, ˈsteɪdiə/ Stadion p. 7
stage /steɪdʒ/ Bühne NHG 6
stair /steə/ Stufe NHG 6
stairs *(pl)* /steəz/ Treppe NHG 6
stake /steɪk/ Pfahl; Pflock p. 111, 7
stall /stɔːl/ Stand NHG 7
stamina /ˈstæmɪnə/ Durchhaltevermögen; Ausdauer p. 85, 5
(to) **stand** *(irr)* /stænd/ stehen NHG 6
(to) stand by /ˌstænd ˈbaɪ/ dabeistehen p. 122, 7
(to) **stand for** *(irr)* /ˌstænd fɔː/ stehen für NHG 6
(to) stand somebody *(irr)* /ˈstænd ˌsʌmbədi/ jemanden leiden können p. 58, 3
(to) **stand up for** *(irr)* /ˌstænd ˈʌp fɔː/ sich einsetzen für p. 89, 9
standing lamp /ˈstændɪŋ læmp/ Stehlampe p. 65, 12
staple food /ˈsteɪpl fuːd/ Grundnahrungsmittel p. 106, 2
star /stɑː/ Stern NHG 5
(to) star /stɑː/ die Hauptrolle spielen p. 149
(to) **stare at** /ˈsteər æt/ anstarren p. 38, 6
start /stɑːt/ Anfang; Beginn NHG 5
(to) **start** /stɑːt/ anfangen; beginnen NHG 5; gründen p. 93, 2
(to) start a fire /ˌstɑːt ə ˈfaɪə/ Feuer machen p. 108, 3
(to) start out /ˌstɑːt ˈaʊt/ anfangen p. 89, 9
starter /ˈstɑːtə/ Vorspeise NHG 7
starting point /ˈstɑːtɪŋ pɔɪnt/ Ausgangspunkt p. 87, 6
starvation /stɑːˈveɪʃn/ Hungertod p. 121, 6
(to) **starve** /stɑːv/ verhungern p. 106, 2
state /steɪt/ Staat; Bundesstaat p. 6

(to) **state** /steɪt/ äußern, aussprechen NHG 7
statement /ˈsteɪtmənt/ Äußerung, Aussage NHG 5
station /ˈsteɪʃn/ U-Bahn-Station; Bahnhof NHG 5
station /ˈsteɪʃn/ *hier:* Station P&P 7
statistics *(pl)* /stəˈtɪstɪks/ Statistik p. 105
the Statue of Liberty /ðə ˌstætʃuː əv ˈlɪbəti/ Freiheitsstatue p. 6
(to) **stay** /steɪ/ bleiben; wohnen NHG 5
(to) **stay away from** /ˌsteɪ əˈweɪ frɒm/ meiden; sich fernhalten von NHG 7
(to) **stay up (late)** /ˌsteɪ ˌʌp ˈleɪt/ lange aufbleiben NHG 7
(to) **steal** *(irr)* /stiːl/ stehlen NHG 7
steam engine /ˈstiːm ˌendʒɪn/ Dampfmaschine NHG 7
steamboat /ˈstiːmbəʊt/ Dampfschiff p. 110, 6
step /step/ Stufe; Schritt NHG 5
(to) **step** /step/ treten; steigen NHG 6
(to) take a step *(irr)* /ˌteɪk ə ˈstep/ einen Schritt machen p. 87, 6
(to) step back in time /ˌstep ˌbæk ɪn ˈtaɪm/ sich in die Vergangenheit zurückversetzen p. 13, 6
(to) step out /ˌstep ˈaʊt/ heraustreten p. 13, 6
(to) **stick with** *(irr)* /ˌstɪk wɪð/ bleiben bei, festhalten an p. 59, 3
still /stɪl/ (immer) noch NHG 5; nach wie vor, trotzdem NHG 7
(to) sit still *(irr)* /ˌsɪt ˈstɪl/ stillsitzen p. 100, 16
(to) **stir in** /ˌstɜːr ˈɪn/ einrühren; unterrühren NHG 7
stomach /ˈstʌmək/ Magen; Bauch NHG 7
stomach ache /ˈstʌmək ˌeɪk/ Bauchschmerzen NHG 7
stone /stəʊn/ Stein NHG 7
(to) **stop** /stɒp/ stehen bleiben; anhalten NHG 5; aufhören NHG 6; stoppen NHG 7
stop /stɒp/ Halt p. 20, 2
store *(AE)* /stɔː/ Laden p. 24, 6
storm /stɔːm/ Sturm p. 108, 3
stormy /ˈstɔːmi/ stürmisch p. 106, 2

story /'stɔːri/ Geschichte, Erzählung NHG 5
straight on /ˌstreɪt_'ɒn/ geradeaus NHG 6
strange /streɪndʒ/ sonderbar; merkwürdig NHG 6
stranger /'streɪndʒə/ Fremde/r p. 34, 2
strategy /'strætədʒi/ Strategie NHG 7
street /striːt/ Straße NHG 5
strength /streŋθ/ Kraft; Stärke NHG 7
stress /stres/ Betonung NHG 6
(to) stress /stres/ stressen NHG 7
stressed /strest/ gestresst NHG 7
stretch /stretʃ/ *hier:* Abschnitt p. 10, 2
(to) stretch /stretʃ/ dehnen, spannen p. 44, 2
strict /strɪkt/ streng NHG 6
strictly speaking /'strɪkli ˌspiːkɪŋ/ streng genommen p. 38, 6
string /strɪŋ/ Schnur; Kordel NHG 6
strong /strɒŋ/ stark NHG 7
structure /'strʌktʃə/ Struktur; Aufbau NHG 7
(to) struggle /'strʌgl/ sich abmühen; sich quälen p. 89, 9
student /'stjuːdnt/ Schüler/in NHG 5; Student/in NHG 7
student council /'stjuːdnt ˌkaʊnsl/ Schülervertretung p. 83, 2
studies *(pl)* /'stʌdiz/ Studium p. 113, 10
study /'stʌdi/ Studie p. 68, 2
(to) study /'stʌdi/ studieren; lernen NHG 7
study hall /'stʌdi hɔːl/ Lernraum; Übungsraum p. 39, 6
study period /'stʌdi ˌpɪəriəd/ Lernstunde; Übungsstunde p. 39, 6
stuff *(informal)* /stʌf/ Zeug NHG 6
stunning /'stʌnɪŋ/ toll, fantastisch p. 13, 6
stupid /'stjuːpɪd/ dumm, blöd NHG 6
style /staɪl/ Stil NHG 6
subject /'sʌbdʒɪkt/ Schulfach NHG 5; Thema; Betreff *(in Emails)* NHG 6
subtle /'sʌtl/ fein; subtil p. 71, 5
subway *(AE)* /'sʌbˌweɪ/ U-Bahn p. 25, 7
(to) succeed /sək'siːd/ erfolgreich sein p. 44, 2
success /sək'ses/ Erfolg NHG 7

successful /sək'sesfl/ erfolgreich NHG 7
such /sʌtʃ/ so; solch NHG 7
such as /'sʌtʃ ˌæz/ wie NHG 7
suddenly /'sʌdnli/ plötzlich NHG 6
sugar /'ʃʊgə/ Zucker NHG 6
(to) suggest /sə'dʒest/ vorschlagen NHG 6; hinweisen auf, andeuten p. 14, 7
suggestion /sə'dʒestʃn/ Vorschlag NHG 6
suit /suːt/ Anzug p. 35, 2
(to) suit /suːt/ passen (zu) p. 100, 16
suitable /'suːtəbl/ geeignet; passend p. 19, 13
suitcase /'suːtˌkeɪs/ Koffer p. 108, 3
(to) sum up /ˌsʌm_'ʌp/ zusammenfassen p. 61, 7
(to) summarize (= summarise) /'sʌməraɪz/ zusammenfassen p. 95, 7
summary /'sʌməri/ Zusammenfassung NHG 7
summer /'sʌmə/ Sommer NHG 5
sun /sʌn/ Sonne NHG 5
Sunday /'sʌndeɪ/ Sonntag NHG 5
(on) Sundays /'sʌndeɪz/ sonntags NHG 5
sunny /'sʌni/ sonnig NHG 5
sunset /'sʌnˌset/ Sonnenuntergang p. 122, 7
sunshine /'sʌnʃaɪn/ Sonnenschein NHG 5
Super Bowl /'suːpə bəʊl/ *Finale der US-amerikanischen American Football-Profiliga* p. 7
superlative /sʊ'pɜːlətɪv/ Superlativ p. 70, 4
supermarket /'suːpəˌmɑːkɪt/ Supermarkt p. 97, 9
support /sə'pɔːt/ Unterstützung; Hilfe p. 34, 2
(to) support /sə'pɔːt/ stützen, unterstützen NHG 7
(to) suppose /sə'pəʊz/ annehmen, vermuten NHG 7
suppression /sə'preʃn/ Unterdrückung p. 14, 7
sure /ʃɔː/ sicher NHG 5
(to) make sure *(irr)* /ˌmeɪk 'ʃɔː/ darauf achten, dass … NHG 6
surf instructor /'sɜːf ɪnˌstrʌktə/ Surflehrer/in p. 93, 2

surf school /'sɜːfskuːl/ Surfschule p. 93, 2
surfing /'sɜːfɪŋ/ Surfen p. 8
surprised /sə'praɪzd/ überrascht; erstaunt NHG 6
surprising /sə'praɪzɪŋ/ überraschend NHG 6
(to) surround /sə'raʊnd/ umgeben p. 135
survey /'sɜːveɪ/ Umfrage NHG 7
(to) survive /sə'vaɪv/ überleben p. 111, 7
sustainability /səˌsteɪnə'bɪləti/ Nachhaltigkeit p. 83, 2
sustainable /sə'steɪnəbl/ nachhaltig p. 93, 2
(to) swap /swɒp/ tauschen p. 75, 10
sweater /'swetə/ Pullover p. 120, 6
sweet /swiːt/ süß NHG 5; Süßigkeit NHG 6
(to) swim *(irr)* /swɪm/ schwimmen NHG 5
swim practice /'swɪm ˌpræktɪs/ Schwimmtraining p. 62, 8
swimmer /'swɪmə/ Schwimmer/in p. 93, 2
swimming /'swɪmɪŋ/ Schwimmen NHG 5
(to) go swimming *(irr)* /ˌgəʊ 'swɪmɪŋ/ schwimmen gehen NHG 6
swimming pool /'swɪmɪŋ puːl/ Schwimmbad NHG 5
(to) be in full swing *(irr)* /ˌbi_ɪn ˌfʊl 'swɪŋ/ in vollem Gang sein p. 34, 2
(to) switch off /ˌswɪtʃ_'ɒf/ ausschalten NHG 7
(to) switch on /ˌswɪtʃ_'ɒn/ einschalten NHG 5
swollen /'swəʊlən/ geschwollen NHG 7
sword /sɔːd/ Schwert p. 121, 6
syllable /'sɪləbl/ Silbe NHG 7
systemic /sɪ'stiːmɪk/ systemisch p. 85, 5

T

table /'teɪbl/ Tisch NHG 5; Tabelle NHG 6
(to) set the table /ˌset ðə 'teɪbl/ den Tisch decken NHG 5
table tennis /'teɪbl ˌtenɪs/ Tischtennis NHG 5

Dictionary

tablespoon /ˈteɪblˌspuːn/ Esslöffel NHG 7

tailgate *(AE)* /ˈteɪlɡeɪt/ Heckklappe; *hier:* Kofferraum p. 48, 7

tailgate party *(AE)* /ˈteɪlɡeɪt ˌpɑːti/ *Picknick von der Ladefläche oder aus dem Kofferraum eines Autos während einer Sportveranstaltung oder eines Konzerts* p. 47, 6

(to) **take** *(irr)* /teɪk/ nehmen; bringen; benötigen; brauchen NHG 5; dauern NHG 6

(to) **take a break** *(irr)* /ˌteɪk ə ˈbreɪk/ eine Pause machen p. 85, 5

(to) take a closer look at *(irr)* /ˌteɪk ə ˌkləʊsə ˈlʊk ət/ sich genauer ansehen p. 148

(to) **take a course** *(irr)* /ˌteɪk ə ˈkɔːs/ einen Kurs machen p. 95, 7

(to) take a dog for a walk *(irr)* /ˌteɪk ə ˌdɒɡ fər ə ˈwɔːk/ mit einem Hund Gassi gehen p. 141

(to) **take a journey** *(irr)* /ˌteɪk ə ˈdʒɜːni/ eine Reise machen p. 121, 6

(to) **take a photo / picture** *(irr)* /ˌteɪk ə ˈfəʊtəʊ / ˈpɪktʃə/ ein Foto machen NHG 5

(to) take a ride *(irr)* /ˌteɪk ə ˈraɪd/ eine Fahrt machen p. 13, 6

(to) **take a seat** *(irr)* /ˌteɪk ə ˈsiːt/ sich setzen NHG 7

(to) take a step *(irr)* /ˌteɪk ə ˈstep/ einen Schritt machen p. 87, 6

(to) take a tour *(irr)* /ˌteɪk ə ˈtʊə/ eine Tour machen p. 26, 8

(to) **take action** *(irr)* /ˌteɪk ˈækʃn/ handeln, Maßnahmen ergreifen p. 81

(to) **take an order** *(irr)* /ˌteɪk ən ˈɔːdə/ eine Bestellung aufnehmen NHG 7

(to) **take an X-ray** *(irr)* /ˌteɪk ən ˈeksreɪ/ eine Röntgenaufnahme machen NHG 7

(to) **take away** *(irr)* /ˌteɪk əˈweɪ/ wegnehmen; mitnehmen NHG 6

(to) take care *(irr)* /ˌteɪk ˈkeə/ *hier:* auf etwas achten p. 77, 15

(to) **take care (of)** *(irr)* /ˌteɪk ˈkeər əv/ sich kümmern um NHG 6

(to) take measures *(irr)* /ˌteɪk ˈmeʒəz/ Maßnahmen ergreifen p. 150

(to) **take notes (on)** *(irr)* /ˌteɪk ˈnəʊts/ sich Notizen machen (zu) NHG 5

(to) take on *(irr)* /ˌteɪk ˈɒn/ übernehmen, auf sich nehmen P&P 5

(to) **take out** *(irr)* /ˌteɪk ˈaʊt/ hinausbringen NHG 5; herausnehmen NHG 7

(to) **take over** *(irr)* /ˌteɪk ˈəʊvə/ übernehmen NHG 7

(to) **take part in** *(irr)* /ˌteɪk ˈpɑːt ɪn/ teilnehmen an NHG 6

(to) **take place** *(irr)* /ˌteɪk ˈpleɪs/ stattfinden NHG 6

(to) take somebody's temperature *(irr)* /ˌteɪk ˌsʌmbədiz ˈtemprɪtʃə/ bei jemandem Fieber messen p. 92, 2

(to) take the initiative *(irr)* /ˌteɪk ðɪ ɪˈnɪʃətɪv/ die Initiative ergreifen p. 96, 8

(to) **take time** *(irr)* /ˌteɪk ˈtaɪm/ Zeit beanspruchen; dauern p. 83, 2

(to) **take turns** *(irr)* /ˌteɪk ˈtɜːnz/ sich abwechseln NHG 6

takeaway /ˈteɪkəˌweɪ/ Essen zum Mitnehmen; Imbissbude NHG 7

tale /teɪl/ Geschichte; Erzählung p. 138

talk /tɔːk/ Gespräch; Vortrag NHG 7

(to) **give a talk** *(irr)* /ˌɡɪv ə ˈtɔːk/ einen Vortrag halten NHG 7

(to) **talk about** /ˈtɔːk əˌbaʊt/ sprechen über NHG 5

(to) **talk (to)** /tɔːk/ sprechen (mit); reden (mit) NHG 5

tall /tɔːl/ groß NHG 6

target task /ˈtɑːɡɪt ˌtɑːsk/ Zielaufgabe p. 19, 13

task /tɑːsk/ Aufgabe NHG 5

Tasmanian Wolf /tæzˌmeɪniən ˈwʊlf/ Beutelwolf p. 132

taste /teɪst/ Geschmack NHG 7

(to) taste /teɪst/ schmecken NHG 6

tasty /ˈteɪsti/ lecker NHG 7

tax /tæks/ Steuer; Abgabe p. 14, 7

tea /tiː/ Tee NHG 5

(to) **teach** *(irr)* /tiːtʃ/ unterrichten NHG 5

teacher /ˈtiːtʃə/ Lehrer/in NHG 5

tear /tɪə/ Träne P&P 1

(to) **tease** /tiːz/ hänseln, ärgern NHG 7

teaspoon /ˈtiːˌspuːn/ Teelöffel NHG 7

technical /ˈteknɪkl/ technisch p. 82, 2

technique /tekˈniːk/ Technik p. 41, 8

technology /tekˈnɒlədʒi/ Technologie; Technik NHG 6

(to) **brush one's teeth** /ˌbrʌʃ wʌnz ˈtiːθ/ sich die Zähne putzen NHG 5

telephone /ˈtelɪˌfəʊn/ Telefon NHG 6

television /ˈtelɪˌvɪʒn/ Fernseher; Fernsehen NHG 7

(to) **tell** *(irr)* /tel/ erzählen NHG 5

(to) **tell** *(irr)* /tel/ *hier:* bemerken p. 65, 12

(to) **tell the truth** *(irr)* /ˌtel ðə ˈtruːθ/ die Wahrheit sagen NHG 7

(to) take somebody's temperature *(irr)* /ˌteɪk ˌsʌmbədiz ˈtemprɪtʃə/ bei jemandem Fieber messen p. 92, 2

tense /tens/ Zeitform p. 66, 13

term /tɜːm/ Trimester; Begriff NHG 5

terrible /ˈterəbl/ schrecklich NHG 5

territory /ˈterətri/ Gebiet; Territorium p. 110, 6

(to) **test** /test/ prüfen; testen p. 25, 7

(to) **text** /tekst/ eine Textnachricht schreiben NHG 5

text (message) /ˈtekst ˌmesɪdʒ/ Textnachricht NHG 5

than /ðæn/ als *(bei Vergleich)* NHG 6

(to) **thank** /θæŋk/ danken, sich bedanken p. 52, 13

thank God /ˌθæŋk ˈɡɒd/ Gott sei Dank p. 110, 6

thank you /ˈθæŋk juː/ danke NHG 5

thanks /θæŋks/ danke NHG 5

(to) **give thanks** *(irr)* /ˌɡɪv ˈθæŋks/ Dank sagen p. 25, 7

thanks a lot /ˌθæŋks ə ˈlɒt/ vielen Dank NHG 5

thanks to /ˈθæŋks tuː/ dank; wegen p. 107, 2

Thanksgiving /ˈθæŋksˌɡɪvɪŋ/ Thanksgiving *(amerikanisches Erntedankfest)* p. 6

that /ðæt/ das; der/die/das (dort); dass NHG 5; so NHG 6

that way /ˈðæt weɪ/ so, auf diese Weise p. 58, 3

that's (= that is) /ðæts, ˈðæt ɪz/ das kostet NHG 5

that's why /ˈðæts ˌwaɪ/ deshalb p. 93, 2

the /ðə/ der/die/das NHG 5

theater *(AE)* /ˈθɪətə/ Theater p. 20, 2

theatre /ˈθɪətə/ Theater NHG 6
their /ðeə/ ihr(e) NHG 5
theirs /ðeəz/ ihre(r, s) NHG 7
them /ðem/ sie; ihnen NHG 5
them /ðem/ ihn / sie *(wird benutzt, um „him" oder „her" zu vermeiden)* p. 23, 5
theme /θiːm/ Thema NHG 6
themselves /ðəmˈselvz/ sich; selbst p. 18, 11
then /ðen/ dann NHG 5
then /ðen/ damals p. 107, 2
theory /ˈθɪəri/ Theorie NHG 7
there /ðeə/ dort; dahin NHG 5
there are/is /ðeərˈɑː/ˌɪz/ dort sind/dort ist; es gibt NHG 5
these *(pl of this)* /ðiːz/ diese; das NHG 5
they /ðeɪ/ sie NHG 5
thin /θɪn/ dünn NHG 7
thing /θɪŋ/ Ding; Gegenstand NHG 5
(to) think *(irr)* /θɪŋk/ denken; glauben NHG 5
(to) think about *(irr)* /ˈθɪŋk ə baʊt/ denken an, nachdenken über NHG 5
(to) think of *(irr)* /ˈθɪŋk əv/ denken an, sich ausdenken NHG 5
third /θɜːd/ dritte(r, s) NHG 5
this /ðɪs/ diese(r, s) NHG 5
This is … speaking. /ðɪs ɪz … ˈspiːkɪŋ/ Hier spricht … NHG 7
this way /ˈðɪs weɪ/ hier entlang NHG 7
those *(pl of that)* /ðəʊz/ diese, jene NHG 5
though *(nachgestellt)* /ðəʊ/ jedoch p. 59, 3
thought /θɔːt/ Gedanke NHG 7
thought bubble /ˈθɔːt ˌbʌbl/ Gedankenblase NHG 7
thousand /ˈθaʊznd/ tausend NHG 6
threat /θret/ Bedrohung p. 69, 2
(to) threaten /ˈθretn/ (be)drohen p. 106, 2
threatening /ˈθretnɪŋ/ drohend; bedrohlich p. 71, 5
thrill /θrɪl/ Nervenkitzel; Kick p. 13, 6
thrilling /ˈθrɪlɪŋ/ aufregend p. 35, 2
sore throat /ˌsɔː ˈθrəʊt/ Halsschmerzen NHG 7

through /θruː/ durch NHG 6
(to) throw *(irr)* /θrəʊ/ werfen NHG 5
(to) throw away *(irr)* /ˌθrəʊ əˈweɪ/ wegwerfen NHG 6
(to) throw out *(irr)* /ˌθrəʊ ˈaʊt/ hinauswerfen p. 106, 2
thumb /θʌm/ Daumen NHG 7
thunder /ˈθʌndə/ Donner p. 111, 7
thunderstorm /ˈθʌndəstɔːm/ Gewitter p. 111, 7
Thursday /ˈθɜːzdeɪ/ Donnerstag NHG 5
(on) Thursdays /ˈθɜːzdeɪz/ donnerstags NHG 5
thus /ðʌs/ folglich; so, auf diese Weise p. 10, 2
ticket office /ˈtɪkɪt ˌɒfɪs/ Fahrkartenschalter p. 130
tidy /ˈtaɪdi/ ordentlich; aufgeräumt NHG 5
(to) tidy (up) /ˈtaɪdi, ˌtaɪdi ˈʌp/ aufräumen NHG 5
tie /taɪ/ Krawatte NHG 7
till /tɪl/ bis NHG 5
time /taɪm/ Zeit; Mal NHG 5
all the time /ˌɔːl ðə ˈtaɪm/ die ganze Zeit NHG 6
at the same time /ˌæt ðə ˌseɪm ˈtaɪm/ gleichzeitig; zur gleichen Zeit NHG 7
for the first time /fə ðə ˈfɜːst taɪm/ zum ersten Mal NHG 6
most of the time /ˈməʊst əv ðə ˌtaɪm/ meistens NHG 7
on time /ˌɒn ˈtaɪm/ pünktlich NHG 5
period (of time) /ˌpɪəriəd əv ˈtaɪm/ Zeitspanne; Zeitraum p. 62, 8
(to) take time *(irr)* /ˌteɪk ˈtaɪm/ Zeit beanspruchen; dauern p. 83, 2
What time is it? /ˌwɒt ˈtaɪm ɪz ɪt/ Wie spät ist es? NHG 5
What's the time, please? /ˌwɒts ðə ˈtaɪm pliːz/ Wie spät ist es, bitte? NHG 5
at that time /ˌæt ˈðæt taɪm/ zu jener Zeit p. 107, 2
for a long time /fər ə ˈlɒŋ taɪm/ lange p. 62, 8
for the time being /fə ðə ˌtaɪm ˈbiːɪŋ/ vorerst p. 59, 3
(to) step back in time /ˌstep ˌbæk ɪn ˈtaɪm/ sich in die Vergangenheit zurückversetzen p. 13, 6

time-saving /ˈtaɪm ˌseɪvɪŋ/ zeitsparend p. 72, 6
timeline /ˈtaɪmlaɪn/ Zeitachse NHG 7
at all times /ˌæt ˌɔːl ˈtaɪmz/ jederzeit, immer p. 72, 6
timetable /ˈtaɪmteɪbl/ Stundenplan NHG 5; Fahrplan NHG 6
tin /tɪn/ Büchse; Dose NHG 7
tiny /ˈtaɪni/ winzig p. 106, 2
tip /tɪp/ Tipp NHG 6
(to) tire out /ˌtaɪər ˈaʊt/ müde machen p. 97, 9
tired /ˈtaɪəd/ müde NHG 6
title /ˈtaɪtl/ Titel; Überschrift NHG 6
to /tə/ (um) zu; in; nach; zu; an; bis; vor NHG 5
today /təˈdeɪ/ heute NHG 5; heutzutage NHG 6
toe /təʊ/ Zeh NHG 5
together /təˈɡeðə/ zusammen NHG 5
(to) get together *(irr)* /ˌɡet təˈɡeðə/ zusammenkommen NHG 5
toilet /ˈtɔɪlət/ Toilette NHG 5
Tokyo /ˈtəʊkiəʊ/ Tokio p. 115, 14
tolerance /ˈtɒlərəns/ Toleranz p. 17, 10
tomato *(pl tomatoes)* /təˈmɑːtəʊ, təˈmɑːtəʊz/ Tomate NHG 5
tomorrow /təˈmɒrəʊ/ morgen NHG 5
tone of voice /ˌtəʊn əv ˈvɔɪs/ Ton p. 71, 5
tonight /təˈnaɪt/ heute Abend p. 117, 2
too /tuː/ auch; zu NHG 5
tool /tuːl/ Werkzeug NHG 7; Mittel; Instrument p. 41, 8
tooth *(pl teeth)* /tuːθ, tiːθ/ Zahn NHG 7
toothache *(no pl)* /ˈtuːθeɪk/ Zahnschmerzen NHG 7
toothbrush /ˈtuːθbrʌʃ/ Zahnbürste NHG 7
top /tɒp/ beste(r, s) NHG 5; oberes Ende; Spitze NHG 6
topic /ˈtɒpɪk/ Thema NHG 5
torch /tɔːtʃ/ Taschenlampe NHG 6
in total /ɪn ˈtəʊtl/ insgesamt p. 34, 2
(to) touch /tʌtʃ/ berühren NHG 5
(to) keep in touch *(irr)* /ˌkiːp ɪn ˈtʌtʃ/ Kontakt halten; in Verbindung bleiben NHG 7
tough /tʌf/ schwierig p. 40, 7
(to) tour /tʊə/ bereisen; erkunden p. 20, 2

Dictionary

(to) take a tour /ˌteɪk ə ˈtʊə/ eine Tour machen p. 26, 8
tour guide /ˈtʊə gaɪd/ Reiseführer/in p. 26, 8
tournament /ˈtʊənəmənt/ Turnier p. 35, 2
towards /təˈwɔːdz/ in Richtung, zu; gegenüber NHG 6
tower /ˈtaʊə/ Turm NHG 6
town /taʊn/ Stadt NHG 5
toy /tɔɪ/ Spielzeug NHG 5
tractor /ˈtræktə/ Traktor p. 93, 2
trader /ˈtreɪdə/ Händler/in p. 25, 7
traditional /trəˈdɪʃnəl/ traditionell NHG 6
traffic /ˈtræfɪk/ Verkehr p. 150
tragic /ˈtrædʒɪk/ tragisch p. 138
trail /treɪl/ Weg; Pfad P&P 1
train /treɪn/ Zug NHG 5
(to) train /treɪn/ trainieren NHG 7; eine Ausbildung machen p. 83, 2
on-the-job training /ˌɒn ðə ˌdʒɒbˈtreɪnɪŋ/ Ausbildung am Arbeitsplatz P&P 6
(to) translate /trænsˈleɪt/ übersetzen p. 75, 11
translation /trænsˈleɪʃn/ Übersetzung p. 71, 5
translator /trænsˈleɪtə/ Übersetzer/in p. 71, 5
transport /ˈtrænspɔːt/ Transport; Verkehrsmittel NHG 6
public transport /ˌpʌblɪk ˈtrænspɔːt/ öffentliche Verkehrsmittel p. 85, 5
trash (AE) /træʃ/ Müll; Abfall p. 86, 6
travel /ˈtrævl/ Reise NHG 6
(to) travel /ˈtrævl/ reisen; fahren NHG 6
travel guide /ˈtrævl gaɪd/ Reiseführer (Buch) p. 9
travelling /ˈtrævlɪŋ/ Reisen NHG 6
(to) treat /triːt/ behandeln NHG 7
tree /triː/ Baum NHG 5
trial /ˈtraɪəl/ Probe; Test p. 35, 2
trick /trɪk/ Trick; Kunststück NHG 5
trip /trɪp/ Ausflug; Fahrt NHG 6; Reise p. 13, 6
(to) trip /trɪp/ stolpern NHG 7
tropical /ˈtrɒpɪkl/ tropisch p. 10, 2
trouble /ˈtrʌbl/ Ärger; Schwierigkeiten NHG 6
(a pair of) trousers /əˌpeər əvˈtraʊzəz/ Hose NHG 5

truck (AE) /trʌk/ Lastwagen p. 93, 2
true /truː/ wahr NHG 5
(to) make one's dream come true (irr) /ˌmeɪk wʌnz ˈdriːm kʌm ˌtruː/ seinen Traum wahr werden lassen p. 149
truly /ˈtruːli/ wirklich, wahrhaftig p. 67, 15
trunk /trʌŋk/ Rüssel p. 65, 12
trunk (AE) /trʌŋk/ Kofferraum p. 48, 7
(to) trust /trʌst/ vertrauen NHG 7
(to) tell the truth (irr) /ˌtel ðə ˈtruːθ/ die Wahrheit sagen NHG 7
(to) try /traɪ/ (aus)probieren; versuchen NHG 5
(to) try on /ˌtraɪ ˈɒn/ anprobieren NHG 7
(to) try out /ˌtraɪ ˈaʊt/ ausprobieren NHG 7
tuberculosis /tjuːˌbɜːkjʊˈləʊsɪs/ Tuberkulose p. 110, 6
Tuesday /ˈtjuːzdeɪ/ Dienstag NHG 5
(on) Tuesdays /ˈtjuːzdeɪz/ dienstags NHG 5
tuition /tjuːˈɪʃn/ hier: Nachhilfe p. 97, 9
Turkey/Türkiye /ˈtɜːki, ˈtʊəkijə/ die Türkei p. 162
Turkish /ˈtɜːkɪʃ/ türkisch p. 162
(to) turn /tɜːn/ abbiegen NHG 6
(to) be one's turn (irr) /ˌbiː wʌnz ˈtɜːn/ an der Reihe sein NHG 5
(to) turn into /ˌtɜːn ˈɪntʊ/ umwandeln in p. 23, 5
(to) turn off /ˌtɜːn ˈɒf/ ausschalten NHG 7
(to) turn out /ˌtɜːn ˈaʊt/ sich herausstellen p. 87, 6
(to) turn over /ˌtɜːn ˈəʊvə/ (sich) umdrehen NHG 7
(to) take turns (irr) /ˌteɪk ˈtɜːnz/ sich abwechseln NHG 6
tutor /ˈtjuːtə/ Nachhilfelehrer/in p. 98, 10
(to) tutor /ˈtjuːtə/ Nachhilfe geben p. 98, 10
tutoring /ˈtjuːtərɪŋ/ Nachhilfe p. 98, 10
TV (= television) /ˌtiː ˈviː, ˈtelɪˌvɪʒn/ Fernsehen; Fernseher NHG 6
(to) watch TV /ˌwɒtʃ tiː ˈviː/ Fernsehen gucken NHG 5

twice /twaɪs/ zweimal NHG 7
twin /twɪn/ Zwilling; Zwillings- NHG 5
Twin Towers /ˌtwɪn ˈtaʊəz/ Zwillingstürme in New York City p. 21, 2
twisted /ˈtwɪstɪd/ verdreht, verschlungen p. 122, 7
type /taɪp/ Art NHG 6; Typ p. 46, 4
typical /ˈtɪpɪkl/ typisch NHG 5

U

ugly /ˈʌgli/ hässlich NHG 6
the UK (= United Kingdom) /ðə ˌjuː ˈkeɪ, juːˌnaɪtɪd ˈkɪŋdəm/ Vereinigtes Königreich NHG 6
ultimate /ˈʌltɪmət/ höchste(r, s); stärkste(r, s) p. 13, 6
umbrella /ʌmˈbrelə/ Regenschirm p. 65, 12
unacceptable /ˌʌnəkˈseptəbl/ inakzeptabel p. 69, 2
uncle /ˈʌŋkl/ Onkel NHG 5
uncomfortable /ʌnˈkʌmftəbl/ unbequem NHG 7
(to) feel uncomfortable (irr) /ˌfiːl ʌnˈkʌmftəbl/ sich unwohl fühlen p. 38, 6
under /ˈʌndə/ unter NHG 5; darunter p. 26, 8
underground /ˈʌndəˌgraʊnd/ U-Bahn NHG 6
(to) underline /ˌʌndəˈlaɪn/ unterstreichen p. 36, 3
(to) understand (irr) /ˌʌndəˈstænd/ verstehen NHG 5
understanding /ˌʌndəˈstændɪŋ/ Verständnis p. 71, 5
underworld /ˈʌndəwɜːld/ Unterwelt p. 141
unemployment rate /ˌʌnɪmˈplɔɪmənt reɪt/ Arbeitslosenrate p. 107, 2
unfortunately /ʌnˈfɔːtʃnətli/ unglücklicherweise NHG 6
unhappy /ʌnˈhæpi/ unglücklich p. 58, 2
unified /ˈjuːnɪfaɪd/ vereint p. 25, 7
unique /juːˈniːk/ einzigartig NHG 7
unit /ˈjuːnɪt/ Kapitel NHG 5
the United States /ðə juːˌnaɪtɪd ˈsteɪts/ die Vereinigten Staaten p. 14, 7
universal /ˌjuːnɪˈvɜːsl/ allgemein; universell p. 71, 5

university /ˌjuːnɪˈvɜːsəti/ Universität NHG 7
unknown /ʌnˈnəʊn/ unbekannt p. 66, 14
unless /ənˈles/ außer wenn NHG 7
unlike /ʌnˈlaɪk/ anders als p. 39, 6
unnecessary /ʌnˈnesəsəri/ unnötig p. 111, 7
(to) **unpack** /ʌnˈpæk/ auspacken p. 48, 7
unrest /ʌnˈrest/ Unruhen; Spannungen P&P 8
(to) **unscramble** /ʌnˈskræmbl/ ordnen, in die richtige Reihenfolge bringen p. 12, 4
until /ənˈtɪl/ bis NHG 6
unusual /ʌnˈjuːʒuəl/ ungewöhnlich NHG 5
up /ʌp/ nach oben; hinauf; oben NHG 5
What's up? *(informal)* /ˌwɒtsˈʌp/ Was ist los? NHG 7
(to) **be up to something** *(irr)* /ˌbiˌʌp tə ˈsʌmθɪŋ/ etwas vorhaben p. 45, 2
up (to) /ʌp tuː/ bis (zu) p. 50, 8
(to) **update** /ˌʌpˈdeɪt/ auf den neuesten Stand bringen p. 97, 9
upper /ˈʌpə/ obere(r, s) NHG 7
upset /ʌpˈset/ aufgebracht; aufgeregt NHG 7
urban /ˈɜːbən/ städtisch p. 150
us /ʌs/ uns NHG 5
(the) US (= United States) /ðəˌjuːˈes, juːˌnaɪtɪd ˈsteɪts/ US, Vereinigte Staaten (von Amerika); US- p. 6
US-American /ˌjuːˌesəˈmerɪkən/ US-Amerikaner/in; US-amerikanisch p. 9
the USA (= United States of America) /ðəˌjuːˌesˈeɪ, juːˌnaɪtɪdˌsteɪtsˌəvəˈmerɪkə/ USA; Vereinigte Staaten von Amerika NHG 6
use /juːs/ Verwendung; Einsatz NHG 7
(to) **use** /juːz/ benutzen NHG 5
used /juːzd/ gebraucht p. 87, 6
(to) **used to** + *infinitive* /ˈjuːst tuː/ früher + *Vergangenheitsform* NHG 6
useful /ˈjuːsfl/ nützlich NHG 5
usually /ˈjuːʒuəli/ gewöhnlich; normalerweise NHG 5

V

vacation *(AE)* /vəˈkeɪʃn/ Ferien; Urlaub p. 34, 2
(to) **vacuum** /ˈvækjuəm/ staubsaugen NHG 5
valuable /ˈvæljʊbl/ wertvoll p. 86, 6
value /ˈvæljuː/ Wert p. 89, 9
variety /vəˈraɪəti/ Vielfalt; Auswahl p. 10, 2
(to) **vary** /ˈveəri/ variieren; verschieden sein p. 26, 8
vegan /ˈviːgən/ Veganer/in; vegan NHG 7
vegetable /ˈvedʒtəbl/ Gemüse NHG 7
vegetarian /ˌvedʒəˈteəriən/ Vegetarier/in; vegetarisch NHG 7
veggie *(informal)* /ˈvedʒi/ Gemüse NHG 7
verse /vɜːs/ Strophe; Vers NHG 6
version /ˈvɜːʃn/ Version, Fassung NHG 5
vertical /ˈvɜːtɪkl/ vertikal; senkrecht p. 150
very /ˈveri/ sehr NHG 5
the very first /ðəˌveri ˈfɜːst/ der/die/das allererste p. 6
very much /ˌveri ˈmʌtʃ/ sehr NHG 6
vet /vet/ Tierarzt/Tierärztin NHG 6
via /ˈvaɪə/ über p. 69, 2
victory /ˈvɪktri/ Sieg NHG 6
(to) **videochat** /ˈvɪdiəʊtʃæt/ einen Videochat machen p. 40, 7
view /vjuː/ (Aus)sicht NHG 6
point of view /ˌpɔɪnt əvˈvjuː/ Ansicht; Perspektive p. 59, 3
Viking /ˈvaɪkɪŋ/ Wikinger/in; Wikinger- p. 121, 6
village /ˈvɪlɪdʒ/ Dorf NHG 7
violence /ˈvaɪələns/ Gewalt p. 14, 7
virtual /ˈvɜːtʃuəl/ virtuell p. 68, 2
visa /ˈviːzə/ Visum p. 106, 2
vision /ˈvɪʒn/ Vorstellung; Vision p. 86, 6
visit /ˈvɪzɪt/ Besuch NHG 5
(to) **visit** /ˈvɪzɪt/ besuchen NHG 6
visitor /ˈvɪzɪtə/ Besucher/in NHG 6
vocational /vəʊˈkeɪʃnəl/ beruflich p. 40, 7
voice /vɔɪs/ Stimme NHG 6
tone of voice /ˌtəʊn əvˈvɔɪs/ Ton p. 71, 5
voice message /ˈvɔɪsˌmesɪdʒ/ Sprachnachricht p. 68, 1
volunteer /ˌvɒlənˈtɪə/ ehrenamtlich p. 87, 6
(to) **volunteer** /ˌvɒlənˈtɪə/ sich freiwillig melden p. 96, 8
volunteering /ˌvɒlənˈtɪərɪŋ/ Verrichten von Freiwilligendienst p. 95, 7
voyage /ˈvɔɪɪdʒ/ Reise; Seereise p. 121, 6

W

minimum wage /ˌmɪnɪməm ˈweɪdʒ/ Mindestlohn p. 17, 10
wagon /ˈwægən/ Planwagen p. 110, 6
wagon train /ˈwægən treɪn/ Planwagenzug p. 110, 6
(to) **wait** /weɪt/ (er)warten NHG 5
waiter/waitress /ˈweɪtə, ˈweɪtrəs/ Kellner/in NHG 7
waiting room /ˈweɪtɪŋˌruːm/ Wartezimmer NHG 7
(to) **wake up** *(irr)* /ˌweɪkˈʌp/ aufwachen NHG 6
walk /wɔːk/ Spaziergang NHG 5
(to) **walk** /wɔːk/ gehen NHG 5
(to) **take a dog for a walk** *(irr)* /ˌteɪk əˌdɒg fərəˈwɔːk/ mit einem Hund Gassi gehen p. 141
walk of life /ˌwɔːk əvˈlaɪf/ Lebensbereich; Gesellschaftsschicht p. 89, 9
walking path /ˈwɔːkɪŋ pɑːθ/ Wanderpfad p. 135
walking tour /ˈwɔːkɪŋ tʊə/ Wanderung p. 27, 10
wall /wɔːl/ Wand NHG 6
Wall Street /ˈwɔːl striːt/ *Straße in New York, auf der sich viele Banken und die weltgrößte Wertpapierbörse befinden* p. 25, 7
wallpaper /ˈwɔːlpeɪpə/ Tapete p. 65, 12
(to) **want (to)** /wɒnt/ wollen NHG 5
(to) **want somebody to do something** /wɒntˌsʌmbədi təˈduːˌsʌmθɪŋ/ wollen, dass jemand etwas tut P&P 8
war /wɔː/ Krieg NHG 7
War of Independence /ˌwɔːr əvˌɪndɪˈpendəns/ (Amerikanischer) Unabhängigkeitskrieg p. 14, 7

Dictionary

ward /wɔːd/ Station p. 92, 2
(to) **warn** /wɔːn/ warnen NHG 7
warrior /ˈwɒriə/ Krieger/in p. 121, 6
(to) **wash** /wɒʃ/ waschen; sich waschen NHG 5
waste /weɪst/ Abfall NHG 7
(to) **waste** /weɪst/ verschwenden NHG 7
waste disposal plant /ˌweɪst dɪˈspəʊzl plɑːnt/ Abfallentsorgungsanlage p. 86, 6
watch /wɒtʃ/ (Armband)uhr NHG 6
(to) **watch** /wɒtʃ/ beobachten; ansehen NHG 5
(to) **watch TV** /ˌwɒtʃ tiːˈviː/ Fernsehen gucken NHG 5
water /ˈwɔːtə/ Wasser NHG 5
water tower /ˈwɔːtə ˌtaʊə/ Wasserturm p. 25, 7
waterfall /ˈwɔːtəfɔːl/ Wasserfall p. 21, 2
wave /weɪv/ Welle p. 109, 5
(to) **wave a flag** /ˌweɪv ə ˈflæɡ/ eine Fahne schwenken p. 40, 7
way /weɪ/ Weg; Art NHG 5
this way /ˈðɪs weɪ/ hier entlang NHG 5
that way /ˈðæt weɪ/ so, auf diese Weise p. 58, 3
way (informal) /weɪ/ viel p. 48, 7
way of living /ˌweɪ əv ˈlɪvɪŋ/ Lebensweise p. 14, 7
we /wiː/ wir NHG 5
weakness /ˈwiːknəs/ Schwäche p. 61, 6
(to) **wear** (irr) /weə/ tragen (Kleidung) NHG 5
weather /ˈweðə/ Wetter NHG 5
Wednesday /ˈwenzdeɪ/ Mittwoch NHG 5
(on) **Wednesdays** /ˈwenzdeɪz/ mittwochs NHG 5
week /wiːk/ Woche NHG 5
weekend /ˌwiːkˈend/ Wochenende NHG 5
on the weekends (AE) /ˌɒn ðə ˈwiːkendz/ an den Wochenenden p. 97, 9
(to) **welcome** /ˈwelkəm/ willkommen heißen p. 34, 2
welcome (to) /ˈwelkəm tʊ/ willkommen (in) NHG 5
You're welcome. /jɔː ˈwelkəm/ Gern geschehen.; Keine Ursache. NHG 7

welding /ˈweldɪŋ/ Schweißen p. 43, 14
well /wel/ nun NHG 5; gut NHG 6
(to) **get well** (irr) /ˌɡet ˈwel/ gesund werden NHG 7
Get well soon! /ˌɡet ˌwel ˈsuːn/ Gute Besserung! NHG 7
well done /ˌwel ˈdʌn/ gut gemacht NHG 6
well-known /ˌwelˈnəʊn/ bekannt; berühmt NHG 7
Welsh /welʃ/ walisisch p. 162
were /wɜː/ hier: würde(st, n, t) p. 17, 10
west /west/ Westen p. 10, 2
west /west/ westlich P&P 1
western /ˈwestən/ West-, westlich p. 122, 7
wet /wet/ nass NHG 6
wetlands (pl) /ˈwetləndz/ Sumpfgebiet p. 11, 2
whale /weɪl/ Wal p. 65, 12
what /wɒt/ was; welche(r, s) NHG 5
What about ...? /ˌwɒt əˈbaʊt ˈ.../ Was ist mit ...? / Wie wäre es mit ...? NHG 5
What's on? (informal) /ˌwɒts ˈɒn/ Was ist los? NHG 6
What's the matter? /ˌwɒts ðə ˈmætə/ Was ist los? NHG 7
What's the time, please? /ˌwɒts ðə ˈtaɪm pliːz/ Wie spät ist es, bitte? NHG 5
What's up? (informal) /ˌwɒts ˈʌp/ Was ist los? NHG 7
What's wrong? (informal) /ˌwɒts ˈrɒŋ/ Was ist los? NHG 7
What time is it? /ˌwɒt ˈtaɪm ɪz ɪt/ Wie spät ist es? NHG 5
whatever /wɒtˈevə/ was (auch immer) NHG 6
wheel /wiːl/ Rad NHG 6
wheelchair /ˈwiːltʃeə/ Rollstuhl NHG 7
when /wen/ wann; wenn; als NHG 5
whenever /wenˈevə/ wann auch immer p. 24, 6
where /weə/ wo; wohin NHG 5
whereas /weərˈæz/ während; wohingegen p. 71, 5
wherever /werˈevə/ wo(her) auch immer p. 25, 7
whether /ˈweðə/ ob p. 42, 11
which /wɪtʃ/ welche(r, s); was NHG 5

while /waɪl/ während NHG 6; Weile NHG 7
for a while /fər ə ˈwaɪl/ eine Weile NHG 7
white /waɪt/ weiß NHG 5
White /waɪt/ *Weiße/r* p. 25, 7
who /huː/ wer; der/die/das NHG 5
whoever /huːˈevə/ wer auch immer p. 25, 7
whole /həʊl/ ganz, gesamt NHG 6
as a whole /əz ə ˈhəʊl/ als Ganzes p. 85, 5
whom /huːm/ wem; wen; der/die/das p. 62, 8
whose /huːz/ wessen NHG 5; dessen, deren p. 11, 2
why /waɪ/ warum NHG 5
wide /waɪd/ weit NHG 7; groß; breit; enorm p. 10, 2
wife (pl **wives**) /waɪf, waɪvz/ Ehefrau NHG 5
wildlife /ˈwaɪldlaɪf/ Tier- und Pflanzenwelt; Flora und Fauna NHG 6
will /wɪl/ werden NHG 6
(to) **be willing to** (irr) /ˌbiː ˈwɪlɪŋ tʊ/ bereit sein p. 89, 9
(to) **win** (irr) /wɪn/ gewinnen NHG 7
(to) **win a scholarship** (irr) /ˌwɪn ə ˈskɒləʃɪp/ ein Stipendium bekommen p. 82, 2
winding /ˈwaɪndɪŋ/ gewunden, sich schlängelnd p. 144
window /ˈwɪndəʊ/ Fenster NHG 5
winged /wɪŋd/ mit Flügeln, geflügelt p. 122, 7
(to) **wish** /wɪʃ/ wünschen, sich wünschen NHG 7
(to) **wish for** (something) /ˈwɪʃ fɔː/ sich (etwas) wünschen p. 90, 11
with /wɪð/ mit; bei NHG 5
within /wɪðˈɪn/ innerhalb, innen p. 26, 8
without /wɪðˈaʊt/ ohne NHG 5
wolf (pl **wolves**) /wʊlf, wʊlvz/ Wolf p. 111, 7
woman (pl **women**) /ˈwʊmən, ˈwɪmɪn/ Frau NHG 5
women's studies /ˈwɪmɪnz ˌstʌdiz/ *Schulfach, das die Rolle der Frau in Geschichte, Gesellschaft und Literatur untersucht* p. 40, 7
won't /wəʊnt/ nicht werden NHG 6

(to) wonder /ˈwʌndə/ sich fragen NHG 6
wonder /ˈwʌndə/ Wunder p. 11, 2
wonderful /ˈwʌndəfl/ wunderbar, wundervoll NHG 6
wood /wʊd/ Holz NHG 6
wooden /ˈwʊdn/ Holz-, hölzern p. 111, 7
woodland /ˈwʊdlənd/ Waldgebiet p. 135
woodworking /ˈwʊdˌwɜːkɪŋ/ Tischlern p. 41, 8
word /wɜːd/ Wort NHG 5
(to) spread the word (irr) /ˌspred ðə ˈwɜːd/ es allen mitteilen p. 87, 6
word web /ˈwɜːd web/ Wortnetz NHG 5
wordbank /ˈwɜːdbæŋk/ Wortsammlung NHG 5
work /wɜːk/ Arbeit; Werk NHG 5
(to) work /wɜːk/ arbeiten NHG 5; funktionieren NHG 6
field of work /ˌfiːld əv ˈwɜːk/ Arbeitsbereich p. 15, 7
(to) work shifts /ˌwɜːk ˈʃɪfts/ Schichtdienst machen p. 92, 2
(to) work on /ˈwɜːk ˌɒn/ arbeiten an p. 96, 8
(to) work out /ˌwɜːk ˈaʊt/ sich entwickeln p. 62, 8
workbook /ˈwɜːkbʊk/ Arbeitsheft p. 10, 1
worker /ˈwɜːkə/ Arbeiter/in p. 93, 2
working /ˈwɜːkɪŋ/ funktionierend NHG 7
working /ˈwɜːkɪŋ/ arbeitend p. 45, 2
working hours (pl) /ˈwɜːkɪŋ ˌaʊəz/ Arbeitszeiten p. 93, 3
worksheet /ˈwɜːkʃiːt/ Arbeitsblatt p. 29, 15
world /wɜːld/ Welt NHG 5
all over the world /ˌɔːl ˌəʊvə ðə ˈwɜːld/ auf der ganzen Welt NHG 6
from (all) around the world /frəm ˌɔːl ˌə ˌraʊnd ðə ˈwɜːld/ aus der (ganzen) Welt NHG 7
from all over the world /frəm ˌɔːl ˌəʊvə ðə ˈwɜːld/ aus der ganzen Welt NHG 5
World War I /ˌwɜːld ˌwɔː ˈwʌn/ Erster Weltkrieg p. 15, 7
World War II /ˌwɜːld ˌwɔː ˈtuː/ Zweiter Weltkrieg p. 15, 7

world-class /ˌwɜːld ˈklɑːs/ Weltklasse- P&P 2
world-famous /ˌwɜːld ˈfeɪməs/ weltberühmt NHG 7
worried /ˈwʌrid/ beunruhigt; besorgt NHG 6
(to) worry /ˈwʌri/ sich Sorgen machen NHG 5
Don't worry. /ˌdəʊnt ˈwʌri/ Mach dir keine Sorgen. NHG 7
worse /wɜːs/ schlechter, schlimmer NHG 6
the worst /ðə ˈwɜːst/ der/die/das schlechteste/schlimmste; am schlechtesten/schlimmsten NHG 6
worth /wɜːθ/ wert p. 86, 6
(to) be worth (irr) /ˌbiː ˈwɜːθ/ (sich) lohnen; wert sein NHG 7
worthy /ˈwɜːði/ würdig p. 89, 9
would /wʊd/ würde(st, n, t) NHG 5
wound /wuːnd/ Wunde NHG 7
wound dressing /ˈwuːnd ˌdresɪŋ/ Verband p. 92, 2
wrist /rɪst/ Handgelenk NHG 7
(to) write (irr) /raɪt/ schreiben NHG 5
(to) write down (irr) /ˌraɪt ˈdaʊn/ aufschreiben NHG 5
writer /ˈraɪtə/ Schriftsteller/in p. 19, 13
writing /ˈraɪtɪŋ/ Schrift; Schreiben NHG 7
written /ˈrɪtn/ schriftlich NHG 6
wrong /rɒŋ/ falsch NHG 6
(to) be wrong (irr) /ˌbiː ˈrɒŋ/ im Unrecht sein NHG 7
(to) be wrong (with) (irr) /ˌbiː ˈrɒŋ wɪθ/ nicht in Ordnung sein (mit) NHG 7
What's wrong? (informal) /ˌwɒts ˈrɒŋ/ Was ist los? NHG 7

X

(to) take an X-ray (irr) /ˌteɪk ən ˈeksreɪ/ eine Röntgenaufnahme machen NHG 7

Y

year /jɪə/ Jahr NHG 5; Schuljahr; Klasse NHG 6
all year round /ˌɔːl ˈjɪə raʊnd/ das ganze Jahr lang p. 10, 2
yearbook /ˈjɪəbʊk/ Jahrbuch p. 33

yellow /ˈjeləʊ/ gelb NHG 5
yes /jes/ ja NHG 5
yesterday /ˈjestədeɪ/ gestern NHG 6
yet /jet/ schon; noch NHG 7
you /juː/ du; dich; dir; man; ihr; euch; Sie; Ihnen NHG 5
young /jʌŋ/ jung NHG 6
your /jɔː/ dein(e); euer/eure; Ihr(e) NHG 5
yours /jɔːz/ deine(r, s); eure(r, s); Ihre(r, s) NHG 6
yours /jɔːz/ mit freundlichen Grüßen (am Ende eines formellen Briefes) p. 75, 11
yours sincerely /ˌjɔːz sɪnˈsɪəli/ mit freundlichen Grüßen (am Ende eines formellen Briefes) NHG 6
yourself /jɔːˈself/ dir, dich; sich NHG 5
yourselves /jɔːˈselvz/ euch; selbst p. 52, 12
youth club /ˈjuːθ ˌklʌb/ Jugendklub NHG 6
youth culture /ˈjuːθ ˌkʌltʃə/ Jugendkultur p. 11, 2
youth hostel /ˈjuːθ ˌhɒstl/ Jugendherberge p. 75, 10

Z

zip /zɪp/ Reißverschluss NHG 7
zoological /ˌzuːəˈlɒdʒɪkl/ zoologisch p. 135

Names

First names

Aaron (m.) /ˈeərən/
Alissa (f.) /əˈlɪsə/
Amy (f.) /ˈeɪmi/
Andrea (m., f.) /ˈændriə/
Andy (m., f.) /ˈændi/
Anna (f.) /ˈænə/
Anne, Annie (f.) /æn, ˈæni/
Anthony (m.) /ˈæntəni/
Anton (m.) /ˈæntɒn/
Arda (m., f.) /ˈɑːdə/
Arnold (m.) /ˈɑːnld/
Asher (m.) /ˈæʃə/
Ashley (m., f.) /ˈæʃli/
Avery (m., f.) /ˈeɪvəri/
Barack (m.) /ˈbæræk/
Belky (f.) /ˈbelki/
Ben (m.) /ben/
Benjamin (m.) /ˈbendʒəmɪn/
Bilal (m.) /ˌbɪˈlɑːl/
Bill, Billy (m.) /bɪl, ˈbɪli/
Bradey (m.) /ˈbreɪdi/
Brandon (m.) /ˈbrændən/
Brendan (m.) /ˈbrendən/
Britt (f.) /brɪt/
Bruno (m.) /ˈbruːnəʊ/
Camila (f.) /kəˈmɪlə/
Carlos (m.) /ˈkɑːlɒs/
Catherine (f.) /ˈkæθrɪn/
Chenoa (f.) /tʃeˈnəʊə/
Christopher (m.) /ˈkrɪstəfə/
Cindy (f.) /ˈsɪndi/
Clive (m.) /klaɪv/
Cody (m.) /ˈkəʊdi/
Damian, Damien (m.) /ˈdeɪmiən/
Dana (f.) /ˈdɑːnə/
David (m.) /ˈdeɪvɪd/
Declan (m.) /ˈdeklən/
Dharna (f.) /ˈdɑːnə/
Ed (m.) /ed/
Eleanor (f.) /ˈelənə/
Elizabeth (f.) /ɪˈlɪzəbəθ/
Ella (f.) /ˈelə/
Emily (f.) /ˈeməli/
Emma (f.) /ˈemə/
Enrico (m.) /enˈriːkəʊ/
Enrique (m.) /enˈriːkeɪ/
Eric (m.) /ˈerɪk/
Fabio (m.) /ˈfæbiəʊ/
Finn (m.) /fɪn/
Gabi (m., f.) /ˈgæbi/
Gabriel (m.) /ˈgeɪbriəl/
George (m.) /dʒɔːdʒ/
Henry (m.) /ˌɒnˈriː/
Jack (m.) /dʒæk/
Jake (m.) /dʒeɪk/
James (m.) /dʒeɪmz/
Janet (f.) /ˈdʒænɪt/
Jasmine (f.) /ˈdʒæzmɪn/
Jayden (m., f.) /ˈdʒeɪdn/
Jean (m., f.) /dʒiːn/
Jeanne (f.) /dʒiːn/
Jenna (f.) /ˈdʒenə/
Jerome (m.) /dʒəˈrəʊm/
Ji-Hoon (m.) /dʒiˈhuːn/
Jo, Joe (m., f.) /dʒəʊ/
John(ny) (m.) /dʒɒn, ˈdʒɒni/
José (m.) /həʊˈzeɪ/
Joshua (m.) /ˈdʒɒʃuə/
Julia (f.) /ˈdʒuːliə/
June (f.) /dʒuːn/
Justin (m.) /ˈdʒʌstɪn/
Katie (f.) /ˈkeɪti/
Kelsey (m., f.) /ˈkelsi/
Kim (f.) /kɪm/
Laura (f.) /ˈlɔːrə/
Lauren (f.) /ˈlɔːrən/
Lea, Leah (f.) /ˈliːə/
Levi (m.) /ˈliːvaɪ/
Li (f.) /liː/
Liam (m.) /ˈliːəm/
Lian (m.) /ˈliːən/
Linda (f.) /ˈlɪndə/
Linh (f.) /lɪn/
Liz, Lizzie (f.) /lɪz, ˈlɪzi/
Lourdes (f.) /lʊəd/
Lucas (m.) /ˈluːkəs/
Lucia (f.) /ˈluːsiə/
Lucy (f.) /ˈluːsi/
Luis (m.) /ˈluːɪs/
Luther (m.) /ˈluːθə/
Lyndon (m.) /ˈlɪndən/
Marcus (m.) /ˈmɑːkəs/
Marian (f.) /ˈmæriən/
Martin (m.) /ˈmɑːtɪn/
Mary (f.) /ˈmeəri/
Mason (m.) /ˈmeɪsn/
Matt (m.) /mæt/
Mia (f.) /ˈmiːə/
Michael (m.) /ˈmaɪkl/
Michelle (f.) /miːˈʃel/
Miriam (f.) /ˈmɪriəm/
Nathan (m.) /ˈneɪθn/
Neil (m.) /niːl/
Nick (m.) /nɪk/
Nihal (m.) /nɪˈhɑːl/
Noah (m.) /ˈnəʊə/
Olivia (f.) /əˈlɪviə/
Patrick (m.) /ˈpætrɪk/
Patsy (f.) /ˈpætsi/
Paul (m.) /pɔːl/
Penny (f.) /ˈpeni/
Pete (m.) /piːt/
Phil, Philip (m.) /fɪl, ˈfɪlɪp/
Rafael (m.) /ˈræfeɪəl/
Ramos (m.) /ˈrɑːmɒs/
Rebecca (f.) /rɪˈbekə/
Reese (m., f.) /riːs/
Reza (m.) /ˈriːzə/
Rhiannon (f.) /rɪˈænən/
Ro(bbie) (m., f.) /rəʊ, ˈrɒbi/
Robert (m.) /ˈrɒbət/
Roberto (m.) /rəˈbɜːtəʊ/
Rosa (f.) /ˈrəʊzə/
Rosanne (f.) /rəʊˈzæn/
Rosemarie (f.) /ˈrəʊzməri/
Ruby (f.) /ˈruːbi/
Ryan (m.) /ˈraɪən/
Samoset (m.) /ˈsɑːməzet/
Sandra (f.) /ˈsændrə/
Sarah (f.) /ˈseərə/
Savannah (f.) /səˈvænə/
Sebastian (m.) /səˈbæstiən/
Simon (m.) /ˈsaɪmən/
Sonia (f.) /ˈsɒniə/
Squanto (m.) /ˈskwɒntəʊ/
Sri (m.) /sriː/
Steve (m.) /stiːv/
Steven (m.) /ˈstiːvən/
Stone (f.) /stəʊn/
Suri (f.) /ˈsuri/
Suzie (f.) /ˈsuːzi/
Tamara (f.) /təˈmɑːrə/
Tami (f.) /ˈtæmi/
Taylor (m., f.) /ˈteɪlə/
Todd (m.) /tɒd/
Tom (m.) /tɒm/
Ulysses (m.) /juːˈlɪsiːz/
Wan (f.) /wɒn/
Wendy (f.) /ˈwendi/

Families

Adams /ˈædəmz/
Alvarez /ælˈvɑːrez/
Armstrong /ˈɑːmstrɒŋ/
Baker /ˈbeɪkə/
Baring /ˈbeərɪŋ/
Beliard /ˌbelɪˈɑːd/
Birk /bɜːk/
Blue /bluː/
Brown /braʊn/
Campbell /ˈkæmbl/
Chang /tʃæŋ/
Chazelle /tʃəˈzel/
Choi /tʃɔɪ/
Colclough /ˈkəʊlkli/
Columbus /kəˈlʌmbəs/
Cruz /kruːz/
Cunningham /ˈkʌnɪŋəm/
Curtis /ˈkɜːtɪs/
de Sousa /dəˈsuːzə/
DeWitt /dəˈwɪt/
Ferris /ˈferɪs/
Flynn /flɪn/
Ford /fɔːd/
Fulton /ˈfʊltən/
Goldschmidt /ˈgəʊldʃmɪt/
Gosling /ˈgɒzlɪŋ/
Graham /ˈgreɪəm/
Grant /grɑːnt/
Hinawy /hɪˈnɑːwi/
Jealous /ˈdʒeləs/
Jean /dʒiːn/
Johnson /ˈdʒɒnsn/
Jones /dʒəʊnz/
Juliana /ˌdʒuːliˈɑːnə/
Kay /keɪ/
Kennedy /ˈkenədi/
King /kɪŋ/
Kracinski /krəˈtʃɪnski/
Legend /ˈledʒnd/
Lighty /ˈlaɪti/
Lincoln /ˈlɪŋkən/
Mars /mɑːz/
McRae /məˈkreɪ/
Miller /ˈmɪlə/
Milligan /ˈmɪlɪgən/
Monterres /ˌmɒnˈterəz/
Moore /mʊə/
Mulvern /ˈmʌlvən/
Nazario /nəˈzɑːriəʊ/
Newman /ˈnjuːmən/
Noor /ˈnʊə/
O'Donnell /əʊˈdɒnl/
O'Toole /əʊˈtuːl/
Obama /əʊˈbɑːmə/
Olson /ˈəʊlsn/

Parekh /'pærek/
Parks /pɑːks/
Pearce /pɪəs/
Poppins /'pɒpɪnz/
Redford /'redfəd/
Rodriguez /rɒ'driːgez/
Roosevelt /'rəʊzəvelt/
Rynhart /'raɪnhɑːt/
Schwarzenegger /'ʃwɔːtsənegə/
Simmons /'sɪmənz/
Spielberg /'spilbɜːg/
Stone /stəʊn/
Strauss /straʊs/
Tammana /tə'mɑːnə/
Tiger /'taɪgə/
Treuer /'trɔɪə/
Washington /'wɒʃɪŋtən/
Webb /web/

Other names
the Adams /ði_'ædəmz/
All-Ireland Senior Championship /ɔːl_ˌaɪələnd 'siːniə ˌtʃæmpiənʃɪp/
American Dream /əˌmerɪkən 'driːm/
American football /əˌmerɪkən 'fʊtˌbɔːl/
b-boy(ing) /'biːˌbɔɪ(ɪŋ)/
b-girl(ing) /'biːˌgɜːl(ɪŋ)/
the Battery /ðə 'bætri/
the Beastie Boys /ðə 'biːsti bɔɪz/
Bewley's /'bjuːliz/
Blarney Castle /ˌblɑːni 'kɑːsl/
Book of Kells /ˌbʊk əv 'kelz/
Brexit /'breksɪt/
Broadway /'brɔːdweɪ/
Brooklyn Bridge /ˌbrʊklɪn 'brɪdʒ/
California Institute of the Arts /ˌkæləˌfɔːniə_ˌɪnstɪˌtjuːt_əv ði_'ɑːts/
Central Park /'sentrəl pɑːk/
Covid /'kəʊvɪd/
Disneyworld /'dɪzniwɜːld/
Dolphin Discovery /'dɒlfɪn dɪˌskʌvri/
Donkey /'dɒŋki/
Dublinia /dʌ'blɪnɪə/
Dumbo /'dʌmbəʊ/
Empire State Building /ˌempaɪə 'steɪt ˌbɪldɪŋ/
EPIC /ˌiː pi_aɪ 'siː, 'epɪk/
European Union /ˌjʊərəˌpiːən 'juːniən/
FBLA /ˌef biˌel_'eɪ/
First Nation /ˌfɜːst 'neɪʃn/
folk /fəʊk/
Founding Fathers /ˌfaʊndɪŋ 'fɑːðəz/
Freedom Tower /'friːdəm ˌtaʊə/
funk /fʌŋk/
Gaelic football /ˌgeɪlɪk 'fʊtbɔːl/
Golden Gate Bridge /ˌgəʊldən geɪt 'brɪdʒ/
Grafton Street /ˌgrɑːftən striːt/
Grand Central Station /ˌgrænd ˌsentrəl 'steɪʃn/
the High Line /ðə 'haɪ laɪn/
Hook Lighthouse /ˌhʊk 'laɪtˌhaʊs/
huckleberry pie /ˌhʌklbəri 'paɪ/
Immigrant Heritage Week /ˌɪmɪgrənt 'herɪtɪdʒ wiːk/
Independence Day / Hall /ˌɪndɪ'pendəns deɪ / hɔːl/
Irish Emigration Museum /ˌaɪrɪʃˌemɪ'greɪʃn mjuːˌziːəm/
the Irish Free State /ðiˌaɪrɪʃ friː 'steɪt/
the Irish War of Independence /ðiˌaɪrɪʃ ˌwɔːr_əv_ˌɪndɪ'pendəns/
Isle of Tears /ˌaɪl əv 'tɪəz/
Jeanie Johnston /ˌdʒiːni 'dʒɒnstn/
Juneteenth /ˌdʒuːn'tiːnθ/
Kool Herc /ˌkuːl 'hɜːk/
Lady Liberty /ˌleɪdi 'lɪbəti/
LaLaLand /'lɑːlɑːlænd/
Lemon Rock /ˌlemən 'rɒk/
the Leonardos /ðə ˌliːəʊ'nɑːdəʊz/
Los Angeles Times /lɒsˌændʒəliːz 'taɪmz/
Marble Arch /ˌmɑːbl_'ɑːtʃ/
Martin Luther King Jr. Day /ˌmɑːtɪn ˌluːθə ˌkɪŋ 'dʒuːniə deɪ/
Massasoit /ˌmæsə'swɑ/
Mayflower /'meɪˌflaʊə/
Merry-Go-Round /'meri gəʊ ˌraʊnd/
the Met(ropolitan Opera) /ðə 'met, metrəˌpɒlɪtn_'ɒprə/
Mickey Mouse /ˌmɪki 'maʊs/
the MoMA, Museum of Modern Art /ðə 'məʊmə, mjuːˌziːəm_əv ˌmɒdən_'ɑːt/
mood board /'muːd bɔːd/
mxmtoon /ˌem_eksˌem 'tuːn/
National Association for the Advancement of Colored People, NAACP /ˌnæʃnəl_əˌsəʊsiˌeɪʃn fə ðiː_əd,vɑːnsmənt_əv ˌkʌləd 'piːpl, ˌen dʌbəl_ˌeɪ siː 'piː/
Navajo /'nævəhəʊ/
Nazi /'nɑːtsi/
NBA (= National Basketball Association) /ˌen biˌ'eɪ, ðə ˌnæʃnəl 'bɑːskɪtbɔːl_əˌsəʊsiˌeɪʃn/
Nevada /nɪ'vɑːdə/
New Year's Day /ˌnjuː jɪəz 'deɪ/
the New York Times /ðə ˌnjuː jɔːk 'taɪmz/
NFL (= National Football League) /ˌen_efˌ'el, ðə ˌnæʃnəl 'fʊtbɔːl_ˌliːg/
9/11 Memorial /ˌnaɪn_ɪˌlevn mə'mɔːriəl/
North Pool /ˌnɔːθ puːl/
North Tower /ˌnɔːθ ˌtaʊə/
Ojibwe /əʊ'dʒɪbweɪ/
One World Trade Center /ˌwʌn ˌwɜːld_'treɪd ˌsentə/
Opening Day /ˌəʊpənɪŋ deɪ/
the Oscars /ðiˌ'ɒskəz/
Oxford Dictionary /'ɒksfəd ˌdɪkʃənri/
Palacio /pə'lɑːsɪəʊ/
Pancake Day /'pænkeɪk deɪ/
Panthers /'pænθəz/
paraclimbing /'pærəˌklaɪmɪŋ/
Parade of Flags /pəˌreɪd_əv_'flægz/
Pennington /'penɪŋtən/
Philly cheesesteak /ˌfɪli 'tʃiːzˌsteɪk/
Pilgrim Fathers /ˌpɪlgrɪm 'fɑːðəz/
Pizza Hut /'piːtsə hʌt/
Powerscourt Estate /ˌpaʊəzkɔːt_ɪ'steɪt/
the Ring of Kerry /ðə ˌrɪŋ_əv 'keri/
Rockefeller Center /'rɒkəˌfelə ˌsentə/
Sea Adventure Waterpark /ˌsiː_ədˌventʃə 'wɔːtəˌpɑːk/
Sedgwick Avenue /'sedʒwɪkˌ'ævənjuː/
the Shamrocks /ðə 'ʃæmrɒks/
Shrek /ʃrek/
Skywalk /'skaɪˌwɔːk/
soul /səʊl/
South Pool /'saʊθ puːl/
South Tower /'saʊθ ˌtaʊə/
St John's Juniors /sənt ˌdʒɒnz 'dʒuːniəz/
St Stephen's Green /sənt ˌstiːvnz 'griːn/
the Statue of Liberty /ðə ˌstætʃuˌəv 'lɪbəti/
Stories from Home /ˌstɔːriz frəm 'həʊm/
Super Bowl /'suːpə bəʊl/
Supreme Court /suˌpriːm 'kɔːt/
Temple Bar /ˌtempl 'bɑː/
Thanksgiving /'θæŋksˌgɪvɪŋ/
Top Tutoring /ˌtɒp 'tjuːtərɪŋ/
Torc /tɔːk/
the Trail of Tears /ðə ˌtreɪl_əv 'tɪəz/
Trinity College /ˌtrɪnəti 'kɒlɪdʒ/
the Troubles /ðə 'trʌblz/
Twin Towers /ˌtwɪn 'taʊəz/
the Universal Hip-Hop Museum /ðə ˌjuːnɪˌvɜːsl 'hɪp hɒp mjuːˌziːəm/
Wall Street /'wɔːl striːt/
Wampanoag /ˌwɒmpə'nəʊæg/

Names

War of Independence /ˌwɔːr_əv_ˌɪndɪˈpendəns/
World Trade Center /ˌwɜːld_ˈtreɪd ˌsentə/
Yankee /ˈjæŋki/
Yankees /ˈjæŋkiz/
Yellowstone /ˈjeləʊstəʊn/

Geographical Names

Africa /ˈæfrɪkə/
Alabama /ˌæləˈbæmə/
Alaska /əˈlæskə/
America /əˈmerɪkə/
Antarctica /ænˈtɑːktɪkə/
Arizona /ˌærɪˈzəʊnə/
Asia /ˈeɪʒə/
Atlantic /ətˈlæntɪk/
Atlantic Ocean /ətˌlæntɪk_ˈəʊʃn/
Australia /ɒˈstreɪliə/
Bath /bɑːθ/
Blarney /ˈblɑːni/
Boston /ˈbɒstən/
Brazil /brəˈzɪl/
Britain /ˈbrɪtn/
the Bronx /ðə ˈbrɒŋks/
Brooklyn /ˈbrʊklɪn/
Buffalo /ˈbʌfələʊ/
Caherdaniel /ˈkəʊəˌdænjəl/
Cahergal /kəˈhɜːɡl/
California /ˌkæləˈfɔːniə/
Campbell County /ˌkæmbl ˈkaʊnti/
Canada /ˈkænədə/
the Caribbean /ðə ˌkærɪˈbiən/
Central America /ˌsentrəl_əˈmerɪkə/
Chicago /ʃɪˈkɑːɡəʊ/
China /ˈtʃaɪnə/
Chinatown /ˈtʃaɪnəˌtaʊn/
Cobh /kəʊv/
Colorado /ˌkɒləˈrɑːdəʊ/
Coney Island /ˌkəʊni_ˈaɪlənd/
Connemara /ˌkɒnɪˈmɑːrə/
Cork /kɔːk/
Davis /ˈdeɪvɪs/
Denmark /ˈdenmɑːk/
Denver /ˈdenvə/
Derrynane /ˈderɪneɪn/
Des Moines /də ˈmɔɪn/
Dingle /ˈdɪŋɡl/
Dingle Peninsula /ˌdɪŋɡl pəˈnɪnsjələ/
Donegal /ˌdɒnɪˈɡɔːl/
Dublin /ˈdʌblɪn/
East River /ˌiːst ˈrɪvə/
Edison /ˈedɪsən/
Ellis Island /ˌelɪs_ˈaɪlənd/
England /ˈɪŋɡlənd/
Europe /ˈjʊərəp/
Everglades /ˈevəɡleɪdz/
Fairbanks /ˈfeəbæŋks/
Florida /ˈflɒrɪdə/
France /frɑːns/
Galway /ˈɡɔːlweɪ/
Germany /ˈdʒɜːməni/
Gettysburg /ˈɡetɪzbɜːɡ/
Grand Canyon /ˌɡrænd ˈkænjən/
Great Britain /ˌɡreɪt ˈbrɪtn/
the Great Plains /ðə ˌɡreɪt ˈpleɪnz/
Harlem /ˈhɑːləm/
Hawaii /həˈwaɪi/
Hawkeye Point /ˈhɔːkaɪ pɔɪnt/
Highland Park /ˌhaɪlənd ˈpɑːk/
Hollywood /ˈhɒliwʊd/
Honduras /hɒnˈdjʊərəs/
Honolulu /ˌhɒnəˈluːluː/
Indiana /ˌɪndiˈænə/
Iowa /ˈaɪəʊə/
Ireland /ˈaɪələnd/
Italy /ˈɪtəli/
Japan /dʒəˈpæn/
Kansas /ˈkænzəs/
Kenmare /kenˈmeə/
Kerry /ˈkeri/
Kilkenny /kɪlˈkeni/
Killarney /kɪˈlɑːni/
Korea /kəˈrɪə/
Lancaster /ˈlæŋkəstə/
Las Vegas /læs ˈveɪɡəs/
Lebanon /ˈlebənən/
Liberty Island /ˌlɪbəti_ˈaɪlənd/
Liffey /ˈlɪfi/
Limerick /ˈlɪmərɪk/
London /ˈlʌndən/
Los Angeles /lɒs_ˈændʒəliːz/
Louisiana /luˌiːziˈænə/
Malta /ˈmɔːltə/
Manhattan /mænˈhætn/
Massachusetts /ˌmæsəˈtʃuːsɪts/
Mexico /ˈmeksɪkəʊ/
Michigan /ˈmɪʃɪɡən/
Mississippi /ˌmɪsɪˈsɪpi/
Missouri /mɪˈzʊəri/
Montana /mɒnˈtænə/
Montgomery /məntˈɡʌməri/
Nashville /ˈnæʃvɪl/
Nevada /nɪˈvɑːdə/
New England /ˌnjuː_ˈɪŋɡlənd/
New Haven /ˌnjuː ˈheɪvən/
New Jersey /ˌnjuː ˈdʒɜːzi/
New Orleans /ˌnjuː ˈɔːliənz/
New York /ˌnjuː ˈjɔːk/
New York City /ˌnjuː jɔːk ˈsɪti/
North America /ˌnɔːθ_əˈmerɪkə/
North Carolina /ˌnɔːθ ˌkærəˈlaɪnə/
Northern Ireland /ˌnɔːðən_ˈaɪələnd/
NYC (= New York City) /ˌen waɪ ˈsiː, ˌnjuː jɔːk ˈsɪti/
Ohio /əʊˈhaɪəʊ/
Oklahoma /ˌəʊkləˈhəʊmə/
Oregon /ˈɒrɪɡən/
Orlando /ɔːˈlændəʊ/
PA (= Philadelphia) /ˌpiː ˈeɪ, ˌfɪləˈdelfiə/
Pacific /pəˈsɪfɪk/
Pacific Ocean /pəˌsɪfɪk_ˈəʊʃn/
Paraguay /ˈpærəɡwaɪ/
Pennsylvania /ˌpentsəlˈveɪniə/
Philadelphia /ˌfɪləˈdelfiə/
Pittsburgh /ˈpɪtsbɜːɡ/
Poland /ˈpəʊlənd/
Portland /ˈpɔːtlənd/
Puerto Rico /ˌpwɜːtəʊ ˈriːkəʊ/
Queens /kwiːnz/
the Republic of Ireland /ðə rɪˌpʌblɪk_əv_ˈaɪələnd/
Rio Grande /ˌriːəʊ ˈɡrænd/
San Diego /ˌsæn diˈeɪɡəʊ/
San Francisco /ˌsæn frənˈsɪskəʊ/
Santa Cruz /ˌsæntə ˈkruːz/
Scandinavia /ˌskændɪˈneɪviə/
Scotland /ˈskɒtlənd/
Shannon /ˈʃænən/
Silicon Valley /ˌsɪlɪkən ˈvæli/
Skagway /ˈskæɡweɪ/
Sligo /ˈslaɪɡəʊ/
Sofia /ˈsəʊfiə/
South Korea /ˌsaʊθ kəˈrɪə/
Spain /speɪn/
St. Louis /sənt ˈluːɪs/
Staten /ˈstætn/
Staten Island /ˌstætn_ˈaɪlənd/
Tegucigalpa /teˌɡuːsɪˈɡælpə/
Tennessee /ˌtenəˈsiː/
Texas /ˈteksəs/
Tokyo /ˈtəʊkiəʊ/
Topeka /təʊˈpiːkə/
Tulsa /ˈtʌlsə/
Turkey / Türkiye /ˈtɜːki, ˈtʊəkijə/
the UK (= United Kingdom) /ðə ˌjuː ˈkeɪ, juːˌnaɪtɪd ˈkɪŋdəm/
the US (= the United States) /ðə ˌjuː_ˈes, ðə juːˌnaɪtɪd ˈsteɪts/
the USA (= United States of America) /ðə ˌjuː_es_ˈeɪ, juːˌnaɪtɪd ˌsteɪts_əv_əˈmerɪkə/
Wales /weɪlz/
Washington, D.C. /ˌwɒʃɪŋtən diː ˈsiː/
Waterford /ˈwɔːtəfəd/
West Virginia /ˌwest vəˈdʒɪniə/
Wexford /ˈweksfəd/
Wisconsin /wɪˈskɒnsɪn/
Wyoming /waɪˈəʊmɪŋ/

Skills	**Wordbanks**	**Grammar**	**Words**

0	oh, zero, nil	/əʊ, ˈzɪərəʊ, nɪl/
1	one	/wʌn/
2	two	/tuː/
3	three	/θriː/
4	four	/fɔː/
5	five	/faɪv/
6	six	/sɪks/
7	seven	/sevn/
8	eight	/eɪt/
9	nine	/naɪn/
10	ten	/ten/
11	eleven	/ɪˈlevn/
12	twelve	/twelv/
13	**thir**teen	/ˌθɜːˈtiːn/
14	fourteen	/ˌfɔːˈtiːn/
15	**fif**teen	/ˌfɪfˈtiːn/
16	sixteen	/ˌsɪksˈtiːn/
17	seventeen	/ˌsevnˈtiːn/
18	**eigh**teen	/ˌeɪˈtiːn/
19	nineteen	/ˌnaɪnˈtiːn/
20	**twen**ty	/ˈtwenti/
21	twenty-one	/ˌtwentiˈwʌn/
30	**thir**ty	/ˈθɜːti/
33	thirty-three	/ˌθɜːtiˈθriː/
40	**for**ty	/ˈfɔːti/
45	forty-five	/ˌfɔːtiˈfaɪv/
50	**fif**ty	/ˈfɪfti/
56	fifty-six	/ˌfɪftiˈsɪks/
60	sixty	/ˈsɪksti/
67	sixty-seven	/ˌsɪkstiˈsevn/
70	seventy	/ˈsevnti/
78	seventy-eight	/ˌsevntiˈeɪt/
80	**eigh**ty	/ˈeɪti/
89	eighty-nine	/ˌeɪtiˈnaɪn/
90	ninety	/ˈnaɪnti/
100	a/one hundred	/ə/wʌn ˈhʌndrəd/
101	one hundred and one	/wʌn ˌhʌndrəd ən ˈwʌn/
200	two hundred	/tuː ˈhʌndrəd/
1,000	one thousand	/ə/wʌn ˈθaʊznd/
1,111	one thousand one hundred and eleven	/wʌn ˌθaʊznd wʌn ˌhʌndrəd ən ɪˈlevn/
2,000	two thousand	/tuː ˈθaʊznd/
10,000	ten thousand	/ten ˈθaʊznd/
100,000	a/one hundred thousand	/ə/wʌn ˌhʌndrəd ˈθaʊznd/
1,000,000	a/one million	/ə/wʌn ˈmɪljən/
1,000,000,000	a/one billion	/ə/wʌn ˈbɪljən/

1st	**first**	/fɜːst/
2nd	**second**	/ˈsekənd/
3rd	**third**	/θɜːd/
4th	fourth	/fɔːθ/
5th	**fif**th	/fɪfθ/
6th	sixth	/sɪksθ/
7th	seventh	/sevnθ/
8th	**eigh**th	/eɪtθ/
9th	**nin**th	/naɪnθ/
10th	tenth	/tenθ/
11th	eleventh	/ɪˈlevnθ/
12th	**twelf**th	/twelfθ/
13th	thirteenth	/ˌθɜːˈtiːnθ/
19th	nineteenth	/ˌnaɪnˈtiːnθ/
20th	twent**ie**th	/ˈtwentiəθ/
21st	twenty-first	/ˌtwentiˈfɜːst/
22nd	twenty-second	/ˌtwentiˈsekənd/
23rd	twenty-third	/ˌtwentiˈθɜːd/
30th	thirt**ie**th	/ˈθɜːtiəθ/
40th	fort**ie**th	/ˈfɔːtiəθ/
50th	fift**ie**th	/ˈfɪftiəθ/
60th	sixt**ie**th	/ˈsɪkstiəθ/
70th	sevent**ie**th	/ˈsevntiəθ/
80th	eight**ie**th	/ˈeɪtiəθ/
90th	ninet**ie**th	/ˈnaɪntiəθ/
100th	hundredth	/ˈhʌndrədθ/

$\frac{1}{2}$	a / one half	/ə/wʌn ˈhɑːf/
$\frac{1}{3}$	a / one third	/ə/wʌn ˈθɜːd/
$\frac{1}{4}$	a / one quarter	/ə/wʌn ˈkwɔːtə/
$\frac{1}{8}$	a / one eighth	/ə/wʌn ˈeɪtθ/
$\frac{3}{4}$	three quarters	/θriː ˈkwɔːtəz/

Jahreszahlen sprichst du so aus:
1939 nineteen thirty-nine
1951 nineteen fifty-one
2010 two thousand and ten

Daten schreibst du im britischen Englisch so:
1 August, 2 January, 5 November

oder so:
1st / 1ˢᵗ August, 2nd / 2ⁿᵈ January,
5th / 5ᵗʰ November

Eine Jahreszahl schreibst du einfach dahinter:
1 August 2024 oder 01/08/24

**Im amerikanischen Englisch ist es umgekehrt!
Hier schreibt man den Monat VOR dem Tag:**
August 1, August 1st oder 08/01/2024

Irregular verbs

infinitive	simple past	past participle	German
(to) be /biː/	was/were /wɒz/wɜː/	been /biːn/	sein
(to) become /bɪˈkʌm/	became /bɪˈkeɪm/	become /bɪˈkʌm/	werden
(to) begin /bɪˈgɪn/	began /bɪˈgæn/	begun /bɪˈgʌn/	anfangen; beginnen
(to) bleed /bliːd/	bled /bled/	bled /bled/	bluten
(to) break /breɪk/	broke /brəʊk/	broken /ˈbrəʊkən/	(zer)brechen; kaputt machen
(to) bring /brɪŋ/	brought /brɔːt/	brought /brɔːt/	mitbringen
(to) build /bɪld/	built /bɪlt/	built /bɪlt/	bauen
(to) buy /baɪ/	bought /bɔːt/	bought /bɔːt/	kaufen
(to) catch /kætʃ/	caught /kɔːt/	caught /kɔːt/	fangen
(to) choose /tʃuːz/	chose /tʃəʊz/	chosen /ˈtʃəʊzn/	wählen; sich entscheiden
(to) come /kʌm/	came /keɪm/	come /kʌm/	kommen
(to) cost /kɒst/	cost /kɒst/	cost /kɒst/	kosten
(to) cut /kʌt/	cut /kʌt/	cut /kʌt/	schneiden
(to) deal with /ˈdiːl wɪð/	dealt with /ˈdelt wɪð/	dealt with /ˈdelt wɪð/	sich befassen mit, umgehen mit
(to) do /duː/	did /dɪd/	done /dʌn/	machen; tun
(to) draw /drɔː/	drew /druː/	drawn /drɔːn/	zeichnen
(to) dream /driːm/	dreamt/dreamed /dremt/driːmd/	dreamt/dreamed /dremt/driːmd/	träumen
(to) drink /drɪŋk/	drank /dræŋk/	drunk /drʌŋk/	trinken
(to) drive /draɪv/	drove /drəʊv/	driven /ˈdrɪvn/	fahren
(to) eat /iːt/	ate /et/eɪt/	eaten /ˈiːtn/	essen
(to) fall /fɔːl/	fell /fel/	fallen /ˈfɔːlən/	fallen
(to) feed /fiːd/	fed /fed/	fed /fed/	füttern
(to) feel /fiːl/	felt /felt/	felt /felt/	(sich) fühlen
(to) fight /faɪt/	fought /fɔːt/	fought /fɔːt/	(be)kämpfen; ankämpfen gegen
(to) find /faɪnd/	found /faʊnd/	found /faʊnd/	finden
(to) flee /fliː/	fled /fled/	fled /fled/	fliehen
(to) fly /flaɪ/	flew /fluː/	flown /fləʊn/	fliegen
(to) forget /fəˈget/	forgot /fəˈgɒt/	forgotten /fəˈgɒtən/	vergessen
(to) forgive /fəˈgɪv/	forgave /fəˈgeɪv/	forgiven /fəˈgɪvn/	vergeben; verzeihen
(to) get /get/	got /gɒt/	got /gɒt/	bekommen; holen; kaufen; kommen, gelangen; werden; bringen
(to) give /gɪv/	gave /geɪv/	given /ˈgɪvn/	geben; angeben, mitteilen
(to) go /gəʊ/	went /went/	gone /gɒn/	gehen; fahren
(to) grow /grəʊ/	grew /gruː/	grown /grəʊn/	wachsen; anbauen
(to) hang (up) /ˌhæŋ ˈʌp/	hung (up) /ˌhʌŋ ˈʌp/	hung (up) /ˌhʌŋ ˈʌp/	hängen, aufhängen
(to) have /hæv/	had /hæd/	had /hæd/	haben; essen; trinken
(to) hear /hɪə/	heard /hɜːd/	heard /hɜːd/	hören
(to) hide /haɪd/	hid /hɪd/	hidden /ˈhɪdn/	(sich) verstecken

infinitive	simple past	past participle	German
(to) hit /hɪt/	hit /hɪt/	hit /hɪt/	schlagen; stoßen gegen; treffen
(to) hold /həʊld/	held /held/	held /held/	(fest)halten; veranstalten
(to) hurt /hɜːt/	hurt /hɜːt/	hurt /hɜːt/	wehtun, schmerzen; verletzen
(to) keep /kiːp/	kept /kept/	kept /kept/	aufbewahren; (be)halten
(to) know /nəʊ/	knew /njuː/	known /nəʊn/	wissen; kennen
(to) lead /liːd/	led /led/	led /led/	führen
(to) learn /lɜːn/	learnt/learned /lɜːnt/lɜːnd/	learnt/learned /lɜːnt/lɜːnd/	lernen; erfahren
(to) leave /liːv/	left /left/	left /left/	weggehen; verlassen, abfahren; (übrig) lassen; zurücklassen; hinterlassen
(to) let /let/	let /let/	let /let/	lassen
(to) lie /laɪ/	lay /leɪ/	lain /leɪn/	liegen
(to) light /laɪt/	lit /lɪt/	lit /lɪt/	anzünden
(to) lose /luːz/	lost /lɒst/	lost /lɒst/	verlieren
(to) make /meɪk/	made /meɪd/	made /meɪd/	machen; (es/etwas) schaffen
(to) mean /miːn/	meant /ment/	meant /ment/	meinen; bedeuten
(to) meet /miːt/	met /met/	met /met/	(sich) treffen; kennenlernen
(to) overcome /ˌəʊvəˈkʌm/	overcame /ˌəʊvəˈkeɪm/	overcome /ˌəʊvəˈkʌm/	bewältigen; überwinden
(to) pay /peɪ/	paid /peɪd/	paid /peɪd/	(be)zahlen
(to) prove /pruːv/	proved /pruːvd/	proved/proven /pruːvd/ˈpruːvn/	beweisen
(to) put /pʊt/	put /pʊt/	put /pʊt/	setzen; stellen; legen
(to) read /riːd/	read /red/	read /red/	lesen
(to) rebuild /ˌriːˈbɪld/	rebuilt /ˌriːˈbɪlt/	rebuilt /ˌriːˈbɪlt/	wieder aufbauen
(to) ride /raɪd/	rode /rəʊd/	ridden /ˈrɪdn/	fahren; reiten
(to) rise /raɪz/	rose /rəʊz/	risen /ˈrɪzn/	aufgehen; steigen
(to) run /rʌn/	ran /ræn/	run /rʌn/	laufen; rennen; leiten, betreiben; durchführen
(to) say /seɪ/	said /sed/	said /sed/	sagen
(to) see /siː/	saw /sɔː/	seen /siːn/	sehen; empfangen, drannehmen
(to) seek /siːk/	sought /sɔːt/	sought /sɔːt/	suchen, streben nach
(to) sell /sel/	sold /səʊld/	sold /səʊld/	verkaufen
(to) send /send/	sent /sent/	sent /sent/	schicken
(to) shoot /ʃuːt/	shot /ʃɒt/	shot /ʃɒt/	schießen
(to) show /ʃəʊ/	showed /ʃəʊd/	shown /ʃəʊn/	zeigen
(to) sing /sɪŋ/	sang /sæŋ/	sung /sʌŋ/	singen
(to) sit /sɪt/	sat /sæt/	sat /sæt/	sitzen
(to) sit down /ˌsɪt ˈdaʊn/	sat down /ˌsæt ˈdaʊn/	sat down /ˌsæt ˈdaʊn/	sich hinsetzen
(to) sleep /sliːp/	slept /slept/	slept /slept/	schlafen
(to) smell /smel/	smelt/smelled /smelt/smeld/	smelt/smelled /smelt/smeld/	riechen

Irregular verbs

infinitive	simple past	past participle	German
(to) speak /spiːk/	spoke /spəʊk/	spoken /ˈspəʊkən/	reden; sprechen
(to) spell /spel/	spelt/spelled /spelt/speld/	spelt/spelled /spelt/speld/	buchstabieren
(to) spend /spend/	spent /spent/	spent /spent/	ausgeben *(Geld)*; verbringen *(Zeit)*
(to) spread /spred/	spread /spred/	spread /spred/	verbreiten; verteilen
(to) stand /stænd/	stood /stʊd/	stood /stʊd/	stehen
(to) steal /stiːl/	stole /stəʊl/	stolen /ˈstəʊlən/	stehlen
(to) stick with /stɪk wɪð/	stuck with /ˈstʌk wɪð/	stuck with /ˈstʌk wɪð/	bleiben bei, festhalten an
(to) swim /swɪm/	swam /swæm/	swum /swʌm/	schwimmen
(to) take /teɪk/	took /tʊk/	taken /ˈteɪkən/	nehmen; bringen; benötigen; brauchen; dauern
(to) teach /tiːtʃ/	taught /tɔːt/	taught /tɔːt/	unterrichten
(to) tell /tel/	told /təʊld/	told /təʊld/	erzählen
(to) think /θɪŋk/	thought /θɔːt/	thought /θɔːt/	denken; glauben
(to) throw /θrəʊ/	threw /θruː/	thrown /θrəʊn/	werfen
(to) understand /ˌʌndəˈstænd/	understood /ˌʌndəˈstʊd/	understood /ˌʌndəˈstʊd/	verstehen
(to) wake up /ˌweɪk ˈʌp/	woke up /ˌwəʊk ˈʌp/	woken up /ˌwəʊkən ˈʌp/	aufwachen
(to) wear /weə/	wore /wɔː/	worn /wɔːn/	tragen *(Kleidung)*
(to) win /wɪn/	won /wʌn/	won /wʌn/	gewinnen
(to) write /raɪt/	wrote /rəʊt/	written /ˈrɪtn/	schreiben

Tipp:

Einige Verben bilden das *simple past* und das *past participle* nach einem ähnlichen Muster. Wenn du sie dir in Gruppen sortierst, kannst du dir die Formen vielleicht besser merken. Findest du weitere Beispiele für diese Gruppen oder andere Gruppen?

bring	brought	brought	mitbringen
buy	bought	bought	kaufen
catch	caught	caught	fangen
fight	fought	fought	bekämpfen
think	thought	thought	denken; glauben
sing	sang	sung	singen
swim	swam	swum	schwimmen

draw	drew	drawn	zeichnen
fly	flew	flown	fliegen
grow	grew	grown	wachsen
know	knew	known	wissen; kennen
throw	threw	thrown	werfen
cost	cost	cost	kosten
cut	cut	cut	schneiden
hit	hit	hit	schlagen
let	let	let	lassen
put	put	put	setzen; stellen; legen

Seite Lernphasen	Inhalte	Kompetenzen	Sprachliche Mittel
6 Quiz			
6 Quiz 1	What do you know about the USA?		
8 Quiz 2	Landscapes and cities in the USA		
9 Unit 1 – Welcome to the USA (Kompetenzschwerpunkt: Hören)			
PART A – Impressions of the USA			
10 Activate	Geographie, Technologie, Natur, Essen und Popkultur in den USA	**Speaking:** darüber sprechen, wie viele US-amerikanische Einflüsse man im eigenen Alltag findet **Reading:** kurze Sachtexte lesen	**Wortschatz** *around the world*
12 Practise	Strukturen bewusst machen und festigen	**Writing:** über Vergangenes berichten	**Strukturen** *simple past (R)* **Aussprache** *the letters -ed*
13 Develop	Sightseeing in den USA Kurze Einblicke in die Geschichte der USA erhalten US-amerikanische Feiertage kennenlernen Der *American Dream*	**Viewing:** einer Präsentation über drei Bundesstaaten gezielt Informationen entnehmen **Reading:** Sachtexte verstehen **Listening:** einem Podcast folgen **Speaking:** die eigene Meinung äußern	**Wortschatz** *around the world, expressing opinions*
18 Practise	Strukturen festigen, Vorbereitung auf die Target task	**Writing:** Lückentexte	**Wortschatz** *numbers*
19 Apply	**Target task** Presenting a state	**Writing:** ein *fact file* gestalten	**Wortschatz** *around the world, numbers*
PART B – New York City			
20 Activate	Mithilfe eines Videoclips einen ersten Eindruck von New York bekommen	**Viewing:** einen Videoclip sehen **Speaking:** New York beschreiben **Reading:** kurze Aussagen lesen	**Wortschatz** *around the world*
22 Practise	Strukturen bewusst machen und festigen	**Speaking:** Fragen stellen und beantworten	**Strukturen** *present perfect (R)*
23 Develop	New York City kennenlernen: Sehenswürdigkeiten, die fünf *boroughs*, Freizeit und Kultur Etwas über die *Immigrant Heritage Week* erfahren	**Viewing:** einem Vlog Informationen entnehmen **Reading:** kurze Aussagen lesen, einen Liedtext verstehen **Writing:** einen Brief schreiben **Listening:** eine Podcastfolge hören **Mediation:** einen Flyer sprachmitteln	**Wortschatz** *around the world*
28 Practise	Strukturen festigen, Vorbereitung auf die Target task	**Writing:** Aussagesätze und Fragen bilden	**Wortschatz** *American and British English* **Strukturen** *passive (R)*
29 Apply	**Target task** A New York travel guide **Check out** Selbsteinschätzung	**Writing:** Eine Seite für einen Reiseführer über New York gestalten	**Wortschatz** *around the world*
30 Challenge	What is the real story of Thanksgiving? Fighting against racism The father of hip-hop – DJ Kool Herc	**Reading:** einen Text über die historischen Hintergründe von Thanksgiving lesen, einen Text über die Bürgerrechtsbewegung in den USA lesen, einen Text über die Anfänge des Hip Hop lesen	

Ausführliches Inhaltsverzeichnis

Seite / Lernphasen	Inhalte	Kompetenzen	Sprachliche Mittel
33	**Unit 2 – High school (Kompetenzschwerpunkt: Sprechen)**		
	PART A – Welcome to high school!		
34 Activate	Aus einem *yearbook* etwas über das Leben an einer US-amerikanischen *high school* erfahren	**Speaking:** Vorwissen über US-amerikanische *high schools* austauschen **Reading:** kurze Beschreibungen verstehen	**Wortschatz** *school life*
36 Practise	Strukturen bewusst machen und festigen	**Writing:** zeitliche Abfolgen beschreiben	**Strukturen** *past perfect* **Wortschatz** *school life*
37 Develop	*High schools* in den USA Über die Erfahrungen einer englischen Austauschschülerin in den USA lesen Das Konzept der *electives* an US-amerikanischen *high schools* kennenlernen	**Listening:** einem Dialog folgen **Reading:** einen Blogbeitrag lesen **Speaking:** sich über Wahlpflichtfächer austauschen, einen Werbespot aufnehmen **Writing:** über den Alltag an einer *high school* schreiben	**Wortschatz** *American and British English* *school life*
42 Practise	Strukturen festigen, Vorbereitung auf die Target task	**Listening:** Unterschiede zwischen amerikanischem und britischem Englisch heraushören, einem Dialog folgen	**Wortschatz** *American and British English* *school life*
43 Apply	**Target task** A yearbook entry	**Writing:** Eine Seite für ein *yearbook* gestalten	**Wortschatz** *American and British English* *school life*
	PART B – After-school activities		
44 Activate	Verschiedene *school clubs* kennenlernen	**Speaking:** sich darüber austauschen, welche AGs es an der eigenen Schule gibt **Reading:** einen Dialog lesen	**Wortschatz** *school life*
46 Practise	Strukturen bewusst machen und festigen	**Writing:** Bedingungssätze bilden	**Strukturen** *conditional clauses type 1* **Wortschatz** *American and British English*
47 Develop	Etwas über ein American-Football-Spiel an einer *high school* erfahren Sport in den USA	**Listening:** einem Gespräch Informationen entnehmen **Reading:** einen Blogbeitrag lesen **Writing:** über ein Ereignis an der eigenen Schule schreiben **Viewing:** Videoclips über Baseball und American Football verstehen **Mediation:** für einen Austauschschüler sprachmitteln **Speaking:** eine typisch amerikanische Sportart präsentieren	**Wortschatz** *school life* *descriptions*
52 Practise	Strukturen festigen, Vorbereitung auf die Target task	**Writing:** Fragen formulieren	**Strukturen** *reflexive pronouns* **Wortschatz** *school life*
53 Apply	**Target task** Interviewing an exchange student **Check out** Selbsteinschätzung	**Speaking:** eine Szene entwickeln und als Rollenspiel präsentieren	**Wortschatz** *school life*
54 Challenge	You should see me in a crown Prom dress	**Reading:** einen Auszug aus einem Jugendroman lesen, einen Liedtext verstehen	

Seite Lernphasen	Inhalte	Kompetenzen	Sprachliche Mittel
57	**Unit 3 – My world today (Kompetenzschwerpunkt: Schreiben)**		
	PART A – Relationships		
58 Activate	Gefühle und Freundschaften	**Speaking:** darüber spekulieren, wie sich jemand fühlen könnte **Reading:** kurze Aussagen zum Thema Freundschaft lesen	**Wortschatz** *feelings*
60 Practise	Strukturen bewusst machen und festigen	**Writing:** direkte Rede in indirekte umformulieren	**Strukturen** *reported speech 2*
61 Develop	Darüber sprechen und lesen, was gute Freunde ausmacht, und welche Probleme es in zwischenmenschlichen Beziehungen geben kann Die Textsorte *six-word story* kennenlernen Ein Liebesgedicht lesen	**Listening:** eine Podcastfolge zum Thema Freundschaft verstehen **Writing:** eine kurze Aussage schreiben, eine *six-word story* schreiben **Reading:** ein Interview lesen, ein Gedicht verstehen **Speaking:** die eigene Meinung ausdrücken **Mediation:** Informationen aus einem Videoclip sprachmitteln	**Wortschatz** *feelings, expressing opinions*
66 Practise	Strukturen festigen, Vorbereitung auf die Target task	**Listening:** Hörübung zum Phänomen *connected speech*	**Strukturen** *reported speech 2* **Aussprache** *connected speech*
67 Apply	**Target task** A friendship tree	**Writing:** kurze Texte zum Thema Freundschaft schreiben	**Wortschatz** *feelings*
	PART B – Digital communication		
68 Activate	Verschiedene digitale Kommunikationskanäle und -gewohnheiten	**Speaking:** darüber sprechen, welche Kommunikationskanäle man selbst benutzt **Reading:** verschiedene Texte zum Thema digitale Kommunikation lesen	**Wortschatz** *digital communication, expressing opinions*
70 Practise	Strukturen bewusst machen und festigen	**Writing:** Steigerungsformen der *adverbs of manner* verwenden und bilden	**Strukturen** *adverbs of manner (R), comparison of adverbs* **Wortschatz** *digital communication*
71 Develop	Über die Entstehung und Verwendung von Emojis lesen Über Vor- und Nachteile digitaler Kommunikation lesen und sprechen Cyberbullying	**Reading:** einen Sachtext lesen, einen Artikel lesen **Listening:** ein Interview verstehen **Speaking:** darüber sprechen, was man gegen Cyberbullying unternehmen kann **Writing:** eine E-Mail schreiben	**Wortschatz** *digital communication*
76 Practise	Strukturen festigen, Vorbereitung auf die Target task	**Writing:** eine Textnachricht schreiben	**Wortschatz** *digital communication* **Strukturen** *prefixes* **Aussprache** *how to pronounce ea*
77 Apply	**Target task** Tips for online communication **Check out** Selbsteinschätzung	**Writing:** Tipps für höfliche und respektvolle digitale Kommunikation sammeln	**Wortschatz** *digital communication seeking and giving advice*
78 Challenge	Every Day Cyberbullying – FAQs	**Reading:** einen Auszug aus einem Jugendroman lesen, FAQs zum Thema Cyberbullying lesen	

Ausführliches Inhaltsverzeichnis

Seite / Lernphasen	Inhalte	Kompetenzen	Sprachliche Mittel
81	**Unit 4 – Our world tomorrow (Kompetenzschwerpunkt: Lesen)**		
	PART A – The power of hope		
82 Activate	Über Hoffnungen und Träume für die Zukunft sprechen und lesen	**Speaking:** über Zukunftsträume für sich selbst und die Welt im Allgemeinen sprechen **Reading:** kurze Aussagen lesen und Schlüsselwörter notieren	**Wortschatz** *hopes and dreams*
84 Practise	Strukturen bewusst machen und festigen	**Writing:** Bedingungssätze bilden	**Strukturen** *conditional clauses type 2* **Wortschatz** *hopes and dreams*
85 Develop	Die vier Handlungsebenen im Klimaschutz Einen jugendlichen Umweltaktivisten kennenlernen Michelle Obama's letzte Rede als First Lady: *The power of hope*	**Writing:** jemandem eine Nachricht mit Ratschlägen schreiben **Mediation:** in einem Gespräch sprachmitteln **Reading:** einen Bericht lesen, Auszüge aus einer Rede lesen	**Wortschatz** *hopes and dreams*
90 Practise	Strukturen festigen, Vorbereitung auf die Target task	**Listening:** kurzen Aussagen über die Zukunft Informationen entnehmen	**Strukturen** *conditional clauses type 2* **Wortschatz** *hopes and dreams*
91 Apply	**Target task** My ideal future world	**Speaking:** die eigene Vision einer idealen Welt präsentieren	**Wortschatz** *hopes and dreams, presenting something*
	PART B – The world of work		
92 Activate	Jobs	**Speaking:** über verschiedene Berufe sprechen **Reading:** kurze Aussagen lesen	**Wortschatz** *the world of work*
94 Practise	Strukturen bewusst machen und festigen	**Writing:** Sätze vervollständigen	**Strukturen** *modal verbs (R)* **Wortschatz** *the world of work*
95 Develop	Hard und Soft Skills Sich für einen Schülerjob bewerben Ein Bewerbungsgespräch	**Reading:** verstehen, was Hard und Soft Skills sind, einem Bewerbungsformular Informationen entnehmen **Listening:** einem Bewerbungsgespräch folgen **Mediation:** eine Anzeige sprachmitteln	**Wortschatz** *the world of work*
100 Practise	Strukturen festigen, Vorbereitung auf die Target task	**Reading:** Personenbeschreibungen lesen und entsprechende Berufsempfehlungen geben	**Strukturen** *conditional clauses type 3 (optional)* **Wortschatz** *the world of work*
101 Apply	**Target task** Our job booklet **Check out** Selbsteinschätzung	**Writing:** eine Seite mit Informationen über einen bestimmten Beruf gestalten	**Wortschatz** *the world of work*
102 Challenge	Interview "Hope is a discipline" Unusual jobs	**Reading:** ein Interview mit einem Klimaschutzaktivisten lesen, Texte über ungewöhnliche Berufe lesen	

Seite Lernphasen	Inhalte	Kompetenzen	Sprachliche Mittel
105	**Unit 5 – New horizons (Kompetenzschwerpunkt: Sprechen)**		
	PART A – Immigration		
106 Activate	Die eigene Heimat verlassen (müssen)	**Speaking:** darüber sprechen, warum Menschen ihre Heimat verlassen **Reading:** über Menschen lesen, die ihre Heimat verlassen haben oder dazu gezwungen waren	**Wortschatz** *around the world*
108 Practise	Strukturen bewusst machen und festigen	**Writing:** indirekte Befehle formulieren	**Strukturen** *reported commands* **Wortschatz** *word families*
109 Develop	Statistiken zum Thema Einwanderung in die USA Die Geschichte einer irischen Einwanderin in die USA Ellis Island Erfahrungen eines südamerikanischen Austauschstudenten in den USA	**Viewing:** einer Präsentation statistische Informationen entnehmen **Reading:** Tagebucheinträge lesen, einen Brief lesen **Listening:** einem Monolog Informationen entnehmen **Speaking:** über Heimweh sprechen	**Wortschatz** *numbers, around the world*
114 Practise	Strukturen festigen, Vorbereitung auf die Target task	**Writing:** Adjektive verwenden, um einen Text interessanter zu gestalten	**Strukturen** *past progressive*
115 Apply	**Target task** An immigration story	**Writing:** aus dem Blickwinkel einer Person schreiben, die in ein anderes Land gezogen ist	**Wortschatz** *around the world*
	PART B – The Republic of Ireland		
116 Activate	Irland heute	**Speaking:** anhand einer Karte Informationen über Irland sammeln **Reading:** kurze Texte lesen und Notizen machen	**Wortschatz** *around the world*
118 Practise	Strukturen bewusst machen und festigen	**Writing:** das *present perfect progressive* anwenden	**Strukturen** *present perfect progressive*
119 Develop	Sehenswürdigkeiten in Irland Etwas über Dublin erfahren Die historischen Hintergründe der Gründung der Republik Irland Gaelic Football	**Listening:** Beschreibungen irischer Touristenattraktionen Informationen entnehmen **Reading:** Auszüge aus einem Reiseführer lesen und Schlüsselwörter notieren **Speaking:** über ein Lied sprechen **Mediation:** Informationen über Gaelic Football sprachmitteln	**Wortschatz** *around the world*
124 Practise	Strukturen festigen, Vorbereitung auf die Target task	**Writing:** Fakten über Irland aufschreiben	**Wortschatz** *presenting something*
125 Apply	**Target task** A five-minute talk **Check out** Selbsteinschätzung	**Speaking:** einen *five-minute talk* halten	**Wortschatz** *presenting something*
126 Challenge	Enrique's journey Annie Moore Isle of Hope, Isle of Tears	**Reading:** einen Auszug aus einer Reportage lesen, einen Text über Annie Moore lesen, einen Liedtext verstehen	
130	**Get together (Kompetenzschwerpunkt: Sprechen)**		

Ausführliches Inhaltsverzeichnis

Seite	Inhalt
148	**Projects**
148	Project 1: Hollywood
150	Project 2: Green cities
152	**Skills**
152	Wortschatzarbeit
153	Hören
154	Mit anderen sprechen
155	Schreiben
156	Lesen
157	Sprachmittlung
158	Videoclips verstehen
159	Im Internet recherchieren
160	Präsentationen halten
161	Eine Szene vorspielen
162	**Wordbanks**
162	Around the world
163	Travelling / Descriptions
164	School life
165	American and British English
166	Feelings / Seeking and giving advice
167	(Digital) communication
168	Expressing opinions / Presenting something
169	Hopes and dreams
170	The world of work
171	Numbers
172	**Classroom phrases**
174	**Grammar**
174	Die einfache Vergangenheit: Aussagen *(revision)*
175	Die einfache Vergangenheit: Fragen *(revision)*
176	Das Perfekt: Aussagen *(revision)*
177	Das Perfekt: Fragen *(revision)*
178	Das Passiv *(revision)*
179	Die Vorvergangenheit
180	Bedingungssätze Typ 1 *(revision)*
181	Reflexivpronomen
182	Indirekte Rede 2
183	Adverbien der Art und Weise *(revision)*
184	Die Steigerung von Adverbien
185	Bedingungssätze Typ 2
186	Modalverben *(revision)*
187	Bedingungssätze Typ 3 *(optional)*
188	Indirekte Befehlssätze
189	Die Verlaufsform der Vergangenheit *(revision)*
190	Die Verlaufsform des Perfekts: Aussagen
191	Die Verlaufsform des Perfekts: Fragen
192	**Words**
192	Erläuterung und richtige Aussprache
194	Bekannte Wörter
195	Wortlisten nach Units
231	*Dictionary*
271	*Names, Numbers*
275	*Irregular verbs*
284	**Bild- und Textquellen**

Bildquellen

|akg-images GmbH, Berlin: 6.2. |Alamy Stock Photo, Abingdon/Oxfordshire: Ammentorp Photography 93.1; anton havelaar 20.3; Antonio Gravante, Antonio 9.3; Antonio Guillem Fernandez 58.3; antony baxter 116.4; B.O'Kane 21.1; Bob Daemmrich 88.1; Brennan, Clark 15.2; Bucknall, Pearl 105.2; Bujdoso, Andor 95.2; Cary T 19.1; Cavanagh, Peter 116.7; Chuck Eckert, Chuck 33.4; Costa, Denise 171.1, 171.2, 171.3, 171.4, 171.5, 171.6, 171.7; Cristino, Carmen 25.1; Cultura Creative Ltd 68.3; DCPhoto 58.1; Dee Jolie 21.2; Desert, Louis-Michel 119.6; Dieterich, Werner 120.3; Dmytro Zinkevych 167.2; Drinkwater, Ros 121.2; Drobot, Vadym 34.1; Durson, Manuela 59.3; Egorova, Olga 167.5; Filimonov, Iakov 93.3; Foy, Kevin 26.1; fStop Images GmbH 105.3; Ghiea, Vlad 9.1; Graham, Jeremy 15.3; Granger - Historical Picture Archive 112.1, 112.2; Henderson, Mark 141.2, 144.1, 147.1; imageBROKER.com GmbH & Co. KG 119.4, 120.4, 130.1, 133.1, 136.1, 139.1, 142.1, 145.1, 166.1; John A Megaw 120.1; Kinovo 167.1; Kmit, Ivan 169.2; Kneschke, Robert 124.1, 168.1; Kruse, Joana 119.1; Lubenow, Sabine 116.6; Lund, Jacob 166.3; makasana photo 119.5; Marije Pama, Marije 104.1; Maskot 24.1; McGouey, Robert 93.2; McLennan, Chris 13.2; Michael Ventura 57.4; Morandi, Tuul and Bruno 121.3; Oleksii Hrecheniuk 170.2; Oleshko, Artem 104.3; Otto, Werner 107.1; Panther Media GmbH 82.2; Parkin, Jim 12.1; passport 122.1; Pearson, Myrleen 59.4; Prostock-studio 58.2; Quality Stock 48.5; Radharc Images 116.1; Samborskyi, Roman 80.1; scenicireland.com / Christopher Hill Photographic 141.1, 144.2, 147.2; Shields, Martin 91.3; Soloman, Andy 121.1; Sparks, Jon 116.5; teddiviscious 116.2; Tetra Images 59.2; The Print Collector 112.3; thislife pictures 106.1; Thornberg, Daniel 8.8; Thornton, Bennie 13.1; tom carter 50.1; ton koene 104.2; Trovo, Paolo 132.2, 135.2, 138.2; Trujillo, Gabriel 74.22; UPI 89.1; Vallecillos, Lucas 116.3; Walker Art Library 120.2; Warren, Scott 33.2; Westend61 GmbH 59.1, 68.4; White, Liam 132.1, 135.1, 138.1; xavierlorenzo 166.2; Zap, Yury 58.4; Zhigalova, Galina 62.1; ZUMA Press, Inc. 104.4. |Alamy Stock Photo (RMB), Abingdon/Oxfordshire: Booth, Mike 128.2; BuddyMays 7.3; Cultura Creative RF 162.1; Dack, Simon 157.1; Garcia, Mariano 6.4; Granger Historical Picture Archive 15.1; grzegorz knec 7.4; Haviv, Joshua 6.3; Hurst, D. 7.2; IanDagnall Computing 31.1; Jannsen, Brian 128.1; Maridav 72.1; Pavone, Sean 20.1; Pictorial Press Ltd 30.1; RTimages 170.1; Shawshots 105.1; Tallec, Tony 92.8. |Bridgeman Images, Berlin: Everett Collection 129.1. |Don Bartletti Photography, Vista, California: 127.1. | fotolia.com, New York: Ints Vikmanis 167.6; Kneschke, Robert 92.7; Wylezich, B. 6.1; zinkevych 92.2. |Getty Images, München: Bloomberg 103.1; Denver Post / Gehring, Karl 164.1; Don Emmert, AFP 20.2; Hill Street Studios 38.2; Hulton Archive 32.1; HUM Images/ Universal Images Group 15.1; Mark Wilson 102.1; MediaNews Group / Orange County Register Archive 34.3; Mirrorpix 32.2; RRP, Team Macarie 7.1; Stock Montage 14.1; Win McNamee 103.2. |Getty Images (RF), München: clu 105.4; coldsnowstorm 83.2; fotografixx 68.2; grandriver 82.1; gremlin 91.8; Jose Luis Pelaez Inc 164.2; kali9 35.1; Marks, George 106.2; Morsa Images 95.1; onurdongel 91.6; RubberBall Productions 35.3; SDI Productions 35.4, 72.2; Stígur Már Karlsson / Heimsmyndir 91.5; wagnerokasaki 39.2. |Gilcrease Museum, Tulsa OK: 16.1. |Harper Collins Publishers Ltd, London: Electric Monkey, Harper Collins Publishers / David Levithan: Every Day / Cover Illustration: Virginia Moura 78.1. |Imago Editorial, Berlin: 54.1; Pond5 Images 119.7. |iStockphoto.com, Calgary: aeduard 92.6; anatoliy_gleb 92.3; Choreograph 16.2; coldsnowstorm Titel; dbstockphoto 34.4; Dufresne, Marc 9.2; dvulikaia 43.2; FatCamera 33.3; freerangestock 7.5; Fudio 11.2; g-stockstudio 68.1; Galan, Roberto 9.4; herkisi 117.4; Inside Creative House 73.1; JackF 57.1; JillianCain 49.1; LDProd 117.3; Le Mauff, Mathieu 11.3, 148.1; lisandrotrarbach 163.1; master1305 43.3; Monkey Business Images 164.3; monkeybusinessimages 37.1, 39.1, 57.2; Nikada 91.2; Nirian 8.3; photoguns 91.1; pixelfit 162.2; reisegraf 119.3; shapecharge 92.9; sl-f 91.4; travelview 148.3; vejaa 57.3; Voyagerix 43.1; White, Don 10.1; YinYang 11.1. |Learned, Brent, Kansas: American Indian artist Brent Learned, Cheyenne and Arapaho Graduate of the university of Kansas 14.2. |PantherMedia GmbH (panthermedia.net), München: Schmid, Christophe 156.1. |Penguin Random House LLC, New York: Enrique's Journey von Sonia Nazario, 9780812971781 / Foto: Don Bartletti 126.1. |Picture-Alliance GmbH, Frankfurt a.M.: akg-images 31.2; Deck, Uli / dpa 83.1; dpa 92.1. |Schwarz, Leonard, Braunschweig: 109.1. |Shutterstock.com, New York: Bilous, Walt 13.3; Castleski 10.2; Chagochkin, Pavel 91.7; charnsitr 165.1, 165.2; ChristianChan 51.1; Eidenweil, Thierry 8.6; fizkes 40.1, 81.1; Fotogrin 81.4; Ground Picture 34.2; Hellebaut, Oskar 81.2; Kumsri, Yongyut 8.7; LightField Studios 33.1; Medbrat_23 167.4; michaeljung 24.4; Motortion Films 166.4; MPH Photos 24.2; Nach-Noth 48.2; Olivier Le Moal 167.3; Pavone, Sean 148.2; Pierucki, Tommy 8.5; pio3 150.1; Rahman, Ryan 81.3; Rawpixel.com 92.5; sam 72 169.3; Sean Locke Photography 48.1; seto contreras 113.1; Sunny studio 169.1; trabantos 119.2; TZIDO SUN 8.2. |Shutterstock.com (RM), New York: ZUMA Press Wire / DeSlover, Daniel 56.1. |stock.adobe.com, Dublin: AlenKadr 171.8; Arid Ocean 8.4; biker3 35.2; DC Studio 61.1; DigiClack 74.2, 74.5, 74.14, 75.1, 75.2, 75.3, 75.19, 75.20, 75.30, 75.38, 75.44; dtiberio 24.5; fizkes 117.2; ilovemayorova 23.1; insta_photos 24.3; lucky-photo 8.1; myvp85 149.1; peregrinus 74.4; pololia 101.1; Production Perig 92.4; seanlockephotography 38.1; streptococcus 74.1, 74.3, 74.6, 74.7, 74.8, 74.9, 74.10, 74.11, 74.12, 74.13, 74.15, 74.16, 74.17, 74.18, 74.19, 74.20, 74.21, 74.23, 74.24, 75.4, 75.5, 75.6, 75.7, 75.8, 75.9, 75.10, 75.11, 75.12, 75.13, 75.14, 75.15, 75.16, 75.17, 75.18, 75.21, 75.22, 75.23, 75.24, 75.25, 75.26, 75.27, 75.28, 75.29, 75.31, 75.32, 75.33, 75.34, 75.35, 75.36, 75.37, 75.39, 75.40, 75.41, 75.42, 75.43, 75.45, 75.46; superlime 117.1; WavebreakMediaMicro 168.2. |Tammana, Sri Nihal, Monroe Township: 86.1, 86.2, 87.1. |ullstein bild, Berlin: Frankenberg 163.2. |Visuelle Lebensfreude - Bodem + Sötebier GbR, Hannover: 44.1, 44.2, 44.3, 44.4, 44.5, 44.6, 44.7, 71.1, 71.2, 71.3, 71.4, 71.5. |Zwick, Joachim, Gießen: 1.1, 2.1; Illustrationen: Ulf Marckwort 2.1.

Textquellen

25 Liedtext „An Open Letter to NYC", Stephen J. JR Bator, Michael Louis Diamond, Adam Keefe Horovitz, John Madansky, Jeff Magnum, Eugene RichardO'Connor, David Lynn Thomas, Adam Nathaniel Yauch, Jimmy Zero. An Open Letter to NYC © Brooklyn Dust Music / Universal-Polygram International Publ. In / WB Music Corp. Neue Welt Musikverlag GmbH, Hamburg Universal Music Publ. GmbH, Berlin. 07.08.2024 https://www.lyricsmode.com/lyrics/b/beastie_boys/an_open_letter_to_nyc.html#!

54/55 „I'm not running for prom queen", Leah Johnson, in: You should see me in a crown, New York: Scholastic Children's Books 2020 © 2020 Leah Johnson.

56 Liedtext „Prom dress", mxmtoon (Maia Xiao-En Moredock-Ting), © Printrechte Hal Leonard Europe GmbH. 07.08.2024 https://www.lyrics.com/lyric-lf/1536209/mxmtoon/prom+dress

65 „On the Discomfort of Being in the Same Room as the Boy You Like", Sarah Kay, in: You Don't Have to Be Everything: Poems for Girls Becoming Themselves, New York: Workman Publishing Company, 2021.

67 „Only a true friend would be that truely honest." (Donkey, Shrek), William Steig, Ted Elliott, SHREK, Hrsg.: The Internet Movie Script Database. 23.05.2024: https://imsdb.com/scripts/Shrek.html

67 „Many people will walk in and out of your life, but only true friends will leave footprints on your heart." (Eleanor Roosevelt), Sandy Rideout, Yvonne Collins: Totally Me: The Teenage Girl's Survival Guide: New Edition (CreateSpace Independent Publishing Platform - ohne Verlagsbindung) © 2020 Yvonne Collins & Sandy Rideout.

67 „It's not enough to be friendly. You have to be a friend." (R.J. Palacio), R.J. Palacio DN: (Der Name Raquel J. Palacio ist ein Pseudonym ihres Namens Raquel Jaramillo). Wonder by Palacio. R.J. (2013) Random House Children's Publisher UK, London.

67 Liedtext „Count on Me" (Bruno Mars), Bruno Mars, Philip Martin II Lawrence, Ari Levine. © BMG Rights Management GmbH, Berlin, Neue Welt Musikverlag GmbH, Hamburg.

78/79 „Every Day" [...], David Levithan, in: Every Day, Dublin: HarperCollins Publishers, 2023.

89 „Remarks by the First Lady at the National School Counselor of the Year Event", Michelle Obama, Washington: The White House Office of the First Lady, 2017. 06.03.2024: https://obamawhitehouse.archives.gov/the-press-office/2017/01/06/remarks-first-lady-national-school-counselor-year-event

102/103 „Hope is a discipline", Dharna Noor for The Guardian, 2023. 06.03.2024: https://www.theguardian.com/us-news/2023/dec/31/alaska-youth-climate-change-activist-nathan-baring-lawsuit-fossil-fuel-government

122 Liedtext „A song for Ireland", Phil Colclough, © Leola Music / BMG Rights Management GmbH, Berlin. 07.08.2024: https://www.lyricsmode.com/lyrics/d/dubliners/song_for_ireland.html

126 „Enrique's Journey", Chapter One: The Boy Left Behind, Sonia Nazario, 2002, Los Angeles Times. 06.03.2024: https://www.latimes.com/nation/immigration/la-fg-enriques-journey-chapter-one-mainbar-story.html

127 „Enrique's Journey", Chapter Three: Defeated Seven Times, a Boy Again Faces 'the Beast', Sonia Nazario, 2002, Los Angeles Times. 06.03.2024: https://www.latimes.com/nation/immigration/la-fg-enriques-journey-chapter-three-mainbar-story.html

127 „Enrique's Journey", Chapter Six: At Journey's End, a Dark River, Perhaps a New Life, Sonia Nazario, 2002, Los Angeles Times. 06.03.2024: https://www.latimes.com/nation/immigration/la-fg-enriques-journey-chapter-six-mainbar-story.html

129 Liedtext „Isle of Hope, Isle of Tears", Brendan Joseph Graham, © Peermusic Ltd./Peermusic (Germany) GmbH, Hamburg. 07.08.2024: https://www.latimes.com/nation/immigration/la-fg-enriques-journey-chapter-six-mainbar-story.html

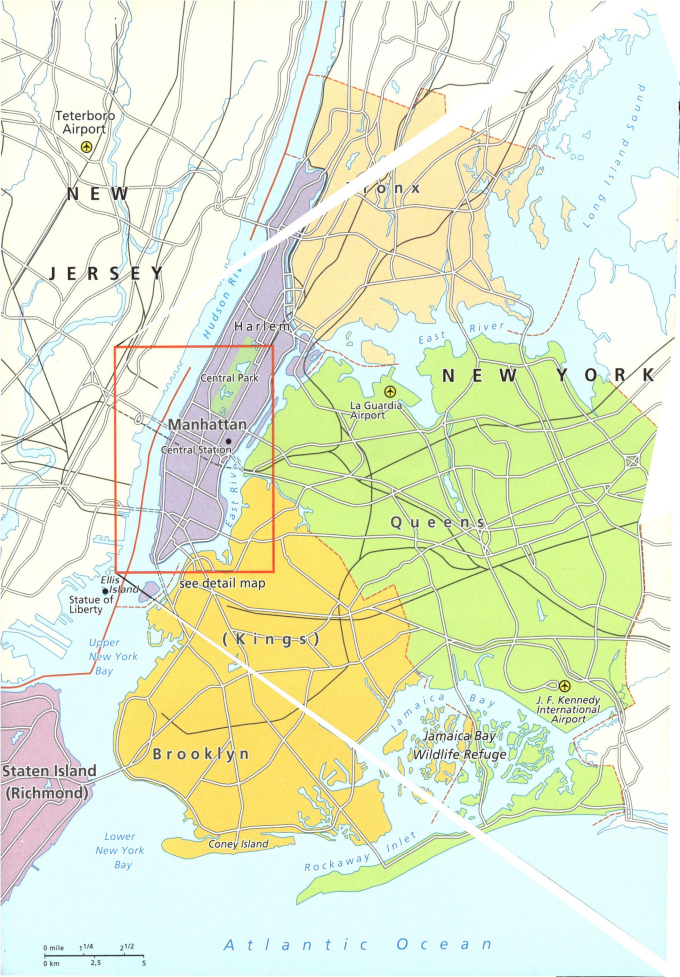